Cops in Lab Coats

Cops in Lab Coats

Curbing Wrongful Convictions through Independent Forensic Laboratories

Sandra Guerra Thompson

ALUMNAE COLLEGE PROFESSOR OF LAW AND
DIRECTOR OF THE CRIMINAL JUSTICE INSTITUTE
UNIVERSITY OF HOUSTON LAW CENTER

CAROLINA ACADEMIC PRESS
Durham, North Carolina

Library of Congress Cataloging-in-Publication Data

Thompson, Sandra Guerra.
 Cops in lab coats : curbing wrongful convictions through independent forensic
laboratories / Sandra Guerra Thompson.
    pages cm
 Includes bibliographical references and index.
 ISBN 978-1-61163-529-4 (alk. paper)
 1. Criminal investigation--Texas--Houston. 2. Forensic sciences--Texas--
Houston. 3. Judicial error--Texas--Houston. I. Title.

 HV6795.H6T46 2015
 363.25'60973--dc23

                        2014044884

CAROLINA ACADEMIC PRESS
700 Kent Street
Durham, North Carolina 27701
Telephone (919) 489-7486
Fax (919) 493-5668
www.cap-press.com

Printed in the United States of America

TO MY PARENTS
ALFREDO AND THELMA GUERRA
Whose passion for justice inspires me.

Contents

Foreword

In 1927, the state of Virginia forcibly sterilized 21-year-old Carrie Buck after scientific "experts" concluded that she was a feebleminded moral delinquent. According to these so-called authorities, Ms. Buck inherited genetic defects from her mother which she, in turn, passed on to her own infant daughter. Based on manufactured—and later thoroughly discredited—"scientific evidence" against Ms. Buck, the U.S. Supreme Court upheld Virginia's mandatory sterilization law. Justice Oliver Wendell Holmes famously justified the Court's decision by quipping that "three generations of imbeciles are enough."

It's tempting to view what happened to Carrie Buck as an unfortunate relic of the unsophisticated past. Surely, we think, the methodology and standards applied by scientists today are far superior to those forced upon the unknowing Carrie Buck. Surely, stringent safeguards are now in place that would have exposed the dishonest "experts" who fabricated evidence against her. Surely, today's judges show more concern for the importance of scientific truth when dealing with fundamental questions of human liberty.

Cops in Lab Coats shatters those assumptions. It begins with the powerful story of twenty-six-year-old George Rodriguez, condemned wrongfully for a rape and sentenced to serve a sixty-year term. A single hair, miraculously preserved when the rest of the evidence was discarded, proved his innocence seventeen years later. But Sandra Guerra Thompson is not simply portraying one man's dramatic rescue from the justice system. She is, instead, describing a broken system—of hundreds, perhaps thousands, of wrongful convictions obtained as a result of shoddy, fraudulent, or otherwise invalid forensic science.

Although this record lends itself to scandal, sensational exposé, and outrage, Professor Thompson instead thoughtfully lays out the causes of those crime lab scandals and argues persuasively that this situation is nothing short of a national crisis. Her analysis of the groundbreaking 2009 report from the National Academy of Sciences casts doubt on the scientific validity of many of the forensic disciplines that shape not only popular crime-scene television dramas but all too real courtroom testimony in which juries determine guilt or innocence.

As I learned from personal experience, however, the release of the NAS report did not dampen the zeal exhibited by some prosecutors to embrace untested "scientific" methods purveyed by self-proclaimed experts in the quest to obtain convictions. Late in 2009, I was horrified to learn that prosecutors planned to use the results of a dog-scent lineup in the upcoming retrial of my client, Anthony Graves, for capital murder. Anthony had been convicted and sentenced to death fifteen years before for the 1992 murder of a family of six in Somerville, Texas. Anthony's conviction was overturned by the Fifth Circuit Court of Appeals in 2005, but rather than release Anthony, the state elected to retry him. At that point, I was one of the lawyers on Anthony's legal team.

Four years after the Fifth Circuit's ruling, however, Anthony still sat in the Burleson County jail, waiting for his retrial. In a last-ditch effort to obtain physical evidence tying Anthony to the crime scene, a deputy sheriff had his dogs smell six items from the burned-out house where the murders had occurred seventeen years before. The deputy reported that after smelling two of the six items, his dogs "alerted" to a gauze pad that had been wiped across Anthony's skin. According to the deputy, this "proved" that Anthony had been present at the crime scene. Had Anthony's life not been at stake, the flimsy melodrama would have been laughable. But the defense team dared not treat it as a joke because a Texas appellate court had already ruled that dog-scent lineup evidence was admissible in court. The prosecutors notified us that the deputy's dog-scent findings would be a key part of the state's case, even though they knew that the deputy had no formal training, followed no scientific protocols and could present no studies to validate his procedures. Soon afterwards, we learned that the deputy had been sued by several people who had been wrongly convicted thanks, at least in part, to his "infallible" dogs. (Ultimately, in 2010, Anthony was exonerated on the grounds of actual innocence, without having to be retried.)

Had I possessed this book in 2009, I would have been better prepared to fight the admissibility of the dog-scent evidence had Anthony's case gone to trial. The book's utility to criminal defense lawyers is obvious. But meaningful criminal justice reforms cannot be achieved simply by educating defense lawyers. This book should be on the must-read list for prosecutors, judges, police officers, forensic scientists, law students, and everyone else affected by the criminal justice system. The solution that Professor Thompson proposes is making crime labs independent of police departments. She does not claim that it will magically solve all problems, but she argues cogently and systematically that it can and will reduce incompetence, unconscious bias toward the prosecution, and improper management in these laboratories. The facts and arguments she presents should reduce the surprising levels of resistance to the concept of crime lab independence among professional organizations within the forensic science community, as well as federal and state prosecutors and law enforcement agencies.

As a Houstonian, I was embarrassed a decade ago by the crime lab failures that seemed to be featured almost daily in the news. Today, nothing makes me prouder about living in Houston than the willingness of our city leaders, our police department, and our citizens to embrace the concept of crime lab independence. It is our good fortune to have Professor Thompson, an acknowledged expert in wrongful convictions as well as a former prosecutor, serving on the board that oversees the new Houston Forensic Science Center. My fondest wish is that Professor Thompson's detailed description of our city's bold crime lab experiment will provide inspiration, as well as a blueprint, for other jurisdictions to free their crime labs from the control of cops in lab coats.

Nicole B. Cásarez, J.D.
Professor, University of St. Thomas
Houston, Texas

Acknowledgments

So many people played a part in supporting this project. I thank my wonderful husband, Jim Thompson, for doing the initial designs of the book's cover and for encouraging me throughout this project. I owe special thanks to my son, Andy Garcia, for his truly brilliant editing of this book. I am blessed to have a dear friend in Nicole Bremner Cásarez, an expert on wrongful convictions and a fellow member of the Board of Directors of the Houston Forensic Science Center, who wrote the engaging foreword for this book.

Many of my colleagues at the University of Houston Law Center also provide me with professional guidance and other support. Michael A. Olivas, my friend and mentor to whom I owe so much, introduced me both to the editors of Carolina Academic Press as well as to Lavina Fielding Anderson, an enthusiastic professional editor. Two other colleagues nominated me for community boards that have inspired my interest in reforming forensic science to better serve the justice system. Law professor David R. Dow nominated me to serve on the Timothy Cole Advisory Panel for Wrongful Convictions at the state level, and sociology professor Tacho Mindiola nominated me to serve on the Houston Forensic Science Center Board of Directors.

On matters of forensic science, I am also fortunate to have Joseph Sanders as a colleague. Joe, a national expert in forensic science, is always generous with this time and expertise. Another colleague, Mon Yin Lung, the Associate Director of the O'Quinn Law Library at the University of Houston Law Center, provided me with invaluable assistance in tracking down the perfect reference books and manuscripts, and she often worked in the wee hours of the night so as to get them to me promptly. Law librarian Matthew A. Mantel, also provided me with an essential bibliography of forensic science research materials relating to cognitive bias for Chapter 4. Finally, my sincere thanks goes to the University of Houston Law Foundation and Deans Raymond Nimmer and Richard Alderman whose generous support made this project possible.

Several chapters of this book were reviewed by legal scholars, to whom I am truly grateful. In June 2013 at the Law and Society Meeting in Boston, Massachusetts, I received important feedback on Chapter 4 from Seth W. Stoughton, a Climenko Fellow and Lecturer on Law at Harvard Law School (now a professor at the University of South Carolina School of Law), and Amna Akbar of the Ohio State University Moritz College of Law. At a workshop at Southern Methodist University's Dedman School of Law in January 2014, I received insightful comments on an earlier version of Chapter 3 from Avlana Eisenberg of Harvard Law School, Andrea Roth of Berkeley Law School, and Laurent Sacharoff, of the University of Arkansas Law School. Jennifer E. Laurin of the University of Texas at Austin School of Law and Andrea Roth of Berkeley Law School also kindly reviewed an earlier version of Chapter 3 and provided me with extremely helpful comments. To Jennifer Mnookin, of the UCLA Law School, I am grateful for her guidance through the complicated Confrontation Clause jurisprudence in Chapter 5. Finally, David A. Harris of the University of Pittsburg School of Law helped me understand some of the issues surrounding information systems in laboratories and the possibility of computerizing much of forensic analysis.

I am blessed to have outstanding law students who worked on this project with me: Nisha Ghosh (J.D. 2013), Darrell Moore (J.D. 2013), Preston Scott Ehlers, and Annalise De Frank. They showed initiative and creativity in tracking down materials in other disciplines, in the press, and in the practice world of forensic science, not to mention in traditional legal research materials. To a person, they will be outstanding attorneys.

Several experts across the country have provided guidance and shared their research with me, and I am indebted to them. At the Innocence Project of New York, Sarah Chu provided me insightful editing suggestions for Chapters 3 and 6. She also generously shared her vast knowledge of reform efforts and research in forensic science. At the Los Angeles County Public Defender's Office, I thank Jennifer Friedman who shared an important table she compiled of the case law on *Daubert* hearings raising issues from the National Academy of Sciences Report. Kathryn M. Kase, Executive Director of Texas Defender Service, helped me understand the law and practice of court-appointed forensic experts. Rick A. Sichta, of the Sichta Law Firm in Jacksonville, Florida, generously shared information and documents regarding the death penalty case of Gerald Murray, which he is handling. Finally, to Carson Guy, Research Attorney for Judge Barbara P. Hervey of the Texas Court of Criminal Appeals, I send my sincere thanks for sharing his important research on crime laboratories nationwide.

In my capacity as a member of the Board of Directors of the Houston Forensic Science Center, I have also had the privilege of working with a dedicated group of people. I am grateful to the Chairman of the Board, Scott Hochberg, for his insightful review of Chapter 7. I also must thank First Assistant City Attorney Tom Allen for his guidance on the history of the creation of the Forensic Science Center and the plan to transform the Houston Police Department Crime Laboratory. I am also indebted to Irma Rios, Director of the Forensic Analysis Division of the Houston Forensic Science Center, for making arrangements for me to tour the FBI Crime Laboratory and for her guidance on a variety of issues related to Chapter 7. She was also diligent in keeping me informed when HPD Crime Laboratory analysts were scheduled to testify so that I might attend. Dr. Daniel D. Garner, the President and CEO of the Houston Forensic Science Center also generously discussed issue of forensic science validity and shared photographs of the Center's inaugural event. I appreciated his feedback on Chapter 7. At the Houston Police Department, I send a special thanks to Executive Assistant Chief Timothy N. Oettmeier for taking the time to discuss his innovative perspectives on laboratory independence with me and for his helpful review of Chapter 7. I am also grateful to Assistant Chief Matthew D. Slinkard for sharing his detailed outline of the tasks that the Houston Police Department completed in order to make the laboratory's independence possible.

Cops in Lab Coats

Chapter One

Bad Science Wreaks Havoc—
The George Rodriguez Story

Raped in Houston

The evening of February 24, 1987, would be a terrible night for Isabel Medina, a 14-year-old girl in the working class neighborhood of Pleasantville in Houston's East End near the Port of Houston Ship Channel.[1] The mostly Latino area, close to nearby oil and chemical refineries, has a putrid chemical smell in the air that makes it an unhealthy and less desirable place to live—but, for those very reasons, it also offers affordable housing for those on the lower end of the economic scale. On this particular night, Isabel was visiting with her 16-year-old friend Bobby Sanchez outside her home in the 7900 block of Kerr Street. Suddenly, two strangers, Manuel Beltran and Isidro Yanez pulled up in Yanez's green-and-white Chrysler Cordoba.[2] First they asked for directions to another location, and then they sought help with a flat tire. The teenagers could see that there was no flat tire, and they quickly realized they were facing dangerous criminals. The two teens started to run away. Bobby got away, but Yanez, a heavy-set man, grabbed Isabel and pushed her into the car.

Beltran and Yanez then drove her to Beltran's house which he shared with his brother, Uvaldo, in the nearby Denver Harbor neighborhood. When the men arrived with the girl, Uvaldo was in the living room watching television. Manuel Beltran, Yanez, and Isabel came in through the kitchen door. Yanez forced her ahead by gripping her neck. Uvaldo could see that she was crying and resisting, yet he did nothing to help her.[3] Manuel and Yanez took Isabel into a bedroom where they slapped her around and threatened to kill her. They ordered Isabel to undress and then took turns raping her.[4]

After the sexual assault, Manual and Yanez told Isabel to get dressed, then blindfolded her by putting a ski mask over her head in such a way that she could not see through the eyeholes. The men drove her to a dirt road behind a Mobil station along the East Freeway and pulled her out of the car. One of them handed her a dollar, telling her, "This is for your trouble." As Isabel started to remove the ski mask, he also warned her not to look at them or they would kill her.[5] Manuel and Yanez then drove away, leaving her on the roadside.

Isabel managed to get help and immediately reported the crime to the Houston Police Department. Police investigators questioned Isabel about the crime, and she characterized her assailants as "the skinny one" and "the fat one."[6] She also described the house and the route the assailants took to get there. One of the assailants had called the other "George," but Isabel thought the name was fake since they had discussed, in front of her, not using their real names.[7] Isabel proved her familiarity with the neighborhood by leading police to the attack site, the home of Manuel and Uvaldo Beltran. Police zeroed in on the one-story, white house with red trim on El Paso Street in Denver Harbor.[8] In addition, the police took Isabel to a local hospital so that medical staff could gather the biological evidence, which here consisted of a semen sample.[9]

Tragic Coincidences

One of the Houston Police Department investigators, Officer Eddie Rodriguez, knew Manuel Beltran and where he lived. In the first of several tragic coincidences, he also happened to know that Beltran at times associated with a man named George Rodriguez, who was on probation for burglary. Officer Rodriguez informed his colleagues that George Rodriguez might be the second rapist.[10] (The two Rodriguezes are not related.[11]) George lived on Abilene Street, three blocks away from the Beltran brothers.[12] Even though Isabel had told the police that she thought "George" was not the second rapist's real name, Officer Rodriguez acted quickly to find George Rodriguez.

George Rodriguez, an eighth-grade dropout, had spent his entire life in the Denver Harbor area of Houston. He came from a large family of modest means. His father was a truck driver, and his mother was a homemaker. George had six brothers, two sisters, and a stepbrother.[13] George was employed in a furniture factory in Houston's East End. He had once been convicted of burglary, and was on probation at the time of the rape.[14] Twice married, he has four daughters and a son. Relatives describe him as quiet and noted that he liked fishing and repairing cars. "He wasn't a rough guy, like the rest of us were," his brother Albert would later tell the *Houston Chronicle*. "He wasn't the type to run the streets like the other kids."[15]

The police needed more specific information about the perpetrators before they could arrest Manuel Beltran. Presumably not wanting to tip Beltran off about their investigation, they asked Isabel to try to identify her attackers from photo arrays *before* they talked to the Beltran brothers.[16] The police had no way of knowing that it was Yanez—and not Rodriguez—who was the second attacker, and so they acted on Officer Rodriguez's theory that the crime had been committed by Manuel Beltran and George Rodriguez. They showed the victim two photo arrays. One included Beltran and five others. The second array included Rodriguez and five others, but not Yanez. In other words, Yanez did not appear in either photo array since the police had no reason to suspect him at this point. In yet another tragic coincidence, Rodriguez and Yanez have similar appearances.[17] Isabel correctly pointed out Beltran but mistakenly identified Rodriguez.[18]

What might have caused the teenage girl to misidentify George Rodriguez as the heavyset rapist? As studies of photo identifications have shown, when the police use suggestive procedures to determine whether a victim can identify a particular suspect, innocent people are put at great risk of misidentification.[19] In this case, we do not know whether the photo spread the police used included at least five other men who looked similar to George Rodriguez. Defense lawyers often challenge photo spreads as being suggestive when the police use a photo of the suspect that "stands out" from the rest because the suspect's face may be larger than the rest because the photo is taken from closer up or the background in the others is different.[20] This tipping of identification can happen when the police use standard mug shots for the "fillers" and use a different type of photo such as a driver's license photo for a suspect who may never have been arrested and thus has no mug shot on record. In other cases, the fillers just do not look anything like the suspect. A photo array also typically only gives a victim like Isabel a view of people's faces, so she does not have the ability to judge height, build or other distinguishing characteristics.

The physical facial resemblance between George Rodriguez and Isidor Yanez turned out to be a coincidence with serious consequences for Rodriguez. This resemblance explains why Isabel picked him out, especially since Yanez's photo was not in the photo array. Psychologist Gary Wells has established that a victim is most likely to make a mistaken identification when she simultaneously views a photo array of six mug shots that do not include that of the true culprit. Eyewitnesses will scan the line of photos looking for the person who most closely resembles her memory of the culprit's face. This method of making judgments by comparison is what psychologists call "relative judgment."[21] Wells further establishes that, when the true guilty person is not present in a simultaneous photo array, the chances that an eyewitness will mistakenly choose the "next best" option—the innocent person who most resembles the guilty person—jumps 300%.[22] These findings are conclusive enough that police departments are switching to a new procedure of showing witnesses photos one at a time in what are called "sequential" photo arrays and lineups.[23]

As part of striving for more accurate identification by witnesses, officers must tell the witness now that the true criminal may or may not be in the lineup. This information dispels the witness's assumption that the police have hard proof implicating one of the people in the group.[24] A victim like Isabel may assume her true job is to confirm the good officer's work and not hamper the case by making a mistake. In this 1987 investigation, such information was not part of general practice, and, in fact, the girl was not told that the criminal's photo might not be in the array. The first DNA exoneration would occur in 1989, and police practices designed to prevent wrongful convictions would not emerge for another decade.[25]

Unsurprisingly, a study in 2008 analyzing the accuracy of witness identifications confirms the intuitive sense that the circumstances typically part of the environment surrounding violent crimes such as rape work against viewing a stranger's face and making an accurate identification later. In a study of the first 214 DNA exonerations, all 214 cases involved a sexual assault, and over 75% included an eyewitness's misidentification.[26] This finding does not mean that rape victims are particularly bad at identifying their culprit—they are not. Rather, they are just as inaccurate as other victims of violent crimes and for the same reasons. During violent crimes, victims will often focus on the weapon with which they are threatened. No weapon was involved in this rape, but other factors made it harder for Isabel to get a good view of her attackers. Events transpired quickly, and the lighting on the street, in the car, and later in the bedroom, was not optimal. There were also two attackers to identify. A witness's extreme fear and stress also significantly reduces her ability to make an accurate identification.[27] Yanez and Beltran forcibly seized Isabel, hit her, and threatened to kill her if she resisted.[28] She later testified at Rodriguez's trial that she had seen his face for only three to four seconds during the attack, effectively admitting that she did not have sufficient time to get a good look.[29]

The mistaken identification of Rodriguez would have terrible consequences. Human memory is not like a video recording. Memory provides only incomplete and malleable images. When Isabel chose Rodriguez's photo, the memory she had of the events of the night of the rape changed forever.[30] Whatever memory she had of Isidor Yanez's face on the night of February 24th became replaced by George Rodriguez's face when she identified him two days later in the second photo array. Without realizing it, she now had a new—and wrong—memory of her attacker. In a similar case in North Carolina, a young woman named Jennifer Thompson* wrongly identified Ronald Cotton as the man who

---

* Jennifer Thompson is not related to this author.

had raped her in 1984. Cotton was quickly convicted based upon her eyewitness testimony. Cotton's lawyers eventually figured out that it was Bobby Poole who had raped Thompson. When Cotton's lawyers later got a court hearing during the appeals process and called Poole to the witness stand, Thompson felt "nothing."[31] She later explained that she did not recognize the actual rapist when she saw him in court—that she felt her memory had been transformed. She could only see Ronald Cotton in her mind. After DNA tests proved her wrong, she asked for a meeting with the innocent man, Ronald Cotton, to remake her memory, disassociating him from the memory of the rape.[32]

In the Rodriguez case, the new memory of the second rapist in Isabel's mind also explains why she would erroneously identify Rodriguez a second time in the following month. The police chose not to arrest Rodriguez based only on her identification of him in the photo array. Instead, erring on the side of caution, they wanted to give Isabel a second opportunity to view Rodriguez, this time in person, so they persuaded Rodriguez to take part in a live lineup.[33] Innocent people often agree to such police requests because they believe their cooperation will help to clear them of suspicion. Unfortunately for Rodriguez, Isabel picked him again, but even then it was less than a firm identification, since she told the police she could identify him in part "by the way he stood,"[34] which is simply not a unique identifying factor.

In the late 1980s, the police and prosecutors were unlikely to know that a first mistaken identification would give rise to a second. They also would not know that a second mistaken identification, as well as the process of preparing for trial with a prosecutor, would increase Isabel's confidence that she had accurately identified her assailant.[35] It is common for witnesses to express some doubt during a lineup only to tell juries a few months later that they were 100% certain.[36] She may even have been told that the crime laboratory had come up with scientific evidence proving his guilt, which would certainly have bolstered her belief that she had fingered the right man.[37]

Beltran's Story Creates a Dilemma

Not long after the rape, police had strong evidence that Yanez, not Rodriguez, had raped the girl. Two days after the attack, during a raid on the suspects' house, the police questioned Manuel Beltran and his older brother, Uvaldo, in separate rooms.[38] Innocence Project attorney Mark Wawro reviewed police reports which show that Manuel confessed to the crime during this initial interview, and, not surprisingly, named Isidro Yanez as his accomplice.[39] Uvaldo Beltran also named Yanez as the second rapist. Officer M.D. Tobar's report states, "During the processing and discussion, it was learned from Manuel (that) the suspect believed to have been George Rodriguez ... was in fact a man by the name of Isi."[40] The police reports give some insight into Manuel's possible motivation for taking part in such a heinous crime. Officer Tobar writes, "When the full weight of the situation was explained to Manuel he broke down into tears and explained that he was afraid of Isi because Isi had a gun and threatened to shoot him if he did not 'get him that girl.' "[41] Further events would prove the truth of Manuel's statement that Isi was a scary, violent man. Manuel Beltran also told police that Isi and Rodriguez resembled each other and were both heavyset,[42] so they had reason to know that the victim might have mistakenly identified Rodriguez when Yanez was the true attacker.

Investigators arrested Manuel, but had no reason to arrest Uvaldo who had simply been present at the scene watching television. It surprises many people to learn that mere presence at the scene of a crime is not itself a crime.[43] Uvaldo sat by idly while his brother and another man assaulted an innocent girl. While morally repugnant, his presence at the scene did not make him an accomplice, at least not in 1987.[44] In most states, the law now requires all witnesses to report certain types of serious offenses such as sexual assaults or child abuse.[45] Uvaldo could have called the police. He did not do it, but since Texas law at the time did not require it, he was not arrested.

Now the police had a genuine dilemma. On the one hand, one of the rapists and his brother, when questioned separately, both named Yanez as the second rapist. Rodriguez resembled Yanez physically, so it seemed possible, even likely, that Isabel might have misidentified Rodriguez. She had said she did not believe the fat rapist was actually named "George" because the men had talked about using fake names.[46] They also learned that Manuel and the second rapist had used Yanez's car to commit the kidnapping.[47] Even Rodriguez's alibi had checked out. The foreman of the furniture factory where Rodriguez worked told the police that he was working at the time of the assault, and time cards supported his statement. However, police noted that workers often punched in and out for each other.[48]

On the other hand, Isabel had chosen Rodriguez's photo and picked him out of the live lineup, the police knew that Rodriguez and Beltran were acquaintances, and she reported that the fat rapist was called "George" by the other. Given the fact that there were two strong competing theories on the table, the police could not justify moving forward by arresting Rodriguez at the same time that they arrested Beltran. The arrest warrant for Rodriguez was withdrawn, but he remained a suspect as the second rapist.

The police were not able to find Yanez initially, so he was not even questioned until almost a month after the attack.[49] They finally caught up with him at his mother's home. He initially identified himself by his own brother's name,[50] in itself an odd thing for an ostensibly innocent person to do. Using fingerprint records, the police learned his true identity, so they returned to question him. He then told officers that he knew nothing about the kidnapping and rape, claiming that he had loaned Manuel Beltran his car. This explained the fact that his car matched the description given by the girl and that Beltran had said the car belonged to Yanez. The police apparently believed that at least one of the Beltran brothers had spoken to Yanez about the police investigation. "Yanez seemed fairly well informed about what had been said to officers about him," the police report said.[51] Yanez had clearly tailored his tale of innocence to fit the information the police already had.

After Isabel's second identification of Rodriguez, the police arrested him and charged him, like Beltran, with kidnapping and rape. Still hoping to prove his innocence, Rodriguez now voluntarily gave the police hair samples which were sent to the Houston Police Department's Crime Laboratory.[52] Since Rodriguez was now under arrest, the Harris County District Attorney's Office took over the case. Police and prosecutors awaited the results of the scientific testing. Meanwhile, Rodriguez sat in jail.

The initial findings seemed to clear Rodriguez. HPD Crime Laboratory Analyst Reidun Hilleman's preliminary microscopic review failed to match Rodriguez's hair to any of the hairs found at the crime scene.[53] Rodriguez was released without charges. Since Beltran had confessed, he would be held in jail pending trial. As for Rodriguez, police reports show that investigators and prosecutors chose to wait until all crime laboratory analysis of the semen, blood, and hair collected in victim's rape kit was completed before deciding whether the evidence supported re-arresting him.[54]

Fighting Tunnel Vision

At about the same time, in April of 1987, one Harris County prosecutor began cautioning the police against focusing on Rodriguez.[55] He tried to prevent them from developing what psychologists call "tunnel vision" regarding Rodriguez and, thus, ignoring Yanez as a suspect. Law professors Keith Findley and Michael Scott have published an influential study that warns about the danger of tunnel vision in police investigations.[56] If police officers (or anyone, for that matter) come to believe that a particular person is guilty, they tend to downplay or reject contrary evidence, to view ambiguous evidence as supporting the leading theory when it may not, and to give greater weight to inculpating evidence than it deserves. Tunnel vision is a natural mental process that enables us to process information more effectively, but in criminal investigations it can make investigators deaf and blind to the possible innocence of a suspect and hamper their ability to weigh evidence accurately.[57]

In the same month that Rodriguez was briefly taken into custody and when the laboratory testing began, Assistant District Attorney Edward Porter informed Sgt. S.L. Clappart that he was investigating a similar case of kidnapping and sexual assault involving Yanez against two women committed by two men about a year earlier in 1986.[58] Two additional similarities weighed heavily. First, in Porter's case Yanez had been implicated not only as a suspect but the driving force behind the crime; and second, the crime also took place in the Denver Harbor area. Porter urged the police "not to rush into an indictment situation" against Rodriguez, according to a police report.[59] The second man in Porter's case was Frank Campos.[60]

Thus, the District Attorney's Office knew, and the Houston Police Department was explicitly warned, that Yanez—not Rodriguez—had committed another crime using the same *modus operandi*. Prosecutors see *modus operandi*—proof that a person has previously committed a different crime in a "peculiar and distinctive" manner, as strong evidence of a criminal's identity.[61] It is often said to be "like a fingerprint" in identifying a person. Police and prosecutors had every reason to believe Yanez was their man.

In an interview with the *Houston Chronicle* in 2004, Campos, who had served three years of a fifteen-year sentence for the 1986 kidnapping and rape, claimed that it was Yanez who insisted on grabbing the women at gunpoint. He added that only Yanez raped the women. Yanez was never charged, even though "everybody knew he was a rapist," Campos told the *Chronicle*.[62]

Even Yanez's mother knew he was a rapist. In July 1987 (five months after the Denver Harbor rape and three months before Rodriguez went on trial), Yanez raped his mother's live-in maid who was five months pregnant at the time. "The suspect pinned her down on the bed and started beating her with his fists on the head and face," the police report said.[63] "The suspect kept yelling at her that if she didn't give in, he was going to kill her." Yanez's mother turned her son in.[64] "She wants charges filed against her son because he, on several other occasions, had assaulted women and nothing has ever been done to him," the police report states.[65] "She thinks her son is mentally ill and needs to be arrested before he hurts someone else."[66]

Prosecutors charged Yanez for raping the maid, but they offered him a reduced charge of attempted sexual assault and a sentence of one year in the county jail in exchange for agreeing to plead guilty. For a violent, sexual predator like Yanez, this must have seemed like a great bargain. Studies of sentencing patterns shows that perpetrators like Yanez are more likely to plead guilty and thus receive drastically reduced sentences.[67] By contrast, when innocent people like Rodriguez are prosecuted, they tend to demand a jury trial and consequently face much harsher punishment upon conviction.[68] It is also true that those who rape poor or minority females, even when they are convicted, tend to receive lighter sentences than when the victims are affluent or white.[69] In this case, the pregnant maid came from a working class neighborhood and was probably Latina.

Thus, by mistakenly arresting Rodriguez for Isabel Medina's rape, the police had also failed to remove a dangerous predator from the community, giving him the opportunity to commit other rapes. To his great credit, Assistant District Attorney Porter pointed to Yanez as the possible rapist in Isabel's case, urging the police to proceed cautiously. Beltran had also named Yanez. And, yet, Rodriguez languished in jail, awaiting trial for a brutal crime he did not commit.

Meanwhile Back at the Lab …

The Houston Police Department Crime Laboratory tested the biological evidence (semen, blood, and hair) that had been collected from Isabel's underwear and body during the medical examination she was given immediately she reported the crime.[70] This material was placed in a "rape kit" so that it could be preserved for testing, then stored, in the police department's evidence room. The investigating officers submitted a standard request for the crime laboratory to test the rape kit, seeking a comparison of the materials found in the kit to the hair and blood samples obtained from Rodriguez and Beltran.[71]

Although Crime Laboratory Analyst Hilleman's initial testing of the rape kit earlier in April found no match to the hair sample, on April 30, 1987, Hilleman now told Detective Clappart that "she had located one pubic hair from the [victim's] panties that was consistent with the hair sample from George Rodriguez"[72] using a process known as microscopic hair analysis. Police departments across the country used this type of analysis routinely in the 1980s, but it has now been proven to be invalid as a means of identifying a specific individual.[73] In a study of DNA exonerations, 75 of the first 200 wrongful convictions—more than a third—involved incorrect hair analysis.[74]

As a matter of scientific methodology, an analyst cannot validly claim that microscopic hair analysis has yielded a definitive "match."[75] Yet the police and prosecutors took statements about a match with Rodriguez's hair as gospel truth. In addition, the girl had by now identified Rodriguez three times. She had also been shown a photo of Yanez among others, and she singled him out as someone who looked like Rodriguez but still maintained that Rodriguez was the attacker.[76] With the crime laboratory's new results, the scientific evidence also conclusively identified Rodriguez. The case was considered rock solid. Whatever similarities Assistant District Attorney Porter may have seen in Yanez's prior crime, and even considering that the Beltran brothers both implicated Yanez, the scientific evidence was viewed as objective, definitive proof that Rodriguez was guilty. The next morning, county prosecutors filed aggravated kidnapping and aggravated sexual assault charges against Rodriguez.[77]

DNA testing was not available to police crime laboratories in 1987, but it was about to burst on the scene.[78] During the time when Rodriguez's case was being investigated, the best a laboratory could do with blood samples taken from the victim's clothing and rape kit was to conduct serology testing. As law professor Brandon Garrett explains in his study of wrongful convictions:

> Conventional serology, using ABO blood-typing, was the most common type of forensic analysis [prior to the advent of DNA analysis]. Unlike some other disciplines, serology was grounded in sound science and empirically validated population data—in other words it was a reliable method. This makes it all the more disturbing that analysts in so many [cases of wrongful convictions] either did not understand or exaggerated the clear boundaries of the science when they offered their conclusions.[79]

In the Rodriguez case, HPD did serology testing in addition to the hair analysis, appraising Rodriguez's blood against the samples in the rape kit. James Bolding, who would later become the supervisor of the DNA laboratory in the HPD Crime Laboratory, gave trial testimony which definitively excluded Yanez as a possible donor but which could not eliminate Rodriguez as a donor.[80] He also testified that Beltran was a possible donor.

Science Convicts

With the test results in, Rodriguez did not stand a chance. The best lawyer at the time would have been hard-pressed to challenge the crime laboratory's findings. The prosecution had serology tests which implicated Rodriguez as a possible culprit, and a hair analysis that found one hair that was "consistent with" Rodriguez's. Even though he was innocent, it would take the justice system over 17 years to reach that conclusion. In 1987 it would not have occurred to most defense lawyers to challenge a crime laboratory's findings. For one thing, few lawyers or judges have the scientific background to fully comprehend an ex-

pert's testimony, and, further, it was unthinkable that crime laboratory analysts could give inaccurate or misleading testimony. The trust in "scientific" evidence was pervasive. Even if a defense lawyer wanted to challenge the forensic
testimony, he would need expert assistance, and poor people like Rodriguez
could not get such help. As was common in cases like Rodriguez's, the judge had
appointed an attorney in private practice to represent him at the county's ex-
pense. Court-appointed lawyers are compensated for their work by the judicial
system, but compensation levels remain notoriously low nationwide. Thus,
court-appointed lawyers often lack the skills and/or the resources to do an adequate job, and at least some members of Rodriguez's family questioned his
lawyer's competence.[81]

After all, by law, the prosecutor should have given the defense attorney a
copy of the police report which included Beltran's statement identifying Yanez
as the second rapist, as this was powerful exculpatory evidence. Whether the
defense was actually given the police report is not clear from the record. Even
if the prosecutor illegally withheld the police report from the defense, any competent defense investigation would have included an interview of Beltran. The
defense should have called him to testify at Rodriguez's trial where he could
have told the jury that Yanez was his accomplice, not Rodriguez. The defense
attorney then could have explained the victim's mistaken identification by pointing out the resemblance between the two men. Yanez had also admitted to police that Beltran was driving his car on the day of the crime, saying he had
loaned it to Beltran, which would have further pointed toward Yanez's guilt.
Finally, Yanez had just been arrested for a similar crime a few months before Rodriguez's trial. Unfortunately, the jury heard none of this evidence.

Nor did Rodriguez's lawyer challenge the lab findings. To do so, he would
have had to ask the trial judge to provide the funds to hire a forensic expert.
The United States Supreme Court recognized a constitutional right to court-
appointed experts in 1985, two years before Rodriguez's trial.[82] Nonetheless,
trial judges typically denied defense requests for experts of any kind, on the
ground that the defense did not need the expert, or they granted the requests but
restricted the right to psychiatric experts.[83] When defense attorneys raised such
denials on appeal, the appellate courts rarely used such denials as the basis for
overturning convictions.[84]

Rich defendants fared better. In the early 1990s, the "dream team" of highly
paid private defense lawyers who handled the O.J. Simpson case included Barry
Scheck, later a founder of the Innocence Project. This team first introduced
Americans to the idea that a forensic laboratory might get it wrong.[85] (Scheck
would also later be responsible for Rodriguez's exoneration.) Simpson's defense team challenged the DNA work of one of the nation's largest commer-

cial laboratories, Cellmark Diagnostics, headed at the time by Dr. Daniel Garner.[86] Their challenge, however, focused on the crime scene unit's handling of the evidence, not Cellmark's work. In an interesting twist, more than 20 years later, Garner, a widely respected forensic scientist would become the first President and CEO of Houston's new independent forensic laboratory which would replace the HPD Crime Laboratory.[87]

Without the benefit of a well-financed lawyer or the assistance of a forensic expert, Rodriguez faced trial with no ability to challenge the forensic evidence, raising only an alibi defense. A jury convicted Rodriguez, and he was sentenced to sixty years in prison for aggravated kidnapping and aggravated sexual assault.[88] Manuel Beltran was separately tried, convicted, and also sentenced to 60 years.[89] At age twenty-six, Rodriguez was headed to a prison within the Texas Department of Criminal Justice where he would probably die before his release date when he was eighty-six.

Rodriguez's only recourse lay in the appellate process, followed by the availability of filing state and federal *habeas corpus* petitions. Like almost all convicted people—innocent or otherwise—Rodriguez lost all his appeals. After the trial, the judge appointed a different appellate lawyer who raised several legal issues on Rodriguez's behalf. In a 1989 decision, the court of appeals rejected all his claims. His lawyer argued, for example, that the evidence did not support a first-degree kidnapping charge.[90] Rodriguez's attorney argued that the victim had not been left in a dangerous place when she was released, as required by a first-degree charge, so he should have been convicted of the lesser charge. The appellate court disagreed.[91] Without new evidence of innocence, the appellate process affords no means of arguing that the conviction should be overturned on grounds of innocence—just on procedural grounds. The appellate lawyer's argument must have seemed grotesque to Rodriguez. He was not guilty of *any* crime, yet his lawyer was arguing that he *had* committed a crime but that he had committed it safely.

Locked Up and Forgotten

It is hard for people in the "free world," as prisoners call it,[92] to imagine the terror Rodriguez felt upon entering a maximum security prison, knowing he was innocent. He knew he would probably die in prison. He was innocent, but how could he prove it? In a speech to law students doing summer work for federal judges in Houston, Anthony Graves, who had proved his innocence after eighteen years on Death Row, reduced many to tears as he described his fear when he walked onto Death Row for the first time.[93] Graves had never committed a violent crime, yet he was surrounded by people who were considered ruthless and bestial killers. One inmate called out to him and said he had something for him. Graves did not know this man and wanted nothing to do with him. Frightened, he ignored the man. Then one day, a book was passed along to him, an unexpected gift from the inmate to help Graves pass the time.[94]

For indigent prisoners like Rodriguez, the law provides an attorney only for the first appeal. Thereafter, he and all indigent prisoners have no constitutional right to a court-appointed lawyer, so they typically fend for themselves drafting petitions in prison law libraries. Rodriguez would spend the next seventeen years behind bars trying to prove his innocence, filing handwritten court papers, and using credit from his commissary account[†] to pay other inmates for legal advice.[95] In years past, inmates were paid a small hourly wage for their prison labor, so that even a prisoner with no support from family or friends could earn some spending money. All inmates are expected to do whatever work they are physically able to do. Many participate in various "prison industries" making furniture, retreading tires, repairing school buses, and farming, among others. During the "get tough" on criminals era of the 1990s, the Texas legislature decided that inmates should work for free. Today, only inmates fortunate enough to have family or friends who send them money have commissary accounts. The commissary sells all the creature comforts not provided by the prison—blankets, heaters, fans, radios, snacks, and more. To give up one's commissary account money for seventeen years is to deprive oneself of the few sources of pleasure and relief in a prison. He also had to give up his free time to work on his case since most of his day was spent doing prison labor.[96]

Spending time with family during weekend visits can also bring much joy. For Rodriguez this source of happiness was often unavailable. He was incarcerated in a prison known as the "Cofield Unit" near Tennessee Colony, Texas, about 175 miles from Houston.[97] Rodriguez's family in Houston would have had to cover the cost of gasoline and a hotel room for an overnight trip, or they would have had to drive nearly 350-miles roundtrip in one day. For a hard-working family of limited means, such a trip would require exceptional sacrifice. Not surprisingly, in 2004 Rodriguez told the *Houston Chronicle* that his family rarely visited.[98] It is not unusual for inmates with no prospect of release to have few visitors.

---

†. Commissary accounts are like bank accounts, which prisoners can use in purchasing items in the prison commissary.

Saved by a Hair

When DNA evidence began making its way into criminal courts in the late 1980s as a means of definitively proving a person's guilt, another group saw its potential to definitively prove innocence. The Innocence Project, a national litigation and public policy group, turned the criminal justice field upside down by taking on cases in which prisoners had reasonable claims of innocence and in which biological evidence could be tested for DNA. One by one, the group obtained the release of wrongly convicted men until their numbers would reach the hundreds. In the process, the Innocence Project uncovered the ugly truth that the criminal justice system—the police, the prosecutors, defense lawyers, judges, and juries—make serious mistakes. Police officers coerced false confessions, eyewitnesses picked the wrong person in lineups, jailhouse informants lied, prosecutors failed to disclose exculpatory evidence to the defense, and crime laboratory analysts gave invalid or misleading testimony.

Nationwide, prisoners with claims of innocence, including Rodriguez, reached out to the Innocence Project, seeking their assistance in getting the evidence in their cases tested for DNA evidence. Rodriguez's luck finally turned when in 2001 when the group agreed to work on his case.[99] Most of the biological evidence had been routinely destroyed in 1995,[100] but the single hair that was supposedly matched microscopically to Rodriguez was miraculously located.[101] This was the same evidence that had convinced the police to focus on Rodriguez and turn away from Yanez. For DNA testing, any biological evidence—hair, semen, saliva, blood, sweat, mucus, skin, and even earwax—can provide the few cells necessary to extract the DNA evidence used to identify a person.

In August 2002, State District Judge Belinda Hill ordered the Houston police crime laboratory to conduct DNA testing on any remaining evidence in the case.[102] This time, the HPD Crime Laboratory mishandled DNA tests on the evidence.[103] Then in December of 2002, the laboratory's DNA section was shut down after an independent audit raised questions about the integrity of the laboratory's work in thousands of cases.[104] Laboratory closures, audits, and a wide variety of scandals in laboratories across the country would throw the entire forensic industry into chaos in the decade to follow. The closure of HPD's DNA laboratory would ultimately be good news for Rodriguez's efforts to clear his name, but meanwhile further progress would be delayed.

In 2003, Rodriguez's lawyers from the Innocence Project again successfully petitioned the State District Court for post-conviction DNA testing on the single strand of hair. This time the hair evidence was sent to a private laboratory, ReliaGene Technologies, in New Orleans. Analysts at ReliaGene complained that the HPD laboratory had not preserved sufficient evidence from the hair to permit them to do the more precise form of DNA testing that they thought was necessary, so the testing was not done.[105]

Finally in April of 2004, the remaining evidence from the hair was sent to yet another laboratory which conducted a less-exact procedure that does not require as much DNA material but which links individuals only through a common maternal ancestor rather than making an exact genetic match with an individual.[106] The testing ruled out Rodriguez as the source of the pubic hair and implicated Isidro Yanez instead.[107] "If (the hair) had been sent to another laboratory in the first place, we could have gotten a profile nailing Yanez to the wall," said Innocence Project lawyer Vanessa Potkin. "But what we have is still extremely powerful."[108]

Additionally, further serological testing ordered by prosecutors on a blood sample taken from Yanez revealed that he had been mis-typed at the time of trial and should never have been excluded as a potential contributor of the semen from the rape kit and the victim's clothing.[109] The Innocence Project arranged for Dr. Robert Shaler, Director of the Department of Forensic Biology at the New York City Medical Examiner's Office, and five other forensic scientists to review the test results as well as the expert testimony given at Rodriguez's trial. All six scientists signed an affidavit stating that James Bolding's testimony "contains egregious misstatements of conventional serology."[110] "These statements reveal that either (he) lacked a fundamental understanding of the most basic principles of blood typing analysis or he knowingly gave false testimony."[111]

The affidavit also stated, "It is reasonable to assume that Jim Bolding and Christi Kim (another analyst) issued many other reports and/or gave testimony in many other cases during their tenure at the Houston Police Department Crime Laboratory…. A serious danger exists that they may have offered similarly false and scientifically unsound testimony/reports in these other cases."[112] Says Barry Scheck: "We've had more than 20 years of bad lab work. Some of the cases may have very well been cases in which people were executed."[113]

Rodriguez was still in prison through late 2004. He gave an interview to a *Houston Chronicle* reporter who wanted his reaction to the Shaler affidavit. In response, Rodriguez declared, "I'm going to keep doing what I'm doing until I prove myself innocent."[114] As he gathered up his legal papers and prepared to return to his cell, he paused to reflect on the people and circumstances that led to his seventeen years in prison. "I'm not really angry," he said, "I just can't believe it happened."[115]

DA Resistance, the Role of the Victim, and Ignoring Occam's Razor

A *Houston Chronicle* editorial on August 26, 2004, urged District Attorney Chuck Rosenthal to keep in mind Occam's Razor, the logical principle that among competing hypotheses one should select the one requiring the fewest assumptions.[116] Two days earlier, Rosenthal had said he found the new DNA evidence in Rodriguez's case unconvincing. "I'm not particularly moved by the DNA findings," Rosenthal said.[117] "We are moving toward a position that HPD was correct—I'm not saying we are there yet, but we are moving toward that position."[118] Rodriguez's lawyers had filed a motion to have his conviction vacated, which the district attorney's office had opposed. While not directly challenging the defense's new forensic evidence, prosecutors conceded only that "further factual investigation may be necessary."[119] Rosenthal stressed the limits of the testing in a desperate attempt to counter the truth of the defense's claims that Rodriguez had been wrongly charged and convicted. It is true that HPD's mishandling of the evidence had restricted the type of DNA testing now possible to one that did definitively identify Yanez. A member of his family could also have been the source of the DNA. "The fact that she had a pubic hair from someone in Mr. Yanez's family on her is not necessarily compelling," Rosenberg said.[120] "We are looking now at the (blood tests), and apparently the experts that filed their so-called peer review didn't have access to everything." Rosenthal added, "We will wait and see what we find."[121]

In his book *Failed Evidence: Why Law Enforcement Resists Science*, law professor David Harris tells us that prosecutorial resistance to DNA tests that exonerate is not uncommon:

> [Prosecutors] appear to love DNA when it supports their efforts, but they deny its legitimacy when it undermines what they have already decided or done. For some prosecutors, the commitment to a set of charges they have brought or a conviction they have already obtained simply overwhelms the ability to accept compelling DNA evidence that stands against their previously adopted positions.[122]

Part of the resistance may stem from the fact that prosecutors work closely with victims, identifying with their suffering and their need for justice, especially in cases of violent crimes. To acknowledge a mistake in prosecuting a violent crime means accepting many unsavory truths. First, it means that prosecutors—who consider themselves "the good guys"—have victimized an innocent person. One senior prosecutor in Harris County once said that if he ever discovered that he had wrongly prosecuted someone, he would consider his entire career to have been a failure.[123] Such emotional commitments are not unique. The burden of DNA exonerations on the prosecutors responsible for the convictions is indeed heavy.

Second, recognizing a wrongful conviction means recognizing that the true culprit—in this case, Yanez—was allowed to remain at large and continue his predatory violence.[124] This is the hidden public safety threat of wrongful convictions: Every innocent person convicted also leaves a criminal on the loose while the public falsely believes the dangerous person to be in custody. In another Texas case, police and prosecutors intentionally hid evidence from the defense (in itself a violation of professional canons, the Constitution, and Texas law), leading to the conviction of an innocent person. Michael Morton was wrongly convicted of beating to death his wife, Christine, the mother of his young son. A jury sent him to prison for life in 1986.[125] The evidence against him included bogus forensic testimony by the medical examiner. In their zeal to convict Morton and reassure the community of its security, the police and prosecutor also failed to apprehend the true killer, Mark Alan Norwood. Two years later, Norwood bludgeoned to death another young mother, Debra Masters Baker, who lived in the same area.[126] Between this second horrific murder in 1988 and 2012, the killer remained free.

Norwood was caught in 2012 after a researcher for Michael Morton's defense team connected Debra Baker's killing to Christine Morton's.[127] He was convicted in 2013 of Christine Morton's murder and received an automatic life sentence.[128] Michael Morton was released in 2011 after spending nearly twenty-five years in prison. The prosecutor in the Morton case, who by 2011 was a sitting judge in the county, was convicted on charges that he intentionally failed to give the defense exonerating evidence during the trial as required by law.[129] Norwood still faces a murder charge in the 1988 killing of Debra Baker.[130] Jesse Baker, Debra's son who was seven at the time his mother was killed, attended the hearings on the prosecutor's malfeasance which had allowed Christine Morton's murderer to kill his own mother. "The thought that (the prosecutors) may have some responsibility in all this and they might not be held accountable is too much to think about," he said.[131]

In the Rodriguez case, a serial rapist continued to terrorize the women of the Denver Harbor area in Houston and amazingly managed to avoid serious punishment the few times that he was actually caught. In 2002, Yanez was arrested for abducting his estranged wife, whom he had allegedly assaulted the day before.[132] "The (victim) stated that she's afraid (Yanez) will hurt her again or kill her," the arresting officer wrote in his report.[133] In July 2003, Yanez pleaded guilty to kidnapping and was sentenced to two years in prison. Because of credit for time served, he was scheduled for release in October of 2004, the year before Rodriguez was eventually exonerated and released.[134] One can readily imaging that someone in District Attorney Rosenthal's position might dread the possibility that a prosecutor had mistakenly sent the wrong man to prison, leaving a predator at large.

Finally, a prosecutor would likely dread the impact that overturning a conviction would have on a victim like Isabel. Rodriguez's innocence meant that the fourteen-year-old rape victim, by now a thirty-one-year-old woman, would learn that she was wrong when she identified Rodriguez and would have to come to terms with that situation in a whole new way. It would require her to re-live the crime that she had surely tried to forget and face the horror and disbelief of having put an innocent man behind bars for almost twenty years. In a case like this, in which the victim's memory was altered due to the misidentification, it would be hard for her not to see Rodriguez when she thought of the crime. For District Attorney Rosenthal, accepting Rodriguez's innocence meant contradicting the victim. He noted that the victim had repeatedly identified Rodriguez as her attacker, adding, "She is convinced of that to this day, and I take that to be significant."[135]

Victims who mistakenly identify a person and contribute to a miscarriage of justice suffer enormous and potentially life-changing guilt and frustration when the truth emerges. In another case, a woman named Michele Mallin learned that she had wrongly identified Timothy Cole as the "Tech Rapist" who had attacked her in 1985.[136] It turned out that Cole, an Army veteran and Texas Tech college student, was innocent, just as he had insisted at trial and as multiple witnesses had confirmed his alibi. Rodriguez also had a solid alibi in his employer, corroborated by his time card. Like the victim in the Rodriguez case, Mallin misidentified Cole, in this case three times, once in a photo array, the next day in a live lineup, and then at trial.[137] Also like the Rodriguez case, the prosecutor presented similar expert scientific evidence (this time from the state police crime laboratory): "consistent" hair samples and blood typing.[138] Cole struggled in prison to get adequate medical care for his asthma but died of an asthma attack after nine years in prison. He was thirty-nine. Cole was posthumously exonerated by DNA evidence and by the confession of the true rapist.[139] The Texas legislature named an advisory panel on wrongful convictions in his honor, and the Timothy Cole Act established a plan to compensate the exonerated.

For her part, Mallin joined the Cole family in clearing his name. She has expressed anger at the police and prosecutors who she believes manipulated her into identifying Cole by repeatedly referring to him as a "low-life hood."[140]

Jennifer Thompson and Ronald Cotton. Dave Kettering/*Dubuque Telegraph Herald*

Mallin expressed the difficult mix of emotions that victims feel as they confront the truth of having sent an innocent man to prison:

> I still feel guilty. I'll always feel guilty about it because, I mean, my testimony sent a man to prison and he ended up dying there. Even though I know I did everything I could in my heart of hearts to do the right thing, still that happened. But I know the police are responsible and the D.A., too, because they knew things I didn't know.[141]

She has since extensively studied the psychology of mistaken identification and travels the country speaking on wrongful convictions.[142]

Jennifer Thompson, the North Carolina rape victim who wrongly identified Ronald Cotton as her rapist, has co-authored a book with him entitled, *Picking Cotton: Our Memoir of Injustice and Redemption*.[143] The two have become good friends and also travel nationwide speaking about their ordeals. In an interview with *60 Minutes*, the two told of their difficult first meeting after Cotton's release at which she apologized for her part in his tragedy, and he gracefully forgave her.[144] It is understandable that a prosecutor, like District Attorney Rosenthal in the Rodriguez case, would have a hard time putting a victim through the experience of realizing that she had destroyed the young adult life of an innocent husband and father.

Free at Last

At long last, the DNA tests had established Rodriguez's innocence, and he was finally released in October of 2004—but he was not exactly free.[145] The trial judge released Rodriguez on bail,[146] but, technically, he was still on bail in the custody of the Texas correctional system pending a possible retrial. With the DNA evidence in hand, Rodriguez's lawyers filed a *habeas corpus* petition, arguing that the use of faulty serological evidence violated his constitutional rights. Facing incontrovertible proof that Rodriguez had not raped the victim, the Texas Court of Criminal Appeals granted his petition in August of 2005.[147] The DNA testing on the pubic hair recovered from the victim's clothing excluded Rodriguez, but the court noted that it "did not exclude Yanez or his maternal blood relatives as possible contributors."[148] The court also found that the testimony from the Houston Crime Laboratory Serology Section Supervisor was "inaccurate scientific evidence and Yanez should not have been excluded as a contributor of semen collected from the victim."[149] Thus, the admission of inaccurate serological evidence violated Rodriguez's due process rights. However, the court absolved the prosecutor of any wrongdoing in presenting the testimony and also found that he had not known that the evidence was inaccurate when he relied on it.[150]

The court's decision had vacated Rodriguez's conviction, but this did not prevent the district attorney from seeking a retrial as Rodriguez had not been found innocent. The court had only determined that the forensic evidence against him was invalid,[151] thus leaving him in a strange legal limbo. Isabel's identification of him could constitute sufficient proof for a second conviction.

At age forty-three upon release, George Rodriguez was no longer the young father and husband he had been at twenty-six when he was arrested.[152] He had lost weight and was going bald.[153] But the changes of heart and soul were more important. He had entered prison as a husband and father. What changes had come to his family in the seventeen years that had passed? Like most DNA exonerees, Rodriguez emerged to a different world. His family had lived without him, with the alternation of belief and doubts about his innocence, with the despair that succeeded each other as he struggled with the legal system. George Bailey, the fictional character played by Jimmy Stewart in the iconic Christmas movie *It's a Wonderful Life*, gains a happier perspective on his current life when his guardian angel shows him how unhappy his loved ones would have been if he had never been born. Unfortunately for George Rodriguez, the world he found upon his absence was complicated and fragmented. His wife had divorced him. In a tragic irony, two of his daughters had been sexually abused by the men their mother had lived with.[154] His twenty-six-year-old namesake

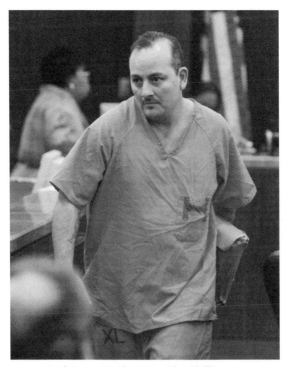

George Rodriguez. AP Photo/David J. Phillip

son was convicted of murder in 1996, nine years after his father's wrongful conviction.[155] George's elder daughter, Esmeralda Estrada commented on her brother's conviction, "I think that if he [her father] would have been out there raising his son, [the son] wouldn't be locked up. When his father left, that is when he started messing up."[156] George's father had also died while he was behind bars.[157] Sitting in prison, Rodriguez must have felt desperate at his thwarted desire to be there for those he loved.

Finally, in November 2004, the month after Rodriguez's release, the district attorney moved to dismiss all charges. Assistant District Attorney Bill Hawkins justified dropping the charges but in a way that resisted the truth of Rodriguez's innocence:

> The defendant has served seventeen years confinement in the Texas Department of Criminal Justice. The State is unwilling to require the victim to relive the 1987 crimes when, even with a life sentence, the defendant would serve less than three years before becoming eligible for parole. As such, the State does not believe that the victim's and

the community's interest would be served by a retrial of the 1987 aggravated kidnapping and aggravated sexual assault.[158]

Thus, the statement assumes, without saying so, that Rodriguez is guilty. The justification for not retrying an ostensibly guilty man, according to Hawkins, is that the benefit of a new conviction would not outweigh the costs to the victim of a retrial.

Rodriguez Sues Houston

After his conviction for rape and kidnapping was set aside by the courts, Rodriguez sued the City of Houston in federal court in 2009 for violating his civil rights.[159] This suit claimed that the police chief had shown "deliberate indifference" to the lack of training and supervision in the crime laboratory and this had allowed for demonstrably false serology testimony to be given against him by the chief of the crime laboratory serology section. Barry Scheck argued the case before a jury of five women and three men.[160] In his opening statement, Scheck told the jury of the loneliness, fear and depression Rodriguez felt after his wrongful conviction and punishment. The jury heard testimony from former Mayor Lee P. Brown, who had been police chief in 1987 when Rodriguez was convicted, as well as from James Bolding, the crime laboratory manager whose testimony landed Rodriguez behind bars. Rodriguez himself also testified. Robert Cambrice, an attorney for the city, blamed the debacle on bad lawyering by the Harris County prosecutor and by Rodriguez's first defense lawyer.[161]

On June 23, 2009, the jury deliberated for six hours. The group then sent a note to the Federal District Judge Vanessa Gilmore informing her that they had reached an impasse on whether Police Chief Lee P. Brown had been deliberately indifferent to the lack of training and supervision of the crime laboratory's staff.[162] The fact that they had reached this question meant that the jury had already agreed that Bolding's testimony played a substantial role in Rodriguez's conviction and that the city allowed the crime laboratory personnel to be inadequately trained and supervised. Judge Gilmore ordered the jury to resume deliberations the following day.[163] If they found that the police chief had been deliberately indifferent, then the last issue they would have to address was whether the laboratory was the "moving force" behind the conviction. If they found that invalid scientific testimony was the "moving force," then the city would be required to pay Rodriguez compensation for the violation of his civil rights. After a second day of deliberations, the jury returned

George Rodriguez (center) with supporters and Houston Mayor Annise Parker (right)
© *Houston Chronicle*/Mayra Beltran. Used with permission.

with a verdict in Rodriguez's favor: the crime laboratory analysts' testimony
had been the "moving force" that caused Rodriguez's wrongful conviction.[164]

On Rodriguez's behalf, Scheck asked the jury to award $35 million in com-
pensation, approximately $2 million for each year he had spent behind bars.
"What was taken away from him was his youth," Scheck told the jury. The jury
awarded him $5 million.[165] Pleased with the verdict, Rodriguez nonetheless
lamented, "Ain't no amount of money is going to even my scale. I lost my dad,
and my girls have been through hell. I am grateful [for the jury verdict], but
no money can replace what I've lost."[166]

Similar lawsuits have been filed around the country by exonerated men,
and multi-million dollar verdicts are the norm.[167] Twenty-nine states and the
District of Columbia also now have compensation statutes that allow exonerated individuals to apply for compensation rather than sue the government.[168] Texas now has the most generous compensation package for exonerees
in the nation, but this program came into effect after Rodriguez's lawsuit.[169]
Not only do wrongful convictions harm innocent individuals and their fam-
ilies, but they also put the community at continuing risk and cost the taxpayers millions.

Despite the jury verdict, by 2011, Rodriguez had still not received a dime from
the city. The city appealed the jury's decision, dragging out the litigation and

disputing the judgment of liability on various legal grounds.[170] The Fifth Circuit Court of Appeals sent the case back to Judge Gilmore's court on June 13, 2011, for another round of legal wrangling.[171] Meanwhile, negotiations between the city and Rodriguez had been ongoing. Finally, twenty-five years after his arrest, the parties settled the case for $3.1 million late the following year.[172] On November 2, 2012, Houston Mayor Annise Parker appeared at a press conference in City Hall. Flanked by George Rodriguez and his family members, on behalf of the city that had done him wrong, she publicly apologized to him. "Anyone with any compassion has to offer a heartfelt apology," said the mayor.[173]

In the aftermath of the Rodriguez conviction debacle and several other cases like it, Houston leaders grappled with a complex problem. How could separate crime laboratory analysts at the Houston Police Department Crime Laboratory give incorrect scientific evidence of three different types against Rodriguez? Were they lying, honestly mistaken, or incompetent? Of James Bolding, who in 2004 was head of the DNA unit, the Innocence Project's lawyer Mark Wawro told the *Houston Chronicle*, "Our experts don't know whether he was lying or completely incompetent."[174] State District Judge Jan Krocker ruled that there was probable cause to believe that Bolding had committed aggravated perjury in a separate 2002 sexual assault trial, and a special court of inquiry was convened.[175] Bolding had interpreted similar scientific evidence in opposite ways in two separate rape cases, each time in ways that supported the prosecution's case. However, the charge against Bolding was later dismissed because the statute of limitations on the perjury offense had expired.[176]

What had become clear is that the crime laboratory had serious problems. The state audit uncovered a dysfunctional organization with untrained staff, contamination problems, and shoddy science.[177] HPD shuttered the DNA unit after discovering that it had "operat[ed] for years without a supervisor, overseen by a technical leader who had no personal experience performing DNA analysis and who was lacking the qualifications required under the FBI standards, staffed by underpaid and undertrained analysts, and generating mistake-ridden and poorly documented casework."[178] As law professor Paul Giannelli describes it, the HPD crime laboratory in the early 2000s was "a paradigmatic example of a failed forensic agency."[179] He quotes one state senator who expressed concerns that "the validity of almost any case that has relied upon evidence produced by the laboratory is questionable."[180]

The worst of the nightmare was over for George Rodriguez, but cases like his had exposed the hidden truth about the deep problems lurking in many police crime laboratories. False, misleading, and exaggerated forensic testimony too often wreaked havoc on the innocent. For Houston, and for so many other cities and states, the efforts to understand the root causes of a dysfunctional police crime laboratory and, more importantly, to identify the solutions, were only beginning.

Notes for Chapter One

1. Steve McVicker, *DNA test review casts shadow of doubt on 1987 rape conviction*, HOUS. CHRON., Aug. 22, 2004, http://www.chron.com/news/article/DNA-test-review-casts-shadow-of-doubt-on-1987-1983999.php. The name "Isabel Medina" is not the girl's actual name. Her name is not disclosed in any media account to protect her privacy as a victim of a sexual assault.

2. *Id.*

3. McVicker, *Crime lab evidence questioned again: Experts dispute testimony in 1987 sex assault case,* HOUS. CHRON., Aug. 5, 2004, http://www.chron.com/news/houston-texas/article/Crime-lab-evidence-again-questioned-1482418.php.

4. *Id.*

5. *Id.*

6. *Id.*

7. *Id.*

8. *See* Steve McVicker, *supra* note 1.

9. Innocence Project, *Know the Cases, George Rodriguez,* http://www.innocenceproject.org/Content/George_Rodriguez.php.

10. *Id.*

11. *Id.*

12. *Id.*

13. *Id.*

14. Andrew Tilghman, *Rape case raises more questions over crime unit,* HOUS. CHRON., Aug. 10, 2004, http://www.chron.com/news/houston-texas/article/Rape-case-raises-more-questions-over-crime-unit-1497561.php.

15. *Id.*

16. *See* Innocence Project, *supra* note 9.

17. *Id.*

18. *See* Tilghman, *supra* note 14.

19. *See* Gary L. Wells, *What do we know about eyewitness identification?*, 48 AM. PSYCHOLOGIST 553–71 (1993).

20. Sandra Guerra Thompson, *Judicial Blindness to Eyewitness Misidentification,* 93 MARQUETTE L. REV. CRIM. L. 639, 660 (2010).

21. *See* Wells, *supra* note 19.

22. *Id.*

23. *Id.; see also* Innocence Project, *News and Information: Sequential Lineups Are More Accurate, According to Ground-breaking Report on Eyewitness Identification Procedures,* http://www.innocenceproject.org/Content/SAVE_Sequential_Lineups_Are_More_Accurate_According_to_Groundbreaking_Report_on_Eyewitness_Identification_Procedures.php (discussing study by American Judicature Society on reliability of sequential lineups).

24. For states that have reformed their eyewitness identification procedures, *see* Innocence Project, *Reforms by State,* http://www.innocenceproject.org/news/LawView5.php; *see*

also Sandra Guerra Thompson, *What Price Justice? The Importance of Costs to Eyewitness Identification Reform*, 41 Tex. Tech Law Rev. 33, 52–53 (2008).

25. *See* Center on Wrongful Convictions, *First DNA Exoneration, Gary Dotson*, http://www.law.northwestern.edu/legalclinic/wrongfulconvictions/exonerations/il/gary-dotson.html (Gary Dotson was the first person exonerated in 1989 by means of DNA evidence.) Reforms in eyewitness identification began in earnest in 1999 when various government and non-government task forces began publishing recommendations. *See* Thompson, *supra* note 24 at 40.

26. *See* Sandra Guerra Thompson, *Beyond a Reasonable Doubt? Reconsidering Uncorroborated Eyewitness Identification Testimony,* 41 U.C. Davis L. Rev. 1487, 1491, 1491 n. 12 (2008).

27. *See* Sandra Guerra Thompson, *Eyewitness Identifications and State Courts as Guardians Against Wrongful Convictions,* 7 Ohio St. J. of Crim. L. 603, 616 n. 73 (2010).

28. *See* McVicker, *supra* note 1.

29. *See* Innocence Project, *supra* note 9.

30. *See* Thompson, *supra* note 26 at 1497–48 (discussing malleability of witness memory).

31. *See* 60 Minutes, Eyewitness Testimony, Part 2, YouTube: http://www.youtube.com/watch?v=GtelV9lmzQc (interview of Jennifer Thompson).

32. *Id.*

33. *See* McVicker, *supra* note 1.

34. *Id.*

35. *See* Sandra Guerra Thompson, Daubert *Gatekeeping for Eyewitness Identifications,* 65 SMU L. Rev. 593, 637 n. 254 (2012).

36. *Id.*

37. *Id.*

38. *See* McVicker, *supra* note 1.

39. *See* McVicker, *supra* note 3.

40. *See* McVicker, *supra* note 1.

41. *Id.*

42. *Id.*

43. *See, e.g.,* State v. Solomon, 49 S.W.3d 356, 361 (Tx. Ct. Crim. App. 2001) (mere presence during commission of a crime is not sufficient to make one an accomplice).

44. Under the Texas Penal Code, as is also true in other states, a person is not considered an accomplice unless he in some way assists another in the commission of a crime. *See* Tex. Penal Code § 7.02 (West 2011).

45. *See generally* Sandra Guerra Thompson, *The White Collar Police Force: "Duty to Report" Statutes in Criminal Law Theory,* 11 William and Mary Bill of Rights Journal 3, 11–12 (2002).

46. *See* Innocence Project, *supra* note 9.

47. *See* McVicker, *supra* note 1.

48. *Id.*

49. *See* Steve McVicker & Andrew Tilghman, *More Crime Lab Troubles Possible, Chief Says,* Hous. Chron., Aug. 6, 2004, http://www.chron.com/news/article/More-crime-lab-troubles-possible-chief-says-1972139.php; McVicker, *supra* note 1.

50. *See* McVicker, *supra* note 1.

51. *Id.*

52. *Id.*

53. *Id.*

54. *Id.*

55. *Id.*

56. *See* Keith A. Findley & Michael A. Scott, *The Multiple Dimensions of Tunnel Vision in Criminal Cases*, 2006 Wisc. L. Rev. 291 (2006).

57. *Id.*

58. *See* McVicker, *supra* note 1.

59. *Id.*

60. *Id.*

61. *See, e.g.,* People v. Bullock, 154 Ill. App. 3d 266, 269 (App. Ct.—Ill. 1987) (*modus operandi* shown "when both crimes share peculiar and distinctive common features so as to earmark both crimes as the handiwork of the defendant").

62. *See* McVicker, *supra* note 1.

63. *Id.*

64. *Id.*

65. *Id.*

66. *Id.*

67. Oren Gazal-Ayal & Avishalom Tor, *The Innocence Effect*, 62 Duke L. J. 339, 348–62 (2012).

68. *Id.*

69. *See* Christopher D. Maxwell, Amanda L. Robinson & Lori A. Post, *The impact of race on the adjudication of sexual assault and other violent crimes*, 31 J. Crim. Just. 523 (2003) (finding harsh punishment of blacks accused of sexual assault of white victims and lenient punishment of blacks who commit sexual assault on other black victims); Rodney Kingsnorth, John Lopez, Jennifer Wentworth, Debra Cummings, *Adult sexual assault: The role of racial/ethnic composition in prosecution and sentencing*, 26 J. Crim. Just. 359 (1998) (same). While most studies involve only comparisons of African-American and white individuals, other studies show that Latinos suffer sentencing outcomes similar to African Americans. *See* Tushar Kansal, Racial Disparities in Sentencing: A Review of the Literature at 4–6 (The Sentencing Project 2005) (Marc Mauer ed.).

70. *See* Innocence Project, *supra* note 9.

71. *Id.*

72. *See* McVicker, *supra* note 1.

73. *See infra* ch. 3.

74. Brandon L. Garrett, Convicting the Innocent: Where Criminal Prosecutions Go Wrong at 90 (Harvard Univ. Press 2011).

75. For a full discussion, *see infra* Chapter 3.

76. *See* McVicker, *supra* note 1.

77. *Id.*

78. *Id.*

79. *See* Garrett, *supra* note 74 at 93–94.

80. *See* McVicker, *supra* note 1.

81. *See* Tilghman, *supra* note 14.

82. *See* Ake v. Oklahoma, 470 U.S. 68 (1985) (recognizing the right of an indigent defendant to the appointment of a psychiatrist if sanity is in issue).

83. *See* Paul C. Giannelli, Ake v. Oklahoma: *The Right to Expert Assistance in a Post-Daubert, Post-DNA World*, 89 Cornell L. Rev. 1305, 1312 (2004) (noting that in a 1990

six-month study, judges in capital cases in the South routinely denied defense lawyers' requests for expert assistance of any type).

84. *Id.*

85. *See Biographical Sketches of Key Players in the O.J. Simpson Trial: Barry Scheck,* http://law2.umkc.edu/faculty/projects/ftrials/simpson/Scheck.htm.

86. *See* Montgomery County, Maryland, *Press Release: Duncan Welcomes Expansion of Germantown's Cellmark Diagnostics,* http://www6.montgomerycountymd.gov/apps/News/press/PR_details.asp?PrID=11714.

87. *See* Houston Forensic Science LGC, Minutes of the Board of Directors, May 24, 2013, http://houstonforensiccenter.com/files/minutes_130524.pdf.

88. Steve McVicker, *Officials Urge Special Probe of HPD Crime Lab,* Hous. Chron., Aug. 7, 2004, http://www.chron.com/news/houston-texas/article/Officials-urge-special-probe-of-HPD-crime-lab-1625012.php.

89. *Prosecutors Want Houston Man's Rape Conviction Dismissed,* KHOU.com, Mar. 3, 2011, http://www.khou.com/news/local/Prosecutors-want-Houston-mans-rape-conviction-dismissed-after-17-years-behind-bars-117313038.html

90. *See* Rodriguez v. State, 766 S.W.2d 360 (Ct. App.—Tex. 1989).

91. *Id.*

92. *See* McVicker, *supra* note 1.

93. Pamela Colloff, *Innocence Found: Why did Anthony Graves spend eighteen years behind bars—twelve of them on death row—for a crime he did not commit?* Tex. Monthly, Jan. 2011, http://www.texasmonthly.com/story/innocence-found.

94. As a member of the panel, I can attest to the power and substance of Graves's talk.

95. 71 *See* Tilghman, *supra* note 14.

96. The information in this paragraph comes from the author's 24 years of annual tours of numerous Texas prisons with students.

97. George Rodriguez, Phone conversation with author (Sept. 15, 2014) (notes on file with author).

98. *See* McVicker, *supra* note 1.

99. *Id.*

100. *Id.*

101. *Id.*

102. *Id.*

103. *Id.*

104. *Id.*

105. *Id.*

106. *Id.*

107. *Id.*

108. *Id.*

109. *Id.*

110. *See* Steve McVicker, *Crime Lab Evidence Again Questioned,* Hous. Chron. , Aug. 4, 2004, http://www.chron.com/news/houston-texas/article/Crime-lab-evidence-again-questioned-1482418.php.

111. *Id.*

112. *Id.*

113. *Id.*

114. *See* Associated Press, *HPD to take second look at Rodriguez case,* Hous. Chron., Aug. 6, 2004, http://www.chron.com/news/article/HPD-to-take-second-look-at-Rodriguez-case-1551669.php.

115. *See* McVicker, *supra* note 1.

116. *See* Editorial, *Unmoved by Injustice DA Should Give Same Weight to Forensic Analysis When it Exonerates or Convicts,* Hous. Chron., Aug. 26, 2004, http://www.chron.com/opinion/editorials/article/Unmoved-by-injustice-DA-should-give-same-weight-1973533.php.

117. *See* Roma Khanna, *DA Unswayed by New Evidence in '87 Rape Case,* Hous. Chron., Aug. 24, 2004, http://www.chron.com/news/houston-texas/article/DA-unswayed-by-new-evidence-in-87-rape-case-1633824.php.

118. *Id.*

119. *Id.*

120. *Id.*

121. *Id.*

122. *See* David A. Harris, Failed Evidence: Why Law Enforcement Resists Science at 71–72 (New York University Press 2012).

123. Sandra Guerra Thompson, Opinion: Brand new era of criminal justice in Harris County?, Hous. Chron., Aug. 5, 2010, http://www.chron.com/opinion/outlook/article/Brand-new-era-of-criminal-justice-in-Harris-1698085.php.

124. *See* McVicker, *supra* note 1.

125. Brandi Grissom, *After 23 Years, A Suspect Emerges and a Family's Wounds are Reopened,* N.Y. Times, Oct. 21, 2011, http://www.nytimes.com/2011/10/21/us/after-23-years-suspect-emerges-in-austin-murder-of-debra-masters-baker.html?pagewanted=all&_r=0.

126. *Id.*

127. *See* Pamela Colloff , *The Guilty Man: Michael Morton spent almost 25 years wrongfully imprisoned for the murder of his wife, until DNA recovered from a blue bandana found near the crime scene helped set him free. A year and a half later, that same piece of evidence finally brought him face-to-face with the real killer,* Tex. Monthly, June 2013, http://www.texasmonthly.com/story/guilty-man/page/0/2.

128. *Id.*

129. *Id.*

130. *See Norwood pleads not guilty in Debra Baker death,* KVUE.com, Jan. 9, 2014, http://www.kvue.com/news/Norwood-pleads-not-guilty-in-Debra-Baker-death-239457951.html.

131. *See* Grissom, *supra* note 125.

132. *See* McVicker, *supra* note 1.

133. *Id.*

134. *Id.*

135. *See* Khanna, *supra* note 117.

136. *See* Innocence Project, *Know the Cases, Browse the Profiles: Timothy Cole,* http://www.innocenceproject.org/Content/Timothy_Cole.php.

137. *Id.*

138. *Id.*

139. *Id.*

140. *Timothy Cole Dies in Prison While Serving Time for Rape he Didn't Commit,* Examiner.com, Oct. 12, 2008, http://www.examiner.com/article/timothy-cole-dies-prison-while-serving-time-for-rape-he-didn-t-commit.

141. Wade Goodwyn, *Family of Man Cleared by DNA Still Seeks Justice,* NPR.ORG, Feb. 5, 2009, http://www.npr.org/templates/story/story.php?storyId=100249923 (quoting Michele Mallin).

142. *See* Innocence Project, *supra* note 136.

143. *See* JENNIFER THOMPSON-CANNINO & RONALD COTTON, WITH ERIC TORNEO, PICK-ING COTTON: OUR MEMOIR OF INJUSTICE AND REDEMPTION (St. Martin's Press 2009).

144. *See* 60 Minutes, *supra* note 31.

145. *See* Rosanna Ruiz, *Rodriguez out of prison but says, 'I'm still not free,'* HOUS. CHRON., Mar. 15, 2005, http://www.chron.com/news/houston-texas/article/Rodriguez-out-of-prison-but-says-I-m-still-not-1924980.php.

146. *See* Innocence Project, *supra* note 9.

147. *See* Ex Parte George Rodriguez, 2005 Tex. Crim. App. Unpub. LEXIS 399 (Aug. 31, 2005).

148. *Id.*

149. *Id.*

150. *Id.*

151. *See* Ruiz, *supra* note 145.

152. *See* McVicker, *supra* note 1.

153. *Id.*

154. *See* Tilghman, *supra* note 14.

155. Roma Khanna, *$5 million award bittersweet for wrongly convicted: Jury awards Ro-driguez,* HOUS. CHRON., June 25, 2009, http://www.chron.com/news/houston-texas/article/5-million-award-bittersweet-for-wrongly-convicted-1720657.php.

156. *Id.*

157. *Id.*

158. Bill Hawkins, Fax to Mark Wawro, Oct. 3, 2005, on file with author.

159. *See* George Rodriguez v. City of Houston, 428 Fed. Appx. 367 (2011).

160. Martha Neil, *Federal Jury Awards $5M to Texas Man Convicted on Bad Crime Lab Evidence,* ABA JOURNAL, Jun. 25, 2009, http://www.abajournal.com/news/article/fedl_jury_awards_5m_to_texas_man_convicted_based_on_bad_crime_lab_evidence.

161. Rodriguez v. City of Houston, Daily Transcripts, June 15, 2008, https://docs.google.com/viewer?pid=explorer&srcid=0B3ulC5gsGYV8ekxKLVcxaG9BTHM&docid=c4d8cadd695f92dc3936643ab40ffaa0%7C620ff377d7eb1075808ae77ce557c238&chan=EQAAAMEZFKbzzVpATXwLTPW/m7S%2BAjk80sMd6EOGPiej2meZ&a=v&rel=zip;z2;June+16+2009+Volume+1+(2).pdf.

162. *See* Neil, *supra* note 160.

163. Mary Flood,*Jury Struggles in Case of Wrongful Conviction,*HOUS. CHRON., Jun. 24, 2009.

164. *See* Neil, *supra* note 160.

165. *See* Daily Transcripts, *supra* note 161.

166. *See* Khanna, *supra* note 155.

167. *See, e.g.,* Stephanie Rice, *County Borrowing $10 Million to Pay Pair Wrongfully Convicted of Rape: Two Men Spent 17 years in Prison for Crime They Didn't Commit,* THE COLUMBIAN (Vancouver, Canada), Oct. 22, 2013, http://www.columbian.com/news/2013/oct/22/clark-county-wrongful-conviction-rape-northrop-dav/; Frances Robles, *Man Framed by Detective Will Get $6.4 Million From New York City After Serving 23 Years for Murder,* N.Y. TIMES, Feb. 20, 2014, http://www.nytimes.com/2014/02/21/nyregion/man-framed-by-new-

york-detective-to-get-6-4-million-without-filing-suit.html; Inside Dateline, *Wrongfully-Convicted Man Awarded $9 Million After Spending Almost 20 Years Behind Bars*, NBC NEWS, Feb. 4, 2014, http://insidedateline.nbcnews.com/_news/2014/02/04/22574079-wrongfully-convicted-man-awarded-9-million-after-spending-almost-20-years-behind-bars.

168. *See* Innocence Project, *Fix the System, Compensation for the Wrongly Convicted*, http://www.innocenceproject.org/fix/Compensation.php.

169. *See* Innocence Project, *Fix the System, State Compensation Laws: Texas* http://www.innocenceproject.org/fix/state1.php?state=TX.

170. *See* Lisa Falkenberg, *Innocent Man Waits for Compensation*, HOUS. CHRON., Jul. 12, 2011, http://www.chron.com/news/falkenberg/article/Innocent-man-waits-for-compensation-1463532.php.

171. *Id.*

172. Lisa Falkenberg, *$3.1 Million Settlement Reached for Man Falsely Imprisoned*, HOUS. CHRON., Nov. 2, 2012, http://www.chron.com/news/houston-texas/houston/article/3-1-million-settlement-reached-for-man-falsely-4003901.php.

173. *Id.*

174. *See* McVicker, *supra* note 3.

175. *See* Roma Khanna, *2 cases, 2 Opinions Equal Trouble for Crime Lab*, HOUS. CHRON., Aug. 29, 2004, http://www.chron.com/news/article/2-cases-2-opinions-equal-trouble-for-crime-lab-1974804.php.

176. *See* McVicker, *supra* note 3.

177. *See* Khanna, *supra* note 175.

178. Paul C. Giannelli, *Wrongful Convictions and Forensic Science: The Need to Regulate Crime Labs*," 86 N.C. L. Rev. 163, 187 (2007).

179. *Id.* at 187–88 (quoting Michael R. Bromwich, the Independent Investigator hired by the City of Houston to conduct an extensive investigation into the quality of the HPD Crime Lab).

180. *Id.*

Chapter Two

A National Crisis

At the turn of the twenty-first century, as a result of the national publicity from cases like George Rodriguez's and several others, the Houston Police Department's Crime Laboratory gained notoriety for extremely incompetent and biased laboratory results. Other scandals emerged at the same time in cities and states across the country, and the pattern has continued unabated since then. The advent of DNA testing uncovered an astounding number of wrongful convictions involving cases that, when reexamined, were found to rest, at least in part, on invalid forensic evidence. Over 50% of the DNA exonerations like that of George Rodriguez were cases that included faulty forensic evidence.[1] Appendix 1 reports the number of DNA exonerations in each state from 1989 to 2009 caused by invalid or fraudulent forensic testimony. It also provides details as reported in local and national media about crime laboratory scandals in those states from 1993 to 2013.

Crime laboratory scandals have exposed analysts who have performed incompetently, lied about their credentials, cheated on proficiency tests, or tampered with drug evidence in order to steal drugs. In some notorious cases, laboratory investigations have unmasked analysts who had engaged in repeated acts of fraud—faking laboratory results, intentionally misinterpreting evidence, and giving flagrantly perjured testimony for many years. The numerous scandals have led cities, counties, states, and even the federal government to conduct independent audits of troubled crime laboratories. Entire laboratories or sections of laboratories have been closed due to a complete breakdown of confidence in the quality of the work product.[2] Analysts have been criminally prosecuted, negligent supervisors have been fired or pressured to retire, and at least two accused analysts have committed suicide.[3] Prosecutors' offices have been forced to review hundreds, and sometimes thousands, of cases in which verdicts were based on forensic testing done by dishonest or incompetent analysts.[4] A single analyst's failings or misconduct can affect an enormous volume of cases, throwing the justice system in these jurisdictions into chaos.

If we account for all the scandals and crises in the past twenty years, troubled crime laboratories have thrown into doubt the outcomes of literally tens of thousands of cases. In 2013, the Boston area alone was reeling from a scandal that cast doubt on 34,000 cases.[5] Erroneous or perjured laboratory reports can and do lead to guilty pleas, even by innocent people whose attorneys likely warn them that they stand no chance of winning in the face of scientific evidence of guilt *and* that the punishment upon conviction at trial will be far greater than what the prosecutor may offer for a guilty plea. Despite such advice, innocent people will more often than not insist on going to trial.[6] George Rodriguez, a non-violent, married man with children, would not agree to plead guilty to a vicious rape. The consequence was a much heavier sentence than he would likely have received if he had pled guilty.[7]

Appendix 2 vividly illustrates the harsh sentences received by innocent people whose trials included erroneous or false scientific testimony. Of the 116 DNA exonerees convicted with faulty forensic evidence, 11 received death sentences. Another 46 were sentenced anywhere from 60 years to life and would surely have died in prison. This might also have been the fate of George Rodriguez had not the Innocence Project agreed to review his case, uncovering the flaws in the police procedures and the forensic testing. In total, 57 out of 116 DNA exonerees (49%) whose trials included flawed forensic science received sentences that virtually guaranteed that they would die in prison or in the death chamber.

These 57 wrongly convicted innocent people were ultimately fortunate, at least compared to other wrongly convicted prisoners. They were lucky that the technology to test for DNA evidence became available at some point during their incarceration, making a much more accurate form of testing available in their cases. They were also lucky that there was some biological evidence still preserved in their case files all those years after conviction, making DNA testing possible. In George Rodriguez's case, the biological evidence had been destroyed, with the amazing exception of a single hair discovered in the evidence files many years later. That single hair ended up setting him free.[8]

Consider these odds. DNA testing is available in only an estimated 5% to 10% of all cases.[9] Police departments regularly destroy biological evidence in old cases,[10] and in many—even most cases—police investigators find no biological evidence at the scene. Consider also the chances that the Innocence Project in New York and similar groups around the country will agree to take on the fight to get DNA testing in cases involving questionable forensic evidence.

What's worse is that these scandals represent the tip of the iceberg. Crime laboratory problems become public news when a new DNA exoneration uncovers the fact that a crime laboratory analyst's testimony caused a wrongful conviction. Since biological evidence is found in only 5%–10% of all cases, this leaves 90–95% of the cases without access to DNA testing.[11] Mistakes or fraud involving ballistics, fingerprints, drug analysis, and many other types of forensic disciplines may never be known unless biological evidence also happens to be present in the file. A few individuals have managed to establish their innocence without DNA evidence, but that feat is rare and typically requires wide media coverage of the case.[12] It is not possible to make more than rough estimates of the numbers of innocent people who plead guilty or who are convicted on the basis of incorrect or false results in laboratory reports.

The following sections provide greater detail on the causes of the various types of scandals and crises seen in police crime laboratories. As this chapter shows, the problems seen in the Houston Police Department Crime Laboratory exist in dozens of laboratories around the country. The reality has begun to sink in nationwide: The police department crime laboratory model does not work.

Choked Budgets, in Good Times and Bad

A major cause of the national crisis in police crime laboratories is the woeful underfunding of crime laboratories. Police departments have generally not had the wherewithal to fund crime laboratories adequately. In a predictable working out of the domino theory, underfunding becomes a major reason why crime laboratories have had limited success attracting analysts and managers with solid scientific education and training. A cascade of additional consequences follows: inadequate quality control measures, inadequate computer support, little computer security, and insufficient laboratory security to preserve evidence. Thus, the severe and persistent underfunding of crime laboratories has quite predictably led to the many scandals in laboratories nationwide involving unchecked fraud, incompetence, and stolen drugs.[13] The National Academy of Sciences has also noted the problem of massive case backlogs initially caused by insufficient resources, but bringing their own problems in analyzing and handling material appropriately.[14] Case backlogs lead to delayed justice for victims whose cases cannot be prosecuted in a timely manner.[15]

Early studies of police departments found severe budgetary issues affecting crime laboratories, which have persisted over the decades. A 1974 report of President Nixon's Crime Commission found that "[t]oo many police crime laboratories have been set up on budgets that preclude the recruitment of professional personnel" and "[t]oo often the laboratory is not considered a primary budget item and is one of the first units to suffer when budgets are trimmed."[16] Almost thirty years later, a 2002 survey by the Bureau of Justice Statistics found that budgets were still quite bleak.[17] Almost half (48%) of the 351 publicly funded crime laboratories had no budget for training staff, and 88%

had no resources for research.[18] A 2006 report by the American Bar Association also identified crime laboratory underfunding as a contributing cause of wrongful convictions.[19]

Historically, part of the underfunding problem has flowed from the fact that these laboratories are located within police departments. Personnel, equipment, laboratory facilities, training programs, evidence storage capacity, quality assurance programs, information technology, and laboratory security all require resources. Crime laboratories, as units within police departments, have not had much political leverage when it comes to setting budgetary priorities. New laboratory equipment ranks low on the list of budgetary needs presented to legislative bodies. Police departments tend to give higher priority to the hiring of new police officers, purchasing new patrol cars, or supplying training on both the basic and expert-investigator levels—items in which legislators and the public can see immediate and direct impact on public safety.

Without sufficient political leverage either within police departments or at the governmental level, crime laboratories often wind up under-resourced. In Los Angeles in 2010, city officials reversed a decision to hire twenty-six staffers for the chronically understaffed LA Police Crime Laboratory.[20] The new positions in the crime laboratory had been intended as an exception to the city's hiring freeze for all city positions. However, the city balked when the police department tried to fill the allocated positions.[21] More recently, in June of 2013, Kansas City leaders announced that the city's budget cuts would reduce the spending for its new police crime laboratory from $40 million to $19 million— cutting it by more than half.[22]

Additionally, since police chiefs tend not to be scientists themselves, they historically have not appreciated the imperative to hire well-qualified scientists as managers and bench analysts. Only recently have crime laboratories begun requiring college degrees in relevant scientific areas.[23] In the past few decades it was not uncommon to find people working in crime laboratories without relevant scientific degrees. Even though at least some had received professional, high-quality on-the-job training, certainly many were learning their jobs from supervisors who, themselves, lacked adequate and up-to-date training. It is still common today to find police officers with no formal science education working in fingerprint (called "latent print") and firearm sections of crime laboratories.[24] Most are surely highly-trained and competent, but they may lack a formal science education.

Even if police chiefs had preferred to hire scientists over non-scientists, the salaries they offered could not compete with those of private laboratories. In 2012, state and local forensic analysts earned median salaries in the mid-$50,000 range, while forensic analysts working in medical and diagnostic laboratories commanded median salaries of $66,000.[25] For this reason, job candidates with science degrees from top universities, who graduate with good grades in their fields, generally have not taken jobs in crime laboratories. This is especially true for scientists with advanced degrees such as master's degrees or doctorates. Even today, individuals with advanced science degrees in crime laboratories are few and far between.[26]

It stands to reason that in tough economic times, city and state budgets might not meet the needs of police crime laboratories, but a locale's economic well-being is not necessarily correlated with the availability of funds for crime laboratories. Houston's crime laboratory scandal erupted in 2002, after more than a decade of prosperity in the city. In fact, the nation as a whole flourished economically throughout the 1990s and early 2000s,[27] yet this is precisely the era when scandals have exposed shoddy crime laboratories nationwide.

The litany of broken laboratories should signal to policy makers a need for immediate, structural change and an infusion of resources. Though the publicized scandals in these crime laboratories have varied, audits in these laboratories have yielded strikingly similar diagnoses. One incompetent or cheating analyst usually signals poor management, weak credentials, insufficient training, and other fundamental failures in the laboratory, many of which result from chronic, severe budget strain.

Fraud in the Laboratory and Perjury in Court

Since the late 1980s, criminal justice authorities have uncovered a number of rogue crime laboratory analysts who regularly and flagrantly faked test results, sending many innocent people to prison in the process. The acts of these individual analysts were heinous and had catastrophic results for the innocent people ensnared by their lies.

One of the earliest and most notorious crime laboratory scandals involved the large-scale fraud committed by State Trooper Fred Zain in the West Virginia State Police Laboratory. A serologist, Zain had provided forensic evidence leading to hundreds of murder and rape convictions over the course of his sixteen-year career as a forensic scientist.[28] In the late 1980s Glen Dale Woodall's wrongful conviction and 335-year sentence for two rapes were overturned when lawyers for Woodall obtained DNA testing on the biological evidence in his case which exposed fraud in Zain's work.[29] Zain's false testimony had also secured the conviction of James Richardson in Cross Lakes, West Virginia. Richardson's conviction and sentence to life imprisonment without parole was overturned in 1989 after lawyers obtained similar DNA testing.

Problems continued to erupt. In 1993 the West Virginia Supreme Court of Appeals appointed retired judge James Holliday to conduct a special investigation into cases where Zain's work had played a significant role in obtaining convictions.[30] Holliday enlisted independent experts to review the evidence in thirty-six of Zain's cases. These experts concluded their five-month review by documenting that Zain had lied about, made up, or manipulated evidence to win a conviction in every single case.[31] A further review of 189 of his cases concluded that "any testimony or documentary evidence offered by Zain at any time should be deemed invalid, unreliable and inadmissible."[32]

He also lied about his credentials in a 1991 double-murder trial.[33] He testified under oath that he had majored in biology and minored in chemistry. His transcript, however, showed he flunked some chemistry classes and barely passed others.[34] He received only the major in biology.

When he was fired in 1993, Zain had worked in a dozen states since beginning his career in 1977. He left West Virginia in 1989 just as authorities there were overturning convictions caused by his wrongdoing. The Bexar County Medical Examiner's Office in San Antonio, Texas employed him for the next four years until he was fired.[35] Seven convictions relying on his testimony have now (2014) been overturned in West Virginia and in Texas. The two states have paid millions of dollars in settlements to some of these wrongly convicted individuals.[36] Special state prosecutors in West Virginia prosecuted Zain for accepting fees and salary under false pretenses because he was systematically falsifying hundreds of test findings. The jury deadlocked, and he was due to be retried in 2002,[37] however, he died of colon cancer first.[38]

Zain should never have been able to perpetrate his fraud on the legal system for so many years. The fact that his incompetence and perjury as a criminalist would go undetected for more than a decade indicates that he worked in laboratories without effective quality assurance protocols. Supervisors at the West Virginia State Crime Laboratory should have administered routine, rigorous proficiency tests to ensure that Zain's skills were up to par. They should also have checked his work by periodically reanalyzing a random sample of casework. Finally, supervisors in the laboratory might have been alert to his lies about his credentials or test results if they had attended some of his trials as part of a quality assurance program. Apparently, none of the laboratories where he worked followed these procedures. In fact, Judge Holliday's investigation found that "there was evidence that Mr. Zain's supervisors may have ignored or concealed complaints of his misconduct."[39] And indeed, Zain's supervisor, Kenneth Blake, received a complaint from two coworkers about his work in 1986, but Blake dismissed the complaint as an office squabble. Jack Buckalew, the superintendent of the State Police, told a special prosecutor who was appointed to investigate the allegation that there was "no need to take any further action," and Buckalew would later tell reporters that he was "satisfied" no one was wrongly convicted as a result of Zain's work.[40] Buckalew left the state police and was elected a state senator in 1995. In July of 2014 the Governor Earl Ray Tomblin reappointed him as a member of the state's ethics commission.[41]

Zain's lies not only failed to produce swift disciplinary action and a review of sentences influenced by his fraud, but he was instead rewarded for his work. According to the *New York Times* coverage of Judge Holliday's commission:

> [I]n 1985, two West Virginia State Police officers who worked under Mr. Zain complained that he was writing laboratory reports based on blank laboratory slides. The two officers told investigators that nothing had been done.

> When one of Mr. Zain's supervisors wrote to the Federal Bureau of Investigation about his concerns about Mr. Zain's test results, the report said, agents "made amusing comments like, 'Fred does not do things by the book,' and called him 'pro-prosecution,'" but recommended no action. The next year, Mr. Zain became head of the crime laboratory.[42]

George Castelle, the chief public defender in Charleston, West Virginia, who was planning to file a lawsuit on behalf of prisoners whose convictions were due to Zain's work, said he was "shocked" to discover that Zain regularly received praise and promotions for his trial work.[43] West Virginia prosecutors continued to hire him as a consultant—even after he had moved to San Antonio—because his results were considered more favorable than those of his successors.[44]

The Washington State Patrol Crime Laboratory system had its share of problems in the early 2000s, at roughly the same time that the scandal exploded over the Houston Police Crime Laboratory. The Washington State laboratory employed Arnold Melnikoff as a drug chemist. In 2003, Innocence Project cofounder Peter Neufeld requested that the Washington Attorney General investigate his work, charging that Melnikoff, in his previous job of hair analysis for the Montana Crime Laboratory he had committed "scientific fraud."[45] Specifically, Melnikoff had "fabricated testimony" on hair analysis that resulted in sentencing Jimmy Ray Bromgard to prison for fifteen years for child rape. Bromgard was exonerated by DNA evidence in 2002.[46] Two other men wrongly convicted due to Melnikoff's testimony were also exonerated by DNA evidence.[47] In 2004, the Washington State Patrol concluded an internal audit of Melnikoff's drug work in 100 felony drug cases, finding troubling flaws in thirty of them.[48] He was then fired.

In 2007, an anonymous tip brought to light other misconduct in the Washington State's toxicology laboratory with regard to drunken-driving cases. The tipster claimed that toxicology laboratory manager, Ann Marie Gordon, employed since 1999, had falsely claimed to have verified solutions used for breath-testing in drunken-driving cases and had also destroyed blood evidence.[49] Gordon twice asserted her Fifth Amendment right not to testify in court hearings. She resigned in July 2007, and the county prosecutor declined to prosecute her, claiming that her misconduct could not be shown to have caused any public harm.[50] In fact, at least 100 cases were dismissed because of her actions.[51] A panel of three Kings County judges ruling on the allegations against Gordon called her a "perpetrator of fraud" in 2008.[52] State police officials shut down the toxicology laboratory.

Three months after leaving Washington State Gordon landed a $105,000-a-year job as the supervising forensic toxicologist in the San Francisco chief medical examiner's office where she vouched for blood-test results in drunken-driving cases for two years until defense attorneys revealed her checkered past.[53] In one San Francisco court hearing, Gordon testified under oath as an expert, and Deputy Public Defender Prithika Balakrishnan asked her during cross-examination about the Washington State controversy. Gordon denied all wrongdoing and said she had never seen the Kings County court ruling that found her to have committed fraud.[54]

In Texas, the Court of Criminal Appeals indicated in 2013 that it would likely overturn all of the nearly 5,000 cases that one rogue analyst handled during his employment from 2006 to 2012 in the Texas Department of Public Safety Crime Laboratory.[55] A co-worker discovered that Jonathan Salvador had produced erroneous results in drug tests in several cases,[56] a finding that led to an investigation into Salvador's other drug tests. This second investigation documented "dry-labbing," meaning that he had submitted false results for a batch of pills that he had not tested.[57] He had instead borrowed the data from another batch of pills tested as part of an unrelated case. To the laboratory's credit, it followed state law and self-reported the problem to the state's Forensic Science Commission.[58] The laboratory ultimately fired him; but during his six-year career, he had been promoted despite concerns about the quality and timeliness of his work.[59]

Boston made national headlines in 2013 for a scandal that tainted the Massachusetts State Crime Laboratory. Chemist Annie Dookhan allegedly inflated drug weights reporting that drugs weighed more than they actually did. [60] She also falsified drug tests to create positive results, for instance, by providing perjured testimony that a defendant's blood showed the presence of a drug when, in fact, it did not.[61] She had handled more than 40,000 cases in her ten years at the crime lab, meaning that these revelations of her misconduct could potentially result in overturning thousands of cases in which her analyses resulted in convictions.[62] In November of 2013, Dookhan pled guilty to twenty-seven counts of misleading investigators, filing false reports, and tampering with evidence. A Boston court sentenced her to three to five years in prison.[63]

Drug Thefts

The city of San Francisco shuttered the drug analysis unit of it crime laboratory in 2010 when an internal audit found that a drug technician, Deborah Jean Madden, had been stealing cocaine for personal use.[64] The scathing audit disclosed a wide range of problems in the laboratory with other personnel as well, including "inconsistencies in the chain-of-custody record-keeping for seized drugs; a potentially dangerous work space, with hazardous chemicals left unlabeled and stored in hallways; a lack of maintenance of microscopes and balances; improperly-sealed drug envelopes; and overworked technicians."[65] The understaffing problem was so severe that working overtime had become mandatory. Technicians were under pressure to complete testing within forty-eight hours to prevent dismissals of criminal charges. The audit also found insufficient training in some areas. Fred Tulleners, a former California Department of Justice crime laboratory manager, described working conditions at the laboratory as "abysmal."[66] Assistant Police Chief Jeff Godown, who took over the laboratory's supervision in April 2010, admitted that the laboratory had suffered from mismanagement, saying "It's just going to take time [to repair the damage]."[67]

Supervisors at the crime laboratory had become aware of the problems with Madden's work as early as 2007 when the *San Francisco Chronicle* reported that four grams of cocaine, evidence in a federal racketeering trial, had disappeared after Madden handled it.[68] She was not investigated, much less fired or prosecuted in 2007 when supervisors first learned of her misdeeds. If Madden stole and tampered with drugs from 2007 to 2010, her misconduct has affected thousands of cases. Says the city's public defender Jeff Adachi: "This is a tsunami of incompetence. There weren't just red flags, there were burning red flags."[69]

After the internal audit, an independent laboratory began retesting drugs in cases where Madden had submitted reports, and by April 2010, more than six hundred cases had been dismissed. Madden was involved in all of them.[70] In the meantime, Madden pled guilty to a drug charge in San Mateo County Superior Court in 2011 and was sentenced to undergo drug counseling.[71] She also pled guilty to a misdemeanor cocaine possession charge in federal court in March 2013.[72] She was sentenced to five years of probation including one year of home custody with an ankle monitoring bracelet, 300 hours of community service, and a $5,000 fine.[73] As for the future of the San Francisco crime laboratory, Tulleners, the former manager of the state's crime laboratory opined, "Ideally, the next best step would be for the state [to] take over that lab. But I doubt that will happen, not in this current budget crisis."[74]

As of this writing (May 2014), the latest drug theft scandal involves Stephen Palmer, drug analyst at the Alaska State Crime Laboratory. In March of 2014, he was charged with six felonies for stealing drugs and adding adulterants to drug reference standards to hide his thefts.[75] He was charged with four counts of tampering with evidence, engaging in a scheme to defraud, and other misconduct. Interviews with Palmer's family revealed that he is addicted to drugs, a problem that might have been discovered if the laboratory had done routine drug testing of employees who analyze drugs for a living.[76] Palmer worked in the laboratory from 1992 until his sudden resignation in 2011, which coincided with the disappearance of a bag of drugs in his custody.[77]

Similar charges of drug thefts have been brought against other drug analysts, including a chemist in the Massachusetts State Crime Laboratory who pled guilty in 2014,[78] a drug chemist at the Florida Department of Law Enforcement crime laboratory in 2013,[79] a Washington State Patrol chemist investigated in 2006 for drug stealing and evidence tampering,[80] and a Houston Police Department crime laboratory chemist convicted in 2010.[81] Similar thefts have been documented in the crime laboratories managed by medical examiners as well.[82]

Incompetence

In 2004, a Seattle newspaper review of documents and court records found errors in the DNA testing done in 23 major cases by four laboratories within the Washington State Patrol.[83] State Patrol laboratories in Spokane, Marysville, Seattle, and Tacoma were implicated in the errors, most of which involved various types of inadvertent contamination of DNA samples. These laboratories tested 1,400 DNA cases per year at that time.[84] Twenty-three errors out of 1,400 may seem inconsequential, but there is reason to think the problems run deeper. According to William C. Thompson, a forensic expert and professor of criminology and law at the University of California-Irvine, "What we're seeing in these 23 cases is really the tip of the iceberg," and he explained that the laboratory is only catching obvious problems, most likely leaving more subtle problems unexposed.[85]

The Washington State Patrol Crime Laboratory also uncovered problems within other units as well. A ballistics analyst, Evan Thompson, resigned in 2007 after an audit found mistakes or documentation problems in more than a dozen cases he handled in 2006 alone.[86] This laboratory is the same one as that in which Arnold Melnikoff had worked in 2003. He was the drug chemist who had fabricated hair testimony in his prior job in a Montana crime laboratory and caused an innocent man to be convicted. It is also the laboratory where Ann Marie Gordon resigned in 2007 after falsely claiming that she had verified solutions used for breath-testing in drunken driving cases and destroyed blood samples to mask her wrongdoing. Despite this flurry of scandals at the State Patrol laboratory, problems persisted. In April 2013, Kevin Fortney, the head of the state laboratory in Cheney, resigned when a three-month internal audit discovered he had lied and mishandled evidence for years.[87] Other analysts in the laboratory informed superiors at the State Patrol that Fortney claimed to have conducted tests that he had not in fact done. This accusation triggered the audit. Fortney had worked as an arson and fire debris analyst from 1991 until 2002 when he became laboratory manager.[88] Thus, the problems at the Washington State Crime Laboratory have continued to pile up.

The Washington State Patrol Crime Laboratory provides just one of numerous possible examples. As Appendix 1 shows, incompetence of a similar magnitude pervades many laboratories in many states around the country. To be pessimistic, states that have comparatively low incidents of fraud and evidence-tampering may not necessarily mean that they have superior standards and performance but rather that they have not yet had the kind of audit, whether internal or independent, that would disclose misbehavior. Given the large number of incompetent analysts, incompetence and fraud may be the most widespread cause of large-scale case reviews and crime laboratory audits.[89] Such problems typically come to light when wrongful convictions are discovered and further investigated.

Cheating on Proficiency Tests and Lying about Credentials

Other wrongdoing by crime laboratory analysts includes committing perjury in court by lying about their credentials. In 2004, Donald Phillips, Washington State Patrol Crime Laboratory analyst, falsely testified to holding a chemistry degree when his degree was actually in agricultural science.[90] In 2006, the San Diego Sheriff's Department Crime Laboratory discovered that criminalist Raymond Cole, who had testified as an expert for over thirty years on the effects of alcohol, had lied about having a degree in "premedical studies." His degree was actually in political science.[91] Joseph Kopera, a twenty-one-year veteran forensic scientist in Maryland, perjured himself for two decades in thousands of criminal cases by falsely claiming he held degrees and certificates that he did not. He resigned and committed suicide in 2007.[92]

Crime laboratory analysts have also cheated on proficiency tests, often to hide their incompetence. In 2002, Inspector Joe Brinson of the Florida Department of Law Enforcement Crime Laboratory found that DNA analyst John Fitzpatrick had switched DNA samples and falsified data in a test designed to test his proficiency.[93] In questioning, Fitzpatrick admitted to the cheating and chose to resign rather than be fired.[94] The Houston Police Department Crime Laboratory also faced a scandal involving proficiency test cheating by its DNA analysts, forcing city leaders to reorganize the unit for a second time in 2008.[95] The head of the unit, Vanessa Nelson, had been hired to head the section when it reopened after its 2002 closure and resigned as the second scandal rocked the laboratory. Even while Nelson was still under investigation in Houston, the Texas Department of Public Safety hired her to work in the DNA section of its crime laboratory.[96] As of 2014, she continued to work in this capacity. She also was elected as secretary of the Association of Forensic DNA Analysts and Administrators.[97]

Massive Backlogs

Newspapers around the country have reported massive backlogs in police crime laboratories, particularly backlogs of rape kits in sexual assault cases. In 2012, Oakland had a DNA backlog of 2,438, including 555 homicides.[98] The Houston Police Department had an even larger backlog—almost 10,000 cases—in 2011.[99] Rape kit backlogs put enormous pressure on crime laboratories, contributing to the chronic state of crisis. So pervasive is the problem of DNA backlogs that the National Institute of Justice provides federal grants to crime laboratories for additional staffing and support. Cities—including Houston—have allocated millions of dollars to outsource DNA backlogs to other laboratories, resulting in the arrest of rapists in old cases.[100] However, the backlogs of DNA cases is a different problem than the cheating, lying, and perjury discussed above that have plagued police crime laboratories. Chronic underfunding is certainly an issue, but the problem is more complex than just a lack of resources.

Defining the problem of rape kit backlogs requires remembering that police crime laboratories are units within larger police departments. The media and even criminal justice experts sometimes fail to distinguish cases in which the investigating officers fail to submit the collected evidence to the laboratory for testing from those in which the request is made but the laboratory does not perform the tests in a timely way to allow arrests or aid prosecutors. Investigators may decide not to seek testing for various reasons such as a victim's refusal to cooperate, judgments about the viability of a prosecution, and the availability of other evidence, among others. If the investigators do not request testing, the evidence does not become part of a crime laboratory's "backlog." Rather, it is part of an inventory of untested rape kits stored in the police department's custody.

The National Institute of Justice defines a backlogged case as "one submitted to a crime laboratory that has not been tested within 30 days."[101] The pertinent testing in rape cases is DNA analysis. Backlogs in DNA testing result from at least three major causes. First, the development of DNA technology has reopened many cases that have gone unsolved, as well as many in which defendants claim innocence.[102] Thus, DNA analysts have caseloads that include both old and new cases. In some places, DNA testing is being done on rape kits in old cases, even though the statute of limitations may have run out on sexual assault prosecution. The Dallas Police Department has received some limited funding to test old rape kits as a way of providing closure to victims of sexual assault.[103] Newer cases of necessity take priority over older cases that cannot be prosecuted; but as more states have embraced DNA testing for prisoners who claim actual innocence, the category of old cases entering the system has grown.

Second, police today have adopted newer forms of DNA testing that enable them to obtain usable evidence in crimes other than sexual assaults. The development of "touch DNA," for example, allows crime laboratories to use forensic evidence to solve a wide array of property crimes.[104] For neighborhoods facing a rash of home or automobile burglaries, such testing could bring needed protection. At present, the use of DNA evidence in property cases remains limited, but there is ample reason to think it will improve. A 2010 study by researchers at Washington State University found that the majority of law enforcement agencies do not routinely collect DNA evidence from property crime scenes.[105] These agencies commonly assume that their crime laboratories do not accept requests to conduct DNA tests in property crimes. However, 75% of local crime laboratories and 88% of state crime laboratories report that they do accept DNA test requests in property crime cases.[106] Thus, while some property crimes and other non-violent crimes may add to the backlog, we can certainly expect the pace of requests to increase as the police learn to make more use of their laboratories' resources.[107]

Third, police departments are addressing issues that previously had deterred investigators from seeking DNA testing in many sexual assault cases. Some experts have noted the ongoing challenge of biases against victims based on "ethnicity, disability, use of alcohol or drugs, or a victim's occupation as a sex worker."[108] To confront these and other impediments to the requesting of DNA testing, some police agencies are now requiring that all rape kits be submitted for testing, regardless of who the victim is. A consequence of these changes in policy—from the perspective of crime laboratories—is an increased workload.

Another study showed that a substantial number of serious unsolved cases such as homicides and rapes contained DNA evidence that was never submitted for testing. The police most often justified the lack of a request by the fact that there was no known suspect whose DNA might prove to be a match.[109] The backlog, combined with the failure to submit evidence for testing, leaves many victims forgotten by the system. For crime laboratories, this study predicts an even heavier deluge of testing requests as departments become more responsive to victims' interests.

The end result is that the number of cases in which police request DNA testing has simply exploded, making it impossible for laboratories to keep up even when they make heroic gains in expanding their testing capacity. The Office of Violence against Women of the Department of Justice convened a workshop in 2010 to address rape kit backlogs. The workshop report cites a National Institute of Justice study showing that "the number of cases coming into crime laboratories has increased three-fold over the past five years, while the number of cases processed has tripled over the same time. Thus, the DNA case backlogs have remained constant."[110]

Nor are DNA backlogs the only type that plagues crime laboratories. News reports around the country tell of overwhelmed laboratories reporting backlogs in all kinds of testing. Laboratory managers point to staffing shortages combined with sharp spikes in test requests, a bad combination for keeping backlogs under control. In 2010, the Baltimore Crime Laboratory had a backlog of 3,100 cases for serology testing, 3,000 cases for drug testing, and 400 for DNA testing.[111] Administrative Judge Pamela White blames these laboratory backlogs for delays in prosecutions.[112] The Maine State Police crime laboratory reported a backlog of 250 cases in its computer crime unit in 2010, including a video in a heinous child pornography case.[113] Also in 2010, the Houston Police Department reported a backlog of more than 300 firearms cases and a staggering 6,000 fingerprint cases.[114] In Rhode Island in 2012, the State Crime Laboratory director sought additional resources to handle a dramatic increase in firearms cases.[115]

The rapid growth of test requests arises partially from the fact that crime laboratories generally do not charge their parent police departments a fee to conduct laboratory tests. Police officers and prosecutors may view laboratory testing as being "free," which encourages more test requests. For example, the police or prosecutors may request the laboratory to conduct multiple checks for DNA on a number of items of evidence in a single case. They may also seek fingerprint evidence and ballistics work for the same case. For serious cases such as homicides or sexual assaults, a large number of tests may be warranted. However, police departments have not implemented any systematic program for prioritizing and limiting the number of tests requested.[116]

Cover-Ups

The miscarriages of justice caused by crime laboratories undoubtedly goes beyond those mentioned in this chapter. As noted above, DNA exonerations have brought many crime laboratory scandals to light, but unfortunately DNA is available in only a tiny fraction of all convictions. Thus, it is widely believed that the true number of people wrongly convicted is much higher. A logical conclusion is that many of those undiscovered wrongful convictions would have involved invalid or erroneous forensic testimony.

Another problem with crime laboratories that are tied to the police stems from the tendency to "whitewash" their crime labs after scandals. Law professor Paul Giannelli is troubled by the "inaction of the forensic scientists and prosecutors" who have worked closely with analysts caught committed fraudulent testing because often they "have ignored or concealed complaints" of misconduct.[117] This protective tendency, though lamentable, is also natural. Scandals threaten to undo large numbers of convictions and bring negative publicity and rebukes. Among the negative consequences are laboratory closures, firings, prosecutions of crime laboratory employees, and occasionally suicides. Laboratory problems also provide evidence for suing cities, counties, and states — strong incentives for all parties to conceal the problems. Crime laboratory scandals put a burden on prosecutors to review hundreds, if not thousands, of old cases in which questionable laboratory testimony was given. Prosecutors must also disclose to defense attorneys the fact that the forensic evidence in their cases has been brought into question. The defense attorneys will use the negative information to impeach the credibility of laboratory analysts when they testify in new cases and will also seek to overturn convictions in old cases.

Thus, it is not uncommon to see laboratory managers and police departments attempt to conceal laboratory problems. They may choose, for example, to conduct internal reviews that they can keep confidential, rather than seeking an independent audit. This was the case in 2003 in Santa Clara when testimony by a 25-year veteran analyst, Mark Moriyama, caused Jeffrey Rodriguez to be wrongly convicted of armed robbery.[118] Moriyama testified that he had found a stain consisting of a mix of vegetable oil and motor oil on Rodriguez's pants. At trial, prosecutor John Luft used this testimony to connect Rodriguez to the loading dock of the auto parts store where the robbery occurred.[119] After serving five years in prison, the courts overturned Rodriguez's conviction due to his trial attorney's bad lawyering. In preparing for a second trial, prosecutors sent the Rodriguez's pants to a different laboratory for re-testing, and the testing done at this laboratory concluded that there had been no oil stain as Moriyama had testified. Prosecutors informed Rodriguez's defense attorneys about the new test results, and the judge ultimately released Rodriguez on grounds of actual innocence. Rodriguez sued the county and settled the lawsuit for $1 million in 2009.[120] The laboratory, upon discovery of such an egregious error or outright lie by a veteran analyst, should have submitted to a review by an independent auditor; the failure to do so suggests an effort to minimize scrutiny and remedial action.

Likewise in Florida, prosecutors complained that the Florida Department of Law Enforcement did not notify them for three months about an analyst who had cheated on proficiency tests. When they did, the laboratory's attorney incorrectly told the prosecutors that it was a personnel matter that need not be disclosed to defense attorneys.[121] In North Carolina, prosecutors in 2012 similarly complained that the state police had not informed them about which analysts had failed proficiency tests.[122] In the same year, when analysts in North Carolina failed certification tests for their disciplines, the state police refused to turn over the information to prosecutors.[123]

In 2008, an accreditation inspection by the Association of Crime Laboratory Directors/ Laboratory Accreditation Board (ASCLD/LAB) raised questions about the competence of a New York State Police Crime Laboratory analyst, Gary Veeder. Further investigation by the state's Inspector General found that Veeder had done "pervasively shoddy forensic work" and had engaged in dry-labbing for fifteen years.[124] The Inspector General's review of his casework found serious problems with twenty-nine percent of his work.[125] Worse still were two other discoveries: (1) the problems in the laboratory had been systemic, and (2) managers in the laboratory improperly concealed the systemic nature of the problems.

When Veeder's competence came into question, the managers of two sections of the laboratory conducted an internal investigation at the laboratory director's request. Veeder informed them that he had received poor training and that widespread problems existed throughout the laboratory with other scientists. The managers challenged and then summarily dismissed his claims, and thus failed to inform the director that the casework of others might be in doubt. The allegations against Veeder were sufficient to trigger an investigation by the state's Inspector General. This investigation substantiated many of Veeder's allegations and found the internal audit to have been "highly flawed" in minimizing the extent of the problems.[126] The Inspector General's report also found that a highly-trained scientist who had complained about Veeder's practices in 1994—one year after he began working in the laboratory—had been removed as a peer-reviewer, and a "patently unqualified" person had been assigned to review Veeder's work instead.[127] As a result, Veeder's wrongdoing went unaddressed for another 14 years. Veeder committed suicide in 2008 during the course of the state's investigation.[128]

Thus, even when analysts have tried to expose problems, managers have preferred to conceal them. Whistleblowers have been ignored, and one can readily see why. In Boston, laboratory colleagues attempted to report analyst Annie Dookhan's misconduct, only to be brushed aside by her supervisor.[129] Even more shocking, when analysts in the Texas Department of Public Safety reported their concerns about Jonathan Salvador's dry-labbing to the lab's managers, they ignored the colleagues' concern, as well as his poor performance reviews, and promoted Salvador.[130] At a later point, the department discovered his dry-labbing "purely by accident," and the laboratory self-reported the problem to the Texas Forensic Science Commission, as required by law.[131]

Conclusion

The state of many police crime laboratories around the country demands serious public policy discussion in cities and states nationwide. Invalid forensic evidence—whether due to fraudulent activity, rushed work, or incompetence—can have tragic results for innocent persons. Delayed testing due to massive backlogs puts the justice system on hold for victims, leaving perpetrators free to victimize others. The sheer volume of scandals in laboratories across the country indicates a crisis of national proportions. The suffering of each DNA exoneree identified in Appendix 2 who was wrongly convicted and harshly sentenced—eleven of whom were on death row—underscores the urgency of the need to address the crisis head-on.

In looking for solutions, one might look first at a large infusion of resources. Certainly, it would fix some problems. Cities and states would do well to fund crime laboratories properly—providing for adequate space, equipment, information management systems, and properly credentialed staff. Quality assurance programs can also go a long way in catching problems early and deterring other problems from occurring. But money alone will not fix broken crime laboratories. As the wrongdoing in crime laboratories and the cover-ups of scandals have shown, the location of crime laboratories within police departments is a structural defect in how forensic science has been organized—a fundament flaw that cannot be fixed with increased funding.

Appendix 1
DNA Exonerations and Crime
Laboratory Scandals by State

State	DNA Exonerations Involving Forensic Evidence 1989 through 2/1/09*	Notable State and Local Police Crime Laboratory Scandals and Major Crises (1993–2013)**
Alabama	0	
Alaska	0	**2014:** Former Alaska crime laboratory chemist Stephen Palmer charged with six felonies relating to drug thefts.
Arizona	1	**2003:** Phoenix Crime Laboratory discovers errors in analyzing DNA evidence in 9 cases dating back to 2001 involved six homicides, two rapes and an aggravated assault. Errors attributed to insufficiently trained technicians using a rare procedure. 500 cases reviewed for errors. **2008:** Tucson Crime Laboratory coordinator Steven Skowron resigns after findings that he stole drugs for personal use and tampered with drug evidence. Review of 400 cases performed.
Arkansas	0	
California	5	**1994:** San Francisco Crime Laboratory Chemist Allison Lancaster accused of faking drug tests reports. Caught by detectives in a sting in which she was given harmless powders which she identified as opiates and cocaine. Approximately 1,000 convictions would require review. **2003:** Santa Clara Crime Laboratory technician testified that a jacket contained drops of motor oil and cooking oil. This evidence contributed to wrongful conviction and sentence of 25 years to life for Jeffrey Rodriguez. Re-testing in 2006 showed the jacket contained no oil stain. Innocence Project faulted police for conducting internal audit of laboratory rather than seeking independent audit as required by federal law. **2004:** Los Angeles crime laboratory chemist Jeffrey Lowe found to have made numerous errors, sparking review of 972 cases.

California (cont.)	5	**2006:** Sacramento County crime laboratory DNA technical reviewer Mark Eastman resigned when it was found he did sloppy work. **2006:** San Diego Sheriff's Department crime laboratory criminalist Raymond Cole, who testified as an expert for over thirty years on the effects of alcohol, was found to have lied about having a "premedical studies" degree when his degree was in political science. **2008:** Los Angeles Police crime laboratory found to have caused numerous wrongful convictions due to shoddy work. **2009:** Sacramento County criminalist Jeffrey Herbert testified that the DNA sample from a defendant matched only one in 95,000 people in the general population, after supervisor had told him the probability was one in 47. An investigation into his work found him to have an "insufficient understanding" of how to analyze mixed DNA samples. **2010:** San Francisco Police Department Crime Laboratory analyst Deborah Madden improperly mishandled drug evidence and stolen drugs for personal use. Over 600 cases were dismissed. Audit found broad systemic problems of understaffing, mismanagement, and a lack of training. The crime laboratory was closed.
Colorado	0	**2010:** Metro Crime Laboratory in Colorado Springs reviewing 1,000 DUI cases after more than 80 DUI suspects possibly falsely accused because tests registered erroneously high results. **2013:** State crime laboratory reports problems with security, training and supervision.
Connecticut	1	**2011:** State crime laboratory loses its accreditation after audits. Governor appoints a 17-member panel to fix state crime laboratory woes which include huge backlogs and insufficient staffing.
Delaware	0	
Florida	6	**2002:** Florida Dept. of Law Enforcement Crime Laboratory DNA Analyst John Fitzpatrick cheated on a proficiency test when realized he had failed it. He resigned rather than be fired. Crime laboratory did not notify prosecutors for three months, ostensibly because Fitzpatrick had agreed to notify them. Laboratory's attorney then told prosecutors that it

Florida (cont.)	6	was a personnel matter that need not be disclosed to defense attorneys. **2007:** Seminole County Sheriff's crime laboratory has fingerprint errors. State reviews hundreds of cases. **2014:** Florida Dept. of Law Enforcement Crime Laboratory drug chemist is charged with drug thefts. District Attorney reviewing 2600 cases and had already found 81 affected cases.
Georgia	4	**2010:** Closing three of seven regional crime laboratories due to insufficient resources, chronic understaffing.
Hawaii	0	
Idaho	1	
Illinois	18	**2001:** Illinois State Police Biochemistry Section Chief Pamela Fish alleged to have given false testimony in nine cases, including at least four that resulted in wrongful convictions and questions were raised in three others. The city settled one lawsuit for $11 million. Other lawsuits also filed. She was removed from casework in 2001 and later fired. In another case, Fish testified that testing was "inconclusive" when it in fact had excluded the defendant as a perpetrator. Police Sgt. Mary Furlong also falsely reported that there was no more biological material to test. **2012:** State Police crime laboratory fingerprint examiner failed proficiency testing, requiring re-testing of examiner's case work. Examiner was reassigned.
Indiana	2	
Iowa	0	**2012:** Department of Public Safety fingerprint examiner of 16 years is fired for nine errors in classifying prints as unsuitable for identification when they could be used.
Kansas	1	
Kentucky	1	
Louisiana	4	
Maine	0	

Maryland	1	**2003:** Baltimore County Police Department Crime Laboratory chemist Concepcion Bacasnot acknowledged in 1987 that she did not understand the science in her forensic tests, making her blood work in a death penalty case "worthless." She left the department at that time. Police reviewed 480 of her cases. In 2003, DNA exonerated one defendant convicted on her testimony. **2007:** Joseph Kopera, a 21-year veteran forensic scientist, first as a firearms examiner for Baltimore Police crime laboratory and then head of the Maryland State Police fingerprint unit, perjured himself for decades in thousands of criminal cases by claiming he held degrees and certificates that he did not hold. He resigned and then committed suicide in 2007.
Massachusetts	4	**2004:** Boston Police Crime Laboratory latent print unit found to have misidentified Stephan Cowans as cop killer in 1998 case. Police Commissioner begins overhaul of the latent print unit after independent review finds fundamental problems. None of the independent experts, including the FBI, could conceive of how error could have been made as it "was not even close." State Attorney General nonetheless declines to prosecute analysts for perjury. **2007:** State police DNA laboratory genetic test results for unsolved rape cases sat on administrator's desk while prosecutors lost their chance to pursue charges. **2012:** State drug laboratory chemist Annie Dookhan is accused of wide-scale misconduct in testing and perjury. 34,000 cases across state in question. Hundreds of cases dismissed. Second chemist in same laboratory, Sonja Farak, charged with drug tampering to hide her thefts of drugs. A prosecutor and laboratory supervisors resign. Dookhan pled guilty in 2013 and was sentenced to serve a prison term of 3–5 years. **2014:** Drug chemist in the State Crime Lab Sonja Farak pleads guilty to drug thefts.
Michigan	1	**2008:** Detroit police crime laboratory closed due to 10% error rate in firearms unit found in random audit of 200 cases. "Shocking level of incompetence" is found. Systemic problems affected other

Michigan (cont.)	1	disciplines as well. Cases transferred to State Police laboratory which reported consequently facing a "real crisis in its ability to complete requested laboratory services in a timely manner …" **2012:** Michigan State Police crime laboratory has numerous procedural problems such as evidence handling, security breaches, and documentation issues that must be corrected before it can obtain accreditation under international standards.
Minnesota	0	**2005:** Minnesota Bureau of Criminal Apprehension, assistant laboratory director David Peterson admits stealing drugs from laboratory. Following his arrest, he is removed as President of ASCLD. **2013:** St. Paul Police crime laboratory recommended for closure after audit by independent consultants. Major errors found in every area of the laboratory. Dirty equipment, poor facilities and incompetent analysts found. Public defenders are reviewing 10,000 cases.
Mississippi	1	
Missouri	3	**2005:** Missouri State Highway Patrol crime laboratory technician pleads guilty to stealing drugs.
Montana	3	**2003:** Montana State Police Crime Laboratory Director Arnold Melnikoff's false and erroneous testimony caused three wrongful convictions, led to review of hundreds of cases.
Nebraska	0	**2010:** Douglas County CSI commander Dave Kofoed sentenced to 20–48 months in prison for planting blood evidence in a double homicide investigation.
Nevada	0	
New Hampshire	0	
New Jersey	1	
New Mexico	0	
New York	13	**2002:** Two NY City crime laboratory examiners lied about drug evidence. They dry-labbed, writing reports on tests they never performed. NY State Inspector General issues report in 2007.

New York (cont.)	13	**2009:** NY State Inspector General report blasts NY State Police crime laboratory. One of its workers Gary Veeder, who had 30 years' experience in trace evidence analysis, was found to have so little training he could not operate a microscope. He engaged in dry-labbing for 15 years. Problems were found in 30 percent of his cases. R. Michael Portzer, the scientist who reviewed Veeder's work, was unqualified to do so. Laboratory managers minimized and downplayed the seriousness of the problems. Veeder committed suicide in 2008. **2009:** Monroe and Erie County Crime Laboratories found to engage in dry-labbing in drug cases, as well as misreporting drug weights and failing to perform vital steps in tests. One Erie County chemist was fired and pled guilty to a misdemeanor of attempted tampering with public records. **2011:** Entire Nassau County laboratory closed. 9,000 drug cases under review. More than 10% of drug cases found to have inconsistent results. Inspector General found chronic "failures at all levels of laboratory management and oversight." Accreditation found 26 areas of noncompliance with universally accepted standards.
North Carolina	2	**2010:** State Crime Laboratory had misleading or false serology reports over a 16-year period. 15,000 reports being reviewed. 190 had serious misrepresentations. FBI was investigating laboratory's practices. **2012:** State Crime Laboratory analysts failed proficiency tests. DA in Buncombe County reviewing 80–90 cases handled by the analysts. DA blames State Police leadership for not informing District Attorneys sooner. Most of the affected cases had been concluded by guilty pleas. **2012:** After a new certification requirement was implemented in the state as a means of addressing problems in crime laboratories, 25 State Crime Laboratory analysts failed tests for certification within their disciplines. The SBI laboratory was refusing to turn over the information regarding the tests to the District Attorneys.
North Dakota	0	

Ohio	1	**2001:** Cleveland Police Crime Laboratory analyst Joseph Serowik testified falsely and caused three wrongful convictions. First of three men exonerated by DNA evidence after serving lengthy prison sentence. Two others exonerated in 2007 after city conducted audit. City paid $1.6 million in lawsuit to first man and agreed to audit 16 years of cases. Other two exonerated men filed lawsuits in 2013.
Oklahoma	9	**2001:** Oklahoma City Crime Laboratory supervisor and chemist Joyce Gilchrist gave misleading testimony in five of eight cases reviewed by the FBI. Prosecutors used her work in thousands of cases, including 23 that resulted in death sentences. She caused numerous wrongful murder and rape convictions which were overturned. She was involved in 11 cases in which defendants were executed. Despite complaints from her colleagues, she had been promoted. She was fired in 2001. Hundreds of cases were under review.
Oregon	0	**2012:** Oregon State Police Crime Laboratory handwriting analysts Ron Emmons and Christina Kelley found to have committed serious error in a killer-for-hire case. Their work had also been used in a high profile bank bombing case in which two people were killed. The handwriting unit was closed in 2012. A routine audit had found they were not independently reviewing each other's work. The two had worked together for 13 years. A review of 35 cases being done in Oregon. Washington State Police also used their services and had begun review of at 40 cases.
Pennsylvania	3	**2002:** Pennsylvania State Police Crime Laboratory chemist Janice Roadcap found to have altered a laboratory report, causing a wrongful conviction and incarceration of Steven Crawford for 28 years. **2003:** A routine check of State Crime Laboratory DNA Analyst Ranae Houtz's work found errors in four cases. DAs in 27 counties reviewed 615 cases. **2007:** Philadelphia crime laboratory chemist Colleen Brubaker pled guilty to charges of theft and tampering with drugs. She had handled hundreds of cases since 1999. Dozens of cases dismissed.

Pennsylvania (cont.)	3	**2012:** Three trace evidence examiners in the Philadelphia crime laboratory failed proficiency test designed to test their ability to identify a particular trace substance, such as blood. Six examiners were tested, and three gave a different answer than the other three. All six were removed from case work until the final results of the test are known. Assuming three examiners gave the wrong answer, the police and District Attorney's office will need to review cases they've handled for mistakes.
Rhode Island	0	**2002:** State Justice Commission publishes report finding forensic services in the state "will ultimately lead to a crisis" if not "rationalized." Call for consolidation under State Police.
South Carolina	1	
South Dakota	0	
Tennessee	0	**2008:** 30-year veteran Nashville Metro Police crime laboratory worker, Police Officer Michael Pyburn, resigned after he was accused of falsifying records to cover a botched ballistics test. The ballistics unit was shut down, and two other officers who worked in the unit were found to be unqualified and resigned.
Texas	16	**1999:** Work of Bexar County Crime Laboratory analyst Fred Zain (who had moved from West Virginia) comes under question. He is fired. DA reviews Zain's cases. **2001:** Department of Public Safety retired fingerprint examiner Diana Boyd Monaghan investigated was indicted in 2000 for falsifying fingerprint reports on evidence she never tested. She allegedly forged 13 reports on cases involving murder, sexual assault and aggravated assault on a police officer. A grand jury in Austin called on the state legislature to investigate "what appears to be a total lack of supervision and managerial oversight" at the state crime laboratory. **2002–2008:** Houston Police Department has major scandals as outlined in Chapter 1. **2003:** Fort Worth Police Crime Laboratory DNA analyst Karla Carmichael performed poorly on a proficiency test. She was fired, the DNA unit was closed. The DA's office was reviewing 100 cases. One

Texas (cont.)	16	man was exonerated by DNA evidence. The laboratory also suffers from backlogs, staff shortages and an inadequate facility. **2008:** Three examiners with the Houston Police Crime Laboratory are forced to resign for cheating in the administration of proficiency tests, including Vanessa Nelson, the head of the DNA section. The DNA section was again shuttered. Nelson had been hired when the DNA section re-opened after its closure in 2002. Even as she was still under investigation in Houston, Nelson was hired by the Texas Department of Public Safety to work in the DNA section. **2011:** El Paso Police Crime Laboratory put on probation by accrediting organization ASCLD/LAB due to one incompetent analyst. **2013:** Texas Department of Public Safety Crime Laboratory narcotics chemist Jonathan Salvador found to have dry-labbed cases. Courts expected to throw out up to 5,000 cases. Salvador had been promoted despite concerns about his work.
Utah	0	
Vermont	0	
Virginia	5	**2005:** DNA exoneration in a death penalty case prompted an audit by ASCLD/LAB of the state's crime laboratory. The limited audit found problems with the work of the DNA analyst being reviewed. The audit called for a wider study to determine whether problems were endemic. The analyst had botched the DNA tests on several occasions, and the "peer review" process to catch errors within the laboratory had also failed several times. The state legislature removed the Division of Forensic Services from law enforcement control and made it an independent state agency.
Washington	0	**2004:** Audit of work done by drug chemist, Arnold Melnikoff, showed troubling flaws in 30 of 100 felony drug cases. **2004:** 23 DNA tests in major criminal cases found to have contamination errors. Work was done in four different State Patrol Crime Laboratories. **2004:** State Patrol crime laboratory analyst Donald Phillips found to have falsely testified to having a chemistry degree when his degree was in agricultural science.

Washington (cont.)	0	2007: State Patrol toxicology laboratory manager Ann Marie Gordon falsely claimed to verify solutions for breath testing in DWI cases & ballistics analysis work by Evan Thompson found mistakes or documentation problems in dozens of cases in 2006 alone. 2009: State Police Toxicology Laboratory found not to meet international standards for accreditation in testing and calibration. Numerous corrective actions were specified. 2013: Manager of State Patrol Crime Laboratory in Cheney, Kevin Fortney resigns upon discovery he had lied about performing work in several cases.
West Virginia	5	1993: West Virginia State Police Crime Laboratory analyst Fred Zain found to have committed repeated perjury causing wrongful convictions. 1999: West Virginia State Police Crime Laboratory chemist Howard Myers found to have falsely testified in a rape trial, stating that he ran tests he could not have run because evidence had been destroyed. 2003: West Virginia State Police Crime Laboratory chemist Todd Owen McDaniel admitted skipping required tests on drug evidence.
Wisconsin	2	2001: State Police Crime Laboratory fingerprint analyst Jack R. Patterson, a 25-year veteran, skipped dye/laser and immersion tests and then claimed in his reports that he had conducted them. He was charged with misconduct in office. 2010: Wisconsin state crime laboratory chemistry supervisor reprimanded for failing to obtain peer reviews in 27 toxicology cases involving drug evidence.
Wyoming	0	

*Sources: Innocence Project, *Wrongful Convictions Involving Unvalidated or Improper Forensic Science that Were Later Overturned through DNA Testing*, available at www.innocenceproject.org.
**Sources by State:

Alaska

Jerzy Shedlock, *Former Alaska crime lab analyst charged in alleged drug thefts,* Alaska Dispatch (Mar. 6, 2014), available at http://www.alaska dispatch.com/article/20140306/former-alaska-crime-lab-analyst-charged-alleged-drug-thefts.

Arizona

Beth DeFalco, *Police Say Lab Made Errors Analyzing Data*, AP Online (May 4, 2003) (Phoenix Police Crime Lab).

2008 *Tucson crime-lab worker resigns; had mishandled evidence in 6 cases,* Arizona Republic (Apr. 13, 2008), available at http://www.azcentral.com/news/articles/0413b10fill0413.html#.

California

Richard C. Paddock, *S.F. Police Lab Worker Accused of Drug Testing Fraud; Law Enforcement: Technician was targeted by internal sting after reports that evidence samples were not properly examined. Defense attorneys say many convictions may be affected,* Los Angeles Times (Sept. 20, 1994) (San Francisco Police Crime Laboratory drug chemist Allison Lancaster).

Tracey Kaplan, *Santa Clara County DA criticized for crime lab failures,* The Mercury News (Mar. 15, 2009), available at http://truthinjustice.org/SantaClaralab.htm.

Anna Gorman, *Case List Turned Over In Drug Lab Errors,* Los Angeles Times (Sept. 03, 2004), available at http://articles.latimes.com/2004/sep/03/local/me-lab3 (errors made by Los Angeles crime laboratory chemist Jeffrey Lowe).

Matt Clarke, *Crime Labs in Crisis: Shoddy Forensics Used to Secure Convictions,* Prison Legal News, available at https://www.prisonlegalnews.org/22698_displayArticle.aspx.

Greg Moran, *Criminalist who testified on DUIs falsified résumé,* San Diego Union Tribune (Mar. 22, 2006), available at http://www.utsandiego.com/uniontrib/20060322/news_7m22duiguy.html.

Moises Mendoza, *Fingerprinting Trouble Plagues Others Besides HPD,* Houston Chron. (Dec. 14 2009), at B1 at http://www.chron.com/news/houston-texas/article/Fingerprint-trouble-plagues-others-besides-HPD-1721098.php (addressing Los Angeles Police Department fingerprint laboratory problems).

Jaxon Van Derbeken, *SFPD Drug-Test Technician Accused of Skimming,* S.F. Chron. (Mar. 10, 2010), at A1 (discussing the San Francisco crime laboratory scandal).

Colorado

M. Alex Johnson, *Already under fire, crime labs cut to the bone*, NBC NEWS.COM (Feb. 23, 2010) (Metro Crime Laboratory, Colorado Springs, Colorado; Georgia Bureau of Investigations regional laboratories).

Jennifer Levitz, *Crime-Lab Woes Snarl Courts: Massachusetts Drug Offenders Demand Release After Chemist's Tampering Charge*, WALL ST. J. (June 23, 2013) at http://online.wsj.com/article/SB100014241278873233000045 78555950950276588.html (state crime laboratory reported problems with security, training and supervision).

Connecticut

Josh Kovner, *Malloy Appoints Panel To Fix State Crime Lab Woes: Governor Wants A Report From Panel By February*, THE HARTFORD COURANT (Aug. 11, 2011) at http://www.rachelbairdlaw.com/Uploads/Malloy%20Names %20Panel%20To%20Fix%20Connecticut%20Crime%20Lab%20-%20 Hartford%20Courant.pdf.

Josh Kovner, *Feds Criticize State Police Crime Lab Operations: Case backlogs, understaffing, DNA evidence control among issues cited*, THE HARTFORD COURANT (Aug. 09, 2011), available at http://articles.courant.com/2011-08-09/news/ hc-crime-lab-audit-0810-20110809_1_dna-evidence-dna-testing-crime-lab.

Courant Staff Report, *State Forensic Lab Loses Accreditation: Malloy Official Says Concerns Being Addressed*, THE HARTFORD COURANT (Aug. 17, 2011), available at http://articles.courant.com/2011-08-17/community/hc-forensic-lab-0818-20110817_1_crime-laboratory-directors-techniques-for-dna-test-tests-in-criminal-cases.

Florida

Anthony Colaross, *Defense calls for new trial in rape case*, ORLANDO SENTINEL (Nov. 26, 2002), available at B2 (Florida Dept. of Law Enforcement Crime Laboratory DNA Analyst John Fitzpatrick).

Moises Mendoza, *Fingerprinting Trouble Plagues Others Besides HPD*, HOUSTON CHRON. (Dec. 14 2009), available at B1 at http://www.chron.com/ news/houston-texas/article/Fingerprint-trouble-plagues-others-besides-HPD-1721098.php (addressing Seminole County Sheriff's Office fingerprint laboratory problems in 2007).

Julie Montanaro, *81 Drug Cases Possibly Affected by Former FDLE Chemist*, WCTV.COM (Mar. 5, 2014), available at http://www.wctv.tv/home/headlines/ FDLE-To-Hold-News-Conference-Regarding-Evidence-Tampering-243009311.html.

Georgia

M. Alex Johnson, *Already under fire, crime labs cut to the bone*, NBC News.com (Feb. 23, 2010) (Metro Crime Laboratory, Colorado Springs, Colorado; Georgia Bureau of Investigations regional laboratories).

Illinois

Steve Mills and Maurice Possley, *Report Alleges Crime Lab Fraud; Scientist Is Accused of Providing False Testimony*, Chi. Trib. (Jan. 14, 2001), at C1 (Illinois State Police Laboratory, Biochemistry Section Chief Pamela Fish).

Steve Mills, *Crime lab analyst moved; Worker who is under fire sent to research post*, Chi. Trib. (Aug. 16, 2001) at 1 (Illinois State Police Laboratory, Biochemistry Section Chief Pamela Fish).

Chris Dettro, State police reassign fingerprint scientist, reviewing cases, The State Journal-Register (Jan 09, 2012) at http://www.sj-r.com/top-stories/x123110627/State-police-reassign-fingerprint-scientist-reviewing-cases

Iowa

Joel Aschbrenner, *Iowa fires crime lab employee for fingerprint error*, Des Moines Register (Jan. 10, 2013) (Department of Public Safety Crime Laboratory Fingerprint Analyst, unnamed).

Maryland

Stephanie Hanes, *Ex-crime lab chemist's work questioned*, Baltimore Sun (Feb. 22, 2003) at 1B (Baltimore County Police Department Crime Laboratory, Forensic Chemist Concepcion Bacasnot).

Jennifer McMenamin, *Police expert lied about credentials*, The Baltimore Sun (Mar. 9, 2007), available at http://www.baltimoresun.com/news/maryland/bal-te.md.forensics09mar09,0,3664583.story?page=1.

Massachusetts

Ralph Ranalli, *Reilly won't charge two police analysts*, Boston Globe (June 25, 2004) at B8 (fingerprint analysts who misidentified Stephan Cowans).

Maurice Possley, Steve Mills and Flynn McRoberts, *Scandal touches even elite labs: Flawed work, resistance to scrutiny seen across U.S.*, Chicago Tribune (Oct. 21, 2004) at C-1.

Maggie Mulvihill & Franci Richardson, *Misfits dumped into key cop unit*, Boston Herald (May 6, 2004) at 2.

Jonathan Saltzman & John R. Ellement, *Mass. DNA Lab's Lapses Draw Beacon Hill Inquiry: Delays, Errors Laid to Lack of Oversight*, Boston Globe (Jan.

17, 2007), at 1A (discussing scandal in DNA laboratory of the Massachusetts state crime laboratory).

Andrea Estes & Scott Allen, *Drug defendants freed in lab scandal; Tainted evidence has 'massive public safety implications,' Suffolk DA says*, BOSTON GLOBE (Sept. 23, 2012) (Chemist Annie Dookhan).

Tovia Smith, *Crime Lab Scandal Leaves Mass. Legal System In Turmoil*, NPR (Mar. 14, 2013).

Rebecca Trager, *Massachusetts crime lab scandal explodes*, CHEMISTRY WORLD (Apr. 4, 2013).

Milton J. Valencia, John R. Ellement and Martin Finucane, *Annie Dookhan, former state chemist who mishandled drug evidence, sentenced to 3 to 5 years in prison*, BOSTON GLOBE (Nov. 22, 2013).

State Crime Lab chemist pleads guilty to theft of drugs, THE LOWELL SUN (Jan. 6, 2014), available at http://www.lowellsun.com/breakingnews/ci_24856098/ state-crime-lab-chemist-pleads-guilty-theft-drugs.

Michigan

Error-prone Detroit crime lab shut down, AP (Sept. 25, 2008) (Detroit Police Crime Laboratory).

Nick Bunkley, *Detroit Police Lab Is Closed After Audit Finds Serious Errors in Many Cases*, N.Y. TIMES (Sept. 26, 2008).

Ben Schmitt & Joe Swickard, *Troubled Detroit Police Crime Lab Shuttered: State Police Audit Results 'Appalling,' Wayne County Prosecutor Declares*, DETROIT FREE PRESS (Sept. 26, 2008), at 1 (discussing the multiple problems that led to the Detroit crime laboratory's closure).

Michigan State Police Crime Lab Woes Persist, FORENSIC MAGAZINE (July 8, 2012), available at http://www.forensicmag.com/news/2012/07/michigan-state-police-crime-lab-woes-persist.

Minnesota

Shannon Prather, *BCA worker had hoped to swap cocaine: Lab employee is charged with possession*, PIONEER PRESS, (Mar. 8, 2005), available at http://www.zoominfo.com/CachedPage/?archive_id=0&page_id=1090700527&page_url=//www.iape.org/Headlines/Headlines2005_03.html&page_last_updated=2008-10-22T16:46:02&firstName=David&lastName=Petersen.

David Hanners, *St. Paul crime lab's fingerprint examiners are trained but not certified*, TWINCITIES.COM (Aug. 20, 2012), available at http://www.twincities.com/localnews/ci_21355966/st-paul-crime-lab-police-chief-will-hire#_=1374525030799&count=vertical&id=twitter-widget-

0&lang=en&original_referer=http%3A%2F%2Fwww.twincities.com%2Flo-
calnews%2Fci_21355966%2Fst-paul-crime-lab-police-chief-will-
hire&size=m&text=St.%20Paul%20crime%20lab's%20fingerprint%20examin
ers%20are%20train.

Madeleine Baran, *Troubled St. Paul crime lab problems even worse than first
thought, probe reveals,* Minnesota Public Radio News (Feb. 14, 2013) (St.
Paul Police Crime Laboratory).

Public defenders review 10,000 cases from St. Paul crime lab, Minnesota Public
Radio News (Jan. 18, 2013), available at http://minnesota.publicradio.org/
display/web/2013/01/18/regional/cases-from-st-paul-crime-lab-under-review.

Missouri

Associated Press, *Lab technician pleads guilty to drug thefts: Mo. highway patrol
employee's thievery forced dismissal of nearly 400 cases,* NBCNews.com (Aug.
4, 2005), available at http://www.nbcnews.com/id/8838826/#.U0R0yU2PKpo.

Montana

Matt Clarke, *Crime Labs in Crisis: Shoddy Forensics Used to Secure Convictions,*
Prison Legal News, available at https://www.prisonlegalnews.org/
22698_displayArticle.aspx.

Ruth Teichroeb, *Oversight of crime-lab has often been lax,* Seattle Post-
Intelligencer (Jul. 22, 2004), available at http://www.seattlepi.com/local/
article/Oversight-of-crime-lab-staff-has-often-been-lax-1149961.php#page-
2 (discussing the audit of the work of Arnold Melnikoff).

Nebraska

John Ferak, *Concern over crime lab hiring plan,* Omaha World-Herald (Dec.
12, 2011), available at http://www.omaha.com/article/20111212/NEWS01/
712129921.

New York

State of New York, Office of the Inspector General, *Investigation of Drug Test
Irregularities at the NYPD Forensic Laboratory in 2002* (Dec. 2007), available at http://www.ig.state.ny.us/pdfs/Investigation%20of%20Drug%20
Test%20Irregularities%20at%20the%20NYPD%20Forensic%20Labora-
tory%20in%202002.pdf.

Murray Weiss, *Criminal Errors,* N.Y. Post (Dec. 4, 2007) (discussing a scandal at an NYPD crime laboratory).

Joseph Fisch, State of New York, Office of the Inspector General, *Report of Investigation of the Trace Evidence Section of the New York State Police Foren-*

sic Investigation Center (Dec. 2009), available at http://www.bulletpath.com/ wp-content/uploads/2011/01/NY-Trace-Doc.pdf.

IG: Serious Misconduct in NY State Police Lab, NORTH COUNTY GAZETTE (Dec. 17, 2009) (NY State Police Crime Laboratory Analysts Gary Veeder and R. Michael Portzer).

Jeremy W. Peters, *Report Condemns Police Lab Oversight*, N.Y. TIMES (Dec. 18, 2009) (NY State Police Crime Laboratory Analyst Gary Veeder).

Brendan J. Lyons, *Probe: Crime data faked*, TIMES UNION (Dec. 18, 2009).

Hicksville Woman's DWI Conviction Tossed Amid Crime Lab Woes Could Be Opening Of Floodgates; Gerdes Case Also In Question, CBS NEW YORK (Mar. 7, 2011), available at http://newyork.cbslocal.com/2011/03/07/ny-judge-rules-on-dwi-case-amid-crime-lab-woes/.

Jay Rey, *Chemist admits to falsifying lab report*, THE BUFFALO NEWS (Dec. 28, 2009), available at http://nl.newsbank.com/nl-search/we/Archives?p_product=BN&p_theme=bn&p_action=search&p_maxdocs=200&p_topdoc =1&p_text_direct-0=12CEAB544B6F0080&p_field_direct-0=document_ id&p_perpage=10&p_sort=YMD_date:D&s_trackval=GooglePM.

Editorial: Nassau lab cleanup a big task, Long Island Newsday, April 23, 2012 at http://www.newsday.com/opinion/editorial-nassau-lab-cleanup-a-big-task-1.3678047.

Frank Eltman, *State report cites failures at NY crime lab*, ASSOCIATED PRESS (Nov. 10, 2011), available at http://www.boston.com/news/nation/articles/2011/11/10/state_report_cites_failures_at_ny_crime_lab/ (citing the results of the retesting of Nassau County laboratory results).

North Carolina

Greg Collard, *N.C. State Crime Lab's Work Draws Scrutiny*, NATIONAL PUBLIC RADIO (Sept. 14, 2010), available at http://www.npr.org/templates/story/ story.php?storyId=129861236.

Paul Giannelli, *The North Carolina Crime Lab Scandal*, CRIMINAL JUSTICE, Vol. 27 (Spring 2012).

Clarke Morrison, *Crime lab failures tied to local cases*, ASHEVILLE CITIZEN-TIMES (Jul. 14, 2012).

Mandy Locke & Joseph Neff, *Inspectors Failed to Find SBI Faults*, CHARLOTTE OBSERVER (Aug. 26, 2010), *available at* http://www.charlotteobserver.com/ 2010/08/26/1643668/inspectorsfailed-to-find-sbi.html.

Mandy Locke & Joseph Neff, *SBI fights district attorneys' attempts to learn about failed tests: Agency won't release data on 25 analysts*, THE NEWS AND OB-

SERVER (Jun. 14, 2012), available at http://www.newsobserver.com/2012/
06/14/2137375/sbi-fights-district-attorneys.html.

Ohio

Cleveland man cleared of rape awarded $1.6 million, AP (Jun. 9, 2004) (Cleveland Police Department Crime Laboratory Analyst Joseph Serowik).

James F. McCarty, *Two Cleveland men seek millions from city for wrongful murder convictions, 13 years in prison,* THE PLAIN DEALER (Mar. 20, 2013) (Cleveland Police Department Crime Laboratory Analyst Joseph Serowik).

Oklahoma

Oklahoma Will Study Capital Cases, N.Y. TIMES (Jul. 18, 2001) (Oklahoma City Police Department Crime Laboratory Analyst Joyce Gilchrist).

Jim Yardley, *Inquiry Focuses on Scientist Employed by Prosecutors,* N.Y. TIMES (May 2, 2001), at 2 (discussing the Joyce Gilchrist Oklahoma scandal).

Oregon

Bryan Denson, *Allegations of sloppy work, dishonesty dog Oregon State Police handwriting unit,* THE OREGONIAN(Nov. 17, 2012) (Oregon State Police crime laboratory handwriting analysts Ron Emmons and Christina Kelley).

Pennsylvania

State won't defend employees who allegedly falsified evidence, KDKA ACTION 2 NEWS (Jun. 4, 2003) (Pennsylvania State Police Crime Laboratory Forensic Chemist Janice Roadcap).

Mark Levy, *Man freed after 28 years in prison,* ALLEGHENY TIMES (Mar. 27, 2003).

Roomy Varghese & Matt Assad, *Crime lab worker's errors could affect cases; Bethlehem scientist's mistakes force the region's Das to review records,* ALLENTOWN MORNING CALL (Jun. 20, 2003) at A1 (State Police laboratory DNA Analyst Ranae Houtz).

Dwight Otts, *Ex-police chemist sentenced for stealing drug evidence,* THE INQUIRER (Nov. 16, 2007) (Philadelphia Police crime laboratory drug chemist Colleen Brubaker).

Tony Hanson, *Philadelphia Crime Lab Examiners May Have Failed Proficiency Test,* CBS PHILLY (May 16, 2012), available at http://philadelphia.cbslocal.com/2012/05/16/philadelphia-crime-lab-evidence-examiners-may-have-failed-proficiency-text/.

Rhode Island

FINAL REPORT OF THE RHODE ISLAND JUSTICE COMMISSION, SUBCOMMITTEE ON STATEWIDE FORENSIC SERVICES (June 2002), available at http://www.

rijustice.state.ri.us/documents/reports/Subcommittee%20on%20Forensic%20Services%20Report.pdf.

Texas

Jane Elliot, *Lawyers seek access to Bexar County Lab; New DA reviews Zain's work*, Texas Lawyer (Aug. 2, 1999) at 1 (Bexar County Crime Laboratory Analyst Fred Zain).

Grand jury seeks inquiry on crime lab, Lubbock Avalance-Journal (Dec. 31, 2000) (Department of Public Safety Crime Laboratory Fingerprint Examiner Diana Boyd Monaghan).

Deanna Boyd, *Crime lab subject of criminal inquiry*, Star-Telegram (Apr. 13, 2003) (Fort Worth Police Crime Laboratory, DNA Analyst Karla Carmichael).

The City of Houston, *Investigation Into Crime Lab Proficiency Test Completed* (Jan. 25, 2008), available at http://www.houstontx.gov/police/nr/2008/jan/nr012508-1.htm.

Rosanna Ruiz & Robert Crowe, *HPD closes crime lab's DNA unit in wake of cheating probe*, Hous. Chron. (Jan. 26, 2008).

Roma Khanna, *State hires DNA chief despite Houston crime lab probe*, Hous. Chron. (Jan. 30, 2008).

Moises Mendoza, *Fingerprinting Trouble Plagues Others Besides HPD*, Hous. Chron. (Dec. 14 2009), at B1, available at http://www.chron.com/news/houston-texas/article/Fingerprint-trouble-plagues-others-besides-HPD-1721098.php (addressing Houston fingerprint laboratory problems).

EP Defense Attorney: Innocent People Could Be In Jail, KTSM News (Jul. 11, 2011), available at http://www.ktsm.com/news/ep-defense-attorney-innocent-people-could-be-in-jail.

One 'root cause' of El Paso crime lab woes: 'analyst's significantly flawed deductive reasoning capabilities,' Grits for Breakfast (Jul. 10, 2011), available at http://gritsforbreakfast.blogspot.com/2011/07/one-root-cause-of-el-paso-crime-lab.html.

Jim Vertuno, *Texas crime lab worker promoted despite poor work*, AP (Apr. 5, 2013) (Dept. of Public Safety crime laboratory chemist Jonathan Salvador), available at http://www.star-telegram.com/2013/04/05/4753940/dps-crime-lab-scientist-was-promoted.html.

Virginia

James Dao, *Lab's Errors Force Review of 150 DNA Cases*, N.Y. Times (May 7, 2005).

Washington

ASCLD/LAB-International, Washington State Patrol Toxicology Division Full Assessment Report (Jun. 9, 2009), available at http://www.waduicenter.com/wp-content/uploads/2010/05/090609-WSP-BAC-FullAssessmentRpt.pdf.

Ruth Teichroeb, *State Patrol fires crime lab scientist*, Seattle Post-Intelligencer (Mar. 23, 2004), available at http://www.seattlepi.com/local/article/State-Patrol-fires-crime-lab-scientist-1140314.php (results of audit of work done by Arnold Melnikoff).

DNA testing mistakes at the State Patrol crime labs, Seattle Post-Intelligencer (Jul. 21, 2004), available at http://www.seattlepi.com/local/article/DNA-testing-mistakes-at-the-State-Patrol-crime-1149846.php (discussing 23 DNA tests with contamination errors).

Ruth Teichroeb, *Oversight of crime-lab staff has often been lax*, Seattle Post-Intelligencer (Jul. 22, 2004), available at http://www.seattlepi.com/local/article/Oversight-of-crime-lab-staff-has-often-been-lax-1149961.php#page-3 (Donald Phillips misrepresentation of credentials).

Jennifer Sullivan, *Lawyers group urges forensic probe of state's toxicology and crime labs*, The Seattle Times (Oct. 17, 2007), available at http://seattletimes.com/html/localnews/2003955621_crimelab17m.html (discussing toxicology laboratory manager Ann Marie Gordon and forensic scientist Evan Thompson).

Police: Eastern Washington Crime Lab Manager Falsified Work, CBS Seattle (Apr. 16, 2013), available at http://seattle.cbslocal.com/2013/04/16/police-eastern-washington-crime-lab-manager-falsified-work/ (Kevin Fortney resignation).

West Virginia

Court Invalidates a Decade of Blood Test Results in Criminal Cases, N.Y. Times, Nov. 12, 1993, at A20 (discussing the Fred Zain West Virginia scandal).

Greg Moore, *Convicted rapist denied retrial despite magistrate's urging to toss convictions*, Charleston Gazette, Aug. 20, 1999 at 1A (West Virginia State Police Crime Laboratory Forensic Chemist Howard Myers).

Supreme court renews crime lab investigation, Williamson Daily News, Jun. 11, 1999, at 12.

Lawrence Messina, *State Police lab review leaves agency with another shiner*, Charleston Gazette, Mar. 13, 2002 at 1A (West Virginia State Police Crime Laboratory Todd Owen McDaniel).

Lawrence Messina, *After testing scandal, State Police lab changes*, Charleston Gazette, Jan. 28, 2002.

Wisconsin

Timothy W. Maier, *Federal Judge Slams Fingerprint "Science,"* Insight on the News, Mar. 18, 2002 at 20 (Wisconsin State Police Crime Laboratory, Fingerprint Analyst Jack R. Patterson).

David Doege, *Former analyst at crime lab is charged*, Milwaukee Journal Sentinel, Oct. 10, 2001. (Fingerprint Analyst Jack R. Patterson).

Agent, analyst accused of stalking, missing errors, The Janesville Gazette, Feb. 13, 2010 at http://gazettextra.com/weblogs/latest-news/2010/feb/13/agent-analyst-accused-stalking-missing-errors/ (discussing chemistry supervisor Dirk Janssen's failure to obtain peer reviews on 27 toxicology cases).

Appendix 2
Sentences Imposed on the Wrongfully Convicted Whose Cases Involved Invalid Forensic Science

Name of Exoneree	State	Sentence (in years)	Years Served
Abdal, Habib Wahir	NY	20–Life	16
Adams, Kenneth	IL	75	17.5
Alejandro, Gilbert	TX	12	3.5
Atkins, Herman	CA	45	11.5
Avery, Steven	WI	32	17.5
Barnes, Steven	NY	25–Life	19.5
Bauer, Chester	MT	30	8
Bibbins, Gene	LA	Life	15.5
Blair, Michael	TX	Death	13.5
Boquete, Orlando	FL	50	12
Bravo, Mark Diaz	CA	8	3
Brewer, Kennedy	MS	Death	7
Briscoe, Johnny	MO	45	23
Brison, Dale	PA	18–42	3.5
Bromgard, Jimmy Ray	MT	40	14.5
Brown, Dennis	LA	Life	19
Brown, Roy	NY	25–Life	15
Bryson, David Johns	OK	85	16
Buntin, Harold	IN	50	13
Byrd, Kevin	TX	Life	12
Charles, Clyde	LA	Life	17
Charles, Ulysses Rodriguez	MA	72–80	17
Cotton, Ronald	NC	Life + 54	10.5
Cowans, Stephan	MA	30–45	5.5
Criner, Roy	TX	99	10
Crotzer, Alan	FL	130	24.5
Dabbs, Chares	NY	12.5–20	7
Dail, Dwayne Allen	NC	Life	18
Danziger, Richard	TX	Life	11
Davidson, Willie	VA	20	12
Davis, Dewey	WV	10–20	7
Davis, Gerald	WV	14–35	8
Daye, Frederick	CA	Life	10

Name of Exoneree	State	Sentence (in years)	Years Served
Dedge, Wilton	FL	Life	22
Diaz, Luis	FL	Multiple Life Sentences	25
Dillon, William	FL	Life	26
Dominguez, Alejandro	IL	9	4
Dotson, Gary	IL	25–50	10
Durham, Timothy	OK	3,200	3.5
Erby, Lonny	MO	115	17
Fain, Charles Irvin	IN	Death	17.5
Fritz, Dennis	OK	Life	11
Fuller, Larry	TX	50	19.5
Good, Donald Wayne	TX	Life	13.5
Gray, Paula	IL	50	9
Green, Michael	OH	20–50	13
Gregory, William	KY	70	7
Halstead, Dennis	NY	33 1/3–Life	16
Harris, William O'Dell	WV	10–20	7
Harrison, Clarence	GA	Life + 40	17.5
Hatchett, Nathaniel	MI	25–40	10
Heins, Chad	FL	Life	11
Hicks, Anthony	WI	20	5
Holland, Dana	IL	11	88
Honaker, Edward	VA	3 Life Sentences + 34 years	9.5
Jackson, Willie	LA	40	17
Jimerson, Verneal	IL	Death	10.5
Johnson, Calvin	GA	Life + 2 terms of 15, to run concurrently	15.5
Jones, Ronald	IL	Death	10
Kogut, John	NY	31.5	17
Kordonowy, Paul	MT	30	13
Krone, Ray	AZ	Death + 21	10
Laughman, Barry	PA	Life	16
Lavernia, Carlos	TX	99	15
Linscott, Steven	IL	40	3
Lowery, Eddie James	KS	11–Life	9.5
McCarty, Curtis	OK	Death	21
McCray, Antron	NY	5–10	6
Miller, Neil	MA	26–45	22
Miller, Robert	OK	Death	6

Name of Exoneree	State	Sentence (in years)	Years Served
Mitchell, Marvin	MA	9–25	7
Mitchell, Perry	SC	30	14.5
Moon, Brandon	TX	75	17
Ochoa, James	CA	2	1
O'Donnell, James	NY	3.5–7	2
Ollins, Calvin	IL	Life	13.5
Ollins, Larry	IL	Life	13.5
Pendelton, Marlon	IL	20	10
Peterson, Larry	NJ	Life + 20	16.5
Pierce, Jeffrey	OK	65	14.5
Pope, David Shawn	TX	45	15
Rainge, Willie	IL	Life	17.5
Restivo, John	NY	33 1/3–Life	16
Reynolds, Donald	IL	55	9.5
Richardson, James	WV	Life	9
Richardson, Kevin	NY	5–10	5.5
Robinson, Anthony	TX	27	10
Rodriguez, George	TX	60	17
Rollins, Lafonso	IL	75	10
Rose, Peter	CA	27	8
Salaam, Yusef	NY	5–10	5.5
Santana, Raymond	NY	5–10	5
Saunders, Omar	IL	Life	15.5
Scott, Calvin Lee	OK	25	20
Sutton, Josiah	TX	25	4.5
Taylor, Ronald Gene	TX	60	12
Tillman, James	CT	45	16.5
Vasquez, David	VA	35	4
Velasquez, Eduardo	MA	12–18	12.5
Waller, James	TX	30	10
Wardell, Billy	IL	55	9.5
Washington, Calvin	TX	Life	13
Washington, Earl	VA	Death	17
Watkins, Jerry	IN	60	13.5
Webb, Thomas	OK	60	13
Webb, Troy	VA	47	7.5
Webster, Bernard	MD	30	20
White, John Jerome	GA	Life	22

Name of Exoneree	State	Sentence (in years)	Years Served
Whitley, Drew	PA	Life	16.5
Williams, Dennis	IL	Death	17.5
Williams, Willie "Pete"	GA	45	21.5
Williamson, Ron	OK	Death	11
Willis, John	IL	100	7
Wise, Kharey	NY	11–15	11.5
Woodall, Glen	WV	2 Life + 203–335	4
Woods, Anthony D.	MO	25	18

Source: Innocence Project, *Know the Cases, Browse the Profiles,* available at http://www.innocenceproject.org/know/Search-Profiles.php?check=check&title=&yearConviction=&yearExoneration=&jurisdiction=&cause=Unvalidated+or+Improper+Forensic+Science&perpetrator=&compensation=&conviction=&x=19&y=5. A search for profiles involving "unvalidated or improper forensic science" as a "contributing cause" yields this list of DNA exonerees. Information about sentences was obtained by reading each of the individual profiles.

Notes for Chapter 2

1. See Innocence Project, *Understand the Causes: Unvalidated or Improper Forensic Testimony,* http://www.innocenceproject.org/understand/Unreliable-Limited-Science.php and *Know the Cases: DNA Exoneree Profiles,* http://www.innocenceproject.org/know/.

2. Crime laboratories that were fully or partially closed include: San Francisco Police Department Crime Lab (California, 2010), Detroit Police Department Crime Lab (Michigan, 2008), St. Paul Police Department Crime Lab (Minnesota, 2013), Nassau County Police Department Crime Lab (New York, 2011), Houston Police Department Crime Lab (Texas 2002 and 2008), and Nashville Metro Police Crime Lab (Tennessee, 2008). *See* Appendix 1.

3. *See infra* notes 28–97 and accompanying text. The two analysts who committed suicide are Gary Veeder (New York) and Joseph Kopera (Maryland). *See* Appendix 1.

4. *See* Appendix 1 for numerous examples.

5. *See infra* notes 60–63.

6. Oren Gazal-Ayal & Avishalom Tor, *The Innocence Effect,* 62 Duke L. J. 339 (2012).

7. *Id.*

8. *See supra* Chapter 1.

9. Innocence Project, *supra* note 1.

10. *See* Innocence Project, *Fix the System: Preservation of Evidence,* available at http://www.innocenceproject.org/Content/Preservation_Of_Evidence.php (discussing limitations of evidence preservation laws that allow many states to destroy crucial biological evidence in criminal cases).

11. *See* Innocence Project, *News and Information: Louisiana Man on Death Row for 15 Years Becomes 300th Person Exonerated by DNA Evidence* (Sept. 12, 2012), available at http://

www.innocenceproject.org/Content/Louisiana_Man_on_Death_Row_for_15_Years_
Becomes_300th_Person_Exonerated_by_DNA_Evidence.php.

12. See, e.g., Pamela Colloff, "Innocence Lost," TEX. MONTHLY (Oct. 2010) (regarding
the Anthony Graves case, published prior to his non-DNA exoneration); "Tulia, Texas,"
Wikipedia, http://en.wikipedia.org/wiki/Tulia,_Texas (noting that the drug convictions of
forty-six innocent African-Americans became a *cause célèbre* that led to the overturning of
their convictions.

13. *See* Paul C. Giannelli, *The Abuse of Scientific Evidence in Criminal Cases: The Need
for Independent Crime Laboratories*, 4 VIRGINIA JOURNAL OF SOCIAL POLICY & LAW 439, 475
(1997); Paul Giannelli, *Independent Crime Laboratories: The Problem of Motivational and
Cognitive Bias*, UTAH L. REV. 247, 260 (2010).

14. *See* NATIONAL ACADEMY OF SCIENCES, STRENGTHENING FORENSIC SCIENCE IN THE
UNITED STATES: A PATH FORWARD at 39–40 (2009) (hereinafter NAS REPORT).

15. *See infra* Chapter 6.

16. *See* Paul C. Giannelli, *Regulating Crime Laboratories: The Impact of DNA Evidence*,
15 J.L. & POL'Y 59, 68 (2007) (quoting NATIONAL ADVISORY COMM'N ON CRIMINAL JUSTICE
STANDARDS AND GOALS, REPORT ON POLICE 304–305 (1974)). An earlier national task force
in 1967 had concluded similarly that "the great majority of police department laboratories
have only minimal equipment and lack highly skilled personnel able to use the modern
equipment now being developed." *Id.* (citing the INSTITUTE FOR DEFENSE ANALYSES, TASK
FORCE REPORT: SCIENCE AND TECHNOLOGY: A REPORT TO THE PRESIDENT'S COMM'N ON
LAW ENFORCEMENT AND ADMINISTRATION OF JUSTICE 91 (1967)).

17. *Id.* at 71–72.

18. *Id.*

19. *See* REPORT OF THE ABA CRIMINAL JUSTICE SECTION'S AD HOC INNOCENCE COMMITTEE
TO ENSURE THE INTEGRITY OF THE CRIMINAL PROCESS, ACHIEVING JUSTICE: FREEING THE
INNOCENT, CONVICTING THE GUILTY, (Paul C. Giannelli & Myrna Raeder eds., 2006).

20. Joel Rubin, *LAPD's Crime Lab Hampered by DNA Backlog, Money Woes*, LOS AN-
GELES TIMES, Jan. 20, 2010, http://latimesblogs.latimes.com/lanow/2010/01/lapd-crime-
lab-hampered-by-backlog-money-woes.html; Kathy Quinn, *New Police Crime Lab Could
Suffer Due to Budget Woes*, Fox4kc.com, http://fox4kc.com/2013/06/27/new-police-crime-
lab-could-suffer-due-to-budget-woes/.

21. *Id.*

22. *Id.*

23. *See* NAS REPORT, *supra* note 14 at 217–18.

24. *Id.* at 36.

25. U.S. DEP'T OF LABOR, BUREAU OF LABOR STATISTIC, *Occupational Employment and
Wages*, http://www.bls.gov/oes/current/oes194092.html.

26. This statement is based on my conversations with leaders of the forensic community, including Dr. Roger Kahn, a former President of American Society of Crime Laboratory Directors.

27. Jeffrey Frankel & Peter R. Orszag, *Retrospective on American Economic Policy in the
1990s*, Nov. 2, 2001, http://www.brookings.edu/research/papers/2001/11/02useconomics-orszag.

28. Francis X. Clines,*Work by Expert Witness Is Now on Trial*, N.Y. TIMES, Sept. 5, 2001,
http://www.nytimes.com/2001/09/05/us/work-by-expert-witness-is-now-on-trial.html.

29. Sau Chan, *Scores of Convictions Reviewed as Chemist Faces Perjury Accusations: Forensics: Fred Zain's expert testimony and lab tests helped put scores of rapists and murderers behind

bars. But college transcript shows he flunked some chemistry classes and barely passed others. He is also accused of evidence-tampering, L.A. TIMES (Associated Press), Aug. 21, 1994, http://articles.latimes.com/1994-08-21/news/mn-29449_1_lab-tests-fred-zain-double-murder.

30. Steve Corris, *Court Asks Officials to Consider Taking Crime Lab from State Police,* W.V. RECORD, Jun. 28, 2006, http://wvrecord.com/news/180999-court-asks-officials-to-consider-taking-crime-lab-from-state-police.

31. N.Y. TIMES ARCHIVES, *Court Invalidates a Decade of Blood Test Results in Criminal Cases,* N.Y. TIMES, Nov. 12, 1993 (hereinafter "*Court Invalidates*"), http://www.nytimes.com/1993/11/12/us/court-invalidates-a-decade-of-blood-test-results-in-criminal-cases.html.

32. Clines, *supra* note 28.

33. Chan, *supra* note 29.

34. *Id.*

35. Clines, *supra* note 28.

36. ASSOCIATED PRESS ARCHIVES *Ex-W. Va. Police Chemist Fred Zain Dies,* ASSOCIATED PRESS, Dec. 3, 2002, http://www.apnewsarchive.com/2002/Ex-W-Va-Police-Chemist-Fred-Zain-Dies/id-c3611a6bee2117e73b21992e16175e9a.

37. *Id.*

38. *Id.*

39. *Court Invalidates, supra* note 31.

40. Chan, *supra* note 29.

41. *See* Associated Press, *7 W.Va. Ethics Commission Members Reappointed,* July 1, 2014, http://www.herald-dispatch.com/news/briefs/x1116648612/7-W-Va-Ethics-Commission-members-reappointed.

42. *Court Invalidates, supra* note 31.

43. Clines, *supra* note 28.

44. Chan, *supra* note 29.

45. Ruth Teichroeb, *They Sit in Prison—but Crime Lab Tests are Flawed,* SEATTLE POST-INTELLIGENCER, Mar. 12, 2004, http://www.seattlepi.com/local/article/They-sit-in-prison-but-crime-lab-tests-are-1139478.php#page-2.

46. *Id.*

47. *Id.*

48. *Id.*

49. Associated Press, *No Criminal Charge for Manager of State Toxicology Lab,* SEATTLE TIMES, Nov. 9, 2007, http://seattletimes.com/html/localnews/2004005066_webgordon10m.html.

50. *Id.*

51. Jaxon Van Derbeken, *Problems of S.F. toxicologist not disclosed,* S.F. GATE, May 26, 2010, http://www.sfgate.com/bayarea/article/Problems-of-S-F-toxicologist-not-disclosed-3263652.php#page-2.

52. Jaxon Van Derbeken, *Toxicologist's Wash. History may taint Calif. cases,* SEATTLE TIMES, May 26, 2010, http://seattletimes.com/html/nationworld/2011952994_coroner26.html.

53. *Id.*

54. Van Derbeken, *supra* note 51.

55. *The Weakest Link: TDCAA Agrees Nearly 5,000 Cases "May All be Jeopardized" by DPS Lab Worker Misconduct,* GRITS FOR BREAKFAST, Mar. 15, 2013, http://gritsforbreakfast.blogspot.com/2013/03/the-weakest-link-tdcaa-agrees-nearly.html?utm_source=feedblitz&utm_medium=FeedBlitzEmail&utm_content=79553&utm_campaign=0.

56. Brian Rogers, *Hundreds of Cases to be Reviewed Because of Errors by Crime Lab Worker*, Hous. Chron., May 1, 2012, http://www.chron.com/news/houston-texas/article/Hundreds-of-cases-to-be-reviewed-because-of-3525028.php.

57. Emily DePrang, *Fake Lab Results Endanger Thousands of Drug Convictions*, Tex. Observer, Jul. 8, 2013, http://www.texasobserver.org/fake-lab-results-endanger-thousands-of-drug-convictions/.

58. *DPS analyst who faked results worked on 4,944 drug cases*, Grits for Breakfast, July 28, 2012, http://gritsforbreakfast.blogspot.com/2012/07/dps-analyst-who-faked-results-worked-on.html.

59. Associated Press, *Agency: Houston Crime Lab Worker had History of Poor Work*, ABC 13 Eyewitness News, Apr. 05, 2013, http://abclocal.go.com/ktrk/story?section=news/local&id=9054336.

60. Tovia Smith, *Crime Lab Scandal Rocks Massachusetts*, National Public Radio, ept. 20, 2012, http://www.npr.org/2012/09/20/161502085/state-crime-lab-scandal-rocks-massachusetts.

61. *Id.*

62. *Id.*

63. *See* Milton J. Valencia & John R. Ellement, *Annie Dookhan Pleads Guilty in Drug Lab Scandal*, The Boston Globe (Nov. 22, 2013), http://www.bostonglobe.com/metro/2013/11/22/annie-dookhan-former-state-chemist-who-mishandled-drug-evidence-agrees-plead-guilty/7UU3hfZUof4DFJGoNUfXGO/story.html.

64. Jesse McKinley, *Hundreds of Drug Cases Are at Risk in San Francisco*, N.Y. Times, Apr. 3, 2010, available at http://www.nytimes.com/2010/04/04/us/04evidence.html?_r=0.

65. *Id.*

66. Paul Elias and Terry Collins, *San Francisco Crime Lab Scandal Growing, Thousands of Criminal Cases May Be Dismissed*, Huffington Post, Apr. 8, 2010, http://www.huffingtonpost.com/2010/04/18/san-francisco-crime-lab-s_n_542102.html.

67. *Id.*

68. *See* McKinley, *supra* note 64.

69. *Id.*

70. *Id.*

71. Bay City News, *Former SF Police Crime Lab Tech Pleads Guilty to Cocaine Possession*, S.F. Examiner, Mar. 15, 2013, http://www.sfexaminer.com/sanfrancisco/former-sf-police-crime-lab-tech-pleads-guilty-to-cocaine-possession/Content?oid=2320882.

72. *Id.*

73. *See Former SFPD Lab Tech Sentenced for Drug Possession*, abc7, Jul. 19, 2013, at www.abc7news.com/archive/9178786/.

74. Elias & Collins, *supra* note 66.

75. Jerzy Shedlock, *Former Alaska Crime Lab Analyst Charged in Alleged Drug Thefts*, Alaska Dispatch, Mar. 6, 2014, http://www.alaskadispatch.com/article/20140306/former-alaska-crime-lab-analyst-charged-alleged-drug-thefts.

76. *Id.*

77. *Id.*

78. *See State Crime Lab Chemist Pleads Guilty to Theft of Drugs*, Lowell Sun, Jan. 6, 2014, http://www.lowellsun.com/breakingnews/ci_24856098/state-crime-lab-chemist-pleads-guilty-theft-drugs.

79. *See* Julie Montanaro, *81 Drug Cases Possibly Affected by Former FDLE Chemist*,

WCTV.com, Mar. 5, 2014, http://www.wctv.tv/home/headlines/FDLE-To-Hold-News-Conference-Regarding-Evidence-Tampering-243009311.html.

80. Tina Potterf, *Crime Lab Junkie? Alleged Theft and Tampering by State Patrol Chemist May Have Jeopardized Thousands of Drug Cases*, SEATTLE WEEKLY NEWS, Oct. 9, 2006, http://www.seattleweekly.com/2001-01-24/news/crime-lab-junkie/.

81. *See Ex-HPD Crime Lab Tech Convicted of Evidence Tampering, Felony Theft*, KHOU.COM, Jul. 7, 2010, http://www.khou.com/news/Ex-HPD-crime-lab-tech-convicted-of-evidence-tampering-felony-theft-97976189.html.

82. *See, e.g.,* Craig Anderson, *21 Defendants Get Notices of Tainted Evidence*, DELAWARE.NEWSZAP.COM, Feb. 27, 2014, http://delaware.newszap.com/centraldelaware/130023-70/21-defendants-get-notices-of-tainted-evidence.

83. *DNA testing mistakes at the State Police crime labs*, SEATTLE POST-INTELLIGENCER, July 21, 2004.

84. Associated Press, *WSP crime labs slip up*, THE SPOKESMAN REVIEW, Jul. 23, 2004, http://m.spokesman.com/stories/2004/jul/23/wsp-crime-labs-slip-up/.

85. *Id.*

86. *See* Associated Press, *Defense Lawyer Group Calls for Investigation of State Crime Lab*, KOMO News, Oct. 16, 2007, http://www.komonews.com/news/local/10590127.html.

87. *See* Associated Press, *Police: Eastern Washington Crime Lab Manager Falsified Work*, THE OREGONIAN, Apr. 16, 2013, http://www.oregonlive.com/pacific-northwest-news/index.ssf/2013/04/washington_state_patrol_says_c.html.

88. *See* Jennifer Pignolet, *Crime Lab Work Went Undone; Worker Accused of Lying about Completing Tests on Evidence*, THE SPOKESMAN-REVIEW, Apr. 17, 2013, at http://www.spokesman.com/stories/2013/apr/17/crime-lab-work-went-undone/.

89. *See* Appendix 1.

90. Ruth Teichroeb, *Oversight of Crime-Lab Staff has Often Been Lax*, SEATTLE POST-INTELLIGENCER, Jul. 22, 2004, http://www.seattlepi.com/local/article/Oversight-of-crime-lab-staff-has-often-been-lax-1149961.php#page-3.

91. *See* Greg Moran, *Criminalist Who Testified on DUIs Falsified Résumé*, SAN DIEGO UNION TRIBUNE, Mar. 22, 2006, http://www.utsandiego.com/uniontrib/20060322/news_7m22duiguy.html.

92. *See* Jennifer McMenamin, *Police Expert Lied about Credentials*, THE BALTIMORE SUN, Mar. 9, 2007, http://www.baltimoresun.com/news/maryland/bal-te.md.forensics09mar09,0,3664583.story?page=1.

93. *See* Rene Stuzman, *Crime-Lab Worker Puts Cases in Doubt*, ORLANDO SENTINEL, Jul. 19, 2002, http://articles.orlandosentinel.com/2002-07-19/news/0207190359_1_fitzpatrick-dna-sanford.

94. Anthony Colaross, *Defense Calls for New Trial in Rape Case*, ORLANDO SENTINEL at B2, Nov. 26, 2002.

95. *See* Rosanna Ruiz & Robert Crowe, *HPD Closes Lab's DNA Unit in Wake of Cheating Probe*, HOUSTON CHRON., Jan. 26, 2008, http://www.chron.com/news/houston-texas/article/HPD-closes-crime-lab-s-DNA-unit-in-wake-of-1536283.php.

96. *See* Roma Khanna, *State Hires DNA Chief Despite Houston Crime Lab Probe*, HOUSTON CHRON., Jan. 30, 2008, http://www.chron.com/news/houston-texas/article/State-hires-DNA-chief-despite-Houston-crime-lab-1785193.php.

97. *See* Association of Forensic DNA Analysts and Administrators, at http://afdaa.org/2013/officers/.

98. *See* Jennifer Inez Ward, *Federal Funds Offer Limited Help for OPD Crime Lab*, Oakland Local, Sept. 11, 2012, http://archive.oaklandlocal.com/article/federal-funds-offer-limited-help-opd-crime-lab.

99. *See Houston Crime Lab Found Hundreds of CODIS 'Hits' in Rape-Kit Backlog*, Grits for Breakfast, Apr. 6, 2014, http://gritsforbreakfast.blogspot.com/2014/04/houston-crime-lab-found-hundreds-of.html?utm_source=feedblitz&utm_medium=FeedBlitzEmail&utm_content=79553&utm_campaign=0.

100. Kevin Quinn, *Effort to Ease Houston's Rape Kit Backlog Pays Off with Arrest of Suspect from 2004 attack*, ABC 13 Oct. 10, 2013, http://abclocal.go.com/ktrk/story?section=news/local&id=9282620; *see also* note 90.

101. *See* U.S. Dep't of Justice, Office of Violence against Women, *Eliminating the Rape Kit Backlog: A Roundtable to Explore a Victim-Centered Approach, Summary of the Proceeding*, at 10 (2010).

102. *Id.* at 7.

103. *Id.* at 15.

104. *See* Joe Minor, *Touch DNA: From the Crime Scene to the Crime Laboratory*, Forensic Magazine, Apr. 12, 2013, http://www.forensicmag.com/articles/2013/04/touch-dna-crime-scene-crime-laboratory.

105. Travis C. Pratt, Michael J. Gaffney, Nicholas P. Lovrich and Charles L. Johnson, *This Isn't CSI: Estimating the National Backlog of Forensic DNA Cases and the Barriers Associated With Case Processing*, 17 Crim. J. Pol'y Rev. 32, 37 (2006).

106. *Id.*

107. *See* Minor *supra* note 104.

108. *See* U.S. Dep't of Justice, *supra* note 101 at 22.

109. *See* Kevin J. Strom and Matthew J. Hickman, *Unanalyzed Evidence in Law-Enforcement Agencies: A National Examination of Forensic Processing in Police Departments*, 9 Criminology & Pub. Pol'y 381 (2010).

110. *See* U.S. Dep't of Justice, *supra* note 101 at 9.

111. *See* Justin Fenton, *City Police Crime Lab is Swamped*, Baltimore Sun, Mar. 14, 2010, http://weblogs.baltimoresun.com/news/crime/blog/2010/03/city_police_crime_lab_is_swamp.html.

112. *Id.*

113. Alex Johnson, *Already under Fire, Crime Labs Cut to the Bone*, msnbc.com, Feb. 23, 2010, http://www.nbcnews.com/id/35319938/ns/us_news-crime_and_courts/t/already-under-fire-crime-labs-cut-bone/.

114. *See* Bradley Olson, *Backlog Woes Continue at HPD Lab*, Houston Chron., Jan. 26, 2010, http://www.chron.com/news/houston-texas/article/Backlog-woes-continue-at-HPD-lab-1709693.php.

115. *See* James Swierzbin, *RI Crime Lab Director Worried about Increased Caseload*, ABC6.com, Oct. 15, 2012, http://www.abc6.com/story/19826411/ri-crime-lab-director-worried-about-increased-caseload (dramatic increase in firearms caseload).

116. *See* John M. Collins, *A Reality Check on Crime Lab Backlogs*, Mich. Bar J. at 36, 37–38 (Oct. 2012).

117. Paul Giannelli, *The Abuse of Scientific Evidence in Criminal Cases: The Need for Independent Crime Laboratories*, 4 Virg. J. of Social Pol'y & L. 439, 445–46 (1997).

118. *See* Tracey Kaplan, *Santa Clara County DA Criticized for Crime Lab Failures*, San Jose Mercury News, Mar. 15, 2009, http://truthinjustice.org/SantaClaralab.htm.

119. Frederic N. Tulsky, *Criminalist Taken Off of Casework, Mistake May Ripple Through Other Cases*, SAN JOSE MERCURY NEWS, Feb. 8, 2007, http://www.mercurynews.com/ ci_5182590.

120. Tracey Kaplan, *Wrongfully Convicted San Jose Man to Receive $1 Million Settlement from Santa Clara County*, SAN JOSE MERCURY NEWS, Aug. 15, 2009, http://www.mercurynews.com/ci_13118342?source=most_viewed.

121. *See* Colaross, *supra* note 94.

122. *See* Mandy Locke & Joseph Neff, *SBI Fights District Attorneys' Attempts to Learn about Failed Tests: Agency Won't Release Data on 25 Analysts*, THE NEWS AND OBSERVER, June 14, 2012 http://www.newsobserver.com/2012/06/14/2137375/sbi-fights-district-attorneys.html.

123. *Id.*

124. *See* Jeremy W. Peters, *Report Condemns Police Lab Oversight*, N.Y. TIMES, Dec. 18, 2009, http://www.nytimes.com/2009/12/18/nyregion/18statepolice.html?_r=0.

125. ROBERT FISCH, REPORT OF THE INVESTIGATION OF THE TRACE EVIDENCE SECTION OF THE NEW YORK STATE POLICE FORENSIC INVESTIGATION CENTER, at 2, Dec. 2009, https:// s3.amazonaws.com/attachments.readmedia.com/files/12426/original/Inspector_General_s_Public_Report_on_NYSP.pdf?1291278511.

126. *Id.* at 1.

127. *Id.* at 2.

128. *Id.* at 8.

129. *See* Sally Jacobs, *Annie Dookhan Pursued Renown along a Path of Lies; Finally Found Fame, As Scandal Engulfed the State Drug Lab*, BOSTON GLOBE, Feb. 3, 2013, http:// www.bostonglobe.com/metro/2013/02/03/chasing-renown-path-paved-with-lies/ Axw3AxwmD33lRwXatSvMCL/story.html.

130. *See* James Pinkerton & Brian Rogers, *Crime Lab Analyst Kept on Job Despite Shoddy Work*, HOUS. CHRON., Apr. 4, 2013, http://www.houstonchronicle.com/news/houston-texas/ houston/article/Crime-Lab-analyst-kept-on-job-despite-shoddy-work-4413046.php.

131. *See* DePrang, *supra* note 57.

Chapter Three

The Complex Critique of Forensic Science

Convicted by Science

Every prosecutor goes to trial with the same objective: to present the evidence so persuasively that jurors will be convinced of the defendant's guilt beyond a reasonable doubt. For decades, forensic science testimony alone was strong enough to supply that persuasion, even in the face of other countervailing evidence such as multiple alibi witnesses or discrepancies in an eyewitness's description of the suspect. "Science" has had the power to persuade juries to reject reasonable defensive arguments and find guilt beyond a reasonable doubt. Indeed, crime laboratory analysts have long purported to prove the incriminating connection between the defendant and the crime beyond *all* doubt. The persuasive power of forensic testimony makes sense. Unlike eyewitnesses and alibi witnesses who may lie or misremember details of an event, scientific proof is—as juries are told—objective, unbiased, and, at least as presented, definitive. The very word "scientific" connotes "definitive" to the layperson. If a crime laboratory analyst says that the fingerprint, blood, bullet casing, or shoeprint could have been left at the crime scene only by the defendant, then the defendant must be guilty. The science is definitive; the science convicts. For jurors struggling to weigh the evidence and concerned about fairness and justice, having such strong reassurance would greatly reduce their anxiety.

Fingerprint examiners have testified to so-called "definitive" matches for over 100 years,[1] and other forensic experts would follow suit as new disciplines were developed for examining crime scene evidence. This concept of a definitive match has been referred to as "individualization," which the National Academy of Sciences defines as "'matching' a specimen to a particular individual or other source."[2] Individualization is a step more precise than "classification," which establishes that a specimen came from a particular category but without tracing it definitively to a particular source or person.[3] (For example, being able to identify a blood sample as Type O, Type AB, etc. was a step that

83

could eliminate some suspects but without establishing that it had come from a particular individual, as DNA matching can do.) So central is the goal of individualization in forensic science that one writer in the 1960s described individualization as being "the essence of forensic science."[4]

The problem is that most forensic science is not actually definitive, nor is it "scientific" in a strict sense of the word. As we now understand, only DNA evidence has the power to yield a virtually definitive conclusion about a match between two specimens of evidence.[5] In the context of fingerprint examination, criminologist Simon Cole reports that for decades "forensic scholars have cast doubt on the concept of individualization, calling it 'not possible' or 'not logically attainable.'"[6] Yet most courts to this day continue to allow forensic experts to testify to definitive matches. More recently, external groups have begun calling on examiners in all forensic disciplines to stop making claims of absolute individualization. Even DNA evidence has an error rate arising from many possible sources such as "coincidental DNA profile matches between different people, inadvertent or accidental transfer of cellular material or DNA from one item to another, errors in identification or labeling of samples, misinterpretation of test results, and intentional planting of biological evidence."[7] Thus, a claim of individualization must be qualified as having a slight possibility of error. Understood in this way, any claim of absolute or definitive individualization is false by definition.[8]

Yet voices from within the National Institute of Justice (a unit of the U.S. Department of Justice) and other individuals and institutions in these forensic disciplines have either given "unabashed defenses" or made no response to the attacks on individualization.[9] Most experts in these fields seem inclined to tweak the language of individualization from the absolute definitive terminology of the past to a more nuanced—if ultimately just as definitive—terminology. For example, the FBI has conceded that statements of absolute certainty in firearms testimony should not be made and now advocates for individualizations to a "reasonable scientific certainty."[10]

To say that individualizations should not be made in most forensic disciplines is not to say that forensic tests have no evidentiary value—they do. But most are not the definitive evidence we once thought they were. One challenge, then, is to make criminal courts aware of the less definitive nature of most forensic evidence so that they will not allow juries to be given the impression that the forensic tests yield "definitive match" results.

Other challenges exist as well, which is what makes unpacking concerns about forensic science so complex. Disciplines with strong scientific support such as serology can still be done improperly or be misreported, and in many cases this has led to numerous wrongful convictions.[11] This problem can be reduced by properly funding and staffing laboratories, by promoting a truly scientific culture in laboratories, and by removing them from oversight by law enforcement agencies where the organizational structure itself promotes psychological contamination by giving the forensic teams strong motivation to confirm certain findings.[12] In other cases, analysts have incorrectly testified that certain forensic tests had an ability to individualize when this was flatly untrue. These situations have led to broad reviews of past convictions to ferret out the "junk science" that may have caused wrongful convictions. Composite bullet lead analysis, bite mark analysis, microscopic hair analysis, and much of traditional arson investigation currently occupy the list of such junk sciences.[13] In short, forensic science consists of a wide array of disciplines, some of which have strong scientific foundations, some of which have unrealized potential to develop scientific foundations, and some of which are simply bogus as a means of making definitive match statements. Good science can be done badly, and good science can be misleadingly reported. Forensic disciplines lie somewhere on a spectrum with DNA evidence on one end of the spectrum and junk science on the other. A variety of responses is needed to address the issues forensic disciplines present. The overarching challenges, then, are how to determine where on the spectrum each lies, how the results of each type of discipline should be characterized in court, cleaning up the mess of junk science used in the past (including the review of convictions based on such testimony), and strengthening the research base and scientific culture of forensic science generally.

Police Departments Invent "Sciences" to Solve Crimes

Over the course of the twentieth century, crime scene evidence became a crucial weapon in the criminal investigator's arsenal. Imagine the aftermath of a shooting on a city street. Police officers find a victim's body lying on the street. On the muddy pavement nearby is the impression of a shoeprint. If other evidence points toward a particular person named Bob Johnson, the police would likely seek to compare Johnson's shoes to the print at the crime scene. If Johnson owned a pair of shoes of the same size and with the same type of tread, a natural response would be, "Aha! He's guilty!" After all, how likely is it that the police would zero in on this person *and* that his shoes would be the exact size and type found at the crime scene? Our gut instincts tell us this evidence strongly points toward Johnson's guilt. Discovering that the suspect's shoes are the same size and tread design as those found at the crime scene, a prosecutor could simply introduce the print as physical evidence and ask the jury to draw whatever probabilistic inferences they thought appropriate. The shoeprint would be strong, circumstantial evidence linking the suspect to the crime. The shoeprint analyst might testify, giving his or her expert opinion about the shoe's "classification," or general type, and this behavior would be appropriate.

But law enforcement officials went further by transforming crime scene evidence into ostensibly scientific evidence. They developed forensic disciplines, which were a natural outgrowth of criminal investigations and other law enforcement needs.[14] Science had the potential to connect physical evidence to a suspect with a degree of conclusiveness that even other strong evidence (e.g., eyewitness identifications) could not. No longer would prosecutors be limited to offering the shoeprint as physical evidence that bears some similarity to the suspect's shoe. Crime laboratories purported to transform the shoeprint into "scientific evidence" with the power to prove without a doubt that a particular person had made the particular shoeprint in the mud. In this way, crime laboratories for decades gave the prosecution ostensibly irrefutable proof of guilt. Whereas the circumstantial evidence of a similar shoeprint could leave jurors wondering whether someone else with a similar shoe might have left the print, the scientific testimony of an individualization or a shoeprint "match" could persuade jurors to hand down a guilty verdict—even in the face of other exculpatory evidence.

Police crime laboratories today typically conduct nuclear or mitochondrial DNA testing, toxicology, serology, drug chemistry, latent prints (commonly referred to as "fingerprints"), firearms/toolmarks (commonly referred to as "ballistics"), and trace evidence (e.g., comparisons of soils, building materials, and fibers). Questioned documents (i.e., handwriting) and a few others may also be found in some laboratories. Some of these disciplines, such as toolmark examination (e.g., whether a knife used in a stabbing had a serrated blade) and trace evidence analysis, can break down into many different types of testing, further increasing the number of possible types of tests conducted in a crime laboratory. Prosecutors also may rely on forensic evidence produced outside the confines of police laboratories by other professionals, such as medical examiners, physicians, sexual assault nurse examiners, arson investigators, forensic odontologists, psychologists, and psychiatrists. Many forensic methods practiced in crime laboratories, such as the analysis of firearms, tire tracks, shoeprints, fibers, and others, were developed for law enforcement purposes and have no purpose beyond assisting in criminal investigations and prosecutions. Thus, police department crime laboratories have been the main locus for the development of modern forensic disciplines. In itself, this is not problematic. However, as I have already argued, tests can be done badly or even faked, forensic experts can give biased or even perjured testimony, and claims of definitiveness can be greatly exaggerated.

Criminal Courts Freely Admit Forensic Testimony

Forensic experts have testified in both civil and criminal cases for over 100 years. In civil lawsuits, experts testify to a wide variety of medical, scientific, and technical issues that affect issues of liability and damages. In criminal cases, most forensic experts testify as prosecution witnesses on such issues as the causes of injuries and the identities of the perpetrators.

In the early 1990s, concerns about junk science abounded in civil tort cases.[15] The courts saw a veritable parade of "experts" whose testimony was being offered in torts cases, many involving class actions.[16] During this time, the U.S. Supreme Court took up this issue deciding the first of three landmark cases addressing the admissibility of expert testimony, and all three involved civil tort cases. The decisions were understood to apply to any case in which an expert would testify, whether civil or criminal. Nonetheless, at that time and for years afterwards, "the 'junk science' debate ... all but ignored criminal prosecutions."[17]

But first, some background. Since 1923, federal and state courts alike had applied a "general acceptance" standard for admissibility of expert testimony, which was established in a D.C. Circuit case called *Frye v. United States*.[18] In *Frye*, a criminal defendant on trial for murder sought to introduce the results of a lie detector test as proof of his innocence. The court pronounced the standard that would prevail nationwide for decades to come:

> Just when a scientific principle or discovery crosses the line between the experimental and demonstrable stages is difficult to define. Somewhere in this twilight zone the evidential force of the principle must be recognized, and while courts will go a long way in admitting expert testimony deduced from a well-recognized scientific principle or discovery, *the thing from which the deduction is made must be sufficiently established to have gained general acceptance in the particular field in which it belongs.*[19]

The rule was meant to screen out "novel" scientific evidence that had not attained the stature of "general acceptance." From the perspective of trial judges, most of whom are not scientists, the rule also had the advantage of avoiding the formidable challenge of having judges evaluate the merits of scientific testimony.

For about fifty years, courts nationwide applied the *Frye* rule. Then in 1975, the Federal Rules of Evidence (FRE) were drafted by Congress and adopted by the Supreme Court to govern the admissibility of evidence in federal trials, including the admission of expert testimony.[20] The FRE were influential in the states as well, with more than four-fifths adopting codes mirroring them.[21] With respect to scientific evidence, the FRE's Rule 702 stated:

> If scientific, technical, or other specialized knowledge will assist the trier of fact to understand the evidence or to determine a fact in issue, a witness qualified as an expert by knowledge, skill, experience, training, or education may testify thereto in the form of an opinion or otherwise.[22]

Rule 702 does not mention "general acceptance," nor was it clear whether the drafters of the FRE intended the *Frye* standard to apply. This rule left the courts in a quandary, with individual judges struggling to determine the meaning of the new rule and whether the *Frye* rule still survived.

Eighteen years later, the Supreme Court finally answered the question of the admissibility of scientific evidence in the three landmark cases. It heard the first, *Daubert v. Merrell Dow Pharmaceuticals, Inc.,*[23] in 1993. This case presented the question of whether the *Frye* standard or the FRE governed the admissibility of expert scientific testimony, an issue on which the lower courts were by then sharply divided.[24]

Finding no mention of *Frye* or the "general acceptance" standard in the text of Rule 702, the Supreme Court concluded that the drafters of the FRE did not intend to continue the practice of admitting expert scientific opinions *solely* on the basis that others in the field generally accepted it as valid.[25] In fleshing out the substance of the admissibility standard in Rule 702, the Court focused on the terms "scientific" and "knowledge" in the Rule in finding a general reliability requirement. Extrapolating from the definitions of those words, the Court required that "scientific knowledge" in testimony "must be derived by the scientific method."[26]

The decision in *Daubert* not only required that the basis of scientific expert testimony be derived by the "scientific method," it also provided a detailed explanation of how this admissibility standard could be applied. As the Court explains, to determine whether the expert testimony conveys scientific knowledge that will assist the trier of fact, the trial court must make a "preliminary assessment of whether the reasoning or methodology underlying the testimony is scientifically valid."[27] With this language, the Court thrust trial courts into the role of judging scientific validity.

The Court identifies as a "key question to be answered in determining whether a theory or technique is scientific knowledge … will be whether it can be (and has been) tested."[28] The testing of a theory or technique enables others to attempt to refute it or, as scientists might say, to "falsify" it. The second consideration the Court identifies is "whether the theory or technique has been subjected to peer review or publication."[29] These factors relate to the ability to test the theory or technique: "submission to the scrutiny of the scientific community is a component of 'good science,' in part because it increases the likelihood that substantive flaws in methodology will be detected [through review and subsequent testing by others]."[30] The Court also notes, however, that merely publishing a paper about a theory or technique "does not necessarily correlate with reliability."[31] It is necessary that the publication provide some data on which the theory or technique rests so that others may attempt to refute the study's results through subsequent testing. The availability of sufficient testing can produce the data needed to determine the "known or potential error rate," which is the statistical information for determining reliability. The known or potential error rate is the third factor identified in *Daubert*.[32] Finally, "general acceptance" should be considered by the trial courts as well.[33] Thus, the *Frye* standard became one of the four factors courts should consider in determining reliability. The four-factor test clarified what the rule meant by "scientific," but it still left the trial judge responsible for deciding whether to accept Expert X as a true expert, and most criminal courts continued to freely admit forensic experts who mostly testify for the prosecution.

In the second case, *Kumho Tire Co. v. Carmichael*, which was heard in 1999, the Supreme Court held that *Daubert*'s requirement that trial courts screen scientific evidence for reliability applied equally to other types of experts.[34] The expert at issue in *Kumho Tire* was an engineer whose testimony was characterized by the parties as "technical."[35] Rule 702 by its terms applies to expertise based on "scientific, technical, or other specialized knowledge," and the Court here clarified that the standard of evidentiary reliability applied to all types of knowledge, regardless of the type of expert.[36] Expertise tied to "specialized experience," just like scientific expertise, requires the judge to determine whether it has "a reliable basis in the knowledge and experience of [the relevant] discipline."[37] The distinction between scientific and technical expertise is important in considering the admissibility of forensic testimony because so many of the disciplines can be viewed as offering technical opinions based on specialized experience, rather than simply conveying the results of a purely scientific laboratory test.

For many forensic disciplines, crime laboratory analysts should be understood as giving expert but non-scientific opinions based on their knowledge and experience. This distinction between scientific and non-scientific expertise could be clearly explained to the jury. A Sixth Circuit case provides an excellent hypothetical to explain the difference between scientific and non-scientific expert testimony, and the appropriateness of each *depending on the conclusions to be drawn by each.* In *Berry v. City of Detroit,* the court explains:

> The distinction between scientific and non-scientific expert testimony is a critical one. By way of illustration, if one wanted to explain to a jury how a bumblebee is able to fly, an aeronautical engineer might be a helpful witness. Since flight principles have some universality, the expert could apply general principles to the case of the bumblebee. Conceivably, even if he had never seen a bumblebee, he still would be qualified to testify, as long as he was familiar with its component parts.
>
> On the other hand, if one wanted to prove that bumblebees always take off into the wind, a beekeeper with no scientific training at all would be an acceptable expert witness if a proper foundation were laid for his conclusions. The foundation would not relate to his formal training, but to his firsthand observations. In other words, the beekeeper does not know any more about flight principles than the jurors, but he has seen a lot more bumblebees than they have.[38]

The U.S. Supreme Court in deciding *Kumho Tire* was aware that much valuable expertise would be screened out if—to use the above hypothetical—beekeepers were held to the same standards as aeronautical engineers. The beekeeper would have highly reliable information about the observed flight patterns of bees, even if he or she could not point to peer-reviewed publications or validation studies of the methodology used. Nor would a beekeeper be able to tell the jury the error rate of the methodology. Training and experience would suffice to give a non-scientific expert of this type a reliable basis upon which to give an expert opinion on bee flight patterns, but it would not suffice to give an opinion conveying scientific knowledge. Applying the *Daubert* factors to experts giving opinions based on "professional studies or personal experience" ensures that they "employ in the courtroom the same level of intellectual rigor that characterizes the practice of an expert in the relevant field."[39] While "general acceptance" may indicate reliability, the Court also warned against relying solely on "general acceptance" within relevant fields "where the discipline itself lacks reliability, as, for example, do theories grounded in any so-called generally accepted principles of astrology or necromancy."[40]

Recognizing the inappropriateness of applying all of the *Daubert* factors in every case, the Court chose to give trial courts wide latitude in deciding which factors to apply.[41] With regard to testimony by non-scientists, the opinion concludes: "*Daubert's* list of specific factors neither necessarily nor exclusively applies to all experts or in every case."[42] In the most sweeping expansion of the trial court's discretion in this area, the Court stated: "[T]he law grants a district court the same broad latitude when it decides *how* to determine reliability as it enjoys in respect to its ultimate reliability determination."[43]

In the third case, *General Electric Co. v. Joiner*, the Court made clear that the appellate courts should take a hands-off approach in passing judgment on the admissibility decisions of the lower courts. Applying the traditional standard for appellate review, the Court directed the appellate courts to affirm a lower court's decision unless the lower court "abused its discretion," which is a highly deferential standard.[44]

Of particular relevance to forensic science, the Court's decision in *Joiner* also addresses the issue of whether the trial court should focus on the principles and methodology applied by the expert or on the conclusions the expert draws from those principles. In *Joiner*, plaintiff had developed small-cell lung cancer, and he sued several companies on the grounds that their products had exposed him to PCBs. The plaintiff argued that, had he not been exposed to the PCBs, he might have contracted cancer years later if at all. He offered the testimony of two doctors. Both of them relied on animal studies rather than epidemiological studies, clinical studies involving testing on humans. The trial court had ruled that the experts could not reasonably draw their conclusions of a probable link between Joiner's exposure to PCBs and his contracting cancer based only on animal studies.

On appeal, Joiner faulted the trial court for focusing on the experts' conclusions, as opposed to the principles and methodology they employed. The Supreme Court saw these as intertwined:

> But conclusions and methodology are not entirely distinct from one another. Trained experts commonly extrapolate from existing data. But nothing in either *Daubert* or the Federal Rules of Evidence requires a district court to admit opinion evidence that is connected to existing data only by the *ipse dixit* [i.e., say so] of the expert. A court may conclude that there is simply too great an analytical gap between the data and the opinion proffered.[45]

Thus, the Court clarified that trial courts should appropriately scrutinize not only the principles and methodology but also the connection between these and the conclusions drawn.

The decade following the *Daubert* decision passed seemingly without the notice of most criminal court judges and at least some defense attorneys, who too frequently failed to challenge invalid or exaggerated forensic testimony offered by prosecutors.[46] Virtually all courts continued to admit testimony about these disciplines on the ground that its admissibility was well established.[47] Despite some efforts by defense attorneys to challenge forensic testimony, the courts almost universally refused to reconsider the admissibility of forensic evidence that had been "generally accepted" for decades.

Forensic Science—and the Justice System's Use of It—Finally Come Under Fire

Ironically, at the same time that criminal courts were ignoring *Daubert's* mandate to screen expert testimony for reliability by using the scientific method as a guide, an ever-increasing flow of wrongful convictions based on invalid forensic science were coming to light. In fact, it soon became apparent that erroneous, false, or misleading forensic testimony was a leading cause of these miscarriages of justice. As of May 2014, invalid forensic science testimony was identified as a contributing cause of 49% of the 316 DNA exonerations.[48]

In 2003, ten years after *Daubert* and amid the ongoing complaints of legal scholars concerned about the lack of scientific rigor in much forensic testimony,[49] research scientists finally took note and began the process of change. *Science* magazine published an influential editorial by Donald Kennedy, the Editor-in-Chief, titled, "Forensic Science: Oxymoron?"[50] Kennedy, a renowned biologist and former president of Stanford University, carried great weight when he questioned the use of hair samples and bullet casings as a means of individualization. He wrote: "The use of hair samples in identification and the analysis of bullet markings exemplify kinds of 'scientific' evidence whose reliability may be exaggerated when presented to a jury."[51] For methods like fingerprint analysis, which he conceded may be reliable, he decried the lack of a statistical model to evaluate its reliability. He further expressed bewilderment about the demonstrated resistance to criticisms shown by the National Institute of Justice, which resides in the U.S. Department of Justice, as evidenced by its unwillingness to take part in "comprehensive evaluations of the science underlying forensic techniques."[52]

The editorial started a dialogue that culminated with the passage of the Science, State, Justice, Commerce, and Related Agencies Appropriations Act of 2006 in which Congress authorized " 'the National Academy of Sciences to conduct a study on forensic science.' "[53] The Senate committee report states:

> While a great deal of analysis exists of the requirements in the discipline of DNA, there exists little to no analysis of the remaining needs of the

community outside of the area of DNA. Therefore ... the Committee directs the Attorney General to provide [funds] to the National Academy of Sciences to create an independent Forensic Science Committee. This Committee shall include members of the forensic community representing operational crime laboratories, medical examiners, and coroners; legal experts; and other scientists as determined appropriate.[54]

The project of providing Congress with a comprehensive assessment of forensic science was well suited for an organization like the NAS which describes itself as

> a private, non-profit society of distinguished scholars. Established by an Act of Congress, signed by President Abraham Lincoln in 1863, the NAS is charged with providing independent, objective advice to the nation on matters related to science and technology.... Nearly 500 members of the NAS have won Nobel Prizes.[55]

Drawn from all fields of science, no more august a body of scientists exists in the country. The committee, which appropriately considered its task of studying all of forensic science in its many forms to be "daunting," responded by holding numerous hearings and soliciting an enormous volume of input from experts in many fields nationwide.[56]

In 2009, after lengthy deliberations, the NAS issued its report, *Strengthening Forensic Science in the United States: A Path Forward*, which had, as its purpose, "chart[ing] an agenda for progress in the forensic science community and its scientific disciplines."[57] The report, published in a 328-page book, reviews the scientific basis and reliability of most forensic disciplines and provides guidance on the governance of forensic science, the improvement of the practice, oversight of the field, and education and training of forensic scientists, among other subjects. The report addresses the following forensic science disciplines: biological evidence (DNA analysis), analysis of controlled substances, friction ridge analysis (fingerprint), other pattern/impression evidence (shoeprints and tire tracks), toolmark and firearm identification, analysis of hair evidence, analysis of fiber evidence, questioned document examination (analysis of handwriting or machine sources of documents), analysis of paint and coatings evidence, analysis of explosives evidence and fire debris, forensic odontology (bite mark analysis), bloodstain and pattern analysis, and digital and multimedia analysis.[58]

With regard to the use of forensic science in the courts, the National Academy of Sciences roundly criticized criminal courts for failing to meaningfully implement the *Daubert* standard of admissibility:

"[T]here is no evident reason why ['rigorous, systemic'] research would be infeasible." However, some courts appear to be loath to insist on such research as a condition of admitting forensic science evidence in criminal cases, perhaps because to do so would likely "demand more by way of validation than the disciplines can presently offer."[59]

"The principal difficulty, it appears, is that many [forensic science] techniques have been relied on for so long that courts might be reluctant to rethink their role in the trial process.... In many forensic areas, effectively no research exists to support the practice."[60]

The NAS Report also makes the case that the adversarial process of the judicial system does not lend itself to the kind of systemic change needed in forensic science. For one thing, the "adversarial process relating to the admission and exclusion of scientific evidence is not suited to the task of finding 'scientific truth.' "[61] Moreover, *Daubert's* optimistic view of the judiciary's ability to evaluate scientific evidence is not shared by the National Academy of Sciences, not only because judges and lawyers "generally lack the scientific expertise necessary," but also because judicial process does not permit collaboration with judicial colleagues nor afford sufficient time for research and reflection.[62] In short, the report concludes, "Judicial review, by itself, will not cure the infirmities of the forensic science community."[63] The report looks instead to Congress to provide support for a broad improvement of the practice of forensic science, as discussed in the next section.

The NAS Review of Forensic Disciplines

The NAS Report provides an important discipline-by-discipline assessment of the field of forensic science, including more than a dozen different forensic disciplines.[64] The NAS committee focused on those disciplines "used most commonly for investigations and trials as well as those that have been cause for concern in court or elsewhere because their reliability has not been sufficiently established in a systematic (scientific) manner ..."[65] Each of these assessments addresses the question of whether the forensic discipline in question produces scientifically reliable results. These assessments provide critical guidance for advocates and the judiciary in determining the reliability of various forensic tests and whether the conclusions drawn from those tests are supported by the underlying test results. Forensic tests can be useful as tools for criminal investigations, but their main purpose is as evidence in criminal trials, almost always on behalf of the prosecution. With regard to the ability of forensic science to yield definitive individualizations, however, the National

Academy of Sciences is clear: "No forensic method other than nuclear DNA analysis has been rigorously shown to have the capacity to consistently and with a high degree of certainty support conclusions about 'individualization' (more commonly known as 'matching' of an unknown item of evidence to a specific known source)."[66] In the entire report, this sentence was the bombshell: *no forensic method*, other than nuclear DNA analysis, supports definitive match opinions. The most prominent group of scientists in the country had just concluded that the "essence" of forensic science—the power of individualization—had no scientific basis, except in DNA analysis.

Trial lawyers and judges who interact with forensic scientists rarely possess much formal education in a scientific field, nor have they worked in a research laboratory (as graduate students in the sciences do), so they will not usually understand what it means for a particular discipline to have a "scientific foundation." Recognizing that many of its readers would not be scientists, the NAS Report provides a primer that is entitled, "The Principles of Science and Interpreting Scientific Data."[67] The primer would be familiar to readers of *Daubert*, but the NAS gives a more thorough explanation of the scientific method and the culture of science.

The Report describes the "scientific method" as a means of testing theories to obtain knowledge. Scientists construct studies to test hypotheses. They incorporate methods to reduce errors, such as errors caused by possible biases.[68] An important element of scientific experimentation is the sharing of data through publication and peer-review. The report explains:

> These theories, and investigations of them through experiments and observed data, are shared through conferences, publications, and collegial interactions, which push the scientist to explain his or her work clearly and which raise questions that might not have been considered. The process of sharing data and results requires careful record-keeping, reviewed by others. In addition, the need for credibility among peers drives investigators to avoid conflicts of interest. Acceptance of work comes as results and theories continue to hold, even under the scrutiny of peers, in an environment that encourages healthy skepticism.[69]

In short, the report identifies the "key elements of good scientific practice" as being:

- precision when defining terms, processes, context, results, and limitations;
- openness to new ideas, including criticism and refutation; and
- protections against bias and overstatement (going beyond the facts).[70]

Disciplines with Solid Scientific Support

The NAS report singles out several forensic disciplines as resting upon solid scientific foundations, calling these "analytically based disciplines."[71] The extent of research validating the underlying premises of analytically based disciplines makes them the most demonstrably reliable of the all the forensic disciplines. Again, only DNA has the research basis for making individualizations, but others have strong scientific foundations nonetheless. As the NAS Report states, "In terms of scientific basis, the analytically based disciplines generally hold a notable edge over disciplines based on expert interpretation."[72] The National Academy of Science includes in the former category "DNA analysis, serology, forensic pathology, toxicology, chemical analysis, and digital and multimedia forensics."[73]

The forensic disciplines identified by the NAS as solidly grounded in science merit such designation because they all share certain common features. First, a critical component of a scientific theory or process is the existence of "validation studies." The search for knowledge through the scientific method means that the new theory or process—and all the underlying data supporting the reliability of the theory or process—has been shared with peers through publication, conferences, etc. The sharing of the data then allows others to replicate the experiments and determine whether the same results are obtained. These validation studies must then be published "in peer-reviewed journals, so that experts in the field can review, question, and check the repeatability of the results."[74] Over time, when sufficient validation studies show the theory or process to be reproducible, it gains acceptance as being scientifically grounded.[75] Not only does the ability to reproduce a method give credibility to the proposition it purports to prove, but it also makes the method "more amenable to systematic improvement than those that rely more heavily on the judgments of the investigator."[76]

The scientific research base for DNA analysis is especially strong. Whereas many forensic techniques were developed within crime laboratories to aid crime scene investigations, "DNA analysis is a fortuitous by-product of cutting-edge science" with far-ranging applications in medicine.[77] As such, "DNA analysis has been subjected to more scrutiny than any other forensic science discipline, with rigorous experimentation and validation performed prior to its use in forensic investigations."[78] Like any other scientific process there is always a "risk of errors in handling that can invalidate the analysis," but, assuming proper handling of the evidence, "the probative power of DNA is high."[79]

To say that a particular type of forensic test rests on a solid scientific basis is *not* to say that the practice of this discipline can yield definitive match information from two physical specimens. While DNA experts will often venture to say that the biological evidence found at a crime scene almost certainly matches that of the defendant, these experts will also usually be expected to state in mathematical terms the probability that the DNA could belong to someone else. Random match probabilities will be higher in some cases, such as those involving degraded samples or mixtures of biological evidence. However, the probabilities of such problems are so astronomically low in a typical case as to make the chance that the DNA is not the defendant's virtually nil.

That said, even the analytically based forensic disciplines are not infallible. They can still produce false conclusions due to human error or incompetence. In law professor Brandon Garrett's study of the first 200 exonerations based on reappraising DNA evidence, 67 included invalid serology evidence and three cases had invalid DNA evidence.[80] When properly performed, DNA analysis provides highly reliable evidence, but, when performed by an incompetent analyst, even it can cause wrongful convictions. To be well-qualified, an analyst should be properly educated, trained and certified, and should pass regular, rigorous proficiency tests. A properly educated and trained analyst will then be capable of following appropriate testing protocols and ensure that laboratory equipment is properly calibrated. The expert should also have the expertise to extrapolate from the test results and produce a conclusion that is valid. The laboratory should utilize properly calibrated equipment and quality control procedures designed to reduce bias, improve consistency, and enhance the validity and reliability of results.[81] Accreditation of the laboratory, which requires that it meet industry standards for quality assurance, is yet another indication that a test was likely conducted properly.[82] These measures greatly reduce the probability of error but cannot eliminate it altogether. Particularly vulnerable to error is the manner in which the tests are conducted and reported. However, numerous indicia of reliability can lend confidence that an analyst conducted the forensic tests properly.

Disciplines with Mid-Range Reliability

Disciplines such as fingerprint analysis, firearms/toolmarks, tire tread analysis, shoe-print analysis, and others provide useful information with evidentiary value, but their reliability cannot yet be determined. The intrinsic reliability of each of these disciplines may fall on a different point on the reliability spectrum. The burning question is just where on the spectrum they fall and how the conclusions drawn by experts in these fields should be characterized. What complicates the issue further is that the reliability *of the discipline* will vary with the experience and training of the analyst, as well as the quality of the recovered evidence. It makes a big difference whether an examiner analyzes a full set of a person's fingerprints as opposed to a partial print from one finger, for example.

Many common forensic disciplines involve comparisons of pattern impressions or physical specimens. The list of these disciplines includes latent prints (fingerprints), toolmark/firearm (ballistics), tire track, shoeprint, voice identification, and handwriting comparison. These disciplines rest on expert subjective comparisons of evidentiary specimens. These types of tests can reliably include or exclude suspects during a criminal investigation, so they are important tools for police investigators. The training and experience examiners develop give them the ability to discern important information from the comparisons of evidentiary specimens that a lay person would not be qualified to find. The best forensic practitioners in these fields bring an impressive amount of knowledge and skill to their work, and their assessments can provide critical information in criminal investigations and in criminal trials.[83]

However, simply because these areas of forensics utilize scientific equipment, such as microscopes, or chemical processes for obtaining usable images of shoeprints, tire tracks or fingerprints, does not necessarily make them "scientific." The use of scientific equipment or processes does not transform the conclusions drawn from a subjective examination of the specimens into "scientifically" valid conclusions. By applying the lessons of *Daubert* and the NAS Report on the scientific method, one can assess the extent to which practitioners in these disciplines have produced scientific knowledge. Testing a hypothesis through unbiased experimentation of a large enough sample to obtain useful data, the sharing of detailed data through peer-reviewed publication or at conferences for purposes, the performance of validation studies by peers in the field, and the discovery of error rates—these are the key elements that, according to the *Daubert* Court itself, mark a field as having a "scientific foundation." In each of these disciplines, however, the NAS Report concludes that finding absolute (zero error rate) individualizations are "not scientifically plausible."[84]

Fingerprint Examination

Latent print examination rests on the presumption that fingerprints (technically called "friction ridge patterns") are unique to each individual and persist unchanged throughout a person's life. Although it is not possible to make this assertion as a categorical fact, the NAS Report finds "some scientific evidence" to support this presumption. [85] This area thus has the potential for solid empirical development given additional research. The larger issue, however, is that the "methodology" used to determine whether prints derive from the same source is not scientific in that it lacks objective measurement and consists of a highly subjective, untestable process.

The accepted process for print examination is known as "ACE-V," which stands for "Analysis, Comparison, Evaluation, and Verification."[86] Although the ACE-V process identifies many factors that examiners should consider in making their determinations, the process remains "largely based on human interpretation."[87] Step 1 of the process involves the "analysis" by the examiner of the features of the crime scene print as well as of the known print (possibly that taken from a suspect). In Step 2, the examiner next visually compares them, looking for similarities and differences, and then "evaluates" (Step 3) whether there is sufficient agreement to say that the two prints come from the same source, or in layman's terms, whether there's a "match." The fourth step, verification, means that a second examiner goes through the same process and reaches the same result. The second examiner is often aware of the first examiner's conclusions before he or she begins working, so this verification is not unbiased in a scientific sense.

As this description shows, fingerprint examination boils down to an expert comparing two things to see if they match. Again, this task is not one that an untrained person could likely do with much success. Experienced and talented latent print examiners provide useful guidance for the judicial system. Nonetheless, the process has no scientific foundation for conclusions with regard to definitive matches.

On the ACE-V process of examination, the NAS Report comments: "Note that the ACE-V method does not specify particular measurements or a standard test protocol, and examiners must make subjective assessments throughout.... As a result, the outcome of a friction ridge analysis is not necessarily repeatable from examiner to examiner."[88] Because "[t]his subjectivity is intrinsic to friction ridge analysis,"[89] it is impossible to develop empirical data about population statistics that would provide objective measurements of fingerprint characteristics. Moreover, there are no objective criteria for determining a match: Fingerprint examiners are simply instructed to declare a match when there are "sufficient features in agreement" to support such a conclusion.[90]

Conversely, with DNA evidence, "[s]tudies have been conducted to determine the range of variation in the sequence of base pairs at each of the 13 [specific segments of DNA samples] and also to determine how much variation exists in different populations."[91] The 13 segments and the procedures to be used have been developed into a standard test protocol with specific, objective requirements. From test data, DNA experts can estimate the probability that two DNA samples from different people will have the same permutations at each of the 13 points of examination.[92] While DNA match statistics are not uncontroversial, they at least have a basis in genetics and have been subject to validation studies.

The subjectivity of fingerprint analysis means that "population statistics for fingerprints have not been developed"; and until some objective means of measurement can be incorporated into the process, it may not be possible to develop such statistics. Thus, the ACE-V method of fingerprint comparison is not one that can be tested, nor can empirical data be published in peer-reviewed journals to facilitate validation studies. How does one empirically validate the accuracy of a purely subjective process involving no objective measurements or criteria? Unfortunately, since judges and attorneys are usually not scientists, their lack of science proficiency not only contributes to the inaccurate evaluation of forensic science in general, but also to the misunderstanding of the factors that determine scientific validity and hence legal admissibility. For example, one court, in deciding on the admissibility of fingerprint examination, mistakenly confused "peer-review" in the *Daubert* sense with a laboratory protocol which required blind verification by a second examiner.[93]

Without population statistics, it is also impossible to know the frequency at which we might find more than one person who share the same set of measurable characteristics within a fingerprint. The error rate for fingerprint analysis increases with each identical pattern found to be shared by different people.[94] Even if we did develop such a database of shared patterns—and, hence, population statistics—we still have no reason to believe that individual characteristics of a single fingerprint are statistically independent from each other. In DNA analysis, the independence of alleles within racial or ethnic groups allows experts to calculate the probability that a given DNA sample could belong to another randomly chosen person of the same racial or ethnic background.[95] Such testimony satisfies the *Daubert* "error rate" prong.[96] For fingerprint analysis, the statistical foundation has not been developed, nor is there scientific proof of the independence of fingerprint characteristics, so the estimated error rate (i.e., how frequently we would expect a fingerprint examiner to declare a false positive match) would need to be determined by other means.

Another means of determining an estimated error rate for fingerprint examination would be to determine how accurate fingerprint examiners tend to be. This might be done by conducting blind proficiency testing at a level of difficulty that represents normal casework. Proficiency testing involves having an examiner compare two prints to determine whether they can be attributed

to the same person. "Blind" testing requires that the known print be introduced into the examiner's casework without the examiner knowing that it is a
test. Proficiency testing has been done for many years in fingerprint examination; however; it has not been conducted in a way that allows the determination of an estimated error rate as a whole.[97] The proficiency testing done to
date has been done on a non-blind, non-proctored, untimed fashion. The level
of difficulty of these tests cannot be determined, nor is there information about
the level of experience or qualifications of test takers.[98] These and other test
design flaws make it problematic to rely on the results of proficiency tests to
determine an error rate that meets the requirements of *Daubert*.

Other aspects of the current approach to latent print examination also do
not provide effective safeguards against possible error in individual cases. As
already described, the "verification" prong of ACE-V has traditionally not been
blind—meaning that the second examiner who goes through the same three
steps (ACE) as the first examiner knows his or her conclusion. Such prior
knowledge tends to influence the second examiner in confirming his or her
colleague's work. As the next chapter shows, blind procedures help to eliminate the inherent cognitive biases that otherwise exist. Fingerprint examination
has traditionally not required the blind procedures that would normally be
used in properly conducted scientific research studies.[99]

Firearms Examination

The same critique of fingerprint examination applies to firearms examination.[100] At present, firearms examination—when used for purposes of *definitive* match conclusions—lacks an adequate scientific foundation, about which
the NAS Report states:

> Toolmark and firearm analysis suffers from the same limitations dis-
> cussed above for [fingerprint and other] impression evidence. Because
> not enough is known about the variabilities among individual tools and
> guns, we are not able to specify how many points of similarity are
> necessary for a given level of confidence in the result. Sufficient stud-
> ies have not been done to understand the reliability and repeatability
> of the methods.[101]

The report also found that "the decision of the toolmark examiner remains
a subjective decision based on unarticulated standards and [with] no statistical foundation for estimation of error rates.... A fundamental problem with
toolmark and firearm analysis is the lack of a precisely defined process."[102]

Moreover, it found that genuine peer-reviewed validation studies have not been done in the area of firearm examination:

> Although some studies have been performed on the degree of similarity that can be found between marks made by different tools and the variability in marks made by an individual tool, the scientific knowledge base for toolmark and firearms analysis is fairly limited. For example, a report from Hamby, Brundage, and Thorpe includes capsule summaries of 68 toolmark and firearm studies. But the capsule summaries suggest a *heavy reliance on the subjective findings of examiners rather than on the rigorous quantification and analysis of sources of variability*. Overall, the process for toolmark and firearm comparisons lacks the specificity of the protocols for, say, 13 STR DNA analysis. This is not to say that toolmark analysis needs to be as objective as DNA analysis in order to provide value.[103]

The last sentence of the quoted passage from the NAS Report underscores the important point that forensic disciplines still provide valuable information and these disciplines *may not need to be* as objective as DNA analysis.

It is also important to note that the Association of Firearms and Toolmark Examiners (AFTE), a professional organization representing the firearm/toolmark community, vigorously rejected this assessment by the National Academy of Sciences. The association's lengthy response listed voluminous publications relating to firearms examination as evidence of underlying empirical research.[104] Whether any of these studies support claims of individualization, however, is another matter. The list includes many studies, for example, in which a researcher examined bullets fired from a certain number of consecutively manufactured guns of the same type, drawing a variety of conclusions but generally supporting the proposition that the markings enable examiners to make individualizations.[105] During the many hearings and other communications before the NAS Report was issued, AFTE representatives had ample opportunity to persuade the National Academy of Sciences that publications of this type established the scientific foundations of firearms examination but apparently failed to convince the committee of the adequacy of the research.[106] The NAS Report does not deny the existence of research studies but found that they did not meet the standards of scientific research because the results were not repeatable due to the "heavy reliance on subjective findings."[107] It is possible the NAS Report gave short shrift to some valuable research in this area. At the same time, because the discipline remains a subjective, comparative technique, it is more likely that the area lacks the objective empirical research needed to support the individualization conclusions firearms examiners routinely make.

Despite the lack of support for definitive individualizations by firearm examiners, many courts continue to allow unrestricted testimony from this type of expert.[108] If courts rigorously applied *Daubert* to firearm examination when used to support definitive individualizations, such testimony would fail all of the *Daubert* reliability factors, but it should probably still be admissible. To be clear, there are two problems at play here. First, some courts misunderstand the *Daubert* standard and misinterpret the meanings of terms like "testable," "validation studies," "peer review," and "error rate." These issues of terminology and conceptualization can and should be addressed by the judiciary. The more challenging problem is that so many forensic sciences at present lack the scientific foundations required by *Daubert* because their processes involve highly subjective assessments and unproven premises.

To see why firearms examination fails all of the *Daubert* factors for scientific evidence, let us examine a 2012 case in which a federal district court (by misapplying the *Daubert* prongs) found that firearm examination did, in fact, *meet* all of the *Daubert* factors. In *United States v. Otero*, the district court found that the methodology of firearm examination met the first prong of *Daubert* because it was "testable." The evidence of testability was the citation of four validation studies.[109] In a logical sleight of hand, the Court recognized that determining whether there is "sufficient agreement" in a comparison of toolmarks (the industry test for determining an individualization) "involves the subjectivity of the examiner's judgment as to matching toolmarks," and yet the Court found the methodology to be "testable on the basis of achieving consistent and accurate results."[110] Presumably, the Court meant that individual examiners who conducted large-scale studies of hundreds of consecutively fired bullets or consecutively rifled barrels reported that they achieved consistent and accurate results.

To say that these studies are "testable," however, makes as much sense—and is as circular—as saying that the subjective decision of a judge in a beauty contest can be "tested" by others because that judge reports achieving "consistent and accurate results" in judging the beauty of the contestants. In the context of a subjective judgment, it is not even clear what "consistent and accurate results" means. The subjectivity of each of those "validation studies" makes it impossible for subsequent researchers to reproduce the results. Thus, these large-scale studies do not "validate" the methodology, nor can they serve as the basis for subsequent validation studies.

The Court in *Otero* also misunderstood the "peer review" or publication prong of *Daubert*. The Court makes the mistake of considering the four "validation studies" published in the industry journal, the *AFTE Journal*, to have been "peer-reviewed." The Supreme Court listed peer-review as a reliability factor because the process itself is designed to operate in an impartial manner to ensure the publication of scientifically sound work *and* because publication of scientific research enables others to replicate experiments so as to test the validity of earlier findings.

While there is not perfect standardization of the meaning of "peer-review" in different settings, within the realm of scientific peer-reviewed journals, the generally understood meaning is that articles submitted for publication will be sent to impartial experts in the field for their review in order to assist the journal's editors in deciding whether to publish the article.[111] These reviewers will not know the identity of the other reviewers. This is thought to eliminate the possibility that they would influence each other, and it better ensures that any consensus among them is impartial and objective.[112] Additionally, the editors of scientific peer-reviewed journals of the type contemplated in *Daubert* generally have no vested interest in establishing the validity of a particular profession or line of research.

In contrast, the leadership of AFTE, including the editor of the *AFTE Journal*, is made up of people who work in the forensic departments of law enforcement agencies.[113] This stands to reason. The field is of interest almost exclusively to law enforcement since this type of forensic work is done almost exclusively within law enforcement agencies. This close connection to law enforcement creates a conflict of interest. A professional organization of this type has a financial interest in advancing the interests of the profession it represents. The subject of firearm and toolmark research is not merely a subject of intellectual interest; rather, applying the discipline—*and defending its validity*—in a real-world setting is how the leaders of *AFTE* earn their living. Each of them as individuals may be ethical, and AFTE's code of ethics requires that members do their work fairly and objectively.[114] The point here is not that the AFTE affiliation renders *the individuals* unethical or biased; it does not. The concern is instead that *their position* in the profession creates an inherent conflict of interest. Until the field attracts academic researchers or researchers from other government agencies or from private industry, the pool of possible reviewers lack individuals who can provide the arms-length impartiality expected of genuine peer-review.

In a 1995 case, a lower federal court considered the similar issue of how to determine the relevant community of experts in deciding whether the discipline was "generally accepted." The court found that the relevant community of experts should reach beyond the practitioner group in a specialized forensic discipline since practitioner groups would be "devoid of financially disinterested parties, such as academics."[115] In a 2005 case, the Florida Supreme Court looked beyond "North American articles ... written by law enforcement" in evaluating whether microscopic knife mark examination had been peer-reviewed and was generally accepted.[116] The court looked instead to "independent and impartial proof" found in publications by European medical professionals which involved rigorous scientific scrutiny and which happened to controvert the previous conclusions.[117]

This reasoning applies equally to the "general acceptance" prong, which is misapplied in *Otero*. The Court found that the reliability of the methodology met the "general acceptance" factor because it is "widely accepted in the forensic community and, specifically, in the community of firearm and toolmark examiners."[118] Forensic sciences derive from broader scientific disciplines, so the relevant community should include professionals from those broader scientific fields as well as those in the narrower forensic discipline at issue. In *Otero,* the Court considered only the narrow group of forensic practitioners, ignoring other scientists such as those at the National Academy of Sciences who had found no scientific basis for individualizations based on this form of testing. As pertains to the issue of "peer-review," some other courts have taken a broader view of the community of experts relevant to firearms examination, in particular looking to experts who have no financial interest in the advancement of the profession.[119]

The *Otero* Court's treatment of the "known or potential error rate" raises a different concern. Since there are no objective, measurable criteria for applying the methodology, there can be no empirical testing of the methodology to determine an error rate. Some prosecutors have turned to studies of the results of proficiency testing to approximate an error rate. In *Otero*, the Court concluded that the error rate was approximately 1–2%, which it found "low," thus assuring that the methodology was sufficiently reliable.[120] However, the Court's evaluation of this estimated error rate does not withstand scrutiny. Most importantly, the vendor of the most widely used proficiency tests for firearms examination, Collaborative Testing Services, Inc. (CTS), clearly states that the results of proficiency tests do not give reliable information about an error rate for firearms examination for three reasons.[121] First, the tests may be purchased by anyone for any type of use, so there are no controls at all on who may take a firearms examination proficiency test. Second, CTS does not grade the tests to determine "correct" and "incorrect" answers. Rather, a test-taker's answers will be judged against the consensus position of the participant pool, and even an answer that disagrees with the consensus may be deemed acceptable based on the explanation given. Third, proficiency tests are designed primarily to assist laboratories in meeting a criterion for accreditation and not to simulate "real world casework-like" samples.[122] Thus, since proficiency tests are designed for purposes completely distinct from measuring an error rate, reliance on any statistic based on these studies is meaningless and can be misleading.

The Court next evaluated whether standards exist to control the technique's operation. Here, too, the Court failed to comprehend what scientists mean by "standards." The Court begins by labeling "the AFTE standard of 'sufficient agreement' [as] the established standard." This was the major criticism of the National Academy of Sciences—"sufficient agreement" is a subjective determination with no measurable criteria for its determination. A description of how something is done is not a measurable "standard" that can be exactly replicated. While the protocols for developing the images to be compared microscopically may involve objective standards, the "match" judgment does not. "Sufficient agreement" is not a standard.

The *Otero* case is representative of a general resistance one sees among trial courts confronting new challenges to evidence of long-standing use—even in the face of the NAS Report. In a 2005 case, a Florida trial judge refused to let the defense even *participate* in the evidentiary hearing, leading unsurprisingly to a reversal on appeal.[123] A California court in 2012 refused to allow the defense to cross-examine the latent print examiner regarding a high-profile case involving an error by others in the field.[124] Courts have also balked at allowing the defense to use the NAS Report during cross-examination, again leading to some reversals.[125] In one case in Utah in 2012, the trial court erroneously barred defense counsel from (1) using the NAS Report to cross-examine the latent print examiner; (2) from questioning the examiner on the changes in the industry guidelines implemented after the NAS Report; or (3) from offering a defense expert on latent print examination who would raise reliability issues.[126]

Why are courts so resistant to the revelations in the NAS Report? One might suspect it is due to confusion about how to proceed. Forensic experts have much expertise to offer; and if beekeepers can testify on the basis of their expertise acquired by observing bees, surely forensic practitioners should also be allowed to testify. One federal court had the temerity to find fingerprint testimony inadmissible on *Daubert* grounds but quickly reversed itself.[127] Total exclusion is not ordinarily warranted. With regard to fingerprint examination, for example, courts should make a specific decision on admissibility based on factors such as the experience and competence of the witness and the clarity and completeness of the print recovered as evidence. Each of these disciplines can provide valuable information that can be helpful in including or excluding someone as a suspect. However, the degree of confidence in an expert's opinion that two prints match should vary. In a 2014 death penalty case in Texas, the court decided to limit the firearms expert's conclusion to stating a "high degree of confidence" in the finding of a match.[128] This case and a few others like it may signal a new recognition by judges that claims of infallibility or even the "practical impossibility" of error cannot be supported. Due to the limitations of the research at this point in time, forensic experts in the disciplines of mid-range reliability should no longer be allowed to make definitive (i.e. zero error rate) individualizations.

The True Battleground: Barring Absolute Individualizations

Curbing the exaggerated testimony currently given by experts in forensic disciplines that lie somewhere in the middle of the reliability spectrum, and the excessive confidence of judges and juries in accepting such testimony, present a formidable political challenge. After the NAS Report, some courts have become savvier about the limitations of these disciplines, but disagreement about how testimony should be adjusted is widespread. Amazingly, even after all the controversy over junk science and wrongful convictions, many courts continue to admit definitive match testimony of fingerprint and firearms examination without limitation, still relying on the long-standing history of admissibility. The courts cannot continue in this approach without eventually losing all credibility.

Responding to critics of individualization claims, industry groups have begun to recognize the need to temper statements of individualization. For example, the Specialized Working Group on Friction Ridge Analysis, Study and Technology (SWGFAST), organized in the early 1990s to provide guidance for fingerprint examiners nationwide,[129] takes the position that experts need to abandon statements of "absolute identification: that *this* person did, *in fact,* make the impression, to the exclusion of all others in the world."[130] According to SWGFAST, "it is now recognized that [examiners'] conclusions are more appropriately expressed as a decision, rather than proof."[131] Thus, examiners are now being trained *not* to testify to an "absolute identification" but instead to state that "the likelihood the impression was made by another (different) source is so remote that it is considered as a practical impossibility."[132] Expert witnesses may appropriately tell juries that "[t]he decision is supported by demonstrable data" and that SWGFAST's standards for "the application of [ACE-V]" procedure have been met."[133] But quite obviously, jurors will see no difference between statements of absolute, factual identification and individualization "decisions" where the error rate is "so remote" as to be a "practical impossibility."[134] Firearms examiners have taken the same approach.[135] In short, the more things change, the more they stay the same.[136]

A few courts, responding to defense challenges based on the NAS Report, have gone so far as to allow only classification conclusions (e.g., testifying to markings on bullet casings that put the evidence within a certain class or sub-class of bullet) but not allowing conclusions of definitive matches.[137] Under this approach, a witness could state an opinion on whether the type of bullet casing, for example, was the type that would be used in a particular weapon, but the witness would not be allowed to state that the particular bullet casing had been fired by a particular weapon. Restricting testimony to this extent constitutes a severe limitation on the evidentiary value of the testimony, but it fits the guidelines set forth in *Daubert*.

The leading approach for responding to the now debunked claims of individualization seems to be to temper "definitive match" statements ever so slightly. Some courts have begun to disallow forensic experts from stating that the methodology they employ is "infallible" or that the evidence shows a "match to the exclusion of all others."[138] Some have also disallowed testimony that an individualization decision has an objective basis or is supported by scientific principles or methods.[139] Rather than stating their opinions in terms of a definitive match with a zero error rate, examiners have adopted new terminology like finding matches to "a reasonable degree of scientific certainty," "a reasonable degree of ballistics certainty," or "a reasonable degree of certainty in the firearms discipline."[140] Some courts also allow the witnesses to state that the risk of error is a "practical impossibility,"[141] although at least one court has balked at the use of this term.[142]

This state of affairs leaves much to be desired. Previously, forensic experts could give "scientific" opinions finding a definitive match to the exclusion of all others and state that the methodology was infallible. Now they will be limited to stating that, "to a reasonable degree of certainty," the two specimens come from the same source. This is still an individualization for which there is no scientific support to validate its reliability, and it is now wrapped in terminology that sounds quite definitive. Indeed, "a reasonable degree of certainty" sounds quite certain. It leads one to ask: in a criminal trial, what is a reasonable degree of certainty and who determines this reasonable degree of certainty? One hopes that defense attorneys will have the wherewithal to use defense experts to inform jurors of the risk of error inherent in these processes so that they might properly weigh a forensic expert's opinion.

The other challenge for the defense arises from the fact that forensic experts do not present themselves as blue-collar workers with specialized skill, similar to a beekeeper. They are presented as *scientific* experts who work in laboratories. Nor are they disinterested witnesses. Crime laboratory analysts work for law enforcement agencies and testify almost exclusively for prosecutors, giving them an inherent pro-prosecution motivational bias. The affiliation between the crime laboratory and the law enforcement agenda led the Florida

Supreme Court to describe individualization testimony as "self-serving."[143] Many forensic disciplines were developed by law enforcement to aid in criminal investigation and prosecution. They have virtually no other purpose. In addition, forensic laboratory methods are not designed to insulate examiners from unconscious cognitive biases.[144] Thus, forensic examiners come to court presenting themselves as neutral scientific experts, but their true orientation is as criminal investigators.

To be fair, jurors may be savvy enough to appreciate the inherent bias that flows from an examiner's connection to law enforcement. For example, some fingerprint and firearm/toolmark examiners are also classified police officers, and they likely identify themselves as such in court. The general connection to law enforcement might also be obvious in the name of the laboratory since it is typically the "police department crime laboratory" of a particular jurisdiction. This is not to suggest that there is any intent to deceive jurors or even to act upon a bias. Laboratory analysts generally approach their work with integrity and fair-mindedness. The problem is that work done by analysts with cognitive biases—combined with laboratory procedures that fail to protect against those biases—produce results influenced by those conscious and unconscious cognitive biases.[145] Combine these problems with the fact that the underlying disciplines lack a scientific basis for ensuring their reliability, that jurors tend to give heightened weight to the testimony of "experts," and that forensic experts tend to give "definitive match" testimony. For all of these reasons, exaggerated conclusions by forensic experts in fields like firearm/toolmarks, fingerprints, and other subjective comparative disciplines present a substantial risk of wrongful conviction, especially in cases where the rest of the prosecution's case is weak. Circumstantial evidence, for example, may be insufficient to prove a defendant's guilt "beyond a reasonable doubt," but if a forensic expert definitively links the defendant to the crime, a guilty verdict becomes a foregone conclusion.

A Separate Problem:
Cleaning Up the Junk Science Mess

The news about wrongful convictions and crime laboratory scandals has evoked many headlines denouncing the epidemic of "junk science" in the courtrooms.[146] Although such headlines are sensational, in truth, only a few types of forensic disciplines have been revealed to be either intrinsically bogus or bogus when used to make definitive individualizations that are utterly unsupportable. Junk science includes invalid and erroneous conclusions about serology testing, hair microscopy, composite bullet lead analysis,[147] and some fiber analysis.[148] These disciplines actually have a scientific foundation when used for purpose of determining classification (not individuation), which can include or exclude a suspect early in the investigation. Blood type testing in serology, for example, has a solid scientific foundation, but it cannot tell us definitively that a particular person left the bodily fluid at issue—there is no scientific support for such individualization. Forensic experts for many years made grossly exaggerated individualizations in these disciplines, transforming good classification procedures into junk science. In addition, some forensic evidence has been shown to be pure junk. In a notorious Chicago case, one now-disgraced analyst linked a defendant in a murder trial to the crime through his "lip prints," even though this has never been considered a reliable form of evidence.[149] Unlike other forms of pattern impression analysis, there exist scant systematic studies of lip shapes and/or wrinkle characteristics to justify the use of such evidence in court.[150]

Junk science performed outside of crime laboratories includes invalid individualizations routinely given by forensic odontologists who have erroneously claimed that they can identify an individual who left bite marks on human skin,[151] as well as various claims made by other medical experts.[152] The use of dogs to provide definitive evidence of guilt has also come under fire. In at least four states, prosecutors have used evidence from "dog sniff lineups" in which a dog ostensibly matches an individual suspect to a scent from a crime scene. The testimony of one such dog sniff lineup expert was estimated to have put fifteen to twenty people behind bars. The courts have now reversed many of those cases because defense attorneys have shown such lineups to be patently bogus as evidence.[153] Dogs may have the ability to track a person effectively or to find things like cadavers or controlled substances, but the process of dog sniff lineups is rife with the possibility of error stemming from the cross-contamination of scents, the use of biased procedures, and a complete lack of scientific foundation for the entire process.[154]

In addition, many arson theories developed in fire departments for determining whether a blaze was set intentionally have turned out to be completely bogus.[155] Fortunately, guidelines based on valid fire science are now available for arson investigations.[156] Researchers in fire science can be found, for example, in the aerospace industry, as well as in university chemistry and fire science programs. Experts in fire science with the National Fire Protection Association have developed a manual for investigators known as *NFPA 921: Guide for Fire and Explosion Investigation* based on scientific principles.[157]

To say that we now recognize various forensic disciplines to be "junk science" is not to say that the mess of injustice they have wrought in the past has been cleaned up or even that junk science is now banned from criminal trials. A first challenge will be to ensure prosecutors, defense attorneys, and courts become more vigilant in keeping patently bogus evidence out of criminal trials.

The more subtle problem is to make judges and criminal lawyers aware that perfectly valid science can be converted into junk science through individualization testimony that has no basis in fact. While fingerprint and firearm evidence may be "good evidence," even if we cannot scientifically validate individualization claims, other areas that rely on expert testimony, such as bite mark analysis, is almost certainly not good evidence. According to a 2010 study published by three researchers in forensic odontology, bite marks on victims cannot be used *even to reliably exclude a person* as a suspect because it has no scientific basis whatsoever and no evidence that it works reliably.[158] Moreover, in such cases, better evidence can often be obtained through DNA testing. Thus, since DNA evidence is usually available in such cases, bite mark evidence should now be considered junk science. Even one forensic odontologist who had worked on about 16,000 cases and testified in 81 trials is now persuaded that courts should stop admitting such testimony.[159] Yet at least some courts continue to reject *Daubert* challenges and admit the testimony, completely ignoring the NAS Report.[160]

A second part of the effort to clean up the mess of junk science is the need to review past convictions to uncover possible miscarriages of justice. In some instances, advocates and public officials have found common ground in recognizing certain types of junk science and in joining forces to uncover possible wrongful convictions. To take one example, efforts are underway to correct for the invalid conclusions regarding the routine performance of microscopic hair analysis in the past that formed such a significant role in wrongfully convicting George Rodriguez as described in Chapter 1. Normal and healthy human beings shed hair frequently, so it is commonly found at crime scenes and is easily transferred from the clothes of one individual to another. The comparison of hair specimens found at a crime scene to those taken from a suspect made by observing the two specimens has limited value. People have hairs that can be grouped into different classes, meaning that they share the same microscopic characteristics. Thus, such an analysis "can be useful in including, or excluding, certain persons from the pool of possible sources of the hair."[161] But microscopic hair analysis cannot uniquely identify one person. Today, individualizations based on hair specimens would be done through nuclear DNA analysis in crime laboratories, as was the case with the single hair found in George Rodriguez's case file many years after his conviction.

Nonetheless, crime laboratory analysts for many years testified to positive "matches," purporting to be able to make an individual identification simply by comparing the two hair samples. Used in this manner, microscopic hair analysis is junk science. Brandon Garrett's study of the first 200 exonerations found that in 75 of the trials, the juries heard evidence about microscopic hair analysis.[162] Across the country, it seems probable that thousands of convictions have rested on microscopic hair analysis, many of which are almost certainly invalid. Each of these cases should be reviewed to determine whether the convictions should be overturned.

Fortunately, some of this revision has recently begun. On July 18, 2013, the FBI and the Department of Justice agreed to join forces with the Innocence Project and the National Association for Criminal Defense Lawyers (NACDL) as a result of growing awareness of the misuse of hair microscopy analysis and the discovery of three wrongful convictions based on such testimony by FBI analysts.[163] In their "groundbreaking and historic agreement" on that date, the FBI and the Department of Justice committed "to review more than 2,000 criminal cases in which FBI analysts gave scientifically invalid microscopic hair analysis testimony."[164] The Department of Justice not only agreed to open its files to review but also agreed to notify defendants of the erroneous testimony in their cases, to refrain from making procedural arguments aimed at barring defendants from raising challenges to their convictions, and to offer free DNA testing.[165] This agreement marks a new and serious commitment to rectify the errors in thousands of cases (including both federal and state cases, but only those in which FBI analysts had testified as expert witnesses). Previously, a 2012 *Washington Post* investigation discovered that the DOJ had begun investigating these same cases in the 1990s but did not notify defendants of the possible errors in their cases.[166]

At the state level, only Texas and New York have announced similar reviews of hair microscopy cases. The two states have another thing in common not found in any other state: a Forensic Science Commission, made up mostly of distinguished scientists. These commissions have proven critical in facilitating the reviews of convictions based on invalid scientific evidence such as those cases involving hair microscopy. Unfortunately, this type of faulty evidence may have sent at least one innocent man to his death. In 2010, DNA evidence proved that Texas may have wrongly executed Claude Jones in 2000.[167] A chemist for the state, Stephen Robertson, had initially concluded that the hair sample was too small to conduct microscopic hair analysis. By the time of trial, however, he testified that the characteristics of the hair left at the scene "matched" hair from Jones and could not have come from the victim or the twelve other people who frequented the liquor store.[168] Postmortem DNA tests showed that the crime scene hair did not belong to Jones.[169]

In a second possible wrongful death sentence, lawyers for Florida inmate Gerald Murray received notice in 2013 of erroneous hair microscopy testimony by an FBI agent in their client's case.[170] The testimony was the only physical evidence placing Murray at the crime scene. Post-conviction hearings will determine whether this conviction should be reversed.[171]

In most states and the federal system, old cases in which convictions rest on invalid forensic science cannot be reviewed by appeals courts due to traditional procedural bars; but all states now have laws allowing reviews when new DNA evidence proves a person's innocence. However, many of these statutes have serious limitations that result in frequent denials of legitimate requests for testing that could prove innocence.[172] Nor can a person claim a constitutional right not to be executed on grounds of factual innocence, as an astonishing 2009 decision of the U.S. Supreme Court held.[173] These new avenues for DNA evidence would also not apply to cases in which forensic evidence turns out to be invalid but in which no new DNA is available to test. In September 2013, Texas became the first—and so far only—state to provide a junk science writ (as it is colloquially called) that gives defendants the right to have their cases reconsidered by the courts if their convictions are based on forensic science that is now considered invalid.[174] Hair microscopy used for purposes of individualization and all bite mark evidence would fall into this category, for example. This procedural right opens the door for private attorneys, public defenders, Innocence Project attorneys, and other state officials to investigate these cases.

In addition to the hair microscopy cases, the Texas Fire Marshall's Office and Texas Innocence Project have collaborated in reviewing arson convictions based on invalid arson evidence.[175] (The original Innocence Project in New York inspired the establishment of numerous other similar organizations that operate autonomously within states or as part of law school programs). As of May 2014, the review has resulted in two overturned convictions, with a third likely soon, and five other cases are still under review.[176]

Individual cases can also be reinvestigated using the junk science writ as well. Recently, four San Antonio women (known in the press as the "San Antonio four") have had their convictions overturned by means of the junk science writ. The four spent nearly 20 years in prison for the alleged sexual assaults of two girls, the nieces of one of the four women. The girls accused the four women of assaulting them as part of a drunken lesbian gathering. Their convictions rested in part on invalid forensic testimony regarding medical proof of sexual assault injuries.[177] The state's expert witness testified that a mark on one of the girls' hymen was a scar indicative of traumatic sexual abuse. Experts now agree that such marks are not signs of abuse.[178] One of the girls has since recanted her allegations of abuse.

A Path Forward

The title of the National Academy of Sciences report rings with optimism: *Strengthening Forensic Science in the United States: A Path Forward.* The very title, however, simultaneously communicates that forensic science has weaknesses and that it the needs to be strengthened. Echoing the blunt 2003 editorial by the renowned scientist Donald Kennedy, the NAS also made the stunning revelation that most forensic disciplines lack scientific support for the sweeping individualizations made by practitioners in court every day. A major challenge outlined in the report is the need to develop a scientific research foundation for most forensic disciplines. Subjective and interpretive forensic disciplines such as fingerprint and firearm examination, while providing extremely valuable information for making definitive class and subclass identifications, have no scientific basis for making statements of a definitive match. The immediate battles in court will be over the appropriate characterization of conclusions that purport to make individualizations.

Valid scientific research and the implementation of computerized processes may someday provide the empirical support for individualization in these disciplines on a level comparable to the reliability of DNA analysis. The NAS Report makes 13 recommendations for taking "the path forward" for forensic science. The first recommendation calls on Congress to create a "National Institute of Forensic Science" (NIFS) to "promote the development of forensic science into a mature field of multidisciplinary research and practice, founded on the systematic collection and analysis of relevant data."[179] The first recommendation would task the NIFS with "promoting scholarly, competitive peer-reviewed research and technical development in the forensic science disciplines and forensic medicine," "developing a strategy to improve forensic science research and educational programs," and "assessing the development and introduction of new technologies in forensic investigations, including a comparison of new technologies with former ones."[180] Of such great concern are the issues of bias, error, and exaggerated conclusions in forensic testing, that the fifth recommendation returns to this related issue and proposes that the NIFS "encourage research programs on human observer bias and sources of human error in forensic examinations," as well as "research conducted to quantify and characterize the amount of error."[181] The goal would be to implement this research in developing standard operating procedures for use within laboratories.

The other goals called for the funding of research into other areas of forensic science, as well as the development of standardized laboratory reports, laboratory protocols and methods, a code of ethics, quality assurance and quality control procedures, and uniform terminology.[182] The report also calls for mandatory accreditation of forensic laboratories and mandatory certification for individual analysts in their respective areas of forensic practice.[183] As discussed in Chapter 6, the NAS report also calls for "laboratory independence from or autonomy within the law enforcement community." The report also urges Congress to provide funding to support the development of graduate educational programs in forensic science, to improve the death investigation system in medical examiner and coroner offices, and to support the development of a nationwide fingerprint data system.[184]

In time, forensic disciplines currently lacking them may develop precise, measurable standards to test their methods for accuracy and determining error rates. However, such standards do not currently exist. Thus for the time being, experts in these subjective, interpretive disciplines "should exhibit a greater degree of epistemological humility," replacing statements of "practical impossibility" of error with more modest claims.[185] The NAS Report's first recommendation even includes a desire to see the proposed National Institute of Forensic Science develop programs to "improve understanding of the forensic science disciplines and their limitations within legal systems."[186]

To clean up the mess created by the past use of junk science, Congress and state legislatures need to adopt junk science writs like that enacted in Texas.[187] Until that time, prosecutors can follow the Department of Justice precedent and waive procedural objections to appellate efforts involving junk science. Indeed, prosecutors and other state officials can play crucial leadership roles in righting the wrongs of junk science. It is not enough to uncover junk science and ban it from the courts for future cases. It is also necessary to review old cases that rest on invalid science. Such reviews are pointless, however, if the wrongly convicted find the courtroom doors closed to them. Clearing the procedural hurdles for courts to review past cases would spur prosecutors, defense attorneys, and innocence projects to set up the large-scale reviews needed to find the wrongful convictions that surely exist.

The search for junk science is a constant one. The process of ferreting out bogus science and bogus individualizations will necessarily be an ongoing process as we develop greater understanding of the many forensic disciplines currently in use, as well as the new disciplines being developed. If society takes to heart the recommendations of the NAS Report, it would foster optimism that forensic laboratories will never again produce junk science.

Notes for Chapter 3

1. *See* Scientific Working Group on Friction Ridge Analysis, Study, and Technology, *Document #4, Guideline for the Articulation of the Decision-Making Process for the Individualization in Friction Ridge Examination (Latent/Tenprint)* 1, posted Apr. 27, 2013, http://www.swgfast.org/documents/articulation/130427_Articulation_1.0.pdf (hereinafter SWG-FAST Doc. #4).

2. *See* NATIONAL RESEARCH COUNCIL, STRENGTHENING FORENSIC SCIENCE IN THE UNITED STATES: A PATH FORWARD at 7 (National Academies Press, 2009) (hereinafter "NAS Report").

3. *Id.*

4. *See* Simon A. Cole, *Individualization Is Dead, Long Live Individualization! Reforms of Reporting Practices for Fingerprint Analysis in the United States,* 13 LAW PROBABILITY AND RISK 117, 117 (2014) (citing P.L. Kirk, *The Ontogeny of Criminalistics,* 54 J. OF CRIM. L., CRIM'Y & POLI. SCI. 235–38 [1963]).

5. *See* NAS Report, *supra* note 2 at 7 ("With the exception of DNA analysis, however, no forensic method has been rigorously shown to have the capacity to consistently, and with a high degree of certainty, demonstrate a connection between evidence and a specific individual or source.").

6. *See* Cole, *supra* note 4 at 1.

7. Each of these causes of error is thoroughly discussed in an article by a leading researcher of forensic science, *see* William C. Thompson, *The Potential for Error in Forensic DNA Testing (and How That Complicates the Use of DNA Databases for Criminal Identification)* at 3, Produced for the Council of Responsible Genetics' national conference (2008), http://www.councilforresponsiblegenetics.org/pagedocuments/h4t5eoyuzi.pdf.

8. *See* Re: In re Richards, Letter Brief of Amici Curiae in Support of Petition for Rehearing, 2012 WL 71060188, p. *3 (Cal. 2012).

9. *Id.* at 2.

10. *See infra* note 140 and accompanying text.

11. *See infra* notes 146–149 and accompanying text.

12. Jennifer L. Mnookin, Simon A. Cole, Itiel E. Dror, Barry A. J. Fisher, Max M. Houck, Keith Inman, David H. Kaye, Jonathan J. Koehler, Glenn Langenburg, D. Michael Risinger, Norah Rudin, Jay Siegel, & David A. Stoney, *The Need for a Research Culture in the Forensic Sciences,* 58 UCLA L. REV. 725 (2011).

13. *See infra* notes 146–157 and accompanying text.

14. *See* MAX M. HOUCK & JAY A. SIEGAL, FUNDAMENTALS OF FORENSIC SCIENCE at 7–8 (2006) (tracing modern origins of fingerprint and body fluid testing to the early twentieth century). Toxicology, or the study of poisons, on the other hand, can be traced back to the nineteen century, although forensic medicine has been around for thousands of years. *Id.* at 7.

15. *See* NAS Report, *supra* note 2 at 89 (discussing Peter Huber's study which, although much criticized, spurred a debate over the use of expert testimony in the courts) (citing P.W. HUBER. GALILEO'S REVENGE: JUNK SCIENCE IN THE COURTROOM [1991]. Ironically, at the same time, the Supreme Court in *Daubert* addressed Merrell Dow Pharmaceutical's "apprehension" that any change from the "general acceptance" standard would usher in a flood of "absurd and irrational pseudoscientific assertions." *Daubert,* 509 U.S. at 595–96.

16. Even after *Daubert*, scholars continued to complain about the admission of junk science in civil cases while reliable evidence was excluded). *See, e.g.*, Victor E. Schwartz & Cary Silverman, *The Draining of* Daubert *and the Recidivism of Junk Science in Federal and State Courts*, 35 HOFSTRA L. REV. 217 (2006) (arguing that junk science continues to be admitted); Henry F. Fradella, Adam Fogarty, & Lauren O'Neill, *The Impact of* Daubert *on the Admissibility of Behavioral Science Testimony*, 30 PEPP. L. REV. 403 (2003) (arguing that *Daubert* should exclude much behaviorial science testimony that they continue to admit); Lisa Heinszerling, *Doubting* Daubert, 14 J. L. & POL'Y 65 (2006) (arguing that courts have excluded too much evidence as unreliable).

17. 17 *See* NAS Report, *supra* note 2 at 89 (quoting Paul C. Giannelli, *"Junk Science": The Criminal Cases*, 84 J. CRIM. L. & CRIM'Y 111 n. 35 [1993]).

18. *Frye v. United States*, 293 F. 1013, 1014 (D.C. Cir. 1923).

19. *Id.* at 1014. Emphasis added.

20. *See* FED. R. EVID. 101(a).

21. *See* MUELLER & KIRKPATRICK, EVIDENCE § 1.2 at 4 (3rd ed. 2003).

22. After *Daubert*, the rule was amended to read:
A witness who is qualified as an expert by knowledge, skill, experience, training, or education may testify in the form of an opinion or otherwise if:
(a) the expert's scientific, technical, or other specialized knowledge will help the trier of fact to understand the evidence or to determine a fact in issue;
(b) the testimony is based on sufficient facts or data;
(c) the testimony is the product of reliable principles and methods; and
(d) the expert has reliably applied the principles and methods to the facts of the case. (FEDERAL RULES OF EVIDENCE FOR UNITED STATES COURTS, P.L. 93-595; 88 Stat. 1926)

23. Daubert v. Merrell Dow Pharmaceuticals, Inc., 509 U.S. 579 (1993). The Federal Rules of Evidence were adopted in 1975. FEDERAL RULES OF EVIDENCE FOR UNITED STATES COURTS, P.L. 93-595; 88 Stat. 1926 (approved Jan. 2, 1975).

24. *Daubert*, 509 U.S. at 585.

25. *Id.* at 589.

26. *Id.* at 589–90.

27. *Id.* at 592–93.

28. *Id.* at 593.

29. *Id.*

30. *Id.*

31. *Id.*

32. *Id.* at 594.

33. *Id.*

34. Kumho Tire Co. Ltd. v. Carmichael, 526 U.S. 137, 147 (1999).

35. *Id.* at 147. The Court refused to apply a different rule for technical experts, finding the task of differentiating between scientific and technical expertise as unwieldy and unnecessary. Instead, the Court purported to apply the same *Daubert* standard to all forms of expertise. *Id.*

36. *Id.*

37. *Id.* at 148–49.

38. Berry v. City of Detroit, 25 F.3d 1342, 1349-50 (6th Cir. 1994).

39. Kumho Tire, 526 U.S. at 152.

40. *Id.* at 151.

41. *Id.*

42. *Id.* at 141. As for the appellate courts, they are directed to take a hands-off approach in judging *Daubert* decisions. *See* General Electric Co. v. Joiner, 522 U.S. 136, 143 (1997).

43. *Id.* at 142.

44. *See* General Electric Co. v. Joiner, 522 U.S. 136, 146–47 (1997).

45. *Id.* at 146.

46. In one study of judicial decisions on *Daubert* challenges, civil defendants were found to prevail most of the time, while criminal defendants almost always lost their challenges to the government's proffer of forensic evidence. *See* D. Michael Risinger, *Navigating Expert Reliability: Are Criminal Standards of Certainty Being Left on the Dock?*, 64 Albany L. Rev. 99, 99 (2000).

An indication of the failure of defense counsel to challenge invalid forensic evidence is found in Brandon Garrett's study of the 93 DNA exonerations that included invalid forensic testimony: "Defense lawyers rarely made any objections and they rarely effectively cross-examined forensic analysts who provided invalid science testimony. Indeed, in forty-seven cases, or half of the ninety-three cases involving invalid forensic testimony, the defense lawyers failed to ask any questions at all about the areas in which the analyst testified erroneously. In at least twelve cases, defense counsel failed to ask for DNA testing that could have proved their client's innocence." Brandon L. Garrett, Convicting the Innocent: Where Criminal Prosecutions Go Wrong at 113 (Harvard Univ. Press 2011). *See also* Peter J. Neufeld, *The (Near) Irrelevance of* Daubert *to Criminal Justice and Some Suggestions for Reform*, 95 Public Health Matters S107 (2005) (noting that "[i]n not one of the half-dozen most sensational forensic-science scandals of the last 20 years, involving serious fraud and gross misconduct, were the transgressions of 'experts' revealed by defense counsel at trial"). One may wonder if these cases are the exceptions in which defense counsel are particularly incompetent, which would also help explain why they produced wrongful convictions. The truth is hard to determine. There are clearly many *Daubert* challenges to evidence in criminal cases, some of which result in hearings. Few result in published opinions, however, especially if the result of the hearing is the dismissal of the case. *See* NAS Report, *supra* note 2 at 97.

47. One study of handwriting analysis found that one federal court of appeals, the Tenth Circuit, upheld a lower court decision admitting the expert to testify only on the similarities and differences between the known exemplar and the questioned document, but disallowing testimony on authorship or a "match." Simone Ling Francini, *Note: Expert Handwriting Testimony: Is the Writing Really on the Wall?*, 11 Suffolk J. Trial & App. Adv. 99, 108–9 (2006). Other than the Tenth Circuit, every other court of appeal found handwriting analysis to be reliable based on its long history of acceptance in the courtroom. *Id.* at 111.

48. *See* Innocence Project, DNA Exoneree Case Profiles, http://www.innocenceproject.org/know/; and *Understanding the Causes: Unreliable or Improper Forensic Science*, http://www.innocenceproject.org/understand/Unreliable-Limited-Science.php (last visited May 18, 2014).

49. *See, e.g.,* Paul C. Gianelli, "Junk Science": The Criminal Cases, 84 J. Crim. L. & Criminology 105 (1993) (observing the disparity in reform efforts as between junk science in civil and criminal cases and calling for more stringent standards in criminal cases).

50. Donald Kennedy, *Editorial: Forensic Science: Oxymoron?*, 302 Science 1625 (2003).

51. *Id.*

52. *Id.*

53. *See* NAS Report, *supra* note 2 at 1 (quoting P.L. No. 109–108, 119 Stat. 2290 (2005).

54. *Id.* (quoting S. Rep. No. 109-88, at 46 [2005]).

55. National Academy of Sciences, *Mission Statement*, http://www.nasonline.org/about-nas/mission/.

56. *See* NAS Report, *supra* note 2 at xix–xx.

57. *Id.* at xix.

58. *Id.* at 127–182.

59. *Id.* at 109 (quoting J. Griffin and DJ. LaMagna, Daubert *Challenges to Forensic Evidence: Ballistics Next on the Firing Line*, The Champion, Sept.–Oct. 2002 at 21).

60. *Id.* at 110 (quoting D.L. Faigman, M.J. Saks, J. Sanders, and E.K. Cheng, Modern Scientific Evidence: The Law and Science of Expert Testimony (2007–2008) at § 1:1, p. 4 n. 9).

61. *Id.* at 110.

62. *Id.*

63. *Id.*

64. *Id.* at 127–82. Other forensic disciplines not examined include: voice comparison and gunshot residue analysis. The report also provides a detailed examination of death investigation systems of medical examiners' and coroners' offices. *Id.* at 241–68.

65. *Id.* at 127.

66. *Id.* at 87.

67. *Id.* at 111–25.

68. *Id.* at 112.

69. *Id.*

70. *Id.* at 113.

71. *Id.* at 87.

72. *Id.*

73. *Id.* at 128.

74. *Id.* at 114. The report further explains:

> These publications must include clear statements of the hypotheses under study, as well as sufficient details about the experiments, the resulting data, and the data analysis so that the studies can be replicated. Replication will expose not only additional sources of variability but also further aspects of the process, leading to greater understanding and scientific knowledge that can be used to improve the method. *Id.* at 114.

75. *Id.* The NAS Report explains validation studies in this way:

> Such studies begin with a clear hypothesis (e.g., "new method X can reliably associate biological evidence with its source"). An unbiased experiment is designed to provide useful data about the hypothesis. Those data—measurements collected through methodical prescribed observations under well-specified and controlled conditions—are then analyzed to support or refute the hypothesis. The thresholds for supporting or refuting the hypothesis are clearly articulated before the experiment is run. The most important outcomes from such a validation study are (1) information about whether or not the method can discriminate the hypothesis from an alternative; and (2) assessments of the sources of errors and their consequences on the decisions returned by the method. These two outcomes combine to provide precision and clarity about what is meant by "reliably associate." *Id.* at 113.

76. *Id.* at 114.

77. *Id.* at 133.

78. *Id.*

79. *Id.*

80. *See* Garrett, *supra* note 46 at 90.

81. *See* NAS Report, *supra* note 2 at 198, 201.

82. *See infra* Chapter 7 (on accreditation).

83. *See infra* Chapter 7 (discussing stringency of certification tests).

84. *See* NAS Report, *supra* note 2 at 142 (addressing friction ridge analysis).

85. *See id.* at 143–45.

86. *See id.* at 137.

87. *Id.* at 139.

88. *Id.*

89. *Id.*

90. *See* SWGFAST Doc. #4, *supra* note 1 at 10.2.

91. *Id.*

92. *Id.*

93. United States v. Council, 2011 WL 1305247 (E.D. Va. 2011).

94. One writer has conservatively estimated the error rate of fingerprint identification to range from 0.2% to 2.5% based on a comparison to studies of the error rates of microscopic hair analysis and of traditional serological testing. *See* Simon A. Cole, *More than Zero: Accounting for Error in Latent Fingerprint Identification,* 95 J. Crim. L. & Criminology 985, 1027 (2005). As Cole acknowledges, this is not a scientifically established error rate, but rather a hypothesis still in need of empirical support.

95. *See* David L. Faigman, Jeremy A. Blumenthal, Edward K. Cheng, Jennifer L. Mnookin, Erin E. Murphy, & Joseph Sanders, Modern Scientific Evidence: The Law and Science of Expert Testimony, (Vol. 4—Forensics) at 250 (2013–14 Ed.).

96. *See Daubert,* 509 U.S. at 594.

97. *See* Cole, *supra* note 94 at 1028–32.

98. *Id.*

99. *See* NAS Report, *supra* note 2 at 138.

100. For similar conclusions regarding shoeprint and tire track analysis, *see* NAS Report, *supra* note 2 at 147 ("[T]here is no defined threshold that must be surpassed (of characteristics required to make a positive identification), nor are there any studies that associate the number of matching characteristics with the probabilities that the impressions were made by a common source."); for questioned document (i.e., handwriting), analysis, *see id.* at 167 ("Although there has been only limited research to quantify the reliability and replicability of the practices used by trained document examiners, the committee agrees that there may be some value in handwriting analysis."). The report also found insufficient scientific research in disciplines that are based on basic chemistry, such as fiber analysis, *see id.* at 163 ("There have been no studies of fibers (e.g., the variability of their characteristics during and after manufacturing) on which to base [a conclusion that two fibers come from the same source]. Similarly, there have been no studies to inform judgments about whether environmentally related changes discerned in particular fibers are distinctive enough to reliably individualize their source, and there have been no studies that characterize either reliability or error rates in the procedures."); and paint and coatings analysis, *see id.* at 170 ("As is the case with fiber evidence, analysis of paint and coatings is based on a solid foundation of chemistry to enable class identification ... However, the community has not defined precise criteria for determining whether two samples come from a common source class.").

101. *Id.* at 154.

102. *Id.* at 155.

103. *Id.* Emphasis added.

104. The firearms examination community vigorously rejected this conclusion in the NAS Report, publishing a response that gave an exhaustive list of publications in the area of firearms examination. *See* AFTE Comm. For the Advancement of the Sci. of Firearm and Tool Mark Identification, *The Response of the Association of Firearm and Toolmark Examiners to the February 2009 National Academy of Science Report "Strengthening Forensic Science in the United States: A Path Forward,"* 41 AFTE J. 204, 205 (2009) ("There is an extensive body of research, extending back over one hundred years, which establishes the accuracy, reliability, and validity of conclusions rendered in the field of firearm and toolmark identification.").

105. *See* Scientific Working Group for Firearms and Toolmarks (SWGGUN), *SWGGUN Responds to SOFS* (May 20, 2011), http://www.swggun.org/swg/index.php?option=com_content&view=article&id=51:swggun-responds-to-sofs-request&catid=13:other&Itemid=43 and http://www.swggun.org/swg/attachments/article/51/SWGGUN_RDTE_Final.pdf.

106. *See* NAS Report, *supra* note 2 at 305–7 (agenda for NAS Meeting of April 23, 2007, on the subject of the science underlying forensic sciences and featuring a report by Peter Striupaitis, Chair, International Association for Identification, Firearm/Toolmark Committee and Member, Scientific Working Group for Firearms and Toolmarks (SWGGUN); Scientific Working Group for Firearms and Toolmarks (SWGGUN), *The Foundations of Firearm and Toolmark Identification,* prepared in response to 2005 request by the National Academy of Sciences, http://www.swggun.org/swg/index.php?option=com_content&view=article&id=66:the-foundations-of-firearm-and-toolmark-identification&catid=13:other&Itemid=43.

107. *See* NAS Report, *supra* note 2 at 155.

108. Reported cases admitting unrestricted fingerprint testimony include, United States v. Stone, 2012 U.S. Dist. LEXIS 8973 (2012) (NAS Report does not provide sufficient basis for excluding fingerprint testimony which is a well-established area of expertise); Webster v. State, 2011 OK CR 14 (Ok. Crim. App. 2011). For similar cases allowing unrestricted firearms testimony, *see, e.g.,* United States v. Casey, 2013 U.S. Dist. LEXIS 34905 (2013); Commonwealth v. Vasquez, 462 Mass. 827 (Mass. 2012) (NAS critiques of bloodstain pattern analysis as subjective goes to the weight of the evidence, not its admissibility); People. v. Eleby, 2012 Cal. App. Unpub. LEXIS 3375 (NAS report on fingerprint analysis states only that more research is needed, not that the methodology is unreliable. Some scholarly criticism does not overcome long-standing general acceptance. Examiner may testify, and defense be prohibited from questioning regarding well-publicized FBI Crime Lab error.); Jones v. United States, 27 A.3d 1130 (2011); State v. McGuire, 2011 WL 890748 (N.J. S.Ct. 2011) (toolmark testimony admissible based on long-standing acceptance despite not making a record on reliability factors); People v. Givens, 2010 WL 5022731 (N.Y.S.Ct. 2010).

109. United States v. Otero, 849 F.Supp.2d 425, 431-35 (D.N.J. 2012).

110. *Id.* at 433.

111. *See* Dale J. Benos, Edlira Bashari, Jose M. Chaves, Amit Gaggar, Niren Kapoor, Martin LaFrance, Robert Mans, David Mayhew, Sara McGowan, Abigail Polter, Yawar Qadri, Shanta Sarfare, Kevin Schultz, Ryan Splittgerber, Jason Stephenson, Cristy Tower, R. Grace Walton and Alexander Zotov, *The Ups and Downs of Peer Review,* 31 Advances in Physiology Education 145–152 (2007).

112. *Id.*

113. *See* Association of Firearm and Toolmark Examiners, *AFTE Contacts,* http://www.afte.org/AssociationInfo/a_contacts.htm.

114. *See* Association of Firearm and Toolmark Examiners, *AFTE Code of Ethics*, http://www.afte.org/AssociationInfo/a_codeofethics.htm.

115. United States v. Starzecpyzel, 880 F. Supp. 1027, 1038 (S.D.N.Y. 1995).

116. State v. Ramirez, 801 So. 2d 836, 850 (Fla. 2001).

117. *Id.* at 850–53.

118. *Otero*, 849 F. Supp.2d at 435.

119. *See supra* notes 115–117 and accompanying text.

120. *Otero*, 849 F. Supp. 2d at 433–34.

121. Collaborative Testing Services, Inc., *CTS Statement on the use of Proficiency Testing Data for Error Rate Determinations* (Mar. 30, 2010), http://www.ctsforensics.com/assets/news/CTSErrorRateStatement.pdf.

122. *Id.*

123. *Ramirez*, 801 So.2d at 841.

124. People. v. Eleby, 2012 Cal. App. Unpub. LEXIS 3375 (2012).

125. State v. Harper, 2012 Wisc. App. LEXIS 629 (2012) (error to exclude NAS Report as hearsay because it is a public record); Gee v. United States, 2012 D.C. App LEXIS 503 (2012) (not error to bar cross-examination based on NAS Report as it is not "a learned treatise").

126. State v. Sheehan, 2012 WL 653653 (Utah App 2012).

127. *Compare* United States v. Llera Plaza, 179 F. Supp. 2d 492 (E.D. Pa., Jan. 7, 2002) *with* United States v. Llera Plaza, 188 F. Supp. 2d 549 (E.D. Pa., March 13, 2002).

128. This information is based on the author's personal notes, taken while attending the hearing in a Fort Bend County, Texas, courtroom on May 14–15, 2014.

129. *See* Scientific Working Group on Friction Ridge Analysis, *About Scientific Working Groups*, http://www.swgfast.org/AboutSWGs.htm.

130. *See* SWGFAST Doc. #4, *supra* note 1 at 2.

131. *Id.*

132. *Id.* at 5.

133. *Id.*

134. For thorough discussions of these issues in the context of fingerprint examination, *see* Cole, *supra* note 4; and Cole, *supra* note 94.

135. The Scientific Working Group for Firearms and Toolmarks (SWGGUN) provides the following guideline for professionals in the field: "The statement that 'sufficient agreement' exists between two toolmarks means that the agreement of individual characteristics is of a quantity and quality that the likelihood another tool could have made the mark is so remote as to be considered a *practical impossibility*." (emphasis added). *See* Scientific Working Group for Firearms and Toolmarks (SWGGUN), *Criteria for Identification* (Guideline 2.2.2, Adopted Jun. 4, 2012), http://www.swggun.org/swg/index.php?option=com_content&view=article&id=28:criteria-for-identification&catid=10:guidelines-adopted&Itemid=6.

136. *See* Cole, *supra* note 4 at 2–3 (arguing that individualization has not died but has simply been reborn in a new and substantively equivalent form).

137. *See, e.g.,* United States v. Dore and Barrett, No. 12 Cr. 45 (RJS) (prohibiting firearms examiner from referring to firearms comparison as a "science" and from stating his opinion that shell casings came from a particular gun with any specific degree of certainty); United States v. Jackson, 1:11-cr-411-WSD (N.D. Ga. July 25, 2012) (firearms examiner testimony limited to reporting "similarities" between crime scene bullet fragments and cartridge casings and those produced by firing the weapon).

138. *See, e.g.,* People v. Greenwood, L.A. Super. Ct. (2010) (disallowing statement by fingerprint expert that opinion is result of an "infallible scientific process"); United States v. Titus Faison, No. 2008 CF2 16636 (D.C. Super. Ct. May 28, 2010). (disallowing fingerprint examiner from stating conclusions in absolute terms, i.e., that a print is unique to one person to the exclusion of all possible others).

139. *See, e.g.,* United States v. Zajac, Slip Copy, 2010 WL 3489597 (D. Utah 2010).

140. For example, the FBI Crime Laboratory currently endorses individualizations that are stated to be at "a reasonable degree of scientific certainty" for firearms testing. *See* Dept. of Justice, Letter to District Attorney Allgood, May 6, 2013, Re: Manning v. Mississippi, 2013-DR-00491-SCT (on file with author).

141. *See, e.g.,* State v. Dixon, 2012 Minn. App. LEXIS 123 (fingerprint expert allowed to testify to identification "to a reasonable degree of scientific certainty").

142. *See* United States v. St. Gerard, United States Army Trial Judiciary, Fifth Judicial Circuit, Germany (2010) (disallowing statement that it was a "practical impossibility" that a cartridge case could have been fired by any weapon other than the one seized).

143. *Ramirez,* 801 So.2d at 836.

144. *See infra* Chapter 5.

145. For more on cognitive bias in forensic science, *see infra* Chapter 4.

146. *See, e.g.,* Jeff Blackburn, Gary Udashen & Cory Session, *It is Time to Ban Junk Science from Texas Courtrooms,* HOUS. CHRON., Oct. 3, 2010, http://www.chron.com/opinion/outlook/article/It-s-time-to-ban-junk-science-from-Texas-1695901.php.

147. *See* Federal Bureau of Investigation, *National Press Releases: FBI Laboratory Announces Discontinuation of Bullet Lead Examinations,* Sept. 1, 2005, available at http://www.fbi.gov/news/pressrel/press-releases/fbi-laboratory-announces-discontinuation-of-bullet-lead-examinations.

148. *See* Justice Dept., FBI to Review Flawed Criminal Forensic Evidence, PBS NEWSHOUR, Jul. 20, 2012, http://www.pbs.org/newshour/bb/law-july-dec12-fbi_07-11/ (announcing review of thousands of cases involving flawed hair and fiber analysis testimony).

149. Steve Mills, Flynn McRoberts, & Maurice Possley, *When Labs Falter, Defendants Pay: Bias toward Prosecution Cited in Illinois Cases,* CHICAGO TRIB., C1 (Oct. 20, 2004).

150. *See, e.g.,* L. Vamsi Krishna Reddy, *Lip Prints: An Overview in Forensic Dentistry,* 2 J. OF ADV. DENTAL RESEARCH 17, 19 (2011) (concluding that "research studies and information regarding the use of lip prints as evidence in personal identification and criminal investigation in forensic dentistry are very much scanty" and urging further study).

151. *See* Innocence Project, *Cases Where DNA Revealed that Bite Mark Analysis Led to Wrongful Arrests and Convictions,* http://www.innocenceproject.org/Content/Cases_Where_DNA_Revealed_that_Bite_Mark_Analysis_Led_to_Wrongful_Arrests_and_Convictions.php.

152. The medical testimony in the "San Antonio Four" case provides just one example. *See infra* note 124 and accompanying text.

153. *See* John Schwartz, *Picked from a Lineup, on a Whiff of Evidence,* N.Y. TIMES, Nov. 3, 2009, http://www.nytimes.com/2009/11/04/us/04scent.html.

154. *Id.*

155. Noted fire scientist John J. Lentini has written about the traditional myths that pervaded arson investigations until recently. *See* John J. Lentini, *The Mythology of Fire Investigation,* http://www.firescientist.com/Documents/The%20Mythology%20of%20Arson%20Investigation.pdf (providing a shorter version of Chapter 8 of the author's textbook SCIENTIFIC PROTOCOLS FOR FIRE INVESTIGATION [CRC Press 2006]). These myths led to

incorrect conclusions in one high-profile Texas case in which a man was executed for committing arson with the intent to kill his daughters. *See* Ethan Bronner, *Executed Texan's
Family Seeks Pardon,* N.Y. TIMES, Oct. 25, 2012, http://www.nytimes.com/2012/10/25/us/
willingham-family-seeks-posthumous-pardon-in-texas.html?_r=0.

156. *See* National Fire Protection Association, NFPA 921: GUIDE FOR FIRE AND EXPLO-
SION INVESTIGATIONS, http://www.nfpa.org/codes-and-standards/document-information-
pages?mode=code&code=921.

157. *Id.*

158. Mary A. Bush, Howard I. Cooper, & Robert B. J. Dorion, *Inquiry into the Scientific Basis for Bitemark Profiling and Arbitrary Distortion Compensation,* 55 J. FORENSIC SCI.
1–8 (2010) (finding that the same dentition does not make reproducible marks, that forensic odontologists should not arbitrarily distort dentition photographs to fit bitemarks and
that bitemark profiling has no scientific basis and should not be used in forensic work);
Mary A. Bush, Peter J. Bush, & H. David Sheets, *Statistical Evidence for the Similarity of
Human Dentition,* 56 J. FORENSIC SCI. 118–123 (2011) (finding statements of dental unique-
ness in an open population is unsupportable).

159. Jerry Mitchell, *Dentist Now Doubts Science of Bite Analysis,* CLARION-LEDGER (Aug.
6, 2012), http://bitemarks.org/2012/08/06/dentist-now-doubts-science-of-bite-analysis/.

160. United States v. Zajac, 2010 WL 3489597 (D. Utah 2010) (Slip Copy).

161. *See* NAS Report, *supra* note 2 at 156.

162. Garrett, *supra* note 46 at 90.

163. *See* Innocence Project, *News and Information: Innocence Project and NACDL Announce Historic Partnership with FBI and Department of Justice on Microscopic Hair Analysis Cases,* http://www.innocenceproject.org/Content/Innocence_Project_and_NACDL_
Announce_Historic_Partnership_with_the_FBI_and_Department_of_Justice_on_
Microscopic_Hair_Analysis_Cases.php# (last visited Jan. 10, 2014).

164. *Id.*

165. *Id.*

166. Spencer S. Hsu, *Convicted Defendants Left Uninformed of Forensic Flaws found by
Department of Justice,* WASH. POST (Apr. 16, 2012), http://www.washingtonpost.com/local/
crime/convicted-defendants-left-uninformed-of-forensic-flaws-found-by-justice-dept/2012/
04/16/gIQAWTcgMT_story.html.

167. David Mann, *DNA Tests Undermine Evidence in Texas Execution,* TEX. OBSERVER
(Nov. 11, 2011), http://www.texasobserver.org/texas-observer-exclusive-dna-tests-undermine-
evidence-in-texas-execution/.

168. *See* Innocence Project, *Press Release: DNA Test Proves Critical Hair Evidence in a
Capital Murder Case Didn't Match Man Executed; General Counsel Memo to President Elect
George Bush Hid the Fact That the Accused Sought DNA Tests That Could Have Spared Him
from Execution* (Nov. 12, 2010), http://www.innocenceproject.org/Content/DNA_Test_
Proves_Critical_Hair_Evidence_in_a_Capital_Murder_Case_Didnt_Match_Man_
Executed.php.

169. *Id.*

170. *See,* John Crabb, Jr., Department of Justice Special Counsel, Re: Florida v. Gerald
Murray (dated Aug. 20, 2013) (on file with author).

171. *See* Rick Sichta, Email correspondence with author (May 30, 2014) (on file with
author).

172. *See* Innocence Project, *Fix the System: Access to DNA Testing*, http://www.innocenceproject.org/fix/DNA-Testing-Access.php (last visited Feb. 23, 2014).

173. *See In re* Davis, 130 S. Ct. 1, 3 (2009) (mem.) (Scalia, J., dissenting); *see also* Joshua M. Lott, *The End of Innocence? Federal Habeas Corpus Law After In re Davis*, 27 GEORGIA ST. UNIV. L. REV. 443-88 (2011).

174. Tex. S.B. 344, http://www.capitol.state.tx.us/BillLookup/History.aspx?LegSess=83 R&Bill=SB344 (effective Sept. 1, 2013).

175. For general information about the Texas arson review, *see* Tim Stelloh, *Old Arson Cases Reviewed in Texas: Is Douglas Boyington an Innocent Man?*, NBCNews.com (Nov. 20, 2013), http://usnews.nbcnews.com/_news/2013/11/20/21370404-old-arson-cases-reviewed-in-texas-is-douglas-boyington-an-innocent-man?lite.

176. *See* Innocence Project of Texas, *State Arson Review*, http://www.ipoftexas.org/statewide-arson-review.

177. Michelle Mondo, *Freedom Comes to Three of the "San Antonio 4,"* SAN ANTONIO EXPRESS-NEWS (Nov. 18, 2013; updated: November 20, 2013), http://www.mysanantonio.com/news/local/article/DA-drops-S-A-Four-cases-4985664.php.

178. *Id.*

179. *See* NAS Report, *supra* note 2 at 19.

180. *Id.* at 19–20.

181. *Id.* at 24.

182. *Id.* at 21–27 (recommendations 2, 3, 6, and 9).

183. *Id.* at 25 (recommendation 7).

184. *Id.* at 27–33 (recommendations 10–13).

185. *See* Jennifer L. Mnookin, *The Validity of Latent Fingerprint Identification: Confessions of a Fingerprinting Moderate*, 7 LAW, PROBABILITY & RISK 127 (2008).

186. *See* NAS Report, *supra* note 2 at 20.

187. *See supra* note 174.

Chapter Four

The Paradox of the Ethical—
and Biased—Analyst

Misplaced Kudos

The minutes of a Houston Police Department Crime Laboratory meeting from September of 2011 include the following commendations for several laboratory analysts:

- Team received kudos from Capt. L. of Special Crimes on serial rapist case—[names of analysts].
- Team received kudos from Sgt. M. on abduction case where woman was taken from her job and her burning body was found by two motorists—[names of analysts].
- [Two analysts] received kudos from Sgt. M. on a post-conviction case.
- [Analyst] received kudos from Officer Y. for her help on a narcotics case where controlled substances were found in a safe from a home invasion.
- Kudos to [analyst]—guilty verdict on case with five counts from Assistant U.S. Attorney S. out of District of Maryland.[1]

At first glance, it may make sense to congratulate a member of a police department who participates in obtaining a guilty verdict for a "serial rapist" or for the assailant of a woman who was abducted and whose body was burned. Anyone who participates in getting violent criminals off the streets should naturally feel a sense of pride. Forensic analysts within crime laboratories have historically played a role in bringing justice to victims as part of a law enforcement team. Indeed, the first thing that visitors see upon arriving at the FBI Crime Laboratory building in Quantico, Virginia, is a statue on the front lawn that pays tribute to crime victims and the search for justice.[2]

Crime laboratory analysts, operating within law enforcement agencies, have traditionally viewed themselves as playing an integral role in the struggle for justice. There is nothing inherently sinister or corrupt about forensic analysts serving law enforcement in the effort to convict guilty criminals and vindicate the rights of victims. The motives are commendable. The goal is to promote public safety. Like police officers, laboratory analysts properly think of themselves as good guys; and with few exceptions, they work hard to help their police colleagues solve crimes. The television show *CSI* and its variants portray such analysts as actively involved in the investigation of crime and the analysis of evidence. In real life, crime scene investigators collect evidence at the scene —such as blood specimens, fingerprints, DNA samples, and the like. Then crime laboratory analysts take the collected evidence and examine the items with microscopes and other laboratory equipment to develop evidence for use in ongoing investigations or at trial. Like the fictional TV portrayal, however, analysts in crime laboratories answer to their law enforcement superiors and do the work requested by law enforcement. They often wear windbreakers emblazoned with the police department's seal or with the words "Police Lab" on the back, looking much like police officers.[3] Crime laboratory analysts are not usually classified as actual police officers and do not make arrests; nonetheless, they identify closely with police officers and consider themselves as colleagues in a joint effort. It stands to reason that police department officials also view laboratory analysts as "their" laboratory analysts and expect that, like all police employees, laboratory analysts will serve the interests of the department.

Prosecutors also come to view crime laboratory analysts in the same way they do other police officers—as "their" witnesses. In the adversary system of criminal justice, crime laboratory analysts are government witnesses like police officers. Police department crime laboratories work exclusively for law enforcement. They do not work for the defense, and they do not testify for the defense. They only testify as prosecution witnesses. Consequently, analysts find themselves being presented to juries exclusively by prosecutors who tout their expertise, their high-quality work, and their credibility as witnesses, while defense attorneys often attempt to attack those same attributes.[4] The adversarial nature of criminal justice pushes laboratory analysts into a pro-prosecution posture.

The Perils of Operating a Laboratory within a Police Department

For a quarter century, scholars have recognized critical dangers created when crime laboratory analysts develop a close association with law enforcement and view themselves as part of the law enforcement team.[5] On the whole, these concerns had historically fallen on deaf ears. That said, as the number of DNA exonerations involving fraudulent or misleading testimony by crime laboratory analysts has grown, the call for the reform of crime laboratories has intensified. In one 2009 study of 137 DNA exonerations, 82 of which involved forensic testimony, law professors Brandon Garrett and Peter Neufeld found that analysts gave incorrect testimony by either "misstating empirical data" or by making assertions "wholly unsupported by empirical data."[6] In other words, an even-handed and proficient reading of the empirical data in these cases would have produced testimony favorable to the defense.

Two main problems lead an analyst to give erroneous or misleading testimony: breaches of ethics and human errors. In the first category are the few malicious or corrupt analysts in crime laboratories who wreak havoc in large numbers of cases, sometimes for years, through fraud.[7] Fortunately, rogue analysts can be detected fairly easily by effective quality assurance programs, which are becoming standard in forensic laboratories. Accreditation protocols require such programs, and police crime laboratories have increasingly sought accreditation. Simultaneously, as the problems have become more apparent, the accreditation process has been made more rigorous. Thus, major cases of fraud will diminish over time if accreditation is mandated for all crime laboratories and if laboratories adopt effective quality assurance protocols for verifying each analyst's work. Yet even the accreditation process itself can be further improved by breaking the close connection between forensic science and law enforcement, as addressed in Chapter 6. However, accreditation is in itself not a panacea. As described in Chapter 2, numerous scandals have occurred in accredited crime laboratories. Without appropriate internal controls, serious problems can occur even in accredited laboratories.

The second category includes cases resulting from simple human error. One might also include errors due to an analyst's lack of proficiency. Crime laboratories also operate under the crush of heavy caseloads that put pressure on analysts to rush their work.[8] The influential 2009 National Academy of Sciences Report describes the inherent pressures built into the day-to-day job of a forensic analyst who faces "a need to answer a particular question related to the issues of a particular case."[9] Naturally, these pressures may produce unintentional errors in an analyst's work. As this chapter details, the location of a forensic laboratory raises concerns that go beyond issues of outright fraud or poor quality due to underfunding. Locating forensic laboratories within police departments represents a structural problem that increases the likelihood of honest error.

Motivational Bias from Group Affiliation

Though rogue analysts who commit outright fraud grab national headlines, these cases should not distract us from the more intractable problem within crime laboratories: the honest mistakes made by ethical analysts. While it is hard to say how often such mistakes are made, we do know that each false positive error creates a high risk of convicting an innocent person and that such mistakes often occur when cognitive and motivational biases affect the interpretation of ambiguous test results.

Numerous types of conscious and unconscious bias may come into play in a crime laboratory—as it does in every setting in which human judgment operates. The National Academy of Sciences explains the concerns about cognitive bias this way:

> Human judgment is subject to many different types of bias, because we unconsciously pick up cues from our environment and factor them in an unstated way into our mental analyses. Those mental analyses might also be affected by unwarranted assumptions and a degree of overconfidence that we do not even recognize in ourselves. Such cognitive biases are not the result of character flaws; instead, they are common features of decisionmaking, and they cannot be willed away.[10]

In the context of a crime laboratory, one type of cognitive bias known as "motivational bias" stems from the mere fact that analysts are part of a police department. The integration of a laboratory into a police department makes it impossible for laboratory analysts to avoid the motivational pressures of group affiliation in two regards. First, as police department employees, laboratory analysts—including the laboratory directors—are subordinates of the chief of police. They maintain their positions and seek advancement by meeting the expectations of their law enforcement superiors. This makes them vulnerable to departmental pressures on how they perform their jobs. Law professor Paul Giannelli's research has shown that some prosecutors can also exert pressure on forensic experts to give favorable testimony:[11]

> For more than a decade, a Texas pathologist worked closely with prosecutors and police "shad[ing] things to follow along with the police theory of the case." As the special prosecutor [appointed to conduct an independent investigation of the pathologist's wrongdoing] remarked: "If the prosecution theory was that death was caused by a Martian death ray, then that is what [the pathologist] reported."[12]

In another case, an Oklahoma Criminal Appeals Court expressed similar concerns: "[W]e are greatly disturbed by the implications that the Oklahoma County District Attorney's Office may have placed undue pressure upon Ms. Gilchrist to give a so-called expert opinion, which was beyond scientific capabilities."[13] These are extreme examples, but they illustrate that, at least in some instances, law enforcement officials may intentionally, or even unintentionally, pressure forensic experts to give supportive testimony.

Second, crime laboratories receive their funding as a line item of the police department's budget. Laboratory directors must depend on the leadership of their law enforcement superiors to obtain adequate funding. Unfortunately, experience has shown that police administrators tend to assign laboratory equipment and salaries a lower priority than hiring and equipping police officers. Thus, a crime laboratory's dependence on its parent police department also motivates laboratory employees to please their superiors within the department.

A similar type of cognitive bias that can affect police laboratory analysts is known as "role effect bias." This is similar to motivational bias, but it can operate more subconsciously. This type of bias develops from the role an individual plays within a group. People naturally feel a need to gain the social support of a group by adopting the attitudes and behavior characteristic of the group.[14] This type of bias can tilt a crime laboratory analyst's conclusions in favor of the prosecution, especially in ambiguous cases. It is hard to evaluate the extent to which crime laboratory analysts view themselves as advocates for law enforcement, but there is every reason to believe that they do.[15] Even if one consciously tries to approach forensic testing in a purely objective manner, role effect bias can still come into play.

The effects of motivational bias have come to light in many crime laboratory scandals around the country. What is striking in these types of situations is that the misleading or inaccurate testimony and inaccurate statements in reports are tilted heavily in favor the prosecution and not the defense, revealing the pro-prosecution bias. For example, in 2002, drug analysts at the Illinois State Police Laboratory withheld negative preliminary results from drug tests from the defense and instead untruthfully reported that the drugs were "not analyzed." Apparently, the untruthful reporting of preliminary findings had become a common practice. Laboratory representatives reportedly had adopted this policy at the request of Cook County prosecutors, although a spokesman for the prosecutors denied knowledge of such a policy.[16]

In 2009, criminalist Jeffrey Herbert in Sacramento County, California, testified that the DNA sample from a particular defendant matched only 1 in 95,000 people in the general population. His supervisor had told him the probability was 1 in 47, but he testified to the higher figure, which was more favorable to the prosecution, despite being warned that it was wrong.[17] A review by the state's Department of Justice found that Herbert's calculations showed "an insufficient understanding" of how to analyze mixed DNA samples.[18] Thus, the official investigation suggests a lack of proficiency, but Herbert's choice to testify according to the calculation more favorable to the prosecution suggests a personal pro-prosecution bias.

In 2010, the North Carolina State Police Crime Laboratory undertook a review of 15,000 cases covering a sixteen-year period after discovering that serologists had given misleading testimony. Of the 15,000 cases, the review found 190 that involved misleading testimony.[19] This means that, in 190 *trials*, analysts made statements under oath about tests done on blood specimens suggesting a link between the defendant and the crime that was not supported by the evidence.

In some cases in which analysts obtain test results favorable to the defense, these results are withheld or misstated in court to favor the prosecution. In Chicago, an Illinois State Police DNA analyst testified against John Willis, charged in 1991 with a being a serial rapist.[20] Eleven victims had identified Willis as their attacker, a fact that may have become known to the analyst. The serology tests showed that Willis's blood type was different from the source of the semen, and thus he was not the rapist. Yet the analyst, Pamela Fish, testified that the results were "inconclusive," meaning that she could neither include nor exclude him as the rapist.[21] A powerful piece of scientific evidence that should have favored the defense was thus transformed into neutral evidence, effectively eliminating it from the case. Willis was convicted and sentenced to 100 years in prison in 1992. DNA evidence exonerated him seven years later.

Even the U.S. Supreme Court has rejected the proposition that crime laboratory analysts merely report the results of "neutral scientific testing," an argument that the State of Massachusetts made in *Melendez-Diaz v Massachusetts*.[22] The majority opinion instead concluded:

> Nor is it evident that what [Massachusetts] calls "neutral scientific testing" is as neutral or as reliable as [the state] suggests. Forensic evidence is not uniquely immune from the risk of manipulation. According to a recent study conducted under the auspices of the National Academy of Sciences, "[t]he majority of [laboratories producing forensic evidence] are administered by law enforcement agencies, such as police departments, where the laboratory administrator reports to the head of the agency." And "[b]ecause forensic scientists often are driven in their work by a need to answer a particular question related to the issues of a particular case, they sometimes face pressure to sacrifice appropriate methodology for the sake of expediency." A forensic analyst responding to a request from a law enforcement official may feel pressure—or have an incentive—to alter the evidence in a manner favorable to the prosecution.[23]

It can be hard to tell whether cases involving misleading or incorrect testimony represent instances of outright pro-prosecution fraud or incompetence combined with a pro-prosecution slant. Either way, the placement of crime laboratories in police departments creates a powerful source of motivational bias that has affected numerous analysts in giving improper testimony.

Unconscious Bias: The Mayfield Affair

In addition to motivational bias, there are other varieties of cognitive bias such as "confirmation bias," also known as "observer bias," as well as context effects that can affect laboratory work when adequate procedures are not in place to protect against them. "Confirmation bias" refers to the natural and unconscious tendency people have to "seek, perceive, interpret, and create new evidence in ways that verify their preexisting beliefs."[24] In other words, people are unconsciously influenced by their expectations and have a tendency to perceive what they expect to see. On the other hand, in the forensic science context, "context effects" refers to the emotional cognitive input caused by the physical evidence being examined.[25] For example, conducting tests on the clothes worn by a murdered child creates emotive influences that can affect an analyst's decision making.

A high-profile international terrorism case involving the country's premiere crime laboratory, the FBI Crime Laboratory, provides a perfect example of how several types of unconscious cognitive bias may have caused a monumental error, leading to the wrongful arrest and two-week incarceration of an innocent man named Brandon Mayfield. The ordeal also included the search of Mayfield's home, not to mention the notoriety he endured when he was publicly accused of being an international terrorist. The Mayfield case reminds us, the lessons on laboratory practice aside, that federal crime laboratories, and even some state and local crime laboratories, do work that has national security implications. It also highlights the imperative to remove law enforcement control of forensic science at the federal level.

On March 11, 2004, a terrorist bombing on a train in Madrid killed 191 people and injured more than 1,400 others.[26] The Spanish National Police (SNP) recovered fingerprints on a bag of detonators connected to the crime and sought the assistance of foreign law enforcement in running the prints through their national databases. On March 13, Interpol Washington received a request for the FBI Crime Laboratory's latent print unit to analyze the prints and attempt to identify the culprit.

The FBI appointed a supervisory fingerprint examiner to conduct the initial analysis. The examiner encoded seven minutiae points of a high resolution image of one of the fingerprints submitted by the SNP, labeled as latent fingerprint #17 (LFP 17). The FBI initiated a search in the American database known as the Integrated Automated Fingerprint Identification System (IAFIS) which contains images of millions of fingerprints.[27] The IAFIS search produced a list of twenty possible candidate prints. The supervisory examiner then began a side-by-side comparison of LFP 17 and the potential matches. Brandon Mayfield's fingerprint was the number four candidate. FBI protocols do not require a minimum number of corresponding points that must be found to determine a match, in contrast to the SNP, which has a ten-point minimum standard for declaring a match. In this case, the FBI examiner found 15 corresponding points of comparison and made the initial determination of a match between Mayfield's fingerprint and LFP 17.[28]

The examiner reported his findings to the FBI unit chief who also then reviewed the on-screen images. He also found that it was a match and assigned the case to a verifier (a retired supervisory fingerprint examiner employed as a contractor). As part of the contextual information, the verifier was informed that LFP 17 had been recovered on evidence connected with the Madrid bombing and that the initial supervisory examiner had declared a match which had been confirmed by the unit chief. The verifier compared LFP 17 and candidate #4 and confirmed the finding of a match. Thus, the erroneous declaration of a "match" was verified by two other examiners. All three examiners were regarded as top experts.

Immediately after Mayfield's identification as a suspect in the Madrid bombing case, the FBI began an intensive investigation, including twenty-four-hour surveillance of Mayfield, who was an attorney in Portland, Oregon. They also learned that he was a Muslim, married to an Egyptian immigrant, and that he had represented a convicted terrorist in a child custody dispute and had contacts with suspected terrorists.[29] These facts became known to the latent print examiners who had identified Mayfield's print as matching LFP 17 at some point *after* the erroneous identification was made.[30]

On March 20, the SNP received the FBI Laboratory's report identifying LFP 17 as matching candidate #4, Brandon Mayfield. The SNP also examined LFP 17 and Mayfield's fingerprint but did not find a match.[31] The FBI, rather than questioning and revisiting their findings, showed absolute confidence in their conclusion and prepared a detailed exhibit delineating their analysis. The unit chief flew to Spain to demonstrate the comparison process, using the images from the FBI's three-page exhibit. According to news reports, the unit chief declined to examine the original print at this meeting and "relentlessly pressed [the FBI's] case anyway, explaining away stark proof of a flawed link—including what the Spanish described as tell-tale forensic signs—and seemingly refusing to accept the notion that they were mistaken."[32] The unit chief left the meeting in Spain believing that the SNP would reexamine the prints and, presumably, revise their decision that the two prints did not match.[33]

The media then became a factor. In early May, the FBI began to receive inquiries from news outlets about a possible American suspect in the case. The agency worried that Mayfield might flee or destroy evidence if his identification as a suspect was publicized before his arrest. As a result, the Department of Justice applied to the United States District Court in Oregon for a warrant to detain Mayfield as a "material witness" and requested a search warrant for his home and office. Mayfield was arrested on May 6 and brought before the court. He denied that the fingerprint obtained from the detonator bag was his and insisted that he had no idea how it got there.[34] Mayfield stated that he had not been out of the country in ten years and did not have a passport. However, on the basis of the FBI Laboratory's identification, the court denied Mayfield's request for home detention and incarcerated him on May 6, 2004.

On May 17, the court appointed an independent examiner to review the FBI's fingerprint identification. This examiner was also informed of the facts of the case, including, presumably Mayfield's religion and associations with known or suspected terrorists. On May 19, the court-appointed expert *confirmed* the FBI's identification. As it turned out, all four examiners—the three FBI examiners *and* the examiner appointed to assist in Mayfield's defense—were wrong.

The very same day that the defense expert confirmed the identification, the SNP informed the FBI that it had positively identified LFP 17 as belonging to an Algerian national named Ouhnane Daoud.[35] On May 24, the FBI Laboratory withdrew its identification of Mayfield, the government dismissed the material witness proceeding, and released Mayfield.

A total of four well-regarded examiners erred, and only the persistence of the SNP brought the error to light. Had it not been for the SNP's dogged refusal to accept the FBI Crime Laboratory's determination of a match, the error may not have been discovered.[36] In turn, the FBI stubbornly resisted the SNP's determination that the two prints did not match. The FBI's resistance in the face of strong evidence of error, in and of itself, was evidence of cognitive bias that affected the laboratory's performance. Fortunately, the error was caught relatively soon, and Mayfield did not suffer a prolonged ordeal. However, had this been an American case prosecuted in a federal court, he might well have been convicted on the basis of the expert testimony of the latent print examiner.[37] This type of testimony "is so powerful that erroneous fingerprint evidence is likely to convict, convict securely, and never be exposed."[38]

How could such errors have occurred? This case involved a terrorist act that caused almost 200 deaths and over a thousand injuries. It is not a case that would have been handled carelessly. There is every indication that the FBI took the task seriously and assigned its best examiners to the case. The supervisory examiner's work was reviewed by the chief of the Latent Print Unit and then by a retired top examiner. Once out of the laboratory, the results went to court where the judge appointed a distinguished examiner on behalf of Mayfield. Even this defense expert ratified the mistaken identification. These examiners were among the best in the country, and they knew the stakes were high. As luck would have it, the error ensnared a man who happened not only to be a converted Muslim married to a Middle Eastern immigrant but one who had also represented a known terrorist in a child custody case. These facts, however, were not known by the FBI examiners at the time his prints were mistakenly identified, and so this information played no part in his mistaken selection, although it likely hardened the FBI's determination to prove they had found the culprit. In the end, these four top latent print examiners made a serious error that simply cannot be explained by carelessness, incompetence, or unethical behavior. These were highly-regarded fingerprint examiners who were aware of the importance of making the right call, and there is no reason to believe they harbored any personal bias against Mayfield. Indeed, one of the examiners was working for Mayfield's defense. The errors they each made are instead traceable to unconscious bias attributable to the methodology used in the examination process.

Reconstructing the chain of errors begins with the coincidence that the two prints were unusually similar, so similar that it is understandable why the IAFIS program found seven points of similarity, followed by additional points identified in live image-to-image comparisons by the three FBI examiners, but the unusual similarity does not tell the whole story. Though unusually similar, the prints were not identical, and the examiners ignored or explained away a number of differences. The Office of the Inspector General of the Department of Justice (OIG), which appointed three distinguished examiners to conduct an investigation into this potential miscarriage of justice, concluded that "[t]he unusual similarity between LFP 17 and Mayfield's known fingerprint was a major factor in the misidentification … [but] the misidentification could have been prevented."[39]

Instead, the reason why an innocent man was erroneously arrested in a case of international notoriety has everything to do with several types of unconscious cognitive bias that infected a subjective process. After the error was discovered, the FBI Crime Laboratory, pursuant to procedures outlined by accreditation authorities, formed an international committee to review the procedures and the factors that contributed to the erroneous identification.[40] Both the OIG and FBI investigations produced reports that provide useful insights into the possible causes of the error, and both reports identify corrective measures of the type that are routinely used in other scientific laboratories to minimize cognitive bias.

The first type of cognitive bias came into play when the supervisory examiner who initially identified LFP 17 as belonging to Mayfield received the LFP 17 image. The examiner began by denoting certain features of LFP 17 for the IAFIS program to compare with prints in the database. The examiner then obtained a set of latent prints for which the IAFIS had found a sufficient degree of correspondence to identify them as potential candidates. As the OIG report noted, "The enormous size of the IAFIS database and the power of the IAFIS program can find a confusing[ly] similar candidate print."[41] When the computer generates a list of potential matches, it creates in the examiner an "expectation bias" that one of these prints is likely to be the culprit. This expectation bias makes it more likely that the examiner will see certain similarities between the most similar potential candidate and LFP 17, when in fact those similarities may not exist. The similarity of the prints will also make it more likely that the examiner will overlook important differences between the prints. The OIG report noted:

> Despite the unusual similarity in the relationship between points on the Mayfield and Daoud prints, however, Mayfield and Daoud did not have identical fingerprints. In several instances, a bifurcation in one print corresponded to an ending ridge in the other. There were also subtle but important differences between the prints in the positioning of the fingers. But the unusual similarity in position and ridge counts was a critical factor that misled four examiners and contributed to their overlooking other important differences between LFP 17 and Mayfield's fingerprint.[42]

Thus, the potential matches found by the computer may have created an expectation bias in the first examiner.

Once the examiner made an initial determination that the two prints seemed to belong to the same person, a confirmation bias came into play.[43] In effect, the IAFIS computer-based match combined with the examiner's initial conclusion of a match created the bias in how the examiner further reviewed the two prints. The focus on Mayfield's print caused the examiner to go back and adjust his initial interpretation of LFP 17 "by reasoning 'backward' from features that were visible in the known prints of Mayfield."[44] As the OIG report states: "Having found as many as 10 points of unusual similarity, the FBI examiners began to 'find' additional features in LFP 17 that were not really there, but rather were suggested to the examiners by features in the Mayfield prints."[45]

Additional layers of confirmation bias affected the subsequent identifications by the unit chief and the retired examiner hired as a "verifier." First, the unit chief was aware of the initial IAFIS selection and that the first examiner had declared a match. The verifier, in turn, was made aware that both the first examiner and the unit chief had declared a match. The court-appointed defense expert was also aware of the IAFIS selection and the positive match by the three FBI examiners. In addition, although no public documentation is available on this point, the defense expert also probably learned about Mayfield's background which seemed to provide strong circumstantial support for the contention that he was a terrorist.

The Inspector General's report also cites Mayfield's religion and prior representation of a terrorist as factors that likely affected the FBI laboratory's resistance to reconsidering their finding after the SNP resisted the conclusion, found a non-match, and raised legitimate questions. The OIG report quotes one examiner who "candidly admitted that if the person identified had been someone without these characteristics, like the 'Maytag Repairman,' the Laboratory might have revisited the identification with more skepticism and caught the error."[46]

Scientific Experiments on Cognitive Bias

The leading researcher on the subject of cognitive bias in forensic analysis is Itiel E. Dror, who with several associates has conducted studies confirming the effects of cognitive bias on forensic scientists. Their studies help us to understand the circumstances that create the greatest potential for causing error and provide guidance on procedural changes designed to reduce cognitive bias in laboratories.

In one important study of fingerprint experts conducted in 2005, the Dror group "employed a within-subject design in which the same experts made judgments on identical pairs of fingerprints, but in different contexts."[47] The aim of this study was to determine what effect contextual information would have on individual scientists when confronted with identical prints for comparison. The researchers obtained the consent of five fingerprint experts to be tested at some point in the subsequent twelve months without their knowledge and in their normal work environment.

The researchers then collected pairs of fingerprints that each of the examiners had found to be a clear and definitive match in 2000, five years before the experiment was conducted.[48] The examiners were given the pair of fingerprints that they had previously judged to be a clear match and were asked for their opinion on whether they matched. In addition, they were also (falsely) told that the pair of prints was the set erroneously found to be a match in the Madrid bombing case that ensnared Mayfield, "thus creating an extraneous context that the prints were a non-match."[49]

The results were as startling as the actual misidentification in the Mayfield case: "Only one participant (20%) judged the prints to be a match." Only one of the five examiners gave a decision consistent with his earlier judgment. The other four, presumably affected by the only new information—that the prints were not Mayfield's—changed their decision from the one they had made five years earlier. Five years earlier they had found a clear and definitive match between the prints, but now three of the examiners completely reversed themselves, finding definite non-matches. The fourth examiner hedged a bit and declared that there was insufficient information to make a definite decision. As the authors of the study note: "The magnitude of the contextual effect and the fact that the [fingerprint] experts had judged the same fingerprints in the past enabled the sample to provide clear findings with a high level of confidence."[50] Additionally, the fact that this study was conducted covertly under conditions in which the experts believed they were providing their opinions within the real world conditions of the criminal justice system means that "if only one expert of five was susceptible to such effects that in itself would have serious implications."[51] The fact that four of five changed their judgments due to the effect of the extraneous contextual information they had received is truly alarming.

Dror and his colleagues concluded that the test results "may reflect cognitive flaws and limitations in conducting objective and independent processing and evaluation" in situations in which compelling contextual information is revealed to the fingerprint examiner. The sources of distortions from a purely objective analysis may include "emotional context, pressure, contextual information, group think, biases, hopes and expectations, self-fulfilling prophecies, and peer pressure."[52]

It is important to note that fingerprint evidence is considered one of the more reliable disciplines. Dror and his colleagues point out that the distortion caused by contextual bias of the type demonstrated in the study will arise "mainly in the more difficult and challenging cases, such as with latent fingerprints collected at crime scenes that are distorted, partially missing, and contaminated."[53] The difficult cases introduce greater potential for subjectivity.

On the other hand, the fact that fingerprint examination is normally such a reliable discipline indicates that the distorting effects observed in this study are likely to be "as prevalent, if not more so, in other biometric and forensic disciplines,"[54] many of which also regularly require subjective analysis.

"Blind" Analysts See More Clearly

As the Mayfield case and Dror's research show, motivational and cognitive biases can be introduced as a result of the relationship that an analyst may have with law enforcement personnel, but they can also result from the particular information about an investigation that the analyst may obtain prior to conducting his or her tests. In the Mayfield case, the FBI experts knew they were investigating a case of international significance. The second and third examiners knew their first colleague had declared a match. Subsequently, learning of Mayfield's background inspired even greater determination to defend the match. The court-appointed defense expert, who was aware of the three match findings and Mayfield's background, also erroneously declared a match.

One might think that organizational changes alone, such as removing a laboratory from the control of its law enforcement parent agency, would be sufficient to eliminate pro-prosecution biases. One lesson from the Mayfield case is that laboratory independence alone is not enough. In fact, the true goal is not laboratory independence *per se*. Laboratory independence, it turns out, is just the means to an end. The true goal is accurate and objective forensic analysis and testimony. Independence may reduce motivational and role effect biases and thus improve testing accuracy, but by itself it is not the solution. Laboratory analysts working in an independent laboratory may still feel susceptible to social expectations or personal hopes regarding a particular forensic test. Such awareness can introduce distortions into what would otherwise be a more objective process. They can also be influenced by the fact that a computer or another analyst in the laboratory has made an initial determination of a match. The fact that another piece of evidence from the investigation points to the suspect in question may also affect an analyst's work on a different piece of evidence.

Equally important to laboratory independence is the adoption of laboratory protocols that reduce the possibility of outside influence affecting an analyst's work. Laboratory protocols should ensure that each item of evidence is analyzed independently in order to minimize laboratory error due to cognitive bias. *Evidentiary* independence is arguably more important than laboratory independence for reducing unconscious cognitive biases. In other words, the findings of testing done on one item of evidence in a single case should not be made known to analysts conducting testing on another item of evidence. Conveying the findings of an initial test will create expectations in the mind of the analyst conducting a subsequent type of test, thus biasing the test.

Even in DNA testing—which is considered the gold standard of forensic testing for its solid scientific grounding—confirmatory bias can infect the process. One group of noted forensic science experts notes that confirmatory bias can distort DNA testing in difficult cases involving ambiguities "such as those that contain mixtures of DNA from two or more individuals, degraded or inhibited DNA, or limited quantities of DNA template."[55] The use of DNA testing in criminal cases will often involve mixtures of DNA in rapes involving multiple assailants or degraded DNA in homicide cases. Moreover, the advances in DNA technology and the demands of law enforcement are pushing in the direction of even more testing of ambiguous samples. Today, DNA testing can be done on "older samples, samples exposed to environmental insult, and limited samples resulting from incidental contact" (commonly called "touch DNA").[56] Thus, cases involving ambiguity are quite common and constitute an expanding proportion of the pool of samples submitted for testing. In difficult DNA cases, confirmatory bias can produce false inclusions or misleading statistical testimony given as a probability ratio that the DNA could belong to another person of the same race or ethnicity.

Information that is not germane to an analyst's work need not be disclosed to the analyst. Positive test results from other items of evidence that link the suspect to the crime need not and should not be disclosed to the DNA analyst.[57] Neither does the analyst need to know other information about the suspects "such as their history or motives, eyewitness identifications, presence or absence of a confession, and the like."[58] When it comes to removing sources of cognitive biases, less is more. The sources of information that can bias an experiment should be eliminated as is standard practice in other scientific experiments. The use of "blind" and "double blind" procedures—a regular feature of proper scientific laboratory protocols—are now gaining acceptance in criminal justice practices such as the administration of eyewitness identification "lineups" as well.[59]

Information on a Need-to-Know Basis

Simply shielding an analyst from extraneous information about a suspect is not enough. Confirmatory bias can come into play within the testing of one item of evidence. With DNA testing, for example, analysts know that their task in every case is to compare a known sample of DNA belonging to the suspect in a criminal case to unknown samples taken from the crime scene. This knowledge can infect the process with confirmation bias. Forensic science experts have developed procedures known as "sequential unmasking" to eliminate this source of bias.[60] The goal of sequential unmasking is to prevent analysts from obtaining information that will bias their comparison of known and unknown samples.

A key component of the sequential unmasking process is the use of a "case manager" who serves as the liaison between the client (whether it be law enforcement or defense counsel) and the laboratory analysts.[61] The case manager, a trained laboratory analyst, may gather any and all evidence related to the investigation that may be relevant to laboratory testing. Even seemingly extraneous information need not be kept from a case manager. He or she evaluates the evidence submitted by an investigator to determine which types of testing will be done and in what order. It is not uncommon for a single item of evidence, such as a backpack, to be tested for more than one type of evidence—for example, latent fingerprints and DNA. One type of testing may destroy or corrupt evidence of another type, so the case manager will determine a sequence of testing that will preserve all the possible types of material present on the item. Armed with full information about the investigation, the case manager can share only the information the analyst needs to know in deciding what tests to perform or the order in which to perform different tests.

Some skeptics of sequential unmasking have concerns that the process will treat analysts like machines, making them "blind" to relevant information which they need to decide how to go about testing an item of evidence. They warn that this process in itself may lead to improper testing and mistakes. In a recent discussion I had with a long-time FBI Crime Laboratory analyst, he described the problem as a "black box" that would encase the analyst in darkness and prevent the analyst from making intelligent decisions about an item of evidence. These concerns seem to ignore the fact that a trained analyst would serve as a case manager who would be in a position to evaluate the evidence from the investigation and make intelligent decisions about how to test the evidence. The case manager would then simply hand off the tasks to an impartial—and "blind"—analyst who would perform the tasks without being influenced by the information that introduces cognitive bias and risk of error.

Proposals for sequential unmasking take into account the fact that some information will determine the particular types of tests or the manner of testing that best suits an individual case. As one group of forensic experts has written, forensic scientists should not "be blind to information that might afford them the greatest opportunity to generate reliable information from evidentiary samples."[62] In DNA testing, for example, "the nature of the substrate associated with a sample may dictate that certain extraction procedures be used."[63] In other words, the analyst may need to better understand the surface (or "substrate") from which the biological matter was collected in order to determine the best procedures to use in extracting the DNA from the biological material. Case managers can decide what to test and how to test it or provide analysts with the information necessary for them to determine the proper tests to conduct.

Once the decision has been made about what to test and how, sequential unmasking procedures should be used to eliminate the inherent confirmation bias that derives from the analyst's knowledge that one sample belongs to the suspect and another was obtained at the crime scene. Keeping in mind that items of evidence should be analyzed independently, sequential unmasking can be accomplished "perhaps most easily by sequencing laboratory workflow such that evidentiary samples are interpreted, and the interpretation is fully documented, before reference samples are compared."[64] Specific protocols should be established in each forensic discipline to accomplish independent sequential analysis that will also minimize cognitive bias.[65]

Verifications of test results should be conducted in blind fashion as well. This is not presently the case in most forensic testing.[66] If test results are verified using a non-blind process, as in the Mayfield case, then the verification will likely be affected by confirmation bias. To eliminate the potential for biasing information that could skew forensic testing, the analysis and verification judgments must be kept independent of each other.

Leaders in the field of forensic science currently take the view that the concerns and proposals relate to cognitive bias implicate their objectivity and ethics, rather than their systemic, unconscious influences.[67] However, cognitive and motivational biases have nothing to do with an analyst's personal virtues or the professionalism promoted through training programs. Efforts to eliminate bias through mission statements and lectures in training programs will not counteract the natural human dynamics of various types of cognitive bias.

Re-imagining the Practice of Forensic Science

The procedural protocols used in police crime laboratories have traditionally served law enforcement purposes, not strictly scientific purposes. Scientists trained to conduct laboratory research routinely take steps to guard against biasing effects. However, forensic scientists in the past did not enter their profession with training in the scientific process and knowledge of the types of protocols used in scientific laboratories. So it should not be surprising that many in the law enforcement establishment have resisted the calls for changes to their laboratory protocols.[68] Increasingly, however, even forensic scientists are calling for fundamental changes in forensic laboratory practices.[69]

At the end of the day, an analyst conducting testing on a "blind" basis may feel that he or she is being treated like a "robot" or as if the work bench is surrounded by a "black box." Doing testing "in a vacuum" and no longer feeling like an integral part of the law enforcement team would understandably make analysts feel as if they are somehow being punished for impropriety or that they cannot be trusted to work impartially. It is understandable that crime laboratory professionals may object to proposals for change. They may also not want to operate like traditional scientists. They may see scientists as "eggheads" while crime laboratory analysts are "cops in lab coats," a much more glamorous role. What they may fail to appreciate is that case managers in the laboratory will continue to work with law enforcement agents to help solve the forensic evidence questions in criminal investigations. If analysts derive personal satisfaction from working in an investigative role, they can apply for positions as case managers or as crime scene investigators. Case manager positions might even be rotated among analysts.

Moreover, analysts need not be completely disconnected from the results of their work. Recognizing the work of analysts and giving them kudos for their work on cases that result in convictions does not necessarily bias the testing process. Laboratory managers can give such information and professional recognition *after* the work is done to remind analysts of the importance of their work. Managers might be well advised to also recognize cases in which an analyst's work *excluded* an innocent suspect. In laboratories that also do work for the defense, kudos should also go to analysts whose testimony assists the defense in obtaining an acquittal. In independent forensic laboratories, analysts have a broader view of the customer they serve. Rather than serving only the police and prosecution, analysts in independent laboratories serve the criminal justice system as a whole.

Notes for Chapter Four

1. Irma Rios, Assistant Director of the Crime Laboratory, City of Houston Inter office Correspondence, Sept. 12, 2012 (on file with author).

2. The author observed the memorial statue during a tour of the FBI Crime Laboratory in October 2012.

3. The author observed such windbreakers hanging on chair backs of some Houston Police Department Crime Lab analysts during a tour of the lab. An online search shows similar jackets for sale. *See* Crime Scene, Forensic Detective Jacket, http://www.crimescene.com/store/index.php?main_page=advanced_search_result&search_in_description=1&keyword=windbreaker&x=0&y=0.

4. As is true on the civil side as well, scientific experts often pick sides and become well known for testifying on behalf of plaintiffs or defendants, etc., in litigation. Unfortunately, there is a widespread perception that litigation—both civil and criminal—has become a "battle of the experts" and that the experts on all sides lack impartiality. *See* Neil Vidmar & Shari Seidman Diamond, *Juries and Expert Evidence*, 66 Brooklyn L. Rev. 1121-80 (2001). A normal part of the process of presenting witnesses at trial is the practice by opposing counsel to "impeach" the credibility of the other side's witnesses. The rules of evidence spell out

the procedure by which this is routinely done. *See* Federal Rules of Evidence for United States Courts, P.L. 93-595; 88 Stat. 1926 (approved Jan. 2, 1975), Rules 607-14.

5. Paul Giannelli, *Independent Crime Laboratories: The Problem of Motivational and Cognitive Bias*, Utah L. Rev. 247, 247 n. 4 (2010) (citing articles dating to as early as 1983).

6. Brandon L. Garrett & Peter J. Neufeld, *Invalid Forensic Science Testimony and Wrongful Convictions*, 95 Va. L. Rev. 1, 1 (2009).

7. *See supra* Chapter 2.

8. National Research Council, Strengthening Forensic Science in the United States: A Path Forward at 39–40 (National Academies Press, 2009) (hereinafter "NAS Report"); *see also* Chapter 2.

9. *Id.* at 23.

10. *Id.* at 122.

11. *See* Giannelli, *supra* note 5 at 257.

12. *Id.* at 258.

13. *Id.* (quoting McCarty v. State, 765 P.2d 1215, 1219 (Okla. Crim. App. 1988)).

14. *See* Giannelli, *supra* note 5 at 252.

15. *See* Paul Wilson, *Lessons from the Antipodes: Successes and Failures of Forensic Science*, 67 Forensic Science International 79, 82–83 (1994) (discussing myth of impartiality of forensic science based on author's experiences in Australia and New Zealand).

16. Steve Mills, Flynn McRoberts, and Maurice Possley, *When Labs Falter, Defendants Pay: Bias toward Prosecution Cited in Illinois Cases*, Chicago Trib., C1 (Oct. 20, 2004).

17. *See* Andy Furillo, *Crime Lab Overseers Split*, Sacramento Bee (Jun. 18, 2010), http://www.mcclatchydc.com/2010/06/18/96147/california-crime-lab-overseers.html.

18. *Id.*

19. Martha Waggoner, *Review Finds Flawed NC Cases, Including Executions*, Associated Press (Aug. 18, 2010), http://news.yahoo.com/review-finds-flawed-nc-cases.html.

20. Steve Mills & Maurice Possley, *Report Alleges Crime Lab Fraud; Scientist Is Accused of Providing False Testimony*, Chi. Trib., Jan. 14, 2001, at C1.

21. *Id.*

22. Melendez-Diaz v. Massachusetts, 129 S.Ct. 2527, 2536 (2009).

23. *Id.* (citations omitted).

24. *See* Saul M. Kassin, Itiel Dror, & Jeff Kukucka, *The Forensic Confirmation Bias: Problems, Perspectives, and Proposed Solutions*, 2 J. Applied Research in Memory & Cognition 42–52, at 44 (2013).

25. *See* Mark Page, Jane Taylor, & Matt Blenkin, *Context Effects and Observer Bias—Implications for Forensic Odontology*, 57 J. Forensic Sci. 108–112 at 109 (2012).

26. Office of the Inspector General, Oversight and Review Division, A Review of the FBI's Handling of the Brandon Mayfield Case, Unclassified Executive Summary at 1 (Jan. 2006) (hereinafter OIG Report).

27. *Id.*; Robert B. Stacey, *Report on the Erroneous Fingerprint Individualization in the Madrid Train Bombing Case*, http://www.fbi.gov/about-us/lab/forensic-science-communications/fsc/jan2005/special_report/2005_special_report.htm.

28. *See* Simon A. Cole, *More than Zero: Accounting for Error in Latent Fingerprint Identification*, 95 J. Crim. L. & Crim'y 985, 1016 (2005).

29. *See* OIG Report, *supra* note 26 at 17.

30. *Id.* at 32.

31. *Id.* at 2.

32. *See* Cole, *supra* note 28 at 1016 (quoting Sarah Kershaw, *Spain and U.S. at Odds on Mistaken Terror Arrest,* N.Y. TIMES, June 5, 2004, at A1.

33. *See* Stacey, *supra* note 27.

34. *See* OIG Report, *supra* note 26 at 70.

35. *Id.* at 3.

36. *See* Cole, *supra* note 28 at 1022.

37. *Id.*

38. *Id.* at 1021.

39. *See* OIG Report, *supra* note 26 at 6.

40. *See* Stacey, *supra* note 27.

41. *See* OIG Report, *supra* note 26 at 7.

42. *Id.*

43. *Id.; see also* Giannelli, *supra* note 5 at 254.

44. *See* OIG Report, *supra* note 26 at 7.

45. *Id.*

46. *Id.* at 12.

47. Itiel E. Dror, David Charlton, & Ailsa E. Peron, *Contextual Information Renders Experts Vulnerable to Making Erroneous Identifications,* 156 FORENSIC SCIENCE INTERNATIONAL 74, 75 (2006).

48. *Id.*

49. *Id.* at 76.

50. *Id.*

51. *Id.*

52. *Id.* at 77.

53. *Id.*

54. *Id.*

55. Dan E. Krane et al, *Letter to the Editor: Sequential Unmasking: A Means of Minimizing Observer Effects in Forensic DNA Interpretation,* 53 J. FORENSIC SCI. 1006, 1006 (2008).

56. *Id.*at 1006.

57. Jonathan J. Koehler & John Meixner, eds.,*Workshop on Cognitive Bias and Forensic Science* (2011) at 30, http://www.law.northwestern.edu/faculty/conferences/workshops/cognitivebias/.

58. *See* Krane et al, *supra* note 55 at 1006.

59. *Id.*

60. *Id.*

61. *Id.*

62. *Id.*

63. *Id.*

64. *Id.*

65. For a delineation of the protocols that should be followed in DNA testing, see *id.*

66. *See* Koehler & Meixner, *supra* note 57 at 11 (summarizing the comments of Glenn Langenburg).

67. *See supra* Chapter 3.

68. *See* OIG Report, *supra* note 26 at 2.

69. Jennifer L. Mnookin et al., *The Need for a Research Culture in the Forensic Sciences,* 58 UCLA L. REV. 725 (2011).

Chapter Five

Safeguarding Justice

Forensic laboratory results dictate outcomes in many criminal cases, yet the judicial system has few safeguards in place to protect against wrongful convictions should those results be wrong. Generally speaking, the legal system offers several possible safeguards to ensure that a defendant receives a fair trial including the right to be represented by legal counsel, allowing the defense to hear live testimony from the witnesses against him or her, and having the right to cross-examine those witnesses.[1] Defense counsel also has a right to obtain such evidence, including witness lists, copies of forensic laboratory reports and to request that the court appoint a forensic expert to assist in reviewing any forensic evidence and possibly to testify. In some cases, the defense may seek to retest the evidence if it is possible to do so.

The courts and the media have paid the most attention to the question of whether a laboratory analyst must testify in order to introduce laboratory results as evidence. Despite three attempts by the Supreme Court to define a clear rule, the relevant case law is currently in shambles. Most courts require some analyst to testify, but it need not be the person who actually tested the evidence. Other procedures allow defense attorneys to waive the right to cross-examine the analyst, meaning that many convictions rest on laboratory reports admitted with no analyst testimony at all.

On the other hand, prosecutors may feel compelled to call one or more analysts to testify out of a concern that jurors expect flashy forensic presentations of the type seen on television shows like *CSI: Crime Scene Investigation* and its variants. While empirical studies do not provide proof of an actual "CSI effect" that television shows have had on juries, there is clear evidence that prosecutors *believe* the shows have affected expectations. Thus, they call several analysts to testify in a single case. They may even seek testimony when the test results do not yield any evidence at all, such as calling a fingerprint expert to testify to the lack of fingerprints found on a weapon, which is sometimes called "negative evidence." They might do this simply to confirm the thoroughness of the forensic investigation.

At the end of the day, it is unclear whether analyst testimony accompanying laboratory reports is helpful at all. Cross-examining the laboratory analyst is neither an effective nor a practical safeguard against wrongful convictions. However, the judicial system can and should put other safeguards into place that will go a long way to protect the innocent from being convicted based on a faulty laboratory report. This chapter discusses three such measures: requiring that laboratories prepare clear and comprehensive reports, that those reports be made available to defense counsel, and that courts provide forensic experts to assist the defense.

Ipse Dixit Guilt

Imagine that an informant tells the police that a guy is selling drugs in a parking lot. The police send the informant to the location with money to purchase drugs, and they keep surveillance from a distance. The suspect is observed selling a white powder to the informant, representing it to be cocaine, so the police arrest the suspect and charge him with possession of a controlled substance. In a drug prosecution, the critical elements the government would have to prove at trial are (1) that the defendant possessed a substance alleged to be a controlled substance; and (2) that the substance in fact proved to be a controlled substance. Laboratory test results—documented in a laboratory report and bench notes—would establish the second critical element. For years, the law in most jurisdictions allowed prosecutors to prove critical elements of this type by means of entering a laboratory report on paper into evidence. The analyst's report could prove the defendant's guilt "*ipse dixit*" (literally meaning, "he himself says it") based on the mere fact that the laboratory report said it was true. In 2009, the laws in forty-five states allowed the admission of laboratory reports without the need for the analyst to testify.[2] Then, in 2009, the Supreme Court struck down this practice as unconstitutional, requiring an analyst to give sworn testimony about the testing procedures and the results. Instead of simply introducing the laboratory report into evidence and reading the results to the jury, the prosecutor from that point on, in all fifty states, was required to call an analyst.

The Court did not, however, answer a critical, related question. Must the prosecutor call the analyst who *actually performed* the important parts of the testing process? The Supreme Court's subsequent decisions on this point in two other related cases since 2009 have so confused the lower courts that practices now vary greatly. In many jurisdictions, for examples, prosecutors offer paper laboratory reports accompanied by the personal testimony of analysts who played a secondary role in the testing process or who conducted routine but not critical portions of the tests. They even call analysts who played no part in the testing at all but who testify as experts, basing their opinions on their reading of the laboratory reports. The principal analysts who performed the actual work of processing the evidence need not testify.

Prosecutors also offer other affidavits—without any supporting testimony—to establish that the controlled substances were kept in safekeeping (the "chain of custody") from the time the police seized them until the time of trial. Affidavits are also used to establish the reliability of the laboratory equipment and procedures for testing. Thus, many of the important activities conducted by crime laboratories that contribute to the ultimate laboratory results are regularly communicated to the jury without any live testimony at all, a condition that most defense attorneys consider as undermining the defendant's right to face his or her accusers in person.

Moreover, in the vast majority of cases, when an analyst produces a report that proves an inculpatory fact, defense lawyers will usually advise their clients to consider pleading guilty, enabling the attorney to bargain a guilty plea against a reduced sentence. The definitive nature of forensic science puts pressure on defendants to plead guilty to avoid the higher sentences meted out upon conviction at trial. All of these situations bring home the same basic point: When a laboratory analyst concludes that a substance tests positive for a controlled substance or that the DNA found at a crime scene matches that of a known person's DNA profile, it is *imperative* that the results be correct.

In short, the reliability of the work done by analysts—how they handle the evidence, how they calibrate the equipment , the knowledge they bring to bear on the process, how accurately and clearly they document their findings, etc.— is absolutely critical. The criminal justice system convicts people on the strength of these laboratory results. Sometimes they are convicted after trial and sometimes by their own guilty plea. Either way, the judicial system, practically speaking, provides few meaningful opportunities to check the accuracy of an analyst's work. The system counts on it being right, without always offering an effective means for challenging the results in court.

Trial by Lab Report

One can understand the desire to expedite cases and get convictions without the time-consuming and sometimes complicated process of lengthening trials by requiring testimony from several laboratory analysts, at least in some types of cases. For example, it is standard practice at trials for prosecutors to call the arresting officer as a witness during cases involving drug possession or drunk driving. As a witness, the police officer explains to the jury the circumstances surrounding the arrest, his or her own role in effecting the arrest, and the evidence upon which the arrest was made. Until 2009, prosecutors would typically also offer the crime laboratory report into evidence, the judge would admit it, and the prosecutor would read the results to the jury: "The substance tested positive for cocaine and weighed two grams." Given a clear chain of custody, which would also be part of the prosecution's information to the jury, nothing more would be needed to establish this critical element of the offense beyond a reasonable doubt. Jurors would have no obvious reason to doubt either the size of the sample nor that the substance consisted of cocaine. In other words, the validity of the laboratory report would be accepted without challenge. The circumstances of the arrest are usually such that most people would assume that the defendants were, in fact, guilty. A defendant who agrees to sell drugs to a person and who is charging the street value for cocaine at that period most likely does, in fact, possess a controlled substance which is being offered for illegal sale. The same would be true in drunk driving cases. A driver who is swerving back and forth across a highway lane late at night, speaks with slurred enunciation, fumbles to find driver's license and registration, looks at the officer with bloodshot eyes, and breathes alcoholic fumes is, most likely, intoxicated. The result of a breathalyzer, which establishes a person's blood alcohol concentration, confirms the arresting officer's testimony. The defendant's intoxication is a foregone conclusion, so jurors have no trouble accepting the laboratory's findings as reported by the prosecutors.

Then between 2009 and 2012, the Supreme Court decided a trilogy of cases addressing the admissibility of crime laboratory reports, correctly recognizing the Constitutional issue but unfortunately leaving the situation lacking a clear ruling.[3]

Supreme Indecision

The first U.S. Supreme Court ruling on whether a crime laboratory report could be used in lieu of the analyst's personal testimony was *Melendez-Diaz v. Massachusetts*, which reached the Supreme Court in 2009. Boston police officers received a tip that a K-Mart employee, Thomas Wright, was acting suspiciously. The informant told police that Wright would receive calls at work after which he would go outside and enter a blue sedan before returning to work. The police officers stopped Wright and searched him, finding four clear plastic bags containing a white powder resembling cocaine. Other officers on the scene arrested Luis Melendez-Diaz and another man in the blue sedan. They put all three men in the police car to transport them to the police station. On route to the station, the officers noticed the men fidgeting and making furtive movements, so after dropping off the men at the station, they searched the police car, finding nineteen small bags containing white powder suspected to be cocaine.[4]

The three men were prosecuted separately, and the Supreme Court's decision pertains only to Melendez-Diaz. Here's how the Court described what happened at his trial:

> At trial, the prosecution placed into evidence the bags seized from Wright and from the police cruiser. It also submitted three "certificates of analysis" showing the results of the forensic analysis performed on the seized substances. The certificates reported the weight of the seized bags and stated that the bags "[h]a[ve] been examined with the following results: The substance was found to contain: Cocaine."[5]

With such strong circumstantial evidence that the bags of powder contained a controlled substance, it is no surprise that the prosecutor could proceed confidently on the basis of laboratory reports to prove the critical element of the crime: possession of a controlled substance. The prosecutor had to prove this element beyond a reasonable doubt, and the only person who could verify the content of the bags was the drug chemist who analyzed the drugs. This analyst did not testify, however, and Melendez-Diaz was convicted on the basis of a piece of paper—a laboratory report. There was nothing strange about this procedure, either in Massachusetts or in forty-four other states. Proving critical facts like these as the basis of determining guilt or innocence with laboratory reports rather than with live witnesses was just business as usual.

Melendez-Diaz argued that he had a constitutional right to cross-examine the drug chemist under the Sixth Amendment which states that "[i]n all criminal prosecutions, the accused shall enjoy the right ... to be confronted with the witnesses against him."[6] On this basis, Melendez-Diaz's appeal went to the Massachusetts Supreme Court, and ultimately to the U.S. Supreme Court. The Court agreed to hear the appeal based on the Sixth Amendment issue. It agreed that the certified laboratory reports, called "certificates of analysis" in the *Melendez-Diaz* case, were the type of "formalized testimonial materials" that "are functionally identical to live, in-court testimony, doing 'precisely what a witness does on direct examination.'"[7] This category of evidence—statements that are "testimonial"—define the limit of the Confrontation Clause as the Court interprets it. If statements are "testimonial," the Clause applies; if not, then there is no problem with using these statements even without live testimony.

In *Melendez-Diaz*, the Court found that, not only were the certificates substituting for critical witness testimony, but also, as its ruling explained, "[U]nder Massachusetts law the *sole purpose* of the affidavits was to provide 'prima facie evidence of the composition, quality, and the net weight' of the analyzed substance."[8] Thus, the prosecution was using the certificates of analysis in lieu of presenting the analyst's testimony against the defendant, a practice that the Court said violated the defendant's rights under the Confrontation Clause.

The State of Massachusetts probably did not realize that the National Academy of Sciences, which had been conducting an extensive study of forensic science since 2006, authorized and funded by Congress, would issue a prepublication copy of its lengthy and detailed report in February 2009, just before the Court's ruling in June that same year. Massachusetts, represented by the state's attorney general, argued that laboratory reports should not be subject to Confrontation Clause restrictions. Its argument was that ordinary witness statements can be "prone to distortion or manipulation," while laboratory reports are objective—merely communicating the "resul[t] of neutral, scientific testing."[9] The Court responded to this argument by noting that the close connection between law enforcement and crime laboratories raises questions about the reliability of forensic evidence produced in crime laboratories. It specifically cited the NAS Report in its rejoinder:

> Nor is it evident that what respondent calls "neutral scientific testing" is as neutral or as reliable as respondent suggests. Forensic evidence is not uniquely immune from the risk of manipulation. According to a recent study conducted under the auspices of the National Academy of Sciences, "[t]he majority of [laboratories producing forensic evidence] are administered by law enforcement agencies, such as police departments, where the laboratory administrator reports to the head of the agency." And "[b]ecause forensic scientists often are driven in their work by a need to answer a particular question related to the issues of a particular case, they sometimes face pressure to sacrifice appropriate methodology for the sake of expediency." A forensic analyst responding to a request from a law enforcement official may feel pressure—or have an incentive—to alter the evidence in a manner favorable to the prosecution.[10]

In light of the revelations in the NAS Report regarding the problematic association of forensic laboratories and police departments, the Supreme Court seemed firm in its decision to require that the analyst who produced the laboratory results in question testify at criminal trials.

The next case that the U.S. Supreme Court heard that dealt with laboratory reports came up in June 2011. Donald Bullcoming in New Mexico, driving a car, rear-ended a pick-up truck, whose driver noticed that Bullcoming had blood-shot eyes and that his breath smelled of alcohol. When the pick-up driver asked his wife, who was a passenger, to call the police, Bullcoming fled the scene. He was soon stopped by a police officer who administered a field sobriety test, which Bullcoming failed.[11] When he refused to take a field breath test, the police officers took him into custody and obtained a warrant to draw a blood sample and have it tested for alcohol to determine Bullcoming's blood alcohol content (BAC). The blood was drawn by a nurse at a local hospital, and then sent for testing at the New Mexico Department of Health, Scientific Laboratory Division (SLD). The SLD analyst, Curtis Caylor, tested the blood, detailing the procedures he followed and the results he found in a laboratory report.

The Supreme Court outlined the results of Caylor's analysis:

> Caylor recorded that the BAC in Bullcoming's sample was 0.21 grams per hundred milliliters, an inordinately high level. Caylor also affirmed that "[t]he seal of th[e] sample was received intact and broken in the laboratory," that "the statements in [the analyst's block of the report] are correct," and that he had "followed the procedures set out on the reverse of th[e] report." Those "procedures" instructed analysts, *inter alia* , to "re-tai[n] the sample container and the raw data from the analysis," and to "not[e] any circumstance or condition which might affect the integrity of the sample or otherwise affect the validity of the analysis."[12]

The laboratory report even included the statement of a "reviewer" who certified that Caylor was qualified to perform the testing and that he had followed the correct procedures. Thus, the report actually included the statements of two separate laboratory analysts. Since Bullcoming had not taken a breath test, the laboratory blood tests provided the critical evidence to establish his level of intoxication.

At trial, the prosecution disclosed to the defense a startling fact: Caylor had recently been put on unpaid leave, so the state would not offer his testimony at trial.[13] (Exactly why, and for how long, Caylor is removed from his position is never made public.) Instead of calling Caylor to testify, the prosecutor informed the defense that he would, with the judge's permission, admit Caylor's report under an evidence rule that allows the business records of organizations to be admitted despite the fact that they are technically hearsay. The prosecutor would also offer the testimony of another SLD analyst, Gerasimos Razatos, who had neither tested nor reviewed Caylor's work. Razatos's testimony established that the report was a business record of the laboratory, and she testified generally to the procedures used in the laboratory to test blood for alcohol content.[14] In effect, the prosecutor offered the laboratory report without any first-hand testimony regarding the testing process. The government used the certificate of analysis as evidence that his blood alcohol content was 0.21 grams per hundred milliliters and thus convicted him of aggravated driving while intoxicated,[15] a misdemeanor that carried a penalty of no less than 48 consecutive hours in jail.

Bullcoming appealed to the New Mexico Court of Appeals, as well as the New Mexico Supreme Court, both of which rejected his Confrontation Clause argument.[16] While the case was pending before the state high court, however, the U.S. Supreme Court decided *Melendez-Diaz*. Thus, the New Mexico Supreme Court, applying the reasoning of *Melendez-Diaz*, rejected the prosecutor's "business records" argument as a clear violation of the rule announced in *Melendez-Diaz*. The laboratory report constituted "testimonial" evidence, the New Mexico court held. Nonetheless, the court approved the use of Razatos's testimony as a proper "surrogate witness," thus finding no Confrontation Clause violation.

The Supreme Court agreed to hear Bullcoming's case to determine whether this use of a surrogate witness violated the Court's recent Confrontation Court ruling in *Melendez-Diaz*. The Court, like the New Mexico high court, classed the laboratory report here as "testimonial," applying the same reasoning it had in *Melendez-Diaz*. As such, the court concluded that Bullcoming had been improperly convicted because using the laboratory report—without giving him the opportunity to cross-examine the preparer of the report—denied him the right to confront the witness giving a "testimonial " statement.[17] Offering the testimony of a surrogate witness who played no role in preparing the report was insufficient.[18] Writing for the majority, Justice Ginsburg also made significant observations regarding the importance of having the relevant analyst available to testify, a condition that Razatos did not meet. Justice Ginsburg's opinion notes:

> Significant here, Razatos [the surrogate witness] had no knowledge of the reason why Caylor had been placed on unpaid leave. With Caylor on the stand, Bullcoming's counsel could have asked questions designed to reveal whether incompetence, evasiveness, or dishonesty accounted for Caylor's removal from his work station. Notable in this regard, the State [prosecutor] never asserted that Caylor was "unavailable" [to testify as a witness]; the prosecutor conveyed only that Caylor was on uncompensated leave.[19]

In other words, the prosecutor may have been able to subpoena Caylor to testify as a witness; there was no evidence that he was unable to appear in court.

The prosecutor did not state a reason why he might not appear such as being dead, extremely ill, or having disappeared or moved to another country. He was simply put on administrative leave, typically indicative of a problem with an employee that prevents the employee from continuing to work pending the outcome of an investigation into the alleged problem. When the employee is a laboratory analyst it suggests that the problem might relate to the quality of the analyst's work or the analyst's ethics, both of which are critical witness credibility issues that defense counsel should have the opportunity to explore on cross-examination. Instead of requiring Caylor's presence as a witness or explaining his unavailability, the prosecutor instead decided simply not to call Caylor as a witness—also raising suspicions.

The prosecution had not given defense counsel adequate notice before trial that Caylor would not be called as a witness, leading counsel to complain that " 'had [she] known that the analyst [who tested Bullcoming's blood] was not available,' her opening, indeed, her entire defense 'may very well have been dramatically different.' "[20] Defense counsel objected to the use of the Caylor's findings, arguing that it violated Bullcoming's Sixth Amendment right to confront the witnesses against him. While a defense attorney may be free to subpoena a witness like Caylor, the Confrontation Clause entitles a defendant to cross-examine every witness that gives testimony against him, and the Constitution also places the entire burden to produce evidence proving a criminal charge on the prosecution. Thus, Bullcoming had no duty to subpoena Caylor himself.

Justice Sotomayor concurred in the decision but betrayed a concern about boxing prosecutors into a requirement to bring the analysts to court in all cases. She takes great pains to "highlight some of the factual circumstances" not addressed in either *Melendez-Diaz* or in *Bullcoming*. She highlights four possible theories under which laboratory reports might be admitted without the accompanying testimony of the analyst who conducted the testing. This is not to say that the reliance on these theories would be constitutional, but only that they fall outside of the practices thus far determined to be unconstitutional. Since constitutional rules develop on a case-by-case basis as the Supreme Court decides new issues presented, the constitutionality of the theories she outlines had simply not yet been decided. In providing the list, her opinion effectively gave prosecutors a set of options for admitting laboratory reports without testimony by the analyst who tested the physical evidence. The four rationales she suggests are:

(1) If the report was not written with the primary purpose of producing evidence, then it is not a substitute for testimony, so the Confrontation Clause does not apply.

(2) If the prosecutor called a supervisor or reviewer to testify instead of the analyst who did the work, unlike the analyst who testified in *Bullcoming* who had a "total lack of connection to the test at issue."

(3) If the prosecutor called an analyst with no connection to the testing as an "expert witness" and the expert offered "an independent opinion" based on the report—but without offering the report itself in evidence.

(4) Reports that contain "only machine-generated results" are not testimonial statements of an analyst, so the Confrontation Clause does not apply.[21]

As subsequent cases would show, prosecutors quickly shifted their argument in offering surrogate witnesses or no witnesses in conjunction with laboratory report results, and now they relied on the rationales Justice Sotomayor had mentioned.

The next year, 2010, the Supreme Court took up the case of *Williams v. Illinois,* a case that hinged on the third rationale outlined in Justice Sotomayor's concurring opinion in *Bullcoming:* offering the testimony of a crime laboratory analyst who did not perform important parts of the forensic analysis but who provided an "expert opinion" based on the results of a laboratory report the expert had reviewed. Unfortunately, the Court was so divided that the decision fails to provide clear guidance to the lower courts.

In the *Williams* case, Sandy Williams had been convicted of raping a 22-year-old woman (known only as "L.J." within the court system) in Chicago, Illinois. As the Illinois Supreme Court summarized:

> L.J. worked until 8 p.m. as a cashier at a clothing store in Chicago. On her way home to the south side of the city, she purchased items at the store for her mother and went toward her home. As she passed an alley, the defendant came up behind her and forced her to sit in the backseat of a beige station wagon, where he told her to take her clothes off. The defendant then vaginally penetrated L.J. The defendant also contacted L.J.'s anus with his penis, but did not penetrate. He then pushed L.J. out of the car while keeping L.J.'s coat, money, and other items. After L.J. ran home, her mother opened the door and saw her in tears, partially clothed with only one pant leg on. After L.J. went into the bathroom, her mother called the police.[22]

Crucial to the prosecution was the DNA testing involved. More than one laboratory and many analysts had been involved in testing the DNA evidence that investigators collected with vaginal swabs that became part of the rape kit in L.J.'s case.[23] The police sent the swabs to the Illinois State Police laboratory for testing and analysis. The first ISP analyst, forensic biologist Brian Hapack had run tests confirming the presence of semen on the swabs taken from the victim. The analyst then sent this vaginal swab to a private laboratory, Cellmark Diagnostics Laboratory, in Germantown, Maryland. The state crime laboratory had outsourced some of its DNA work to private laboratories like Cellmark, in an effort to keep its backlog of sexual assault evidence under control.

Cellmark produced a male DNA profile, sending the swab and the profile back to the ISP.[24] The ISP entered this profile into the DNA database, checking for a possible match to a known subject. This process identified Sandy Williams, who had become part of the database in 2000 when he was arrested on an unrelated charge. Another ISP analyst had developed Williams's DNA profile in 2000 when he had previously been arrested.

When it came time to go to trial, the prosecutor called as witnesses three ISP analysts to testify regarding their roles in the testing process, but not the Cellmark analyst. The first witness testified to collecting the evidence for the rape kit. The second witness testified about developing Williams' DNA profile for the database in 2000. The third analyst, Sandra Lambatos, testified as an "expert witness," explaining to the jury the process of sending evidence to Cellmark for testing and receiving the DNA profile in return. She gives the critical piece of testimony: her expert opinion that the DNA profile developed for Williams in 2000 matches the DNA profile derived from the semen found in LJ.'s rape kit. Under the rules of evidence, experts have wide latitude to testify in the form of opinion and may base their opinions on any information that other experts in the field may reasonably rely on. Here, Lambatos relied on the laboratory report prepared by the analyst at Cellmark who had created the DNA profile from the semen specimen provided by the swab. Thus, she gave her "opinion" that the defendant's DNA profile matched the DNA collected from the rape victim and processed by Cellmark.

In a case like *Williams*, the state might have possessed sufficient physical evidence to retest the DNA—re-doing the work done by Cellmark—so as to offer the testimony of an ISP analyst who had performed the work. Doing so would have completely eliminated any Confrontation Clause concern. Or the state might have brought the Cellmark analyst to testify. But instead the state chose to go to trial without the testimony of any analyst who had been directly involved in the critical work of developing a DNA sample from the evidence obtained from L.J.

The U.S. Supreme Court justices voted 5–4 to affirm the defendant's conviction, but for different reasons. The case produced four opinions, none of which got the five votes needed for a majority. In an opinion written by Justice Alito, four justices agreed with the state's theory that an expert (i.e., Lambatos from the ISP) could rely on a laboratory report (i.e., from Cellmark) that she had played no role in producing and that such reliance did not give the defendant a right to confront the Cellmark analyst.[25] Justice Alito's opinion also sketches out an alternate theory: that Cellmark's report was not testimonial and thus involved no Confrontation Clause issue because it was not written "for the primary purpose of accusing a targeted individual."[26]

Justice Thomas agreed to uphold the conviction, finding that the Confrontation Clause did not apply to Cellmark's report. He also agreed that, unlike the laboratory reports in *Melendez-Diaz* and *Bullcoming*, Cellmark's laboratory report was not "formalized testimonial material" because it was "neither a sworn nor a certified document."[27] By this reasoning, as long as the laboratory analyst does not "formalize" the report by notarizing it or in any way certifying its reliability, then the document is not a substitute for testimony. Thus, the report can be freely admitted without any supporting testimony to prove the truth of its contents. Since he considers an informal laboratory report not to be "testimonial" evidence, a defendant would not have a right to confront a witness in that case since the report would not constitute a substitute for testimony. Thus, under Justice Thomas's reasoning, offering an informal laboratory report without analyst testimony does not violate the Confrontation Clause whereas a certified, "formal" report would.

Justice Breyer also concurred in the outcome but argued for an exception for laboratory reports for two reasons. First, as the DNA testing in the *Williams* case showed, multiple analysts may participate in the process of extracting, testing, and analyzing DNA evidence. He includes an appendix illustrating the fact that up to twelve analysts may play a role in processing DNA evidence and determining a match to a known DNA profile (of a suspect or of a person identified in a DNA database). Justice Breyer questioned the limits of a rule requiring all participating analysts to testify: If up to twelve people played a role in testing DNA evidence, did the government have the responsibility of calling all twelve to testify? Justice Breyer believed that this important issue had not been adequately considered by the Court in deciding *Williams*. More fundamentally, he rejects the premise of *Melendez-Diaz* and considers laboratory reports not to be "testimonial" when produced by professional laboratory analysts working in accredited laboratories such as Cellmark Diagnostics. He does not view these reports as the type of accusatory statements to which the Confrontation Clause was directed.[28]

These opinions represented a shaky majority that agreed to uphold the conviction—but all for different reasons. In a dissenting opinion authored by Justice Kagan and joined by three other Justices, she rejected the state's portrayal of Lambatos's role as anything other than a surrogate witness for the missing Cellmark analyst whose statements were, in fact, being introduced through Lambatos's testimony.[29] In the end, the *Williams* ruling created no clear guidance but suggests several possible approaches to admitting laboratory results without calling the analyst who performed the testing.

At first glance, one can understand the urge to dispense with calling analysts in routine drug cases or DWI prosecutions. Taking analysts away from the laboratory to testify in court means that they will do less laboratory work which creates a greater need to hire more analysts. In a case like *Williams* where the missing analyst worked for a private laboratory in another state, the state prosecutor's office may not be able to afford the analyst's fee and travel expenses to appear in court. Budgetary pressures almost certainly must be factored into a prosecutor's decision.

However, Justice Ginsburg (writing for herself and three other Justices) in the previous case of *Bullcoming* rejected financial considerations as a compelling concern that the Court should take into account. First, she noted correctly that only a "'small fraction'" of criminal cases actually go to trial and that not all of them involve forensic evidence. Of cases that go to trial, some defendants will stipulate to the findings of the laboratory report rather than have a live witness to highlight the forensic evidence. Thus, the number of instances in which analysts will be needed to testify is extremely small. She also notes that the practice in many laboratories is to retest evidence whenever an analyst involved in testing is unavailable to attend a trial.[30] If a jurisdiction could not afford to bring in an analyst from a private laboratory, the other option would be to have a local analyst (here presumably in the ISP) retest the evidence and testify.

Justice Ginsburg is surely correct in her view that—in the few cases that actually go to trial (as opposed to being resolved through guilty pleas)—either defendants will waive their right to cross-examine a laboratory analyst *or* the prosecutor will prefer to call the analyst in order to fully inform the jury about the forensic testing. Either way, the Confrontation Clause requirement requiring a right to cross-examine a laboratory analyst should not be overly burdensome for the prosecutor.

Ultimately, however, *Williams* yielded neither a new principle nor a clarification of the *Melendez-Diaz* and *Bullcoming* cases. The lower courts, including the lower federal courts, have faced the challenge of interpreting *Williams* in order to apply it in subsequent cases. The federal Second Circuit Court of Appeals states the pre-*Williams* rule: "[A] laboratory analysis is testimonial if the circumstances under which the analysis was prepared, viewed objectively, establish that the primary purpose of a reasonable analyst in the declarant's position would have been to create a record for use at a later criminal trial." [31] What, if anything, did *Williams* add? The Second Circuit takes the view that the decision added nothing, explaining:

> The question then becomes whether the Court's later decision in Williams changed that rule. We agree with Justice Kagan that this problem is intractable. No single rationale disposing of the Williams case enjoys the support of a majority of the Justices. Ordinarily, "[w]hen a fragmented Court decides a case and no single rationale explaining the result enjoys the assent of five Justices, the holding of the Court may be viewed as the position taken by those members who concurred in the judgments on the narrowest grounds." But what is the narrowest ground in the disposition in Williams?
>
> The Williams plurality's first rationale—that the laboratory report there was offered as [the] basis [of an expert's opinion] ... and not for [the report's] truth—was roundly rejected by five Justices.... Nor do we think we can apply the plurality's narrowed definition of testimonial, which would require that the analyst had "the primary purpose of accusing a targeted individual of engaging in criminal conduct[.]" Again, five Justices disagreed with this rationale, and it would appear to conflict directly with Melendez–Diaz, which rejected a related argument. For similar reasons—lack of support among the Justices and conflict with prior precedents that did command majority support—we do not think either Justice Thomas's concurrence on the ground that the analysis was not sufficiently "formalized," or Justice Breyer's new approach to application of the Confrontation Clause, is controlling.
>
> Williams does not, as far as we can determine ... yield a single, useful holding relevant to the case before us. It is therefore for our purposes confined to the particular set of facts presented in that case. We think it sufficient to conclude that we must rely on Supreme Court precedent before Williams to the effect that a statement triggers the protections of the Confrontation Clause when it is made with the primary purpose of creating a record for use at a later criminal trial.[32]

In contrast to the Second Circuit's approach of essentially finding *Williams* to be so much pointless verbiage, the Fourth Circuit takes the surprising and counter-intuitive approach of upholding a conviction based on the assessment that the Supreme Court would cobble together the same five-vote majority as in *Williams* upholding the conviction, even if those votes would not agree on the rationale.[33] In short, the case law now gives little guidance on whether the

Confrontation Clause requires the in-person testimony of the analysts who process the evidence in crime laboratories.

To summarize the current situation, the Confrontation Clause gives every person accused of a crime the Constitutional right to "confront" the witnesses against him or her by means of observing their sworn testimony in person and cross-examining them. The *Melendez-Diaz* case seemed to be a clear ruling that the Supreme Court would prohibit *ipse dixit* prosecutions and require the laboratory analyst who personally performed the tests to testify. The *Bullcoming* ruling agreed, and rejected the attempt to offer a surrogate witness rather than the one who performed the forensic tests. These cases nonetheless left open many possible avenues for avoiding the prohibitions they establish. The Court's decision in the *Williams* case addressed one of those open questions, but it produced no clear rule, instead raising doubt about how strictly the rulings in *Melendez-Diaz* and *Bullcoming* should be applied.

The next sections summarize the lower court decisions applying the Supreme Court's Confrontation Clause decisions. The case law reveals the different ways in which prosecutors continue to obtain convictions by means of laboratory reports without offering the testimony of the analyst who tested the evidence.

Ipse Dixit Convictions Keep Coming

After the Supreme Court's confusing decision in *Williams*, a few lower courts have found Confrontation Clause violations when prosecutors have called as a witness an analyst with no connection to the testing but who "recites" the findings in the reports generated by other analysts—a situation similar to *Bullcoming*.[34] The vast majority of the cases, however, permit surrogate witnesses to testify or laboratory reports to be admitted without testimony under one of several rationales. Without attempting to provide a complete doctrinal analysis of this complicated area of law, the following six sections illustrate the different ways in which it is still possible in some jurisdictions to obtain convictions that rest heavily on the laboratory work performed by analysts who are not then called as witnesses at trial: (1) if the primary purpose of the analysis was not accusatory; (2) when the report is not "formalized"; (3) when the laboratory report is machine-generated; (4) when a different analyst testifies about the results as part of an "expert opinion"; (5) an analyst performs a review of the testing analyst's work; and/or (6) when the defense waives a Confrontation Clause challenge.

Laboratory Reports Are Not Testimonial
When Primary Purpose Was Not Accusatory

In this first situation, the *Melendez-Diaz* ruling found that laboratory reports documenting the testing of evidence were "testimonial" because they substituted for the in-person testimony of the analyst-witness. In *Williams*, however, the plurality opinion stated that a laboratory test conducted during the investigative stage of a criminal investigation was not testimonial because it did not have the "primary purpose of accusing a targeted individual."[35] Under this narrower reading of "testimonial," although an analyst might reasonably foresee that the test results would later be used at trial, the report would not be testimonial since its use at trial was not the analyst's motivation at the time the tests were conducted. This rationale has been applied by some courts following *Williams*.[36]

Courts have also allowed prosecutors to introduce laboratory records (not supplemented by a witness's testimony) to prove such facts as the proper calibration of laboratory equipment and that the analytical procedures conform to "best practices."[37] This evidence helps to establish the reliability of the laboratory testing done in the case, which is part of the necessary foundation for the admissibility of scientific evidence. Courts have found it unnecessary to require an analyst to testify to these facts because they are part of the laboratory's ordinary business and not done specifically to create testimony for a particular case.

Laboratory reports generally also include sworn statements to establish the chain of custody, meaning that evidence has been properly handled from the time it was seized until the time it was brought into court for trial. Establishing the chain of custody involves tracing the whereabouts of the item from the time it was taken into police custody until the time it appears in court to determine which persons have had possession of it and how it was handled and stored. This must be shown prior to admitting an item of evidence to assure that no one has tampered with the item of evidence in question. Thus, it is normally necessary to call as witnesses all of the persons who have handled the evidence to testify under oath to the actions they have taken in handling the evidence. For evidence like drugs, chain of custody is crucial. Too many crime laboratories have had drug chemists who engaged in "dry-labbing" and who have stolen drugs.[38] Yet courts have allowed prosecutors to prove the chain of custody by means of an affidavit, with no inquiry into the credibility and credentials of the drug chemist or others who may have handled the evidence.[39]

Laboratory Reports Analyzing Evidence Are Non-Testimonial Because They Are Not "Formalized"

As the second example growing out of the *Williams* case, a Maryland Court of Appeals applied Justice Thomas's approach to find that the admission of a laboratory report was not "testimonial" because "[n]owhere on either page of the report … is there an indication that the results are sworn to or certified or that any person attests to the accuracy of the results."[40] While purporting to be consistent with *Melendez-Diaz* and *Bullcoming*, both of which involved certified documents, it is clear that these cases did not rest on that theory, and the theory garnered only one vote—Justice Thomas's—in *Williams*.

The California Supreme Court reached the same conclusion in applying Justice Thomas's "not formalized" argument.[41] It stated that it need not address the fact that the crime laboratory report's "primary purpose" was to create accusatory material against a targeted individual (reflecting a majority view on the Court) because the report had not been formalized.[42] Thus, lower courts' reliance on this rationale represents a departure from *Melendez-Diaz* and *Bullcoming*.

Laboratory Report Not Testimonial Because Machine-Generated

The third approach—that a laboratory report is not testimonial if it is "machine-generated"—is one of the approaches suggested in Justice Sotomayor's concurring opinion in *Bullcoming* as a possible rationale for admitting a laboratory record without the testimony of the person operating the machine.[43] Some courts both before and after the Supreme Court's crime laboratory trilogy have taken this approach.[44] For example, the California Supreme Court explains why machine-generated data involves no statement by a person:

> Turning first to the laboratory report's pages 2 through 6, they consist entirely of data generated by a gas chromatography machine to measure calibrations, quality control, and the concentration of alcohol in a blood sample.… Even though nontestifying analyst Peña's signature appears on the laboratory report's second page (the printout of the machine's calibrations) and the remaining pages bear the handwritten initials "JRP" (presumably Jorge Peña's initials), no statement by Peña, express or implied, appears on any of those pages.[45]

This reasoning ignores the fact that the reliability of the data depends in part on whether the analyst followed appropriate protocols in operating the machinery that produced the data. No data is "entirely" machine-generated; human involvement is required in at least one stage of the process. One critique finds that this rationale fails to give due respect to Confrontation Clause values as applied "in the modern, technological era in which guilt or innocence can turn on data generated by technicians in processes open to mistake and fabrication."[46]

A Different Analyst Testifies to the Results as the Basis of an Expert Opinion

A fourth direction suggested by the plurality in *Williams* is the argument that an uninvolved analyst could use another laboratory's results but arrive at her own independent "expert opinion" without running afoul of the Confrontation Clause. Five Justices actually believed that an analyst who did not test the evidence should be allowed to give an independent expert opinion *based on* the results found by the analyst who did the testing. This reasoning effectively allows the prosecution to use the testifying analyst to prove the results found by the analyst who did the testing, a practice ostensibly disallowed in *Bullcoming*.[47] The five did not muster a majority, however, because one of the five (Justice Thomas) believed the Confrontation Clause did not apply to the laboratory report for a different reason. So the Court was effectively split 4–4 on this issue.

Some lower courts nonetheless apparently read the *Williams* plurality opinion as permitting the practice, as if it had announced a new rule. In a Maine case, *State v. Mercier*, Jay Mercier faced murder charges. The state offered the expert testimony of the Chief Medical Examiner Dr. Margaret Greenwald. She had not conducted the autopsy or authored the autopsy report at issue, yet the trial court allowed her to give her expert opinion on the cause of the victim's death based on her reading of the autopsy report. The Maine Supreme Court approved the practice in a 2014 decision, stating:

> The Supreme Court [in *Williams*] held that the expert's testimony was admissible because she was not purporting to testify that the sample analyzed by the outside lab had in fact come from the victim, but was instead merely testifying that the DNA profile obtained from the lab matched that of the defendant. The Court reasoned that an expert witness may testify as to her own opinion and the facts on which that opinion is based "without testifying to the truth of those facts."[48]

A Washington Supreme Court decision came out the same way.[49]

A Missouri Court of Appeals reached this same conclusion, but this time emphasizing that the testifying analyst was making an "independent" assessment and not merely acting as a conduit for the other laboratory's results:

> Had [the analyst] Karr's testimony merely recited the findings presented in the laboratory report, we would have Confrontation Clause concerns as Karr would be testifying as to findings made by a technician who was not available to the accused for cross-examination. But such is not the case here. Instead, Karr's testimony was based on her personal knowledge of the DNA testing and results. Karr specifically testified that the conclusions she made regarding the DNA found in Galbreath's vehicle were independent of the findings of the technician who drafted the laboratory report, and of the report itself. As recently noted by the U.S. Supreme Court, the Confrontation Clause, as interpreted in [the landmark case called] *Crawford*, bars only testimonial statements by declarants who are not subject to cross-examination.[50]

The Supreme Court of New Hampshire also reached the same conclusion, giving additional guidance on what the courts mean by "independent" analysis.[51] The court defines an expert's opinion as "independent" if it does more than merely transmit the other analyst's conclusions. The testifying analyst must be shown to have applied her own "training and experience" in order for the opinion to be considered "independent."[52] Presumably it requires some "training and experience" to understand the meaning of the results contained in laboratory reports, whereas an untrained person could not speak intelligently about the laboratory report. It is not merely "reading the results" when another analyst reads the report and then gives her "expert opinion." It involves some "independent judgment."

For example, in this particular case, an apartment fire had killed four people in a building twenty-one years prior to David McLeod's arrest. Shortly after the fire, twenty-one years earlier, a witness named Sandra Walker made certain statements to fire investigators implicating defendant as having started the fire. The investigator wrote a report that included these statements, along with the results of his examination and testing of materials at the premises. A grand jury investigation did not result in an indictment of the defendant, so the government did not pursue charges against McLeod at that time. A Cold Case Unit re-examined the case twenty-one years later, sending the investigator's report to federal fire experts from the U.S. Bureau of Alcohol, Tobacco, and Firearms. Based on this re-examination of the case file, McLeod was indicted for murder by arson in the deaths of the four people who had died in the fire. By now the witness, Walker, had died. At trial, the court allowed the federal fire experts to give their opinions that McLeod had started the fire, explaining to the jury that their opinions were based, in part, on Walker's statements.[53] While Walker was not a forensic analyst who had done any testing, the case shows the extent to which courts will allow a non-testifying witness's prior statement to be communicated to the jury as undergirding the expert's opinion.

In a New Mexico case, an analyst read aloud the machine readings from a drug test run by a different analyst, and the testifying analyst then explained them. This was deemed acceptable. The court wrote:

> *Williams, Bullcoming,* and *Melendez-Diaz* do not support the notion that a defendant has the right to confront a laboratory analyst who, having participated in some aspect of evidence analysis, nevertheless did not record any certifications, statements, or conclusions that were offered as evidence ... Here, as in *Williams,* no inculpating report of the testing process or conclusions of a non-testifying analyst were offered or admitted into evidence. In both cases, the testifying analyst assumed the accuracy of a result that was not in evidence, but testified only to his or her independent conclusion when determining whether the test result matched another test result.[54]

An Analyst who Performs a Review Suffices

In a fifth variation, drawing an exception to *Bullcoming,* a Pennsylvania prosecutor offered only the testimony of an analyst who had not tested the evidence but who had reviewed the raw data generated by a first analyst. The second analyst then analyzed the data (but without retesting it) and authored the laboratory report. The defendant objected to the fact that the government did not call the analyst who actually did the work of handling the evidence and testing it.[55] A Pennsylvania Superior Court found sufficient difference to distinguish *Bullcoming* from the present case:

> We concede that Dr. Blum is in a similar position as the testifying witness[] in *Bullcoming* that he did not personally handle the defendant's blood sample, prepare the aliquots, or physically place the aliquots in the testing apparatuses. However, unlike the testifying witness[] in *Bullcoming,* Dr. Blum did certify the results of the testing and author the report sought to be admitted as evidence against [the defendant]. We conclude [that] this distinction is dispositive of the issue presented.[56]

Other courts have arrived at the same conclusion in allowing a technical reviewer to testify in lieu of the testing analyst.[57] It is not clear, however, why it should be sufficient with regard to the Confrontation Clause to call an analyst who performs a review of the results generated by another analyst's testing, nor does the Pennsylvania court try to give a rationale. This case may differ from that in *Bullcoming*, but it may be just as much of a Confrontation Clause violation.

In a similar situation, a court of appeals in Michigan goes so far as to say that the analyst who ran DNA testing on the evidence was only a "chain of custody" witness, and not a witness who needed to testify to satisfy the Confrontation Clause:

> Good [the analyst who tested the DNA] primarily executed data collection on defendant's buccal swab sample and did not write the report, instead giving the information and data to Morgan, who made her own conclusions after comparing defendant's buccal sample to the DNA recovered from the button. Good did not formulate his own opinions or conclusions from the data; he simply extracted the data and ran it through the genetic analyzer to obtain a DNA profile. The fact that Good processed the evidence relates more to the chain of custody, which goes to the weight of the evidence and not its admissibility, and the Confrontation Clause does not require the prosecution to call as a witness "anyone whose testimony may be relevant in establishing the chain of custody." Comparing the respective responsibilities of Good and Morgan, the laboratory report in this case was not prepared by a nontestifying analyst. It was Morgan's analysis and report that linked defendant's DNA to the DNA found on a button at the crime scene, and she testified at trial and was amply cross-examined, affording defendant the right to "be confronted with the analyst[ ] at trial." Accordingly, the admission of the laboratory report and Morgan's testimony did not violate the Confrontation Clause.[58]

What these decisions allow a laboratory to do is to put a supervisor in charge of "reviewing" the work of the testing analysts and then "author the reports." Analysts who test evidence on a daily basis would never give testimony in court under this approach. Instead, a laboratory can assign a more highly credentialed and experienced supervisor to perform the "review" function, and only this person would ever testify in court. Whether such a review truly constitutes a separate independent analysis of the evidence depends on the type of forensic tests being run and whether the review consists of a close examination of the evidence specimens themselves. In one case involving firearms examination, the reviewer inspected the evidence under the microscope in conducting his review.[59] In most cases applying this approach, the review may consist of simply reading the findings of the tests in the analysts' bench notes or machine-generated printouts. The defense has no ability to cross-examine the person actually handling the evidence and the laboratory equipment, nor would the defense know whether the analyst who tested the evidence has the credentials, training, and experience to do reliable work. Rejecting this approach, the Supreme Court of Maryland found that the defendant is entitled under *Bullcoming* to cross-examine the testing analyst.[60]

Defense Attorneys May Waive Confrontation Clause Challenges

As a final situation, courts have often ruled that defense attorneys have waived valid Confrontation Clause rights either by failing to follow the requirements of state "notice and demand" statutes that set out certain requirements defendants must meet,[61] by failing to object at trial to certain testimony,[62] or by objecting on the wrong ground.[63] Sometimes defense attorneys simply make strategic decisions not to object when the government introduces a laboratory report without offering the testimony of the analyst who tested the evidence.[64] In the final analysis, it is still often true that laboratory reports will be used with no supporting testimony.

****

The Confrontation Clause cases prove one thing: Defendants often do not have the opportunity to cross-examine the analyst who conducts forensic testing in their cases. When analysts do testify, it is not clear that innocent defendants are better off for it. Too many wrongful convictions, including George Rodriguez's, involved faulty forensic testimony, and the opportunity to cross-examine those analysts did not make a difference. When crime laboratory analysts do testify, other pressures may operate to make their testimony problematic for other reasons as the next section highlights.

The Drive to Dazzle — the Real "CSI Effect"

Drunk driving and drug cases lend themselves more readily to *ipse dixit* convictions since the evidence is largely handled by machines using generally reliable scientific processes that do not involve a subjective comparison by the analyst. In contrast, different forms of forensic evidence may play a role in other types of serious cases such as homicides, sexual assaults, or robberies. Forensic disciplines such as such as firearms examination, latent print examination, and other types of trace evidence examination require examiners to conduct a subjective comparison of two specimens to make an assessment of whether the two derive from the same source. In these cases, the guilt of the defendant may not be obvious *except for* the forensic test that connects the defendant to the crime. In such a case, a prosecutor would want the analyst who did the testing to testify in court with the expectation that such testimony will persuade the jury of the defendant's guilt. If the prosecutor failed to call the analyst to testify, jurors might have cause to acquit. In these cases, prosecutors will not only want the analyst who conducted the testing to appear as a witness, but the witness may be expected to live up to the standards set by fictional characters on television shows like *CSI*.

Here is an amazing statistic: In 2005, six of the twenty most viewed prime-time television shows were forensic crime dramas: *CSI: Crime Scene Investigation; CSI: Miami; Without a Trace; NCIS; Cold Case;* and *CSI: NY*.[65] Not surprisingly, at about this same time, media attention to the so-called "CSI effect" reached its peak.[66] The CSI effect, as it turns out, means different things to different groups of people depending on their role. In their comprehensive review of the literature, Simon Cole and Rachel Dioso-Villa identify several different purported effects.[67] Initially, prosecutors tended to view television shows like *CSI: Crime Scene Investigation* as beneficial to the prosecution because it depicts prosecutors and forensic scientists favorably.[68] They appreciated that the show also seemed to help jurors understand forensic testimony more readily, an effect also touted by the show's producer.[69] Defense attorneys tend to agree with this characterization of the CSI effect but complain that it has a negative effect on the defense by unduly elevating the status of forensic scientists and giving the impression that their work is more accurate than it actually is.[70] Over time, however, prosecutors were increasingly likely to complain about the effects on jurors' expectations. Prosecutors came to worry about a perceived heightening of the burden of proof, meaning that jurors would not be as willing to convict without impressive forensic evidence.[71]

In its strongest version, the CSI effect refers to the belief expressed by some prosecutors that the shows have induced unrealistic juror expectations, resulting in wrongful acquittals.[72] As a result, prosecutors have tried to counter this perceived effect by "questioning jurors about the show during voir dire [ie., jury selection], explaining the absence of forensic evidence in opening and closing arguments, and calling on experts to explain why evidence was not found or why results may have been found inconclusive."[73] Some prosecutors also call forensic experts to explain the absence of forensic evidence—for example, if testing for fingerprints fails to produce any. Prosecutors present the testimony of these "negative evidence" witnesses out of concern that, without such an explanation of the lack of evidence, jurors will view the failure to introduce such a fingerprint as a sign that the investigation lacked thoroughness.

In their survey of the available empirical data, however, Cole and Dioso-Villa found no evidence that any of the various "CSI effects" actually exist,[74] a finding also made by other scholars.[75] They reviewed three large surveys, one of 53 prosecutors, public defenders, and private defense attorneys, a second survey of 102 prosecutors, and a third involving 290 prosecutors, defense attorneys, and trial judges. Another study they reviewed involved simulated jurors. The surveys of prosecutors and defense attorneys did not provide any useful evidence of actual effects on juror behavior.[76] The various studies of simulated jurors reviewed by Cole and Dioso-Villa, on the other hand, found no difference between viewers of the shows and non-viewers in terms of how they would judge a criminal trial.[77] At least from the data currently available, it appears that whatever effects the shows may have on their viewers, jurors continue to decide criminal cases in about the same way they did before the shows began.

While Cole and Dioso-Villa do not find any untoward effects on jurors from viewing the *CSI*-type shows, of keener interest is how *prosecutors* have responded to their own beliefs about jurors' unrealistic expectations. The National Academy of Sciences reports that some prosecutors now believe that the "conclusiveness and finality of the manner in which forensic evidence is presented on television" may exaggerate how much credence jurors give to real forensic experts.[78] It is reasonable to assume that prosecutors might seek to elicit testimony from crime laboratory analysts in terms that stress that the findings are "scientific," conclusive, and definitive. The TV shows have also persuaded some prosecutors that jurors now expect their presentations of forensic evidence to be more visually appealing with charts, PowerPoint presentations, and simulations.[79] As a consequence, the *real* CSI effect may be that it exerts new pressures on prosecutors to call as witnesses only those crime laboratory analysts who can put on a good show with visual depictions and conclusive statements of laboratory test results. Such cases would logically include serious cases like homicides involving such evidence as firearms and fingerprint evidence. When forensic scientists work for law enforcement, the risk that the analyst will attempt to cooperate by distorting the evidence only increases. As DNA exonerations and common sense suggest, distorted presentations of forensic science put innocent defendants at risk.

Interestingly, the concern over the CSI effect may wane in the years to come. Whereas six shows pertaining to forensic science ruled the Neilsen ratings in 2005, only one show, *NCIS*, ranked in the top ten during in 2013.[80] If the day should come when TV shows featuring forensic laboratory heroes no longer top the primetime charts, prosecutors may set aside their concerns about unrealistic juror expectations. In the meantime, policy-makers should consider measures to give laboratory analysts greater independence from law enforcement influence to protect against the possibility of pressures to exaggerate forensic findings.

The Risks of Wrongful Convictions

Laboratories can make mistakes, and some analysts may engage in fraudulent activity. The many crime laboratories that have experienced problems (see Chapter 2) provide evidence of this lamentable situation. The Rodriguez case exemplifies the way in which the justice system can go awry when a laboratory gets it wrong, but many other types of cases may be harder to uncover.

Prosecutors often rely on laboratory reports alone or use surrogate witnesses in drug cases, and these practices present an increased risk of wrongful convictions that will likely never come to light. *Melendez-Diaz* involved drug tests, and, like in many drug cases, the defendants seemed to be caught red-handed. The laboratory report's findings were considered a foregone conclusion given the circumstances in which the white powder was found. However, as unlikely as it may seem, in some cases the substances believed to be drugs turn out not to be drugs. For example, some drugs are pain-killers or drugs in liquid form that can be easily confused for a controlled substance by an arresting officer. The Texas high court recently granted the petition of a woman who had been convicted of attempting to obtain a controlled substance by prescription fraud. It later turned out that the drug she was attempting to obtain was Naproxen, which is an over-the-counter drug akin to aspirin, so the court overturned her conviction.[81]

The weight of the drugs is also of critical concern since the seriousness of the offense and the punishment ranges vary according to the amount of the substance in the accused's possession. If the laboratory finds a greater amount of the substance than he or she actually possessed, the defendant may indeed be guilty of a drug crime but still be incorrectly convicted of a higher level of offense and likely to receive stiffer punishment than is merited.

Too many drug analysts have been caught manipulating drug weights, stealing drugs, and engaging in fraudulent "dry-labbing" as documented in the notorious cases in crime laboratories of Boston, San Francisco, and the Texas Department of Public Safety.[82] One news report on a dry-labbing case noted that forensic laboratory reports often indicate what type of controlled substance the arresting officer believes the substance to be; as a result, this opinion can contribute to the occurrence of dry-labbing.[83]

Additionally, defendants may "voluntarily" choose to plead guilty (and hence to end up wrongly convicted) when their lawyers explain the options. Defense attorneys gauge the likelihood of acquittal when advising their clients about whether to accept a guilty plea offer. Once defense attorneys know that the laboratory test results implicate their clients, they know that those results will be virtually impossible to challenge—even if the test results are wrong. If they go to trial, the prosecutor will either use only the laboratory report or will produce an analyst to testify. Either way, defense attorneys are not usually able to effectively challenge the results unless the lawyer can obtain a sufficient amount of the evidence, and has the wherewithal, to have the evidence re-tested by a defense expert.

In most cases, the lawyer can be expected simply to advise the client to accept the prosecutor's guilty plea offer and obtain a reduced sentence. Over 90% of all criminal cases end in guilty pleas.[84] Sentences imposed upon conviction after a trial are typically longer than those imposed in response to a defendant's guilty plea. However, prosecutors have less incentive to offer a serious reduction in sentence when the forensic evidence seems to clinch the case, assuring a jury conviction. Thus, cases that involve forensic evidence reduce the risk that an innocent person will plead guilty because the sentencing discount offered is not likely to be great.

One study in 2014 of court records and interviews found that twenty-one innocent people in one state had pled guilty to drug charges *before* laboratory results had even been received.[85] Fourteen of those convictions had occurred in the previous two years alone. Also in 2014, the Public Defender's Office in Houston received over 300 such cases of premature guilty pleas in which people pled guilty to drug charges before laboratory testing occurred. Attorneys later learned that the substances were not controlled substances. In some cases, the defendants had been in jail for weeks or months after pleading guilty.[86] In these cases, the police had submitted the suspected drugs to crime laboratories for testing, but the results were not ready when the cases went to court. Tests can be delayed due to backlogs, but sometimes defendants are simply eager to plead guilty before laboratories can realistically be expected to complete testing. Many people arrested on drug charges remain in jail pending disposition of their cases because they are too poor to post the financial bond required by the court. Frequently, prosecutors offer to release them immediately if they plead guilty to the charges and accept a sentence of "time served." For individuals in this position, they often prefer immediate release to the prospect of remaining incarcerated pending the completion of laboratory testing. Some of these individuals may have attempted to sell drugs, knowing the substances were not drugs, so they would be guilty of attempted distribution of drugs. Others, however, may have been actually innocent or only guilty of a lesser crime based on the laboratory's calculation of the drug weight.

In another study by Brandon Garrett and Peter Neufeld of the first 232 DNA exonerations, three involved wrongful guilty pleas in which invalid forensic science played a part.[87] Remarkably, cases in which DNA evidence exonerates people almost always involve sexual assault or murder.[88] Those convicted of these crimes receive some of the most severe punishments in the entire criminal justice system.[89] Yet three innocent people chose to take the guilty plea deal offered by the prosecutor rather than exercising their constitutional right by demanding a jury trial, even when facing serious punishment.

Safeguards besides Cross-Examination

It may not be practical for the courts to require the analysts who perform the laboratory test in question to testify in person. Considering this issue, Justice Breyer went so far as to attach an appendix to one of his opinions with a chart showing how up to twelve analysts might take part in testing a DNA sample.[90] Most cases would not involve so many analysts, but good laboratory protocols should mean that more than one analyst has played a role in the testing, analysis, or verification of testing for a single item of evidence. From the perspective of providing the best possible evidence, we would want to encourage multiple analysts to work on a single item of evidence. Science should be a collective enterprise in which colleagues can observe and question each other. Best laboratory procedures involve having other analysts review each other's work and conduct verification testing. Having more analysts work on an item of evidence can enhance the reliability of the work and deter fraudulent activities. However, if all participating analysts were required to testify in all cases, scheduling difficulties would cause delays or increase the pressures for prosecutors to offer plea bargains to dispose of cases because witnesses are unavailable.

Even if we could get every analyst on the witness stand, cross-examination would probably fail to bring to light every testing error or act of fraud. The notorious perpetrators of forensic fraud described in Chapter 2 testified often and became adept at persuading juries to believe their lies.[91] Moreover, the judicial system — and possibly also the perceived effects of TV shows like *CSI* — pushes prosecutors and crime laboratory analysts into an adversarial posture that can encourage an overstatement of test conclusions.

Thus, legal reformers should explore other options in putting safeguards into place. At least three possibilities exist: (1) a requirement that laboratory reports be comprehensive, including all bench notes; (2) that prosecutors should supply defense attorneys promptly with copies of laboratory reports; and

(3) that legislatures and courts provide adequate funding for forensic experts to advise the defense.

First: Clear, Comprehensive Laboratory Reports

No current standards mandate what information laboratory reports should contain. Efforts are currently underway at the National Commission on Forensic Science to develop standards for the terminology used in laboratory conclusions.[92] The reports should also convey sufficient information to enable a defense expert to conduct a meaningful review of the data. The National Academy of Sciences Report urges that reports be "complete and thorough."[93] According to the NAS Report's findings, some laboratory reports provide no information about the exact methods used in testing the evidence and no discussion of measurement uncertainties. They will contain only basic information and definitive conclusions. Such reports typically "contain only identifying and agency information, a brief description of the evidence being submitted, a brief description of the types of analysis requested, and a short statement of the results (e.g., 'the greenish, brown plant materials in item #1 was identified as marijuana')."[94] To avoid such vagueness, the NAS Report advocates that laboratory reports "should contain, at a minimum, 'methods and materials,' 'procedures,' 'results,' 'conclusions,' and, as appropriate, sources and magnitudes of uncertainty in the procedures and conclusions (e.g., levels of confidence)."[95] Additionally, any "bench notes" in which a laboratory analyst documents the steps in the testing process such as measurements, equipment readings, etc. should be included in the documents that comprise the "laboratory report."

Second: Enabling the Defense to Review Laboratory Reports

The purpose of a comprehensive and clear laboratory report is to give the defense full information about the prosecution's evidence. Most jurisdictions give the defense the right to review the prosecutor's evidence, although some places make it harder than others. Ideally, the sharing of a prosecutor's evidence (in legal jargon, the "discovery" process) is handled informally between the defense attorney and the prosecutor, and the defense will receive laboratory reports as a matter of course. In other jurisdictions, the defense attorney must file a formal discovery motion; and, too often, it seems that defense attorneys fail to make such requests.

The New York State Justice Task Force in 2012 considered the procedural rules in that state governing the disclosure of laboratory reports to the defense. It concluded that practitioners, both prosecution and defense, should be reminded of the defense's right to obtain copies of laboratory reports. The report found that the law adequately provided for the defense to obtain laboratory reports, but defense attorneys did not seem aware that they needed to make formal requests for them.[96] As for the additional case file materials such as bench notes, the commission concluded that both prosecutors and laboratories should notify defense attorneys about the existence of such materials and that, when requested, that they can also obtain copies. Defense attorneys could (and, arguably, should) review the laboratory's standard operating procedures (SOPs)—the most voluminous items the laboratory would have to produce. Laboratories are increasingly providing electronic copies of their SOPs, thus reducing the burden of making copies.

Third: Providing Adequate Funding for Forensic Experts to Assist the Defense

Most defense attorneys lack the expertise to fully comprehend laboratory reports. Even if they did have the expertise themselves, they would still need scientific experts to explain the reports to the jury through expert testimony. In 1985, the Supreme Court recognized that indigent defendants in some cases have a constitutional right to the appointment of a psychiatrist or some other defense expert to assist in their defense.[97] From the start, however, the right to defense experts was severely limited and woefully underfunded.[98] The failure to fully support defense access to forensic experts puts criminal defendants at a severe disadvantage in a system in which prosecutors have access to a wide variety of experts.[99] The proposal to create publicly-funded, independent forensic laboratories to provide services for both the prosecution and the defense[100] has an incidental advantage of providing an affordable source of defense experts.

****

Wrongful convictions, crime laboratory scandals, and the tough critique by the National Academy of Sciences have fostered the political momentum to improve the practice of forensic science. The judicial system could play a role by providing new rules that would require that the prosecution and laboratories disclose comprehensive information to the defense and provide adequate funding for defense experts so that defense attorneys would be better equipped to guard their clients against wrongful convictions.

Notes for Chapter Five

1. The Sixth Amendment of the Constitution states:
In all criminal prosecutions, the accused shall enjoy the right to a speedy and public trial, by an impartial jury of the State and district wherein the crime shall have been committed, which district shall have been previously ascertained by law, and to be informed of the nature and cause of the accusation; to be confronted with the witnesses against him; to have compulsory process for obtaining witnesses in his favor, and to have the Assistance of Counsel for his defense.
U.S. Const., amend. 6.

2. *See* Pamela R. Metzger, *Cheating the Constitution*, 59 Vand. L. Rev. 475, 478 n. 9 (2006) (listing the laws of forty-five states that admit a forensic certificate in at least one type of prosecution).

3. For a thorough analysis of the Supreme Court's trilogy of crime laboratory cases, *see* Jennifer Mnookin & David Kaye, *Confronting Science: Expert Evidence and the Confrontation Clause*, 2012 S.Ct. Rev. 99 (2013).

4. Melendez-Diaz v. Massachusetts, 129 S.Ct. 2527, 2530 (2009).

5. *Id.* at 2531.

6. *Id.*

7. *Id.* at 2532.

8. *Id.*

9. *Id.* at 2536

10. *Id.* (citations omitted).

11. Bullcoming v. New Mexico, 131 S.Ct. 2705, 2710 (2011).

12. *Id.* (citations omitted).

13. *Id.* at 2711–12.

14. *Id.* at 2712.

15. *Id.* at 2711.

16. *Id.*

17. *Id.* at 2715.

18. *Id.* at 2715–16.

19. *Id.*

20. *Id.* at 2712.

21. *Id.* at 2722 (Sotomayor, J., dissenting).

22. People v. Williams, Docket No. 107550, at 2 (Jul. 15, 2010), http://www.state.il.us/court/Opinions/SupremeCourt/2010/July/107550.pdf.

23. Williams v. Illinois,132 S.Ct. 2221 (2012).

24. *Id.* at 2229.

25. *Id.* at 2233.

26. *Id.* at 2243.

27. *Id.* at 2255 (Thomas, J., concurring).

28. *Id.* at 2250 (Breyer, J., concurring).

29. *Id.* at 2269 (Kagan, J., dissenting).

30. Bullcoming, 131 S.Ct. at 2719.

31. *See* United States v. James, 712 F.3d 79, 94 (2d Cir. 2013).

32. *Id.* at 95–96 (citations omitted).

33. United States v. Shanton, 513 Fed.Appx. 265, 267 (4th Cir. 2013) (per curiam).

34. *See, e.g.*, Commonwealth v. Lezynski, 466 Mass. 113, 115–16 (Mass. S. Ct. 2013); Miller v. State, 2013 OK CR 11, 313 P.3d 934, 968–70 (2013) (finding error to be harmless); Jenkins v. United States, 75 A.3d 174, 176 (D.C. 2013).

35. Williams, 132 S.Ct. at 2243.

36. State v. Dotson, 2013 WL 4728679, 63–66 (Tenn. Crim. App. 2013); People v. Leach, 980 N.E.2d 570 (Ill. 2012).

37. *See, e.g.*, McCarthy v. State, 285 P.3d 285, 287 (Ala. Ct. App. 2012); Chambers v. State, 424 S.W.3d 296, 302–303 (Ark. 2012); Jones v. State, 982 N.E.2d 417 (Ind. Ct. App. 2013); People v. Pealer, 20 N.Y.3d 447, 985 N.E.2d 903 (2013) cert. denied, 134 S. Ct. 105, 187 L. Ed. 2d 77 (U.S. 2013); Anderson v. State, 2014 WY 13, 317 P.3d 1108 (Wyo. 2014).

38. *See supra* Chapter 2.

39. Commonwealth v. Dyarman, 73 A.3d 565 (Pa. 2013), *cert. denied,* 134 S. Ct. 948, 187 L. Ed. 2d 785 (U.S. 2014) (allowing certificates to establish both calibration and chain of custody).

40. Cooper v. State, 434 Md. 209, 236 (Md. Ct. App. 2013).

41. People v. Lopez, 55 Cal. 4th 569, 584–85 (Cal. 2012).

42. *Id.*

43. Bullcoming, 131 S.Ct. at 2722 (Sotomayor, J., concurring).

44. *See, e.g.*, Lopez, 55 Cal. 4th at 570; State v. Ortiz-Zape, Case No. 329PA11 (NC S.Ct., Jun. 27, 2013); United States v. Moon, 512 F.3d 359, 362 (7th Cir. 2008); United States v. Washington, 498 F.3d 225 (4th Cir. 2007).

45. *Lopez*, 55 Cal. 4th at 570.

46. *See* Comment: *Evidence. Confrontation Clause. Fourth Circuit Holds That "Machine-Generated" Analysis Is Not Testimonial Evidence. United States v. Washington, 498 F.3d 225 (4th Cir. 2007),* 121 Harv. L. Rev. 1937 (2008).

47. For a thorough discussion of this issue, *see* Mnookin & Kaye, *supra* note 3 at 117–142.

48. State v. Mercier, 87 A.3d 700 (Me. 2014) (citations omitted).

49. State v. Lui, 179 Wn. 2d 457, 462 (Wash. 2014).

50. Littleton v. State, 372 S.W.3d 926 (Mo. Ct. App. 2012).

51. State v. McLeod, 166 A.3d 1221,1224 (N.H. 2013).

52. *Id.*

53. *Id.* at 1225.

54. State v. Huettl, 2013-NMCA-038, 305 P.3d 956, 964-65, *cert. granted,* 300 P.3d 1182 (N.M. 2013).

55. Commonwealth v. Gatlos, 76 A.3d 44, 65 (Pa. Super. Ct. 2013) (citations omitted).

56. *Id.*

57. *See* Galloway v. State, 122 So. 3d 614, 636 (Miss. 2013); United States v. Turner, 709 F.3d 1187 (7th Cir. 2013).

58. People v. Farley, 2013 WL 6084198 (Mich. Ct. App. 2013) (unpublished).

59. Miller v. State, 2013 OK CR 11, 313 P.3d 934, 973 (2013).

60. Martin v. State, 60 A.3d 1100, 1109 (Del. 2013).

61. *See, e.g.*, Jones v. State, 2013 Ark. App. 466 (Ark. Ct. App. 2013); Watson v. State, 828 N.W.2d 326 (Iowa Ct. App. 2013); State v. Dennis, 303 P.3d 726 (Kan. Ct. App. 2013) (unpublished); State v. Hayes, 108 So. 3d 360, 366 (La.App. 4 Cir. 2013); State v. Rosario, 2012 WL 6027715 (N.J. Super. Ct. App. Div. 2012); State v. Whittington, 753 S.E.2d 320, 321 (N.C. 2014); State v. Kinslow, 257 Or. App. 295, 306 (Or. Ct. App. 2013); Brown v. State,

01-12-01040-CR, 2014 WL 60965 (Tex. App. Jan. 7, 2014); Whitehurst v. Commonwealth, 63 Va. App. 132, 138 (Va. Ct. App. 2014).

62. *See, e.g.,* Moore v. State, 294 Ga. 682, 755 S.E.2d 703 (Ga. 2014) (defendant failed to preserve error for review by making a timely objection).

63. *See, e.g.,* Oehling v. State, 109 So. 3d 1199 (Fla. Dist. Ct. App. 2013) *review denied,* 123 So. 3d 559 (Fla. 2013) (objection raised on hearsay ground, not Confrontation Clause).

64. *See* Bullcoming, 131 S.Ct. at 2718–19 (noting that defense attorneys make strategic decisions not to insist on live forensic testimony).

65. Maricopa County District Attorney's Office, *CSI: Maricopa County, The CSI Effect and Its Real-Life Impact on Justice, A Study by the Maricopa County Attorney's Office* (June 30, 2005), http://www.ce9.uscourts.gov/jc2008/references/csi/CSI_Effect_report.pdf.

66. A number of studies were done. *See Id.*; Karin H. Cather, *The CSI Effect: Fake TV and its Impact on Jurors in Criminal Cases,* THE PROSECUTOR (Mar./Apr. 2004) ; Simon A. Cole & Rachel Dioso-Villa, CSI *and Its Effects: Media, Juries, and the Burden of Proof,* 41 NEW ENGLAND L. REV. 435, 444 (2007).

67. *Id.* at 447–52.

68. *Id.* at 442.

69. *Id.* at 442, 451.

70. *Id.* at 449.

71. *Id.* at 447–48,465–68.

72. *Id.* at 447–48. Police chiefs raise a concern that does not implicate the accuracy of criminal trials. They report the concern that criminals have learned to use techniques for avoiding detection by watching the show. *Id.* at 452.

73. *Id.* at 448.

74. *Id.* at 463.

75. *See* Tom R. Tyler, *Viewing CSI and the Threshold of Guilt: Managing Truth and Justice in Reality and Fiction,* 115 YALE L. J. 1050, 1083 (2006).

76. *Id.* at 457–59.

77. *Id.* at 459–61.

78. *See* NATIONAL ACADEMY OF SCIENCES, STRENGTHENING FORENSIC SCIENCE IN THE UNITED STATES: A PATH FORWARD at 48–49 (2009) (hereinafter NAS REPORT).

79. *Id.* at 48.

80. *Tops of 2013, TV and Social Media, Top Ten Primetime TV Programs of 2013—Regularly Scheduled,* NIELSEN (Dec. 17, 2013), http://www.nielsen.com/us/en/newswire/2013/tops-of-2013-tv-and-social-media.html.

81. *See Ex Parte* Donna G. Klohn, No. WR-81,294-01 (Ct. Crim. App.—Tex. May 21, 2014) (per curiam).

82. *See supra* Chapter 2.

83. *See* Ken Lazar, *How Chemist in Drug Lab Circumvented Safeguards,* BOSTON.COM (Sept. 29, 2012), http://www.boston.com/news/local/massachusetts/2012/09/30/how-chemist-drug-lab-scandal-circumvented-safeguards/A29LZnAw1eW4hvjn4xX7rL/story.html.

84. *See* Richard Birke, *Reconciling Loss Aversion and Guilty Pleas,* 1999 UTAH L. REV. 205, 207 (1999).

85. *Report: Crime Lab Delays Lead to False Drug Convictions,* STAR-TELEGRAM (Apr. 20, 2014). http://www.star-telegram.com/2014/04/20/5751844/report-lab-delays-lead-to-false.html.

86. Robert Wicoff, Assistant Public Defender, Harris County Public Defender's Office, Email correspondence with author (Sept. 28, 2014) (on file with author).

87. Brandon L. Garrett & Peter J. Neufeld, *Invalid Forensic Science Testimony and Wrongful Convictions*, 95 Virg. L. Rev. 1, 15 (2009).

88. *Id.* at 13

89. *See supra* Chapter 2, app. 2.

90. Williams v. Illinois, 132 S.Ct. 2221, 2253 (2012) (Breyer, J., concurring).

91. *See supra* Chapter 2.

92. *See infra* Chapter 6.

93. NAS Report, *supra* note 78 at 21. The participants at a 2012 Stakeholders Meeting sponsored by the Texas Forensic Science Commission reached the same conclusion. *See Texas Forensic Science Commission Stakeholder Roundtable Meeting Report* (Jun. 6, 2012), http:// www.fsc.texas.gov/sites/default/files/documents/files/StakeholderRoundtableReport-June62012.pdf.

94. NAS Report, *supra* note 78 at 21.

95. *Id.*

96. New York State Justice Task Force, *Recommendations Regarding Discovery of Case File Materials*, Oct. 21, 2012 (on file with author).

97. *See* Ake v. Oklahoma, 470 U.S. 68, 74 (1985).

98. *See, e.g,* David A. Harris, *The Constitution and Truth Seeking: A New Theory on Expert Services for Indigent Defendants*, 83 J. Crim. L. & Crim'y 469, 471–72 (1992); Paul C. Giannelli, *Ake v. Oklahoma*: The Right to Expert Assistance in a Post-*Daubert*, Post-DNA World, 89 Cornell L. Rev.1305, 1312–1313 (2004).

99. Scholars have proposed a variety of models for reducing the funding disparity between prosecutors and appointed counsel, including the disparity in the provision of expert assistance. *See, e.g.,* Darryl K. Brown, *Rationing Criminal Defense Entitlements: An Argument from Institutional Design*, 104 Columbia L. Rev. 801 (2004); Ronald F. Wright, *Parity of Resources for Defense Counsel and the Reach of Public Choice Theory*, 90 Iowa L. Rev. 219 (2004).

100. *See supra* Chapter 4.

Chapter Six

Resisting Independence

The NAS Call for Independent Forensic Laboratories

Years of crime laboratory scandals, wrongful convictions, and concerns about the validity of forensic sciences spurred legislative efforts to improve the quality of work done in police crime laboratories. As Congress became increasingly interested in the improvement of forensic science, industry leaders hoped that the federal government would provide greater resources for staff, training, equipment, and research.[1] Indeed, the NAS Report did recommend increased federal financial support, but it also made clear that increasing budgets alone would not solve the *structural* problems inherent in the practice of forensic science.[2] The main problems with forensic science—the lack of a scientific research culture, the persistent overstatement of test results in many disciplines, the chronic underfunding of crime laboratories, scandals due to incompetence and fraud, and the official foot-dragging and whitewashing following discoveries of serious problems—can all be attributed, at least in part, to the affiliation of crime laboratories with police agencies. Throughout the report, the National Academy of Sciences makes repeated calls for the independence of forensic laboratories.[3]

Converting police crime laboratories into independent forensic laboratories offers advantages that should be attractive to those in the crime laboratory industry. Independence would extricate managers and analysts from the pressures of law enforcement and allow them to work in a more purely scientific environment. This independence would reduce the influences that create motivational bias and unconscious cognitive biases. Independent forensic laboratories would also be better positioned to obtain adequate funding, while crime laboratories constantly compete within police departments against other seemingly more pressing police priorities.

Furthermore, police administrators may not be competent to supervise a scientific laboratory. The Houston Police Department is a good police department in a major city, and there is no logical reason to think that the police chiefs would be negligent in this one aspect of their administration and not others. The same is surely true for the many other mismanaged laboratories around the country. The truth is simple: One cannot properly supervise what one does not understand.

To develop independent forensic laboratories requires that lawmakers at every level of government—federal, state, county, and municipal—take steps to transfer the assets of police crime laboratories to the control of new entities that operate independently of law enforcement.[4] At the federal level, "law enforcement" usually refers to the Department of Justice (DOJ), overseen by the U.S. Attorney General. The DOJ includes the Federal Bureau of Investigation and numerous other law enforcement agencies, each with its respective crime laboratories. Other federal crime laboratories also exist as part of federal law enforcement agencies within other departments, such as the Secret Service, which is part of the Treasury Department, and in the criminal investigation departments of the armed services.[5] State law enforcement agencies are generally structured much like the federal DOJ, with state attorneys general at the helms. Local police departments and sheriff's offices also typically operate crime laboratories; and in some jurisdictions (e.g., Sacramento, California), the District Attorney's Office also operates a crime laboratory.[6]

Following scandals similar to that within the Houston Police Department Crime Laboratory, a few laboratories severed ties with their law enforcement agencies, including those for Nassau County, New York; and the State of Virginia.[7] In a few other jurisdictions, the crime laboratory systems had developed independently of law enforcement as accidents of history rather than by design. Alabama has one of the oldest state forensic laboratories, originally established in the 1930s as an independent state agency.[8] The Rhode Island State Crime Laboratory was founded in 1952 by a faculty member at the University of Rhode Island and still operates as an independent laboratory within the university today.[9] None of these independent laboratories have been implicated in fraud or perjury scandals, even though all of them share the common complaint of being understaffed and underfunded.

The fact that a few independent forensic laboratories exist in this country provides evidence for two propositions. First, the existence of independent forensic laboratories proves that law enforcement's needs for forensic evidence can be met by laboratories that have been removed from within law enforcement agencies. Second, the small number of police crime laboratories that have been emancipated also underscores that the vast majority of jurisdictions have not yet heeded the call of the National Academy of Sciences Report (2009) to remove crime laboratories from the jurisdiction of police agencies. Given the national scandal caused by law enforcement control of forensic laboratories and the fact that the nation's most prestigious scientific entity has firmly recommended removing laboratories from police agencies, the question should be why *not* remove them?

Reconsidering the Crime Laboratory Model

With all of the advantages offered by independence, one might think that repositioning crime laboratories from police departments might be welcomed by those who administer and work in crime laboratories. Unfortunately, nothing could be further from the truth. Most forensic science professional organizations have soundly rejected the recommendation to make forensic laboratories independent. The question is why? One reason is that such fundamental changes may be unsettling to those currently in leadership positions. Second, anecdotal evidence, and my personal observations, suggests that some crime laboratory analysts prefer to work for police departments. Many analysts like being cops in lab coats, like the characters in TV shows. Who wouldn't find great personal satisfaction in helping to put criminals behind bars? Receiving praise and merit awards for their help in getting convictions carries great satisfaction.

As this book has documented, however, even without the problems of overt fraud and perjury, a work environment that fosters motivational and other unconscious cognitive biases in favor of the prosecution inevitably creates the potential for a slanted reading of ambiguous test results. These effects can tilt forensic evidence in the dangerous direction of persuading a jury to convict an innocent person.

However, the resistance to independence runs deeper than simply a preference to work with law enforcement. A third reason is that the industry suddenly found itself on the receiving end of a broad array of criticisms that cumulatively painted an ugly and unprofessional picture. Predictably, the reaction of forensic scientists was defensive. Professionals in the field, though they may be experienced, competent, and ethical, likely perceive these proposals for fundamental change emerging from a period of sustained negative publicity as personal criticism. Understandably, they have rejected the concerns about motivational and unconscious cognitive biases, viewing these observations as attacks to their integrity. Factoring into this defensiveness is the NAS Report's major blow to the profession by refuting so many of the basic precepts of various forensic disciplines. In this highly charged atmosphere, and in light of the growing awareness of notorious cases of scientific fraud, it is understandable that leaders in forensic science interpret valid concerns about cognitive bias as accusations of bad ethics, but the point I have argued is that cognitive biases can cause even an ethical person to make mistakes.[10]

A number of professional organizations represent the forensic science profession when Congress considers legislation. These organizations also provide such services as certification testing and education, accreditation for laboratories, proficiency tests, and research on forensic science. The American Society of Crime Laboratory Directors (ASCLD), the American Academy of Forensic Science (AAFS), and the International Association for Identification (IAI) are three important forensic science professional organizations. A spin-off organization of ASCLD is the American Society of Crime Laboratory Directors/ Laboratory Accreditation Board (ASCLD/LAB), which provides accreditation services for forensic laboratories. ASCLD and IAI both testified in hearings before the Senate Judiciary Committee that they opposed moving crime laboratories out of law enforcement agencies. Another accrediting body, Forensic Quality Services (FQS), took no position on the issue of removing crime laboratories from police departments, but it did support greater independence for crime laboratories *within* police departments.[11] Only the AAFS released a statement in 2009 endorsing *all* of the recommendations of the NAS Report. However, this statement is general, making no specific mention of the NAS recommendation to make laboratories independent.[12]

Representatives of ASCLD took the position that law enforcement agencies should be required to support—and document their support of—good ethics in their crime laboratories. In their testimony to the Senate Judiciary Committee, ASCLD representatives stated, "The practice of forensic science is built on a foundation of ethics and objectivity that must be supported at all levels in the organization."[13] Therefore, Congress "should not remove crime laboratories from parent agencies if the parent agency is required to document how the crime laboratories have scientific freedom to conduct testing and report results without pressure from activity, interest, or influence."[14] On its face, this position is both reasonable and highly professional, yet it does not address why simple documentation requirements would be preferable to laboratory independence as a means of minimizing police influences. ASCLD also recommended that Congress fund research on "the potential for influence or biases that could affect the quality of results of forensic laboratory operations."[15]

The IAI, the oldest and largest professional forensic association in the world, founded in 1915 in Oakland, California, also opposed the removal of crime laboratories from police agencies.[16] Like ASCLD, the IAI also rejected the concern about motivational and cognitive bias in forensic science, viewing the issue solely as one of "integrity." Its position simply ignores the research on the effects of cognitive biases on forensic science, as seen in the notorious Brandon Mayfield debacle, of which it was certainly well aware. Rather than addressing these concerns in any way, IAI representatives diminished the problem by characterizing the concerns about cognitive bias as acts of intentional wrongdoing. They stated, "It is a great stretch to believe that a professional analyst would risk their [sic] integrity and jeopardize the rights and freedoms of the innocent to satisfy some desire to be 'accepted' by clients and client agencies."[17] While thus rejecting the need for independent crime laboratories as improbable, IAI took the position that "there needs to be a separate funding structure for crime labs and identification units so they don't compete with public safety and first responder resources."[18] Thus, the IAI agreed that there should be significant funding separation between the law enforcement agency and the crime laboratory but not to organizational independence.

ASCLD/LAB, the accrediting authority, also opposes the removal of crime laboratories from police departments. It acknowledges the problem of motivational bias but puts its faith in accreditation checks as the solution. Accreditation is part of a laboratory's quality management system by which an independent organization such as ASCLD/LAB provides ongoing support, education, and oversight of a laboratory's policies and operations.[19] The ASCLD/LAB Board, in a letter to Congress written by its chair, Jami St. Clair, supported most of the NAS Report recommendations, but protested:

> One of the few recommendations that ASCLD/LAB is not prepared to support is the removal of laboratories from law enforcement agencies or prosecutor's offices. While we agree that crime laboratories must have scientific autonomy from their parent agencies and the freedom to report non-biased results without external pressure, accreditation standards under ISO 17025 already require that laboratories be guarded against undue influence in the work of the scientist by the parent agency or any other interested party. We believe that this standard, as enforced by ASCLD/LAB, addresses the concerns expressed by the report and achieves the goal of the NAS.[20]

(ISO 17025 refers to the widely-accepted accreditation standard for scientific laboratories set by the International Organization for Standardization or "ISO".[21]) In other words, the accreditation standards require laboratories to follow procedures that adequately safeguard against the possibility that superiors' undue influence might affect test results. So long as the laboratory is accredited and continues to meet accreditation standards, the ASCLD/LAB tells us, we can rest assured that its standard operating procedures give those laboratories "scientific autonomy" from their law enforcement superiors.

The organizations representing federal and state prosecutors also oppose the recommendation to create independent laboratories. Both the DOJ, as well as the National District Attorneys Association (NDAA), rejected the NAS proposal, arguing mainly that it was essential to integrate the laboratory's investigation with the criminal investigation in its early stages.[22] This argument presumably refers to the work of the Crime Scene Investigation Units (CSIs or CSUs) which intimately intersects with the work of police detectives and investigators during the early stages of an investigation, and the need to involve the laboratory's case manager(s) who work directly with the investigating officer(s). The concern for effective access to forensic specialists early in an investigation is valid, but this relationship is not prohibited or even hampered by having an independent crime laboratory. Making laboratories independent of law enforcement does not in and of itself change anything about how a laboratory collects and processes evidence. In fact, one benefit of having CSUs operate from an independent laboratory (as opposed to operating from a police department) is that CSUs can act as a liaison between the police department and the laboratory, providing sound evidence collection, and facilitating the provision of forensic resources early in the investigation.

Like the IAI, the NDAA also rejected NAS's argument, which it paraphrased as asserting that laboratory independence could "guarantee unbiased service." Of course, the NAS Report did not suggest that laboratory independence alone would "guarantee" the removal of bias. However, the NDAA's insistence that these issues can be better addressed by promoting "autonomy"—rather than actual independence—for laboratories housed within police departments is difficult to understand.[23] The argument in favor of creating "autonomy" for laboratories while maintaining crime laboratories within police departments stems from two unfortunate words in the NAS Report. The report states: "Ideally, public forensic science laboratories should be independent of or *autonomous within* law enforcement agencies."[24]

What it means for a laboratory to be part of a police department and yet be "autonomous within" the organization is not clear, and the report's authors do not define what they see as the difference. The NAS report mentions budgetary autonomy, by which it means that a laboratory should set its own priorities about resource management and expenditures,[25] but a laboratory in a police department would still have to negotiate its budget with the police chief, who would certainly have the last word and who presumably would still be the laboratory director's supervisor. In such a situation, "autonomy" would be virtually meaningless. The report also recommends as a description of autonomy that the laboratory director "would have an equal voice with others in the justice system on matters involving the laboratory and other agencies."[26] Again, it is simply not possible for a laboratory director to have an "equal voice" with a police chief supervisor. Despite the confusing language about "autonomy within" a police agency, the NAS Report's actual recommendation is clear:

"Recommendation 4" states that the goal should be "removing all public foren-sic laboratories and facilities from the administrative control of law enforce-ment agencies or prosecutors' offices."[27]

Representatives of police departments also rejected the call for independent laboratories. The International Association of Chiefs of Police (IACP) issued a "Forensics Policy" in 2009 responding to the NAS Report. The IACP policy is "strongly opposed to the removal of crime laboratories and other forensic serv-ices from law enforcement agencies."[28] The one-page policy paper gives no ra-tionale for the strong opposition.

In sum, the arguments for keeping crime laboratories as subunits of law enforcement agencies do not withstand scrutiny. Experience has shown that situating a forensic laboratory in a police department can create systemic struc-tural obstacles to achieving objective results in scientific testing. This negative influence holds true regardless of the credentials, experience, or ethics of in-dividual analysts. True objectivity—unaffected by the drive to obtain convic-tions—may be impossible to obtain in an atmosphere steeped in a police culture with a close emotional connection to crime victims. Thus, the NAS Report's recommendation to remove forensic laboratories from police juris-diction is a logical response to this fundamental concern.

Another point worth reiterating here is that an independent crime laboratory is not, in and of itself, a barrier against other types of cognitive bias that have plagued crime laboratories in the past.[29] Other quality assurance procedures such as se-quential unmasking and blind verifications are necessary as well (see Chapter 4). These procedures are used in other kinds of scientific laboratories, such as in university research laboratories or pharmaceutical research laboratories, to minimize cognitive bias from affecting the results of laboratory testing.

The NAS Report's Support for Independent Forensic Science Research

Before the NAS Report in 2009, observers had noted that the agenda of fed-eral law enforcement agencies favored law enforcement interests in forensic science research rather than a broader interest in pursuing scientific truths. For example, an article in *Issues in Science and Technology* in 2003 complained that "we have a growing body of unreliable research funded by law enforce-ment agencies with a strong interest in promoting the validity" of techniques such as fingerprints, fiber analysis, hair analysis, firearms and tool marks, and bite marks.[30] The current state of research on these particular areas is not re-assuring that the results will stand up to rigorous inspection.[31]

Even with regard to DNA testing which can and does produce far more dependable results, Paul Giannelli reports numerous attempts by DOJ officials to "withhold data from the general scientific community, selectively share information with scientists it approve[s], and underwrite their research."[32] One important battle arose in the early 1990s over whether the FBI Crime Laboratory would make its DNA database information available to the defense experts in a particular case to evaluate the FBI laboratory's DNA test results. The FBI objected to making the disclosure. A Minnesota court of appeals was troubled by the defense's contention that "the FBI does not allow members of the scientific community general access to its databases."[33] When the court ultimately ordered the FBI to disclose, the defense's expert, Seymour Geisser, a professor of statistics at the University of Minnesota, reported:

> The form in which the databases were surrendered by the FBI was unusable for a proper analysis by the defense. However, the material was supplied, in the form requested, to one of the prosecution experts. Hearing my complaint, this expert generously sent me an appropriate diskette, to the chagrin of the FBI.[34]

Geisser has also complained about experts with close connections to the DOJ who have interfered with the peer-review process when he has submitted academic papers on the forensic use of DNA statistics for publication in journals.[35] He also reports that the FBI has denied him access to its databases for scientific research purposes while apparently allowing its use for the scholarly work of other scientists with ties to the DOJ.[36] Such partisan gamesmanship interferes with the process of scientific discovery and has no place in scientific research, but it can occur—and at least in these cases, does—when law enforcement agencies have control of scientific information pertinent to the criminal justice system.

The DOJ has also opposed legislative efforts to reform forensic science in an apparent attempt to maintain its control of the field. At a 2008 subcommittee hearing one Senator Richard Shelby, Republican of Alabama, complained that individuals at the National Institute of Justice (NIJ), an agency within DOJ, had "attempted to derail" the legislative directive calling for the NAS study of forensic science when it was being considered in 2005.[37] Apparently, the NIJ also convened a summit conference in 2008 for the purpose of undercutting the NAS study.[38] Ironically, these high-level attempts to preclude the NAS investigation and ultimately to diminish the validity of the report's arguments may have convinced the NAS committee of the need to remove forensic science from the control of law enforcement. In its first recommendation, the NAS Report called for the creation of a strong and "independent" national entity to govern forensic science. The recommendation states in part: "To promote the development of forensic science into a mature field of multidisciplinary research and practice, founded on the systemic collection and analysis of relevant data, Congress should establish and appropriate funds for an *independent* federal entity, the National Institute of Forensic Science (NIFS)."[39] The report continues:

> There was also a strong consensus in the committee that no existing or new division or unit within DOJ would be an appropriate location for a new entity governing the forensic science community. DOJ's principal mission is to enforce the law and defend the interests of the United States according to the law. Agencies within DOJ operate pursuant to this mission. The FBI, for example, is the investigative arm of DOJ and its principal missions are to produce and use intelligence to protect the Nation from threats and to bring to justice those who violate the law. The work of these law enforcement units is critically important to the Nation, but the scope of the work done by DOJ units is much narrower than the promise of a strong forensic science community. Forensic science serves more than just law enforcement; and when it does serve law enforcement, it must be equally available to law enforcement officers, prosecutors, *and* defendants in the criminal justice system. The entity that is established to govern the forensic science community cannot be principally beholden to law enforcement. The potential for conflicts of interest between the needs of law enforcement and the broader needs of forensic science are [sic] too great.... In sum, the committee concluded that advancing *science* in the forensic science enterprise is not likely to be achieved within the confines of DOJ.[40]

The national entity proposed by the NAS would be tasked with promoting valid scientific research in the forensic sciences, developing uniform national guidelines for conducting testing, documenting laboratory work, and reporting test results. What the NAS Report makes perfectly clear, however, is that the DOJ should not control this national research entity.

In the end, Congress gave the DOJ a prominent role in shaping the future of forensic science in the United States by assigning DOJ to co-chair a new "National Commission on Forensic Science."[41] Announced in early 2013, this national commission will develop policy recommendations regarding the intersection of forensic science and the criminal justice system. According to the Department of Justice press release:

> Members of the commission will work to improve the practice of
> forensic science by developing guidance concerning the intersections
> between forensic science and the criminal justice system. The com-
> mission also will work to develop policy recommendations for the
> U.S. Attorney General, including uniform codes for professional re-
> sponsibility and requirements for formal training and certification.[42]

Fortunately, the commission's large size and the diversity of its members (including academics, judges, forensic scientists, and defense attorney, in addition to prosecutors) bode well for a balanced consideration of the critical issues
that will face the commission. The members also include some critics of DOJ's
past handling of scientific research.[43]

Other developments at the national level give additional cause for optimism.
To govern the *practice* of forensic science, Congress assigned the responsibility to the Director of the National Institute of Standards and Technology (NIST),
who was appointed as co-chair of the National Commission on Forensic Science. NIST is a non-regulatory agency in the Department of Commerce whose
mission is "to promote U.S. innovation and industrial competitiveness by advancing measurement science, standards, and technology."[44] NIST members include several Nobel Prize winners and winners of the National Medal of Science.
The NAS Report mentions NIST more than fifty times.[45] The NAS Committee on Identifying the Needs of the Forensic Science Committee included one
Senior NIST Fellow, Sheldon M. Wiederhorn.[46]

In the past, the governance of individual areas of practice was loosely governed by "Scientific Working Groups" ("SWGs") within each discipline. As of
2014 the FBI Crime Laboratory oversaw twenty-one 21 SWGs in various forensic disciplines, and another had been organized under the leadership of the
U.S. Drug Enforcement Administration.[47] The SWG model left much to be desired, largely because the federal government had no jurisdiction to control
state and local crime laboratories. For example, each SWG has published guidelines for analysts in their respective disciplines for reporting test results, but
these were merely recommendations. The guidelines include no mechanisms
for validation and/or enforcement. Regarding these SWG guidelines, the NAS
Report states:

> Despite the proliferation of standards in many of the forensic science
> disciplines, their voluntary nature and inconsistent application make
> it difficult to assess their impact. Ideally, standards should be consis-
> tently applicable and measurable. In addition, mechanisms should be
> in place for their enforcement, with sanctions imposed against those
> who fail to comply.[48]

Under its 2013 Memorandum of Understanding with the DOJ, NIST will oversee a new centralized governance structure to replace the current SWGs for each discipline which currently have no organizational connection to each other.[49] NIST will create new "Organization of Scientific Area Committees" (OSACs), which will be a practice-focused effort.[50] OSACs will guide the practice of forensic science by providing best practices and guidelines and a registry of approved standards.[51] For example, OSACs may publish quality control standards that would be recommended for all forensic laboratories. It might also establish standards for the practice of forensic disciplines such as fingerprint or firearm examination which currently lack measureable standards.[52]

It should be noted that the current SWGs are comprised mainly of law enforcement representatives who work in crime laboratories across the country. This situation will not change under NIST leadership. By and large, the current practitioners of forensic science work within law enforcement agencies. Thus, the NIST effort will not be completely "independent" of law enforcement in that sense. It will be headed by scientists who *are* independent of law enforcement, but the work will be done in cooperation with the leaders in forensic science, most of whom are members of law enforcement agencies. To bring a more balanced diversity to the enterprise, NIST has given advisory roles to other stakeholders such as defense attorneys and representatives of innocence projects as part of this effort.

Two bills pending in Congress as of 2014 would improve the quality of forensic science in different ways. As originally written, the bills would have placed control of the research agenda in federal science entities like the National Science Foundation (NSF). In later revisions however, the law enforcement establishment has been given greater control. The first bill would create a NSF Research Initiative (the Initiative) to coordinate federal research in forensic science and will be managed by the National Forensic Science Coordinating Office at the Office of Science and Technology Policy. Leadership of this office will rotate among members of the Interagency Forensic Science Committee carrying out the Initiative and would include the National Science Foundation, NIST, DOJ, the Department of Homeland Security, the Department of Defense, and other federal agencies and offices participating in the Initiative.[53] Having an entity within the Office of Science and Technology Policy that would coordinate the diversity of federal entities with an interest in forensic science should ensure the development of a uniform set of goals through the Initiative, and the distribution of federal grants for forensic science research would provide the badly needed foundational scientific support for many areas of forensic science that currently lack an adequate research basis such as fingerprint and firearms examination. This legislation would address additional pressing needs identified by the NAS Report—the lack of a "unified strategy for developing a forensic science research plan" and "extremely limited opportunities for research funding."[54]

The second bill would create a federal "Office of Forensic Science" overseen by an advisory board that would establish accreditation standards for forensic laboratories that would be required to make a laboratory eligible to receive federal funding. The Office of Forensic Science would also set standards for the certification of individual analysts, set research priorities, dispense research grants, and establish standards for best practices.[55] At the time of this writing (May 2014), it remains to be seen whether Congress will pass either piece of legislation.

Wrongful convictions caused by invalid forensic science serve as sharp reminders of the need for integrity in the search for scientific truths.[56] Will the new national commission, the leadership role played by NIST, and the pending legislation to fund research succeed in fostering the kind of research and enforceable standards so badly needed in forensic science? The present outlook at the federal level is cautiously optimistic.

Forensic Science Commissions at the State Level

Two states currently have Forensic Science Commissions, Texas and New York. These commissions are assigned such tasks as investigating allegations of negligent or fraudulent conduct by analysts, developing policies and procedures about the relationship of crime laboratories to the criminal justice system, and facilitating reviews of convictions involving forensic evidence that is later discovered to be invalid. Unfortunately, efforts in Arizona to create a forensic science commission failed in 2010 due to resistance from law enforcement and crime laboratory entities.[57] Despite a series of promising meetings and widespread support, the Arizona Supreme Court shelved the proposal to create the commission after representatives of the Office of the Attorney General met with the Supreme Court in a closed meeting. Larry A. Hammond, an attorney in Phoenix and past president of the American Judicature Society, took part in the negotiations and had this reaction:

> The Arizona crime laboratories were not enthusiastic about the prospect for "outside" involvement. The forensic science community in Arizona has at least two distinct parts: the government-run crime labs, and the rest of the criminal law-related forensic science community. Many of the most articulate voices in the community are, and have been,

distrusted or ignored by their crime lab colleagues. Sadly, this is true both of the way private laboratories and some academicians have been treated.[58]

The failure in Arizona to establish independent laboratories is a reminder that any attempts at major institutional reform will elicit suspicion and resistance from those within the institutions. The phenomenon of wrongful convictions has given political leverage to criminal justice reformers who previously had little success in challenging the law enforcement establishment. Thus, we see some success in advancing improvements in the administration of forensic science, but we can expect to see some political defeats as well.

Independence Promotes Rigor in Accreditation, Proficiency Testing, and Certification

A major topic of discussion within forensic science today is "quality assurance."[59] Most laboratory managers include a number of important safeguards under the rubric of quality assurance, including accreditation, proficiency testing, and certification.[60] All three of these components of quality assurance represent critical safeguards that a laboratory's work can be trusted, so it is especially important that the safeguards themselves can also be trusted. The integral connection between crime laboratories and law enforcement, however, calls into question the trustworthiness of all of these safeguards.

Legislators in some states have required laboratory accreditation as a means of promoting laboratory reliability.[61] Accreditation review verifies that the laboratory follows accepted standards and employs qualified personnel. This type of review is conducted by assessors with organizations such as the American Society of Crime Laboratory Directors/Laboratory Accreditation Board (ASCLD/ LAB) and Forensic Quality Services (FQS). Accreditation, which must be renewed through re-inspection every five years, examines the laboratory's standard operating procedures, quality assurance practices, the quality of laboratory equipment, and practices for ensuring the competence of analysts.

Changes implemented in the past fifteen years suggest that the forensic science profession has recognized the need to increase the rigor of quality assurance tools. It has become more common for crime laboratories to employ quality assurance managers.[62] The standards for accreditation have been increased substantially as well. The main accrediting body, American Society of

Crime Laboratory Directors/Laboratory Accreditation Board (ASCLD/LAB) increased the standards for accreditation in 2006 by requiring that laboratories seek initial accreditation or renewals of accreditation to meet the international standards applicable to all scientific laboratories known as ISO 17025. This standard is now supplemented with certain elements unique to forensic laboratories.[63] For example, ISO 17025 may provide a general standard for proper estimation of measurement uncertainty, and this will be supplemented through ASCLD/LAB with specific guidance for applying the general standard to particular forensic disciplines, such as firearms.[64] The process begins with a required internal audit. The laboratory's managers will follow a "field assessment guide" provided by ASCLD/LAB or FQS to conduct a self-assessment and then take corrective actions, prior to applying for accreditation. If Houston's experience is any indicator, it is no small feat to obtain accreditation under the new standards. The laboratory in Houston spent more than a year gearing up to undergo the accreditation process.[65]

Despite the adoption of more stringent standards for accreditation, a study conducted by one prominent critic finds fault with what he argues is the pro-prosecution makeup and orientation of ASCLD/LAB. Marvin E. Schechter, a member of the New York State Commission on Forensic Science, and also a member of the committee that produced the NAS Report, surveyed newspaper reports between 2005 and 2011. He found reports of at least fifty major laboratory failures such as fraudulent activity by analysts, destruction of evidence, failing proficiency tests, misrepresenting test results in court testimony, drug tampering, etc. Twenty-eight of them (56%) involved laboratories accredited by ASCLD/LAB.[66] (The news reports did not provide accreditation information for the other twenty-two laboratories, so Schechter excluded them from his study.) Based on his review of the statements and actions of ASCLD/LAB representatives during several of these scandals, Schechter documented a disturbing tendency of ASCLD/LAB to err on the side of covering up and downplaying incidents. He states:

> ASCLD/LAB could more properly be described as a product service organization which sells for a fee, a "seal of approval," … which laboratories can utilize to bolster their credibility through in-court testimony by technicians plus ancillary services such as protection from outside inquiry, shielding of internal activities and where necessary, especially in the event of public condemnation, a spokesperson to buffer the laboratory from media inquiry.[67]

Public trust in the process demands that accreditation standards be meaningful and that laboratory incidents result in thorough corrective action. Schechter's study points to a troubling tendency for ASCLD/LAB to minimize or hide problems from public scrutiny.

He attributes this problem to the close connection of ASCLD/LAB to law enforcement. He states:

> Far worse than the culture of tolerance is the culture which values laboratory product produced for law enforcement as opposed to the criminal justice system. This is not surprising since its entire Board, save one person, appears to have an extensive relationship with law enforcement. The ASCLD/LAB Board has no advisory board of independent scientists (certainly not one listed on its website). It has no defense lawyers with scientific backgrounds as Board members, though it does have at least one former prosecutor.[68]

Schechter has begun a further investigation of the accreditation process on behalf of the National Association of Criminal Defense Lawyers, which will present the report to the National Commission on Forensic Science.[69]

Proficiency testing raises similar concerns. Ostensibly, laboratory managers administer annual proficiency tests to individual analysts, one of the requirements for a laboratory's accreditation. Analysts within each discipline take proficiency tests to measure their competence to practice the discipline. Laboratories obtain proficiency tests from external vendors approved by the accreditation board and then administer them internally to analysts. Laboratories also administer proficiency tests that they design themselves.

Proficiency tests should require an individual analyst to perform a sample test such as to determine whether two fingerprints belong to the same person, as might be required in real casework. Externally sourced proficiency tests may not capture a true measure of competence, however. Criminologist Simon Cole cites several problems both with the design and administration of proficiency tests in his study of the field of fingerprint examination. First, laboratories administer the exams themselves—even the exams provided by external vendors. Thus, they are "conducted by mail, under unproctored, untimed conditions."[70] It is not known whether they are completed by individuals or "by committee."[71] Instead, proficiency testing should be proctored by disinterested parties rather than by internal personnel. Second, testing should be sufficiently rigorous to meaningfully test competence.[72] Cole states that, at least in the fingerprint area, "no metric exists for measuring the degree of difficulty."[73] Thus, there is "no way of determining the level of difficulty of these tests relative to casework."[74]

One group raised this concern with the National Academy of Sciences. The American Statistical Association Board of Directors recommends a number of improvements to proficiency testing. In a statement responding to the NAS Report, the Board of Directors recommended that forensic science proficiency tests should "mirror the level of complexity found in actual practice" and that they should be conducted in a double-blind fashion, which is standard operating procedure in medical research.[75] Double-blind proficiency testing would mean that neither the examiner nor the laboratory manager would know when a test specimen was being assigned; they would both believe it was a real case assignment.

The same concerns exist for internally produced proficiency tests. With regard to an internal proficiency test administered by the FBI Laboratory for its fingerprint examiners, at least one observer found the test to be extremely easy. Cole recounts the sworn testimony given by one fingerprint examiner in an American federal court:

> Retired Scotland Yard examiner Allan Bayle testified that the simulated latent prints in the test were "nothing like" typical crime-scene latent prints, that Scotland Yard examiners would "fall about laughing" if given the FBI's tests, and that the tests were "a joke."[76]

More rigorous testing would be implemented if it was required for laboratory accreditation, but it is not. ASCLD/LAB requires that all analysts take at least one proficiency test each year, but only one analyst in each section of a forensic discipline must take an externally obtained proficiency test. The rest can take an internally developed test.[77] Obviously, these standards cannot ensure that all of the analysts in a laboratory are competent. Moreover, even if externally produced proficiency tests were required of all analysts, groups like the American Statistical Association echoed the NAS Report in voicing concerns about proficiency tests that do not reflect the difficulty and ambiguity found in real casework.[78]

One can readily appreciate why accrediting bodies might not require rigorous proficiency testing. As test difficulty increases, there is a greater likelihood that analysts will fail to meet the requisite standards, a situation that creates headaches for crime laboratories and prosecutors. It usually necessitates removing the analyst from bench work in the laboratory so that he or she can be retrained and tested, thereby usually requiring increased workloads for those analysts who did pass the proficiency test. Such incidents can create strain, resentment, and damaged morale within a laboratory.

Laboratories will generally also undertake a review of the actual casework that the non-proficient analyst had done for a defined period of time (i.e., usually several months but sometimes as long as the analyst has worked in that laboratory). Laboratory managers will gather all the case files for which the analyst in question has conducted forensic testing. If possible to retest evidence (such as drugs) or to test remaining evidence (such as biological evidence), the evidence in these cases will be retested. If retesting produces the same results, then the new test results will be available to the prosecution, and the non-proficient analyst's work will not impede a pending prosecution. If the evidence cannot be retested, the prosecution will be notified that the laboratory cannot produce credible evidence of that type for the case in question.

For cases that have already resulted in convictions, the laboratory will turn over a list of the affected cases to the prosecutor for further review to ensure that no injustice occurred as a result of the analyst's work. In some cases, retesting may also be possible. The laboratory should also notify the defense attorneys and defendants if the forensic evidence figured in their specific cases, although not all prosecutors' offices have instituted policies requiring such notification.[79]

Besides current and past cases, there is the question of whether a non-proficient analyst can be a credible expert witness in future cases on which he or she may perform forensic testing. An analyst's failing performance on a proficiency test becomes information that must be disclosed to defense attorneys in future cases in which the analyst performs forensic work. Such information is known as "*Brady* material," named after the Supreme Court decision recognizing a criminal defendant's right to learn exculpatory information, including information bearing on a government witness's credibility.[80] Defense attorneys can use this information in two ways: (1) to argue that the judge should not find the analyst qualified to testify as an "expert witness" due to a lack of competence; and (2) during cross-examination to show the jury that the witness's conclusions may not be sound. A proficiency test failure can taint an analyst's testimony long into the future.

Forensic practitioners may also sit for certification exams offered by various organizations within most forensic fields. Certification also involves testing individual analysts for proficiency in their fields. This type of testing resembles licensing exams such as the bar exam for attorneys. While it would be desirable to implement a requirement that analysts become certified, policy-makers currently face numerous practical challenges in implementing the NAS Report's recommendation to make analyst certification mandatory.[81] The Texas Forensic Science Commission published a 2013 white paper supporting a mandatory certification requirement and addressing some of the obstacles that policymakers would face in implementing such a requirement. Pending federal legislation would task new federal offices with developing certification requirements,[82] so we should see progress on this front if the legislation passes.

Independent Laboratories Can
Serve the Entire Justice System

About 80% of the "crime laboratories" in the United States operate as subunits of law enforcement agencies, and almost all work exclusively for law enforcement.[83] This need not be the case. Jurisdictions—federal, state, and local—can remove forensic laboratories from their parent law enforcement organizations. Independent forensic laboratories could continue to operate as governmental agencies of the political jurisdiction, but laboratory directors would not report to police chiefs.

Independence would free forensic laboratories to work for the defense as well as prosecutors. A small number of independent forensic laboratories already operate in this fashion.[84] Laboratories that work for both defendants and the prosecution offer two advantages. First, working for the defense as well as for the prosecutor broadens the laboratory's client base, enabling it to generate fees that the defendant would otherwise pay to a private laboratory. Second, when laboratory analysts work for the defense, both in the laboratory and in the courtroom, it dissolves the psychological ties to law enforcement that analysts may previously have had. When analysts testify on behalf of defendants as well as on behalf of the prosecution, they would naturally come to view the trial process from a more neutral perspective. Too many scientific experts in both civil and criminal cases give testimony that is sharply slanted in favor of the side for which they regularly testify. Truly independent, objective, and high-quality forensic laboratories that do work for both the prosecution and the defense have great potential to ameliorate the adversarial slant in trial testimony often encountered in the criminal justice system today.

Providing services to the defense as well as law enforcement would also make defense attorneys clear stakeholders in the quality of work done in the laboratories. Defense attorneys could assist in a laboratory's quality assurance programs such as their testimony monitoring programs or in mock trials.[85] However, accepting defense attorneys as "customers" of a forensic laboratory would require the laboratory to take special safeguards such as measures to ensure that defense testing information remains private, as court rules require, and does not get turned over to the police. At the same time, laboratory staff members face challenges in communicating with defense attorneys about testing requested by prosecutors, primarily because the laboratory must first confirm that the attorney requesting the information has a legal right to receive it. For this reason, laboratories often transmit information to prosecutors who then turn over the information to the defense attorneys.

Since most crime laboratories do not currently work for the defense, the result is that they are disconnected from the defense attorneys in a number of respects. Laboratory managers do not view defense attorneys as stakeholders in their operations, nor do they include them in their quality assurance programs. Even when defense attorneys seek information about tests performed in the cases they are handling, laboratory managers will usually transmit the information via the prosecutor and not directly. Thus, there is little direct communication or interaction between crime laboratory staff members and defense attorneys.

A critical recommendation of the NAS Report was that crime laboratories should be removed from their parent law enforcement agencies. Yet at the time of this writing (May 2014), five years after the report's publication, the status quo persists almost everywhere. Only a couple of laboratories have been extricated from their law enforcement parent institutions and converted into independent forensic laboratories.[86] The hundreds of police crime laboratories elsewhere continue their status as integral units within law enforcement agencies. The sole job of virtually all police crime laboratories continues to be to serve the needs of law enforcement.

Homeland Security: The Imperative to Reform Crime Laboratories

America has a vital interest in the existence of effective forensic laboratories at every level of government, not only to serve the criminal justice system but increasingly to protect national and international security as well. Many federal and military forensic laboratories already specialize in forensic practices that concentrate on investigating terrorist acts. One example is the National Biodefense Forensic Analysis Center established in the Department of Homeland Security.[87] The FBI Crime Laboratory's involvement in the investigation of the Madrid train bombing in the Mayfield case illustrates the critical role forensic science plays in addressing acts of terror around the world in an era of global policing.

State and local forensic scientists can also play a role in the protection of homeland security. The NAS Report quotes Barry A. J. Fisher, Director of the Scientific Services Bureau of the Los Angeles County Sheriff's Department:

[C]onsider a situation where there are multiple [terrorism] events in the US and abroad occurring simultaneously. Resources could be stretched to the breaking point.... There is *not* an unlimited supply of forensic scientists available to the FBI. But there are probably 5,000+ public forensic scientists at State and local crime labs who could be enlisted to help.[88]

The report concluded that "a strong and reliable forensic science community is needed to maintain homeland security."[89]

* * * *

The publication of the NAS Report represents a turning point in the development of forensic science. The political momentum that it has generated has already spurred a flurry of legislation at the federal and state levels. The recommendation to make crime laboratories independent, however, has not yet made headway. Reformers should give this recommendation a closer look; otherwise they risk squandering a historic opportunity to give the practice of forensic science a much-needed fresh start.

Notes for Chapter Six

1. *See* National Institute of Justice, Status and Needs of Forensic Science Service Providers: A Report to Congress (2004), https://www.ncjrs.gov/pdffiles1/nij/213420.pdf (forensic science leaders identify personnel shortages as the greatest challenge of forensic science and support an increase in federal funding to address the problem).

2. *See* National Research Council, Strengthening Forensic Science in the United States: A Path Forward at 78–79 (National Academies Press: 2009) (hereinafter "NAS Report").

3. *Id.* at 16, 18–20, 23–24, 79, 183–84.

4. *Id.* at 16–17. Others have also called for independent forensic laboratories. *See, e.g.*, The Justice Project, Improving the Practice and Use of Forensic Science: A Policy Review, at 1, http://ag.ca.gov/meetings/tf/pdf/Justice_Project_Report.pdf.

5. *See* Secret Service Forensic Services, at http://www.secretservice.gov/forensics.shtml; U.S. Army Criminal Investigation Laboratory, at http://www.cid.army.mil/usacil.html.

6. *See* Sacramento County District Attorney's Office, Crime Lab (Laboratory of Forensic Sciences), http://www.sacda.org/divisions/crime%20lab/crime%20lab.php.

7. Nassau County's crime lab shut down in 2011 in the wake of a scandal that threw thousands of cases into questions. A new civilian lab opened under the county medical examiner in 2012. *See* Shelly Feuer Domash & Christopher Twarowski, *Nassau County Taxpayers Secretly Charged Millions for Police Crime Lab Scandal*, Long Island Press.com (Dec. 31, 2012), http://www.longislandpress.com/2013/12/31/exclusive-nassau-county-taxpayers-secretly-charged-millions-for-police-crime-lab-scandal/. In Washington, D.C., the Metropolitan Police Lab was transformed into the "Consolidated Forensic Laboratory" in the Department of General Services, whose mission is to advance and improve "public safety support, homeland security, crime investigation capabilities, and public health and science in the District." *See* The District of Columbia, Department of General Services, Consolidated Forensic Laboratory, http://dgs.dc.gov/page/consolidated-forensic-laboratory.

8. *See* Alabama Department of Forensic Sciences, History of the Alabama Department of Forensic Sciences, http://www.adfs.alabama.gov/About.aspx.

9. *See* The University of Rhode Island, Rhode Island State Crime Lab, History, http://web.uri.edu/riscl/about/history/.

10. *See* Chapter 4.

11. *See* Sudhir Sinha, *Re: "Strengthening Forensic Science in the United States: A Path Forward,"* (2009) (president of Forensic Quality Services, a forensic laboratory accreditation firm's response to the NAS Report) (on file with author).

12. *See* AMERICAN ACADEMY OF FORENSIC SCIENCES, *"The American Academy of Forensic Sciences Approves Position Statement in Response to the National Academy of Sciences: Forensic Needs' Report,"* Sept. 4, 2009, http://aafs.org/sites/default/files/pdf/AAFS_Position_Statement_for_Press_Distribution_090409.pdf.

13. SENATE JUDICIARY COMMITTEE, THE NEED TO STRENGTHEN FORENSIC SCIENCE IN THE UNITED STATES: THE NATIONAL ACADEMY OF SCIENCES' REPORT ON A PATH FORWARD, Hearing before the Committee on the Judiciary, United States Senate at 25–26 (2009) (hereinafter Congressional Hearing) (letter from Dean Gialamas and Beth Greene, American Society of Crime Lab Directors /Laboratory Accreditation Board [ASCLAD/LAB] President and President-Elect, respectively), http://www.gpo.gov/fdsys/kpg/CHRG-111shrg54304/pdf/CHRG-111shrg54304.pdf.

14. *Id.*

15. *Id.* at 26.

16. *See* International Association for Identification, *History*, at http://www.theiai.org/history/.

17. *See* Congressional Hearing, *supra* note 11 at 44 (letter from Robert J. Garrett, President, International Association for Identification [IAI]).

18. *See* Robert J. Garrett, President of International Association for Identification (IAI), Correspondence to Senator Leahy of the Senate Committee on the Judiciary, at 3 (Mar. 18, 2009) (on file with author).

19. *See* ASCLD/LAB-International, Program Overview (2010 ed.), http://www.ascld-lab.org/wp-content/uploads/2013/09/AL-PD-3041_Intl_2010_Program_Overview_v2.2_unmked.pdf.

20. Congressional Hearing, *supra* note 13 at 23 (May 16, 2009) (letter from Jami St. Clair, Chair, ASCLAD/LAB Board).

21. *See* International Organization for Standardization, ISO/IEC 17025:2005 (2010), http://www.iso.org/iso/catalogue_detail.htm?csnumber=39883.

22. Paul Giannelli, *Independent Crime Laboratories: The Problem of Motivational and Cognitive Bias*, UTAH L. REV. 247, 249, 259–60 (2010).

23. *See* National District Attorneys Association (NDAA), *NDAA Comments Provided to the Consortium of Forensic Sciences Regarding the National Academy of Sciences Report* (April 2009) (on file with author).

24. *See* NAS Report, *supra* note 2 at 184.

25. *Id.*

26. *Id.*

27. *Id.* at 190–91.

28. *See* International Association of Chiefs of Police (IACP), *Forensics Policy* (approved by the IACP Governing Body on Apr. 18, 2009) (on file with author).

29. Roger Koppl, *CSI for Real: How to Improve Forensic Science,* Reason Foundation, Policy Study No. 364 at 20 (2007), http://reason.org/files/d834fab5860d5cf4b3949fecf86d3328.pdf.

30. *See* Paul C. Giannelli, *Regulating Crime Laboratories: The Impact of DNA Evidence*, 15 J.L. & Pol'y 59, 65 (2007) (quoting D. Michael Risinger & Michael J. Saks, *A House with No Foundation*, Issues in Sci. & Tech., Fall 2003, at 35, 35.).

31. *See* Chapter 3.

32. Paul C. Giannelli, *Daubert and Forensic Science: The Pitfalls of Law Enforcement Control of Scientific Research*, 2011 U. Ill. L. Rev. 53, 66 (2011).

33. *Id.* at 70 (quoting State v. Alt, 504 N.W.2d 38, 48–49 (Minn. Ct. App. 1993)).

34. *Id.*

35. *Id.* at 70–71

36. *Id.* at 71–72.

37. *Id.* at 88.

38. *Id.*

39. *See* NAS Report, *supra* note 2 at 19. Emphasis added.

40. *Id.* at 17–18. Emphasis in original.

41. Justice Department, *Notice of Establishment of the National Commission on Forensic Science and Solicitation of Applications for Commission Membership*, A Notice by the Justice Department, Feb. 22, 2013, Fed. Reg., http://www.federalregister.gov/articles/2013/02/22/2013-04140/notice-of-establishement-of-the-national-commission-on-forensic-science-and-solicitation-of.

42. Dep't of Justice, *U.S. Departments of Justice and Commerce Name Experts to First-Ever National Commission on Forensic Science*, Jan. 10, 2014, http://www.justice.gov/opa/pr/2014/January/14-at-029.html.

43. *Id.* One report found that the creation of the National Commission "was widely hailed as a step in the right direction, albeit a small one." *See* Mark Hansen, *Crime Labs under the Microscope after a String of Shoddy, Suspect, and Fraudulent Results*, ABA Journal (Sept. 1, 2013), http://www.abajournal.com/magazine/article/crime_labs_under_the_microscope_after_a_string_of_shoddy_suspect_and_fraudu/.

44. *See* National Institute of Standards and Technology (NIST), proposed Organization of Scientific Area Committees (OSAC), Presentation for National Commission on Forensic Science (Feb. 4, 2014), http://www.nist.gov/forensics/upload/NIST-OSAC-Plan-NCFS-Feb-4-2014-2-3-14-FINAL.pdf.

45. *Id.*

46. *See* NAS Report, *supra* note 2 at v.

47. *See* NIST, *Scientific Working Groups*, http://nist.gov/forensics/workgroups.cfm.

48. NAS Report, *supra* note 2 at 205–6. The NAS Report also called for coupling the standards of each discipline with accreditation and/or certification requirements. *Id.* at 206.

49. *See Memorandum of Understanding between the Department of Justice and the National Institute of Standards and Technology in Support of the National Commission on Forensic Science* (signed Mar. 25, 2013) (on file with author).

50. *See* National Institute of Standards and Technology, *Organization of Scientific Area Committees, Role and Responsibilities* (April 11, 2014), http://www.nist.gov/forensics/osacroles.cfm.

51. *Id.*

52. See Chapter 3.

53. *See* Forensic Science and Standards Act of 2014, S. 2022, at https://www.govtrack.us/congress/bills/113/s2022/text. This legislation unanimously passed out of Senate Commerce, Science and Transportation Committee by voice vote on April 9, 2014.

54. *See* NAS Report, *supra* note 2 at 78.

55. *See* Criminal Justice and Forensic Science Reform Act of 2014, S. 2177, at https://beta.congress.gov/113/bills/s2177/BILLS-113s2177is.pdf. (accessed Aug. 11, 2014).

56. *See* Hansen, *supra* note 43.

57. *See* Larry A. Hammond, *The Failure of Forensic Science Reform in Arizona*, 93 JUDICATURE 227 (2010).

58. *Id.* at 228.

59. In 2001, because of a growing concern about quality assurance in forensic science, the Association of Forensic Quality Assurance Managers was established. *See* Association of Forensic Quality Assurance Managers, http://afqam.org/wp12/.

60. *Id.*

61. *See, e.g.,* TEX. GOV'T CODE ANN. §411.0205 (West 2012) (legislation establishing the state's Crime Laboratory Accreditation Process and mandating that all police crime laboratories be accredited). The main accrediting organization, ASCLD/LAB lists 405 accredited forensic laboratories nationwide. *See* American Society of Crime Lab Directors / Laboratory Accreditation Board, Accredited Laboratory Index (as of March 27, 2014), http://www.ascld-lab.org/accredited-laboratory-index/.

62. *Id.*

63. See American Society of Crime Laboratory Directors/Laboratory Accreditation Board, (ASCLD/LAB) History, http://www.ascld-lab.org/history/; and its Legacy Program, http://www.ascld-lab.org/legacy-program/.

64. *See* American Society of Crime Laboratory Directors/Laboratory Accreditation Board, *ASCLD/LAB-International, ASCLD/LAB Guidance on the Estimation of Measurement Uncertainty–ANNEX C Firearms/Toolmarks Discipline Firearms Category of Testing, Example-Overall Length of a Firearm* (approved May 22, 2013), http://www.ascld-lab.org/wp-content/uploads/2013/06/AL-PD-3064-Guidance-Measurement_Uncertainty-Firearms_v1.0.pdf.

65. The author has followed the activities of the former Houston Police Department Crime Laboratory, which has now become the independent Houston Forensic Science Center, of which the author is a member of the Board of Directors.

66. *See* Marvin Schechter, Memorandum to the New York State Commission of Forensic Science, *ASCLAD/LAB and Forensic Laboratory Accreditation: An Analysis*, Mar. 25, 2011, http://newenglandinnocence.org/wp-content/uploads/2011/07/ASCLD-Lab-and-Forensic-Laboratory-Accreditation.pdf.

67. *Id.*

68. *Id.* at 24.

69. Sarah Chu, Innocence Project Forensic Policy Advocate, Email correspondence with author (May 16, 2014) (on file with author).

70. *See* Simon A. Cole, *More than Zero: Accounting for Error in Latent Fingerprint Identification*, 95 J. OF CRIM. L. & CRIMINOLOGY 985, 1029 (2005).

71. *Id.*

72. Jonathan J. Koehler & John Meixner, eds., *Workshop on Cognitive Bias and Forensic Science* (2010) at 16, http://www.law.northwestern.edu/faculty/conferences/workshops/cognitivebias/.

73. *See* Cole, *supra* note 70 at 1029.

74. *Id.*

75. *See* American Statistical Association, Position Statement on the NAS Report (May 3, 2010) (on file with author).

76. *See* Cole, *supra* note 70 (citations omitted).

77. *See* American Society of Crime Laboratory Directors/Laboratory Accreditation Board (ASCLD/LAB), *Proficiency Testing and Review Program* at 4–5 (Oct. 31, 2011), http://www.ascld-lab.org/wp-content/uploads/2013/04/AL-PD-1020_Proficiency_Testing_Review_Program_v1.0.pdf.

78. *See* American Statistical Association, *supra* note 75 at 65; NAS Report, *supra* note 2 at 147–48.

79. *See, e.g.,* Texas Forensic Science Commission & Texas Criminal Justice Integrity Unit, *Defendant Notification after Major Forensic Nonconformance* (Nov. 27, 2013).

80. *See* Brady v. Maryland, 373 U.S. 83, 87–88 (1963).

81. *See* NAS Report, *supra* note 2 at 208–10.

82. *See* Texas Forensic Science Commission & Texas Criminal Justice Integrity Unit, *Certification of Forensic Examiners in Texas: Our Path Forward* (Nov. 27, 2013).

83. Roger Koppl, *How to Improve Forensic Science,* 20 European J. of L & Econ. 255, 260 (2005).

84. *Id.* at 260 (80 percent of crime laboratories work exclusively for law enforcement).

85. *See* Texas Forensic Science Commission Stakeholder Roundtable Report (Austin, Texas, June 6, 2012), http://www.fsc.texas.gov/sites/default/files/documents/files/StakeholderRoundtableReport-June62012.pdf.

86. *See* Chapter 7.

87. *See* NAS Report, *supra* note 2 at 281.

88. *Id.* at 284.

89. *Id.*

Chapter Seven

Houston's Laboratory Experiment

In the wake of the scandals involving George Rodriguez and others, the Houston Police Department closed the DNA section of its laboratory in 2002.[1] The number of untested sexual assault kits in 2002 was estimated at an astonishing 19,500 and included not only those backlogged in the laboratory but also kits for which investigators had never requested testing. Like so many places around the country, the Houston Police Department had accumulated a large backlog of rape kits. Many of these rape kits were not tested because investigators had never requested it, usually because they viewed testing as unnecessary due one of several possible reasons such as the victim's refusal to cooperate, an inability to locate the victim, or because the identity of the alleged perpetrator was not in question.[2] In Houston, the number of untested rape kits was so large that it suggested a failure to test in thousands of viable cases.

On November 11, 2002, reporters David Raziq and Anna Werner, of local television station KHOU, did extensive reporting on the problems in the HPD Crime Laboratory.[3] As a result of the serious questions raised in the reports, HPD closed its DNA section and commissioned an outside audit of the section. Houston resident, Carol Batie, also reacted to the news reports. She sent an email to Raziq and Werner, desperate to help her twenty-year-old son, Josiah Sutton, who had been convicted of rape three years earlier in 1999 and sentenced to twenty-five years in prison based in part on the HPD Crime Laboratory's DNA testing.[4] The KHOU reporters took interest in the case and sent the DNA report from Sutton's case to William C. Thompson, of the University of California-Irvine, a professor of criminology and an expert on forensic science. Thompson found serious and obvious mistakes in the report which a review by any qualified supervisor should have immediately identified.[5] When the reporters presented this new information to local officials, HPD agreed to an immediate retest of the DNA evidence, and this re-test clearly demonstrated that the DNA collected in the case did not belong to Sutton. He was released from prison in March 2003 and given a full pardon in 2004.[6]

The public scandal caused by such an obvious miscarriage of justice resulted in the retirements and dismissals of many laboratory employees. A new director, Irma Rios, was hired in October 2003, seven months after Sutton's release.[7] Rios had worked in forensic science for nineteen years, the last nine as manager of the DNA section of the state crime laboratory. The previous year, in December 2002, HPD leaders tapped her as one of three auditors for the DNA section of its laboratory, in the wake of the Josiah Sutton scandal.[8] The results showed numerous and fundamental problems: poorly trained analysts, insufficient documentation of the testing process, and improper storage of physical evidence resulting in some contamination.[9] As a result of the audit, HPD sent 407 DNA cases in which convictions had already been handed down to other laboratories for retesting.[10] In March 2003, the *New York Times* article reported that legal experts considered HPD's laboratory the "worst in the country."[11]

One of the analysts involved in the 1998 rape case in which Josiah Sutton was convicted had been subsequently terminated for incompetence related to the case (e.g., using outdated methods and formulas for DNA testing) by then-Mayor Lee Brown in December 2003. However, through the civil service process, she was reinstated to her previous position less than a month later in January 2004.[12] Some HPD supervisors, including Timothy Oettmeier, who had become Executive Assistant Chief in 2002 as well as other expert observers called for more stringent disciplinary actions against Crime Laboratory employees whose analyses showed they had used improper procedures or whose testimony misrepresented forensic evidence during trials.[13]

The bad publicity continued in 2004, but this time it centered on which agency would review old convictions obtained with faulty serology evidence performed by the HPD Crime Laboratory. The Harris County District Attorney Chuck Rosenthal resisted calls by the county criminal court judges that he appoint an independent "special master" to review the cases and insisted that his prosecutors could conduct the review. A *Houston Chronicle* editorial called for an independent inquiry to detect other possible miscarriages of justice caused by the unreliable crime laboratory, citing the Rodriguez case.[14] By mid-2004, the political firestorm proved too much, and Rosenthal stopped insisting that his office could handle the reviews and, where necessary, the motions for new trials and/or dismissals.[15] As a result, local officials decided that the local criminal court judges would appoint three defense attorneys to review the 180 cases involving questionable serology testing.[16]

The problems in the serology division were so glaring that they had tarnished the reputation of the entire laboratory. State Senator Rodney Ellis and Innocence Project founder Barry Scheck jointly called for an audit of approximately 5,000 to 10,000 serology cases spanning decades.[17] Scheck also argued for a comprehensive review of cases in which convictions had been obtained based on the crime laboratory's reports of toxicology, serology, ballistics, fingerprint, and hair and fiber analysis.[18] Elizabeth Johnson, the Director of the DNA laboratory at the county medical examiner's office before moving to a private laboratory in 2003, commented in the press as a local expert on the kind of testing that needed to be done. According to Johnson, the undertaking would be "daunting" and that, if cases from other sections of the laboratory were included in retesting and reviews, the number of cases could be "off the board."[19]

Two successive HPD Police Chiefs called for a moratorium on executions until the laboratory's DNA work in prior capital cases could be reviewed. Clarence Bradford, who had resigned in January 2004, called for a moratorium in 2003. In October 2004, the new HPD Chief of Police Harold Hurtt made a similar plea in a joint statement with a state high court judge, and several state legislators.[20] DNA evidence had been first introduced in criminal courts in the late 1980s, less than twenty years earlier, and it tended to be used primarily in serious cases such as rapes and homicides. Thus, it was quite feasible to review all past cases in which HPD crime laboratory analysts had performed DNA testing that led to a conviction and death sentence. A spokesman for Mayor Bill White supported this recommendation, stating that the mayor wanted "to make sure that there are not innocent people locked up. And [his] number one concern is that the jurors in our community have confidence in our evidence so that criminals don't get off."[21]

Throughout this period of intense turmoil in 2002–04, Rios's direction in the DNA lab made significant progress in improving the quality of its work, facilitated by HPD's improved funding of the DNA section. She hired new supervisors and analysts, many of whom were relatively fresh from their academic training, bright, and enthusiastic. The laboratory had re-written all of its standard operating procedure manuals. HPD increased funding for training and hired a new quality assurance and quality control manager. In May 2005, HPD announced that the laboratory had received national accreditation through the American Society of Crime Laboratory Directors/Laboratory Accreditation Board (ASCLD/LAB) for every area of the laboratory except DNA.[22] This accreditation status was earned under the previous "Legacy" standards that are considered less rigorous than the newer ISO standards applied by ASCLD/LAB, but accreditation nonetheless indicated improved quality controls. The DNA section did not qualify for accreditation, even under these weaker standards. After the serious problems found in the DNA section following the exonerations of Josiah Sutton and George Rodriguez, the HPD undertook a large-scale effort to rebuild the DNA section, essentially starting from scratch, and these efforts had not progressed by 2005 to a point where the section could gain accreditation.

On March 30, 2005, City Council approved the hiring of Michael Bromwich, a former Inspector General with the U.S. Department of Justice, who would conduct a comprehensive, independent investigation of the entire HPD laboratory. Bromwich enlisted a team of attorneys and seven forensic scientists to conduct the investigation. A Scientific Advisory Board of three renowned crime laboratory managers who had since retired provided guidance to the investigative team.[23] Between 2005 and his final report in 2007, this team undertook a review *and reanalysis* of over 3,500 cases involving DNA, serology, toxicology, firearms, controlled substances, trace evidence, and questioned documents. Bromwich would later reflect on this investigation in a 2012 op-ed piece, noting:

> It was the most comprehensive investigation of a crime lab ever conducted. No limits were placed on our investigation, and we were permitted to expand its scope once we learned that there were profound problems in the way that serology (blood) analysis had been conducted going back more than 20 years.[24]

The investigation into past practices confirmed huge problems in the serology and DNA cases and significant problems in a number of controlled substances cases. As Bromwich recounted:

> These problems called into question close to 200 cases in which defendants had been incarcerated based, at least in part, on blood evidence. When our final report was published in the summer of 2007, we expressed grave concern over the quality of DNA and serology analysis that had been performed in the lab—major problems with close to one-third of the DNA cases we reviewed, one-quarter of the capital (death penalty) DNA cases, and one-fifth of all the serology cases. By any measure, these were unacceptably high numbers.[25]

The retesting done by Bromwich's team showed that, of 1,100 samples reviewed, 40% of DNA samples and 23% of blood evidence samples had serious problems. The Bromwich study also showed 147 cases involving major issues in the controlled substances section. The rest of the laboratory—the firearms section, trace evidence, toxicology, and questioned documents—proved to do good work. Nonetheless, Bromwich stated that "the appalling DNA and serology statistics captured the attention of the public and confirmed some of its worst fears."[26] The audit blamed the problems on a lack of support and resources (e.g., low salaries, little training), ineffective management of the crime laboratory (i.e., incompetent managers, low morale, difficult personalities), lack of adequate quality control and quality assurance, as well as the isolation of the DNA/serology section from the rest of the crime laboratory which caused supervisors to fail to recognize the serious problems affecting the section.[27] Likewise, the laboratory had not been accredited because the section manager recognized that without greater resources they could not make the changes needed to meet accreditation standards.

By the time Bromwich concluded his review in 2007 the laboratory had shown much improvement, including the announcement that the DNA section had finally gained accreditation on June 11, 2007. Still issues such as space, resource constraints, and the never-ending pressure of huge caseloads made it difficult for the laboratory to show truly dramatic improvements, despite sincere efforts to do so, and the public did not regain confidence in the laboratory even after many years.[28]

Only four months after Bromwich reported the newly rebuilt DNA section's accreditation, a cheating scandal erupted, again reinforcing the public's skepticism. On October 5, 2007, the *Houston Chronicle* published allegations that analysts had cheated on a routine open-book proficiency test.[29] An investigation that fall revealed widespread problems in the DNA section, which resulted in the resignation of the section chief who stepped down to avoid termination.[30] The HPD hired an outside consultant in February 2008, Dr. Charlotte Word, to oversee the casework being done within the DNA section, and she would continue in this role throughout 2008. A new technical leader, Laura Gahn, assumed management of the section on June 4, 2008. With the assistance of an additional outside consultant, Dr. Robin Cotton, who began work on December 2008, the HPD continued to transform the DNA section into a well-functioning operation. Dr. Cotton would continue in that role until 2010.[31] In the meantime, sexual assault kits continued to pile up, further increasing an already-enormous backlog, evoking outrage over rape victims whose cases may have been ignored.

More wrongful convictions stemming from the poor work done years before came to light in 2008, continuing the onslaught of negative publicity. These included those of two men wrongly convicted of rapes. Gary Alvin Richard had spent twenty-two years in prison, and Ronald Gene Taylor had served twelve years of a sixty-year prison sentence.[32] Subsequent DNA testing exonerated both men. Reviews of their convictions showed that in both cases the police department's analysts had reported the evidence as favorable to the prosecution even though the actual results would not support their testimony. William C. Thompson, a professor and forensic expert, found a pattern of statistical errors, misleading testimony, and scientific errors that tended to favor the prosecution, leading him to conclude, "It's like team spirit. They see the defense counsel as their enemy and tend to be kind of secretive and not want to disclose things outside of the family."[33]

Then outside auditors discovered problems in other sections of the laboratory. A special audit conducted in December 2009 found major problems with the fingerprint unit, including staff shortages, poor training and supervision, failure to meet industry standards and a backlog of six thousand cases. The audit was conducted as a measure to move the identification unit of HPD closer to attaining accreditation. As a result, the HPD fired one temporary employee, and placed one supervisor and two examiners on administrative leave, later investigating one of those examiners for other workplace irregularities.[34]

In July 2011, the HPD crime laboratory faced yet another scandal that broke out when a former HPD laboratory supervisor, Amanda Culbertson, testified during a hearing in a DWI case that she had quit because she could not trust the accuracy of field breath tests for alcohol at traffic checkpoints. These tests used equipment and supplies transported to each site by police breath alcohol testing (BAT) vans. Culbertson testified to having disciplined officers, as well as civilian technicians, who had not followed strict rules designed to keep the machines from overheating, but also stated that she feared retaliation from laboratory director Irma Rios for requiring adherence to these rules.[35] (Culbertson alleged that Rios was more interested in keeping the statistics on sobriety checks high.)

In an odd twist, Culbertson's testimony led to a grand jury investigation into possible wrongdoing by members of the District Attorney's Office. Grand jury investigations are secret so there is no public record of the proceedings, and participants are required to keep the proceedings secret. Presumably, however, the grand jury investigated whether members of the District Attorney's Office may have known about the problems with the BAT van tests and nonetheless prosecuted people based on the test results without disclosing the issues to defense counsel. The political intrigue intensified when Assistant District Attorney Rachel Palmer was called to testify in December 2011, and she surprisingly invoked the Fifth Amendment, thereby suggesting that she would have incriminated herself by testifying.[36] Then District Attorney Pat Lykos herself testified before the grand jury during the investigation a month later, raising the question whether the grand jury might indict her. After a six-month investigation, no indictments resulted from the grand jury proceedings.[37] Then in February of 2012, Lykos announced that she was asking the Texas Department of Public Safety to replace the HPD in providing quality assurance and supervision of the BAT vans.[38] In the end, the finger-pointing became so intense that only the insiders in this particular scandal would ever know the truth about possible problems with the BAT vans. What was clear was that the HPD laboratory continued to generate negative publicity.

During the same time period when the scandal over the BAT vans captured headlines, the press also reported yet another crime laboratory problem, this time regarding the backlog of sexual assault kits. The DNA section, which by now had vastly improved its performance, had worked hard to reduce the backlog which was believed to number about four thousand. Then in December of 2011, the *Houston Chronicle* reported that the actual figure was between 6,000 and 7,000.[39] These figures included both cases for which testing had been requested and those for which it had not, which normally are not counted as an estimate of *a laboratory's* backlog. In 2011, the Texas legislature enacted a law requiring the testing of all sexual assault kits received by law enforcement agencies within thirty days of receiving them, thus increasing the demand for testing.[40] Sexual assault kit backlogs are a national problem, and the federal government provides grants to crime laboratories to hire personnel and purchase equipment so that crime laboratories can reduce their backlogs, yet such additional resources had apparently not improved Houston's ability to work through its massive backlog. The logistical problem was real, but it was exacerbated by the community relations problem. Houston citizens were weary of abysmal stories about its crime laboratory.

The troubled laboratory's failings had first gained national attention in 2002, followed by many years of negative headlines. The NAS Report in 2009 embarrassed the city further by featuring the HPD Crime Laboratory prominently in its discussion of crime laboratory "errors and fraud."[41] After almost ten years of unrelenting bad press, leaders at HPD and City Hall yearned for a drastic change.

Don't Fix It — Reinvent It

In 2010, Houston's new mayor, Annise Parker discovered that, when she traveled around the country, her mayoral colleagues and journalists did not ask about Houston's thriving economy, strong cultural scene, or diversity. Rather, the city was identified primarily with the troubled crime laboratory. She resolved to turn the laboratory from a political liability to a genuine asset. But what, exactly could city leaders do that they had not already tried? Major personnel overhauls, massive internal and external audits, and an expanded budget for training, quality assurance, and equipment had resulted in accreditation for almost all of the entire laboratory in 2005 and later the now-improved DNA section in 2007. The crime laboratory was now functioning about as well as those in most major U.S. cities, yet the perception of a broken system still lingered. What the laboratory needed was a paradigm shift that would not only improve the laboratory's quality but also reverse its community image.

During the summer of 2011, some county officials proposed the establishment of a "regional" crime laboratory.[42] City leaders talked to county officials about merging the HPD crime laboratory with that of the Harris County Medical Examiner's Office, which already had a solid reputation. The county already had plans for the construction of a new forensics building in Houston's world-class Texas Medical Center, so a plan to further expand by joining forces with the city seemed to make sense.[43] In the end, county officials seemed willing to consider taking over the HPD laboratory, but the plan ultimately failed to reach agreement about shared authority in governing a joint laboratory.[44]

Committed to the mayor's resolution of permanently fixing both procedural and public relations problems, high-ranking members of the HPD, Executive Assistant Chief Oettmeier and Crime Laboratory Director Rios, returned to the National Academy of Sciences' 2009 recommendation and proposed that the laboratory be removed from HPD's control and become an independently governed unit. In contrast to the almost knee-jerk resistance to independent laboratories from law enforcement and crime laboratory leaders nationally, the police department and crime laboratory in Houston provided the leadership driving this proposal. One reason was their recognition that police officials have not and never have been trained to effectively manage forensic disciplines. More importantly, they acknowledged that the goals and objectives of a forensic operation will always take a back seat to those of police operations.[45] Because the laboratory's funding would also be assigned a lower priority than the hiring of new officers and buying new equipment, it would never get proper funding. And finally, HPD's administrators had learned the lesson of history: HPD's forensic operations began deteriorating long before the DNA debacle; the laboratory was simply underfunded, underdeveloped, and more or less ignored.[46] But more than that, HPD officials truly believed in the value of independence for a forensic laboratory. Thus, they presented the proposal to Mayor Parker who, after thorough study, agreed that creating an independent forensic science laboratory was most likely to result in a first-class laboratory that could regain public confidence.

Political Negotiations

The plan to remove the HPD Crime Laboratory from police control faced a number of political and practical challenges. Politically, the mayor needed buy-in, not only from Charles McClelland, who became the acting police chief in March 2010 until his promotion to Police Chief in 2014, but also from the head of the Houston Police Officers' Union, Ray Hunt. Houston has had strong police union leadership for many years, and Hunt wanted assurances that no classified police officers would lose their jobs, benefits, or civil service protections. This requirement was not a deal-breaker. Only about half of the lab's employees were classified police officers, as opposed to the other half which consisted of civilians. After city leaders assured Hunt that the positions of classified police officers would be protected, he endorsed the city's plan for an independent laboratory.

The next step was achieving buy-in from rank-and-file police officers. Houston learned a few lessons from the recent troubles faced in Washington, D.C. The Metropolitan Police Department had long operated a small forensic laboratory, relying mostly on the FBI Crime Laboratory to provide the district's forensic services. In 2006, the FBI proposed that the district should establish its own laboratory.[47] Congress eventually authorized and funded the development of a state-of-the-art forensic laboratory that would operate independently of law enforcement.

In October 2012, a new, independent forensic laboratory in Washington, D.C. opened to much fanfare. The new laboratory occupies a state-of-the-art $210 million building, and its director, Dr. Max Houck, enjoys an outstanding national reputation for excellence in forensic science.[48] Yet bitter in-fighting over the plans for the new laboratory attracted as many headlines as the design for the impressive new building. The police department found itself at odds with its local union, the Fraternal Order of Police. The dispute arose when the department decided to reassign eighty veteran crime scene investigators to other police duties and replace them with civilian scientists.[49] After the first twenty police officers had been reassigned as of February 2013, the remaining sixty were temporarily assigned to the new laboratory where they were expected to handle the work *and* train their replacements before being reassigned to positions within the department.[50] The president of the police union bitterly opposed this plan.[51] The *Washington Times* in March 2013 criticized the laboratory and published photographs showing the shoddy handling of blood-stained evidence. Houck challenged the authenticity of the photographs.[52] The president of the police officers' union stated: "The lack of a functioning crime lab is a serious threat to public safety.... Sloppy, unprofessional practices can result in criminals going free."[53] The real story was clearly the no-holds-barred management dispute and possible efforts to embarrass the District's administration. Leaders in Washington, D.C. had moved forward with a plan that rankled the police union, and the dispute played out in the media. Houston leaders looked for ways to avoid those conflicts.

In most places, the approval of the county district attorney is a political necessity for any significant change in criminal justice administration. In Houston, however, the district attorney, Pat Lykos, was completely at odds with the police department, as well as a significant number of her assistant district attorneys who disagreed with her leadership style and policies.[54] Because Lykos had little to no political clout, they could proceed without her involvement. In fact, according to comments I heard while these negotiations were ongoing, if she had been included in the negotiations about creating a new laboratory, the police may have backed out. Thus, the alliances forged between the mayor, city council, the police department, and the police union were sufficient to move forward with the plan.

The Process of Transition

Houston then faced the next step, which is the issue of governance. Once the decision is made to remove a laboratory from police control, what entity will control it? The city decided to create a "local government corporation" overseen by a board of community volunteers. On June 6, 2012, the Houston City Council approved the formation of the Houston Forensic Science Center, Inc.[55] The Center operates as a unit of city government, but it enjoys a larger measure of political independence since it operates as a "corporation." An "FAQ" prepared by the Center's attorney, Tom Allen, gives this insight into the reasoning behind the decision to create a local government corporation:

> Texas law provides that "[a] local government corporation may be created to aid and to act on behalf of one or more local governments to accomplish any governmental purpose...." Like other non-profit corporations, a local government corporation is an independent business entity with its own directors, officers, and employees. Current plans call for the City Council to name the directors of the proposed "Houston Forensic Science LGC, Inc." (the "LGC") but also to approve articles of incorporation prohibiting the removal of a director unless he or she has engaged in intentional, unlawful behavior directly related to official duties. The LGC structure will go far to insulate the Center from inappropriate influence by police, prosecutors, elected officials, or special interest groups.[56]

With the basic structure for the administration of the new laboratory in place, representatives of the City Attorney's Office assisted the mayor, who would appoint the members of the Board of Directors. They made informal inquiries at local universities, within law enforcement, business, and political circles, searching for the right combination of people to tap for these positions. One June 20, 2012, the board held its first organizational meeting at City Hall at which the mayor greeted the nine board members she had appointed, of which I am one.[57] One might assume that any board of directors for a forensic laboratory should include forensic scientists who could bring their expertise to bear on the management of the new laboratory. However, the Memorandum of Understanding contemplates that board members could come from fields other than forensic science to serve on the board.[58] The governance structure provides that a separate "Technical Advisory Group" (TAG) would advise the board on scientific matters,[59] so board members need not specialize in forensic science, and none of the mayor's appointees had such expertise.

What the board did bring was diversity of many kinds. It had gender and racial diversity, important in a city such as Houston. The board included five women and four men, of whom two were African-Americans, three were Hispanics, one was Asian-American, and three were whites. Equally important, however, was the diversity of expertise that would be useful to the board, such as in wrongful convictions, law enforcement, the judicial system, laboratory practices, and business management. Each person on the board brought an important perspective and skill set that enabled the Center to navigate the challenging terrain it faced in making fundamental changes to an ongoing enterprise without disrupting the daily flow of work. The initial board included four academics, Nicole B. Cásarez, Enrique V. Barrera, Marcia Johnson, and me, each from a different local university. Cásarez and I, both licensed attorneys, specialize in wrongful convictions. She teaches in an undergraduate journalism program, whereas I teach at a law school. Johnson specializes in business law and had prior experience serving on a board for the city. Barrera was a renowned scientist in materials science and nanoengineering. Catherine Lamboley, another board member, was a retired attorney who had worked for a large oil company and was experienced in business law. Donna Fujimoto Cole was an entrepreneur who had started her own chemical company. She was familiar with managing a business and, in particular, with operating a business involving scientific processes. Removing a laboratory from a police department essentially entails setting up a new business, so expertise in law, business, and laboratory management becomes critical.

Despite having the support of HPD leaders and the Police Union, the Board would have little political legitimacy in criminal justice circles unless it also included representatives of law enforcement and the judiciary. To represent law enforcement, the mayor chose Hiram A. ("Art") Contreras, who had risen to the rank of Assistant Chief in the HPD in July 1991 and then became U.S. Marshal for the Southern District of Texas, a position from which he retired in

2002. Representing the judiciary was retired judge Willie Blackmon. The appointment of retired members of law enforcement and the judiciary proved a clever political move. They could speak knowledgeably about the effects of the board's activities on their constituencies, but being retired enabled them to act with greater independence and without conflicts of interest.

The most important appointment was that of Scott Hochberg, a businessman and former state legislator, whom Mayor Parker tapped for the position of Chairman of the Board. Hochberg was well known in Texas for facilitating the passage of important legislation on education and criminal justice. He was known as both book-smart and politically brilliant. Hochberg accepted the appointment as chair while heading a software company and teaching courses at Rice University. Time would prove Hochberg to have been the right choice to lead the transition.

Setting Up Shop

When the board started its work in June 2012, nothing actually changed at the HPD Crime Laboratory. The actual crime laboratory, housed within HPD's headquarters in a downtown skyscraper, remained in the same building under the management of HPD until the details of the transition would be worked out. City Council had approved a small budget of about $500,000 for the new Houston Forensic Science Center (HFSC) to cover the board's minor administrative expenses and to hire a top executive for the laboratory who would help guide the board during the transition. The initial tasks included such mundane matters as opening a bank account for the new corporation, obtaining office space, hiring a secretary, setting up a website, and training the new board members on open meeting laws and the rules on conflicts of interest. With these general housekeeping tasks out of the way, the board then undertook its most important task: hiring a president and CEO for the forensic science center.

Hiring a leader to transform a laboratory from a unit of law enforcement into an independent institution requires a visionary person with good managerial skills and a solid background in laboratory work. The nine members considered whether this person should be an outsider to forensic science, and who could therefore bring a different perspective to the task, or would such a person flounder for a lack of knowledge about forensic practice? These were some of the issues the board members discussed as they created a job description and began to consider candidates. After two rounds of interviews during April and May of 2013, the new director was hired in June of 2013.

In the meantime, a working group of the board defined the criteria for the new Technical Advisory Group (TAG), which would be composed of up to nine members and which would include both university science professors and forensic practitioners. The board members structured the TAG this way to strike a balance between those who work in the "research culture" of academic science and those who work in the rough-and-tumble world of forensic practice. The academics could help the board put the laboratory on a path toward greater scientific integrity while the forensic scientists would help the board better understand the demands and needs of the profession. TAG members hailed from universities and forensic laboratories from across the nation. The board hosted lengthy meetings of the TAG at which TAG members provided guidance and information on a wide variety of issues. Individual TAG members have also given presentations on cutting-edge advances in forensic disciplines.

The board also spent the next few months learning about the laboratory and the interests of the community. HPD hosted tours for board members of the crime laboratory, the identification unit (which included the fingerprint section, the polygraph section and others), the property building (where evidence is stored), the crime scene unit, and the digital forensics laboratory (where analysts investigate crimes committed online). Chairman Hochberg invited community stakeholders to attend board meetings to share their concerns and advice. For example, speakers included local criminal defense leaders, a representative from the Innocence Project, a toxicology professor from a local university, a county leader, a local assistant district attorney, and independent investigator Michael Bromwich. The board hired Bromwich in March of 2013 to conduct another audit of the laboratory as part of the board's new oversight activities. This audit found no major areas of concern, a marked improvement over past audits.

While the new board of directors was defining and refining its new tasks, the employees of the HPD Crime Laboratory continued their work, but now the managers also attended board meetings to learn more about how their workplace would be transformed. Laboratory managers provided the board with regular updates on their activities.

One of the most ambitious items on HPD's agenda was to upgrade the accreditation status of the laboratory. The laboratory's initial accreditation in 2005 had been granted under criteria that did not meet the international standards for laboratories provided by the world's largest developer of standards, the International Organization for Standardization (ISO).[60] The national crises in crime laboratories also tarnished the reputation of the accrediting bodies that had accredited many of those laboratories—mainly ASCLD/LAB. Since 2005, ASCLD/LAB had firmed up accreditation standards for crime laboratories by offering the rigorous ISO 17025 accreditation. This accreditation process incorporates different requirements, such as the use of ISO accredited vendors to calibrate equipment and more procedural detail in the written standard operating procedures for the various disciplines. In a 2009 national survey of public forensic laboratories, only 19% of the laboratories surveyed had obtained ASCLD/LAB international accreditation and 8% had achieved international accreditation through the other major accrediting organization, FQS.[61] The Houston laboratory would work toward ISO 17025 accreditation for several more years until finally completing the process successfully in September 2014.

As laboratory managers worked toward accreditation, the board's international search to hire a president and CEO for the new laboratory continued. The process involved two highly competitive rounds of interviews, one via Skype and then in-person meetings with the three finalists in Houston in May 2013. In the end, the board unanimously voted to hire Dr. Daniel Garner, whose qualifications include many years of experience in forensic science and in establishing and improving forensic laboratories.[62] Garner had directed the forensic laboratory for the U.S. Bureau of Alcohol, Tobacco, and Firearms, leading its successful effort to become the first federal laboratory to earn ASCLD/LAB accreditation. He had also worked in private industry as president of Cellmark Diagnostics, Inc., the laboratory that processed the DNA evidence in the O. J. Simpson case during Garner's tenure. He also led Cellmark to become the first commercial laboratory to achieve ASCLD/LAB accreditation. Most recently, he worked internationally on behalf of the U.S. Department of Justice in an effort to improve forensic science laboratories in foreign countries.[63]

Garner started work in Houston in August of 2013. Though gentle and soft-spoken, Garner nonetheless presented a vision for the new laboratory that was even bolder than the board members had imagined. He grasped the national significance of the Houston experiment in laboratory independence and knew that people around the country were watching to see how things would go in Houston. He viewed this national attention as an opportunity. Garner expressed a desire to build a laboratory that could serve as a role model for the future of forensic science in the United States by providing training services for other laboratories and by engaging with academia in forensic research. He began hosting public lectures in forensic science by national experts to engage the public and to broaden the perspectives of local forensic practitioners and law enforcement. He also immediately began work on plans for a new facility.

Once Garner was employed, negotiations began to actually transition the laboratory out of HPD's organizational control. The Memorandum of Understanding between the City of Houston and the HFSC provided a bare-bones outline of how the assets of the HPD Crime Laboratory would be transferred to the HFSC. Over the course of 2013 and early 2014, the board and its attorney, Tom Allen, worked with other city officials to negotiate the terms of the final "Interlocal Agreement," which would outline the specific terms under which the laboratory would become independent of HPD.

To finalize the Interlocal Agreement required the parties to make tough decisions. For one thing, it had been determined that the Crime Scene Unit (CSU) and Identification Unit (which included the latent print group) would become part of the HFSC. These units employed classified police officers, so the agreement had to find a way for an agency other than the police department to employ a police officer. The agreement reached with the Houston Police Officers Union required that classified police officers remain employees of HPD but be contracted to the HFSC. The police officers would answer to the civilian director of the laboratory, but the director could not actually fire or even discipline a police officer. In the event of a need to discipline or terminate a classified police officer, the director would have to refer the police officer to HPD,[64] effectively removing the police officer as an employee of the laboratory and sending the officer back to HPD which would be the entity with the authority to discipline and retain within HPD, or terminate, the officer.

The board also faced the challenge of which divisions within HPD would become part of the HFSC and which would stay with HPD. Early HPD plans recommended that—in addition to the Crime Laboratory—the Identification Unit, the CSU, the Polygraph Unit, and the Digital and Video Laboratories should become part of the HFSC.[65] Board members expressed uneasiness about keeping the Polygraph Unit as part of the HFSC. Polygraph technology is used either to screen applicants for jobs as police officers or as part of the interrogation of suspects. Some board members objected to including a discipline considered so unreliable and "unscientific" that courts will not allow its results in trial.[66] Fortunately, the HPD officials decided to refocus the mission of the Polygraph Unit for screening new employees rather than for questioning suspects, making it purely a resource for use in hiring new employees, not in forensic investigations. Thus, its inclusion in the HFSC was withdrawn from the plan.[67]

Board members also considered whether the CSU should be part of the HFSC or whether it should stay in HPD. It was no secret that at least some crime scene investigators were reluctant to accept the idea of not working in the police department. They had gone through the police academy to become classified police officers, and they relished their status as officers, yet they were in no position to protest the move since both HPD and the union favored it. Still, the board considered the question because it was not immediately clear whether this group should be part of the laboratory or of the police department.

In many ways, crime scene investigators genuinely act in dual roles as both police officers and as scientists. Unlike most analysts in crime laboratories, most members of CSUs are classified police officers. Their work begins in the field when they are called to the scene of a serious crime such as a murder. The job can involve police work such as securing crime scenes and interacting with people in the area. CSUs will learn the police investigator's working theory of a case and may contribute to further developing the theory. Together, the CSU and the investigating officer decide what evidence to collect. Thus, CSUs are intimately involved in the investigation—a uniquely police-specific role.

On the other hand, CSU members also apply scientific knowledge to the process of collecting the evidence—a uniquely scientific role. Like crime laboratories, CSUs can seek accreditation under an ASCLD/LAB program specially designed for such organizations. No less than laboratory analysts, members of CSUs should follow proper scientific protocols in handling evidence and fully documenting their work. They should also receive on-going training in scientific techniques, and their supervisors should periodically conduct proficiency testing as well. All of these considerations ultimately satisfied board members that it was more important that the crime scene investigators be included as part of the HFSC. Thus, HPD's proposal to include the CSU as part of the new laboratory was approved without much discussion by the board.[68]

Heavy Lifting by HPD

HPD officials did a great deal to prepare for the transfer of the parts of the department that would move to the HFSC.[69] Among the tasks included were a number of changes to the HPD organizational chart such as repositioning units not relating to forensic science out of the divisions into new slots in HPD. The fingerprint database, AFIS, was also moved to the Jail Division, with the HFSC retaining access to the database as part of its fingerprint identification operation. The Central Evidence Receiving Unit did not become part of the HFSC but remained under HPD management as part of the Property Division. This step assured that law enforcement retains possession of all controlled substances except those being analyzed by the laboratory.

The HPD administration showed a genuine commitment to making dramatic improvements to the laboratory prior to its transfer. HPD officials had a vested interest in having a high-quality laboratory since it would continue to do the department's forensic work. Still, it is remarkable that an agency that knew it would be losing a major section of its organization would devote as many resources to improving the section prior to losing it. When a local university decided to close its toxicology laboratory, HPD purchased all of the equipment and hired the staff. The department also obtained $1.5 million in funding to hire sixteen new criminalists for the DNA section of the laboratory and a toxicology manager. HPD built a CSU training room and added storage space in the section of the building dedicated to the HFSC. This floor plan allowed crime scene investigators to have individual work-stations, a requirement of ISO accreditation. HPD also built a new suite of offices for the executive staff of the new HFSC.

Further investments by HPD reduced backlogs in many disciplines, allowing the new center to begin unencumbered by the pressure of delayed casework. Among its top priorities was eliminating the gigantic backlog of sexual assault kits that had caused the most public furor. When an internal audit conducted in 2012 determined that 6,662 sexual assault kits remained untested, the HPD proposed a plan to the mayor and city council that would eliminate this backlog, as well as the backlog of DNA evidence in other types of crimes— a total of about 10,000 cases. Under the proposal, HPD would send the kits to three private laboratories that could collectively handle the large volume of tests required. City leaders approved a plan to spend $4.4 million to clear the DNA backlog, coming up with $2.2 million from the city's general fund and a matching $2.2 million grant. As of April 2014, the department had received results on nearly 8,000 DNA tests and made several arrests in old cases as a result. The testing effort was one of the largest DNA clearance efforts conducted in the nation.

Backlogs were reduced or eliminated in other areas as well. HPD spent $700,000 to expand and renovate its antiquated latent print processing laboratory. This remodeled laboratory enables the HFSC to operate its own latent print laboratory rather than continuing to outsource most of the work to private contractors. By eliminating the latent print backlog, the HFSC laboratory could process prints in new violent crime cases within forty-five days.

HPD also hired additional analysts and acquired new gas chromatographs and mass spectrometers for its controlled substances unit, enabling the staff to reduce the backlog from an astonishing 30,000 cases in December 2009 to a manageable load of just over 4,000 by early 2011.

As a final and important updating step, the HPD installed a laboratory information management system (LIMS), converting more than 200,000 laboratory files for older crimes into electronic format so that the paper copies could be put into storage. This action better positioned the laboratory to manage files and reduce its reliance on hard-copy files.

The intensive effort to improve the laboratory received high praise from Michael Bromwich in his audit report of January 2014. He remarked that the laboratory as of that time was "a very different place" than it had been during the 2005–2007 audit review. He concludes that the laboratory had survived all the challenges of the intervening years "because of an impressive set of senior supervisors under Director Irma Rios, all new in their positions since 2007, who have brought talent, experience, and good judgment to the task of improving the operations of the Crime Lab."[70]

HPD and the HFSC continued to make decisions regarding every aspect of the laboratory assets that would be transferred to the HFSC. The long process of defining the exact terms of the Interlocal Agreement, which had been ongoing since the HFSC was formed in 2012, culminated in its approval by the city council on February 26, 2014. A little over one month later, all of the pieces were finally in place for the City of Houston to commence its independent forensic laboratory.

A New Day Dawns at the Houston Forensic Science Center

On April 3, 2014, the HPD Crime Laboratory ceased to exist, and the Houston Forensic Science Center came into being with a modest cake-and-punch reception in the laboratory meeting room.[71] The two most striking things about its inaugural event were the impressive congratulatory talks by HPD's top brass and the fact that reporters were not invited. The HPD Crime Laboratory had become so notorious that even a positive story like the transition to the HFSC would simply have given the press another opportunity to remind the public of the laboratory's troubled past.

One of the first speakers was Timothy Oettmeier, HPD's Executive Assistant Chief, who had put much work into realizing the department's vision for

Logo of the Houston Forensic Science Center, April 3, 2014.

HPD Executive Assistant Chief Tim Oettmeier at the opening celebration for the Houston Forensic Science Center—April 3, 2014. Photograph courtesy of Houston Forensic Science Center.

an independent laboratory. He greeted the crowd of laboratory staff, board members, and other guests by wishing the laboratory a "happy birthday." He reassured the staff, among some whose concerns were by now well known, that they would find the change to be a good one and that this move gave them the chance to be a part of something important in forensic science nationwide. The HPD would become the laboratory's "customer" and would still have an interest in seeing the laboratory thrive. In a strikingly candid moment, he conceded that the HPD had not looked out for the laboratory as it should have.

Board Chairman Hochberg said the laboratory had come a long way and quipped that the media now struggles to find something about the laboratory to complain about. He thanked Chief Oettmeier, as well as another key figure in the transition, Assistant Chief Matthew Slinkard, for their hard work, saying that the creation of an independent laboratory had been "their dream."

"There are people watching who hope you fail ..."

Many in Houston celebrated the opening of the HFSC, but not everyone hoped for the laboratory's success. On May 28, 2014, the HFSC hosted the first event of its Forensic Lectureship Series at Rice University. A national expert, Larry D. Depew, former FBI digital forensics analyst and founder of Digital Forensics US LLC, gave a speech on cybercrime. He praised Houston's decision to make its forensic laboratory independent of law enforcement and championed the importance of independence. On a more ominous note, he articulated what some in the audience already suspected: "There are people watching who hope you fail because it will bring down the kingdom,"[72] by which he probably referred to bringing down the structure of police-controlled forensic laboratories.

Exactly who would like to see the HFSC fail has not become public knowledge. The national resistance to independence among law enforcement and forensic scientists is no secret, so it stands to reason that at least some detractors would be found in those groups. Even if they do not want the Houston experiment to fail, at least they might not be eager to lend it a hand.

For example, things might be easier for the HFSC if federal law and DOJ policy were either changed or interpreted more flexibly. Crime laboratories, as part of the law enforcement establishment, have access to federal law enforcement databases such as CODIS for DNA profiles. Such access allows a laboratory's DNA analysts to enter crime scene DNA profiles into the federal database to search for a possible match. By federal law, however, access to the database is limited to law enforcement purposes. This limitation presented a problem for the HFSC recently which as of yet remains unresolved.

One aspect of the plan for the laboratory was that it might someday provide forensic services for defense attorneys as well as law enforcement. This part of the plan had not been a top priority, but board members had discussed it during interviews with candidates for the president's position and with local defense attorneys who attended a board meeting by invitation in October 2012.[73] The board's hopes to include defense work met an obstacle in May of 2014 when the Board of Directors learned that, under federal law, the laboratory cannot have access to the FBI's CODIS unless its agrees not to provide DNA services to any party other than law enforcement.[74] The HFSC attorney had assured the FBI attorney that the laboratory would implement strict measures to limit access to the database for only law enforcement use. However, the FBI attorney took the position that the law required the board to amend its Certificate of Formation to state that it would only do work for law enforcement. Board members expressed frustration over the FBI's demand as it did not seem to be legally required for the laboratory to adopt such a limit.

Federal agency internal policies also prevented several analysts from federal laboratories from serving on the HFSC's Technical Advisory Group (TAG), thus blocking invitations that members of the HFSC board had issued to several forensic scientists at federal laboratories.[75] A manager at the FBI Crime Laboratory said that the invitation in question would have to be cleared through Department of Justice channels and that she believed it would not be approved. A manager at the Secret Service laboratory did not return a phone message regarding an invitation to join the TAG. In the end, the TAG included highly regarded managers of forensic laboratories from across the country, including *former* federal laboratory analysts, but no current federal laboratory analyst was permitted to assist the Houston laboratory.

These federal limitations regarding CODIS and the TAG do not indicate hostility to the HFSC per se, but rather identify federal laws and policies that currently impede the improvement and independence of a local forensic laboratory. This situation is unfortunate. The National Forensic Science Commission and Congress should reconsider laws and policies that interfere with efforts to make forensic laboratories independent.

To date, the Houston experiment in laboratory independence has been so well planned and executed that it seems a foregone conclusion that the laboratory will not fail. In fact, police representatives from other states have already visited the HFSC to learn more as they consider the possibility of doing the same.[76] As more jurisdictions follow Houston's lead, the need for adjustments to federal law and policy becomes more important.

Glimpsing the Rewards of Independence

In a rural county just outside of Houston in May of 2014, a prosecutor questioned a firearms expert from the Houston Forensic Science Center who was testifying during a hearing in a death penalty case. The defense attorney challenged the reliability of the firearms examiner's conclusions. The prosecutor rebutted this challenge by pointing out that the analyst worked in a well-functioning and *independent* forensic science center. The independence of the laboratory does not yet carry much sway because it is such a recent development and memories of the HPD laboratory's many broken pieces still linger. The defense attorney noted that the change had been spurred by the serious problems in the HPD Crime Laboratory and made the point that the "new" laboratory employed mostly the same employees and was housed in the same building, within HPD headquarters. The firearms examiner later commented that she wished the prosecutor had mentioned that HPD no longer controlled access to the laboratory. It is indeed still located in the same HPD building for the time being, but it is now a secure facility with the HFSC controlling who may enter. It was too soon for the laboratory's independence to be a great benefit to the prosecutor at this particular trial, but as time goes on, having experts who have no perceived conflict of interest with law enforcement will be a feature that prosecutors can use to bolster the reliability of HFSC's forensic work.

Moreover, the independence of the HFSC can facilitate major changes in the organization's culture over the course of the long run. In a remarkable collaborative effort, a group of thirteen prominent forensic researchers, forensic practitioners, and law professors, co-authored an article calling for the development of a "research culture" in the forensic sciences. They explain:

> [W]e believe that a significant culture shift is required: Forensic science needs to focus more on science than on law, to shift from a quasi-adversarial perspective to a research orientation. In short, we call for the development and instantiation of what we will term a *research culture* within forensic science. The emergence of a research culture would affect how evidence is understood, change analysts' relationship to empirical data, and alter how evidence is reported.[77]

Corporate cultures do not change overnight. Change takes place slowly over time as office practices, managerial attitudes, and unit priorities change. Independence changes perspectives, and having a leader with the vision to inculcate a research culture makes a difference, too. On May 28, 2014, the HFSC sponsored its first lecture featuring a national expert on digital forensics, held in a major university. This event brought together law enforcement officers, forensic scientists, and members of the public. With this small step, hopefully the first of many, the Houston Forensic Science Center has begun the process of cultural change.

Notes for Chapter Seven

1. *See supra* Chapter 1.

2. *See supra* Chapter 2.

3. *See* Rebecca Leung, *DNA Testing: Foolproof?*, 60 Minutes, May 27, 2003, http:// www.cbsnews.com/news/dna-testing-foolproof/.

4. *See* Adam Liptak, *Worst Crime Lab in the Country—Or is Houston Typical?*, N.Y. Times, Mar. 11, 2003, http://truthinjustice.org/suttonDNA.htm; Mary Ann Fergus, *Josiah Sutton: One Year Later*, Hous. Chron., March 7, 2004, http://www.chron.com/life/article/Josiah-Sutton-One-Year-Later-1976295.php.

5. *See* Roma Khanna, *Governor Pardons Josiah Sutton*, Hous. Chron., May 14, 2004, http:// www.chron.com/news/houston-texas/article/Governor-pardons-Josiah-Sutton-1633572.ph.

6. *Id.*

7. *See* Liptak, *supra* note 4; Roma Khanna & Steve McVicker, *Early Critic Named Director of Houston's New Crime Lab*, Hous. Chron., Oct. 9, 2003, http://archives.lists.indymedia.org/

imc-houston/2003-October/007757.html.

8. *Id.*

9. *See* Nick Madigan, *Houston's Troubled DNA Crime Lab Faces Growing Scrutiny*, Hous. Chron., Feb. 9, 2003, http://www.nytimes.com/2003/02/09/us/houston-s-troubled-dna-crime-lab-faces-growing-scrutiny.html.

10. *See* Office of the Independent Investigator for the Houston Police Department Crime Laboratory and Property Room, *Background of the Investigation*, http://hpdlabinvestigation.org/about.htm#From%20Home.

11. *See* Liptak, *supra* note 4.

12. *See* Roma Khanna & Steve McVicker, *Fired DNA Analyst to Return to Work at Crime Lab*, Hous. Chron., Jan. 28, 2004, http://www.chron.com/news/houston-texas/article/Fired-DNA-analyst-to-return-to-work-at-crime-lab-1609733.php.

13. *Id.*

14. *See* Editorial, *Crime Lab: How Many Cases of Incompetent Analysis Must Come to Light?*, Hous. Chron., Aug. 9, 2004, http://www.chron.com/opinion/editorials/article/Crime-lab-How-many-cases-of-incompetent-analysis-1505063.php.

15. Steve McVicker, *Officials Urge Special Probe of HPD Crime Lab: Famed Attorney Weighs In on Call for Major Reforms at HPD Facility*, Hous. Chron., Aug. 7, 2004, http://www.chron.com/news/houston-texas/article/Officials-urge-special-probe-of-HPD-crime-lab-1625012.php.

16. *See* Roma Khanna & Steve McVicker, *Panel will Review 180 HPD Crime Lab Cases*, Hous. Chron., Oct. 12, 2007, http://www.chron.com/news/houston-texas/article/Panel-will-review-180-HPD-crime-lab-cases-1796314.php.

17. Statement from the Office of State Senator Rodney Ellis, *DNA Testing Proves George Rodriguez Innocent: Forensic Scientists Call for an Audit of HPD's Serology Cases*, Aug. 5, 2004, http://www.senate.state.tx.us/75r/Senate/Members/Dist13/pr04/s080504a.htm.

18. Barry C. Scheck & David R. Dow, *Falsification of Evidence Can Only Be Called Corruption: The Scope of the Scandal*, Editorial, Hous. Chron., Jul. 10, 2005, http://www.chron.com/opinion/outlook/article/Falsification-of-evidence-can-only-be-called-1925384.php; McVicker, *supra* note 15.

19. *See* Adam Liptak & Ralph Blumenthal, *New Doubt Cast on Testing in Houston Police Crime Lab*, N.Y. Times, Aug. 5, 2004, http://www.nytimes.com/2004/08/05/us/new-doubt-cast-on-testing-in-houston-police-crime-lab.html.

20. *See* Roma Khanna, *Judge Again Urges Moratorium*, Hous. Chron., Oct. 26, 2004, http://www.chron.com/news/houston-texas/article/Judge-again-urges-moratorium-1982619.php. For Bradford's 2003 recommendation, *see* Liptak, *supra* note 4.

21. *See* Khanna & McVicker, *supra* note 12.

22. *See* Houston Police Department, News Release: *HPD Crime Lab Receives National Accreditation*, http://www.houstontx.gov/police/nr/2005/may/nr051105-4.htm; Michael R.

23. *See* Office of the Independent Investigator for the Houston Police Department Crime Laboratory and Property Room, Scientific Advisory Board, http://www.hpdlabinvestigation.org/sci_adv_board.htm.

24. *See* Michael Bromwich, *Crime Lab Proposal is a Major Step Toward Independence*, Hous. Chron., Mar. 23, 2012, http://www.chron.com/opinion/outlook/article/Crime-lab-proposal-is-a-major-step-toward-3430904.php.

25. *Id.*

26. *Id.*

27. *See* Michael R. Bromwich, *Final Report of the Independent Investigator for the Houston Police Department Crime Laboratory and Property Room* (Jun. 13, 2007), http://www.hpd labinvestigation.org/reports/070613report.pdf.

28. *See* Brian Rogers, *Criticism Continues to Dog HPD Crime Lab,* Hous. Chron., Jul. 29, 2011, http://www.chron.com/news/houston-texas/article/Criticism-continues-to-dog-HPD-crime-lab-2077794.php.

29. *See* Steve McVicker, *HPD's Crime Lab Faces Proficiency-Test Inquiry,* Hous. Chron., Oct. 5, 2007.

30. *See* Roma Khanna, *Problems Persisted at Reformed HPD Crime Lab,* Hous. Chron., Feb. 22, 2008, http://www.chron.com/news/houston-texas/article/Problems-persisted-at-reformed-HPD-crime-lab-1610556.php.

31. The Bromwich Group, *Looking Back to Move Forward: The Houston Police Department Crime Laboratory's Implementation of the Independent Investigator's 2007 Recommendations* at 15 (Jun. 29, 2014) (on file with author).

32. *See* Roma Khanna, *Houston Man Walks Free after 22 Years in Prison,* Hous. Chron. (Aug. 29, 2009), http://www.chron.com/news/houston-texas/article/Houston-man-walks-free-after-22-years-in-prison-1736190.php; Innocence Project, *Know the Cases: Browse the Profiles: Ronald Gene Taylor,* http://www.innocenceproject.org/Content/Ronald_Gene_Taylor.php.

33. *See Grits for Breakfast, Houston Crime Lab Reports Only Prosecution Friendly Evidence,* (Apr. 30, 2009), http://gritsforbreakfast.blogspot.com/2009/04/houston-crime-lab-only-reported.html; Grits for Breakfast, *Crime Lab Workers Suffer from "Team Spirit" Mentality,* (July 10, 2008), http://gritsforbreakfast.blogspot.com/2008/07/crime-lab-workers-suffer-from-team.html.

34. *See* Moises Mendoza & Bradley Olson, *Major, Costly Overhaul Likely in HPD Fingerprint Unit,* Hous. Chron., Dec. 1, 2009, http://www.chron.com/news/houston-texas/article/Major-costly-overhaul-likely-in-HPD-fingerprint-1739953.php.

35. *See* Brian Rogers, *HPD Crime Lab Workers Quit over Faulty Testing Vans,* Hous. Chron., Jul. 28, 2011, http://www.chron.com/news/houston-texas/article/HPD-crime-lab-workers-quit-over-faulty-testing-2081382.php.

36. *See* Brian Rogers, *Assistant DA Refuses to Testify about BAT Van Evidence,* Hous. Chron., Dec. 15, 2011, http://www.chron.com/news/houston-texas/article/Assistant-DA-refuses-to-testify-in-grand-jury-2405482.php.

37. *See* Brian Rogers, *Harris County DA Testifies in Grand Jury Probe,* Hous. Chron., Jan. 17, 2012, http://www.chron.com/news/houston-texas/article/Harris-County-DA-testifies-in-grand-jury-probe-2584972.php.

38. *See* Ted Oberg, *Latest Large-Scale Reversal by DA Pat Lykos,* ABC13 Eyewitness News (Feb.14, 2012), http://abc13.com/archive/8542367/.

39. *See* Zain Shauk, *More Rape Kits Than Thought Remain Untested,* Hous. Chron., Dec. 17, 2011, http://www.chron.com/news/houston-texas/article/HPD-rape-kit-backlog-more-than-6-000-2403903.php.

40. *See* Tex. Gov't Code § 420.041-043.

41. *See* National Research Council, Strengthening Forensic Science in the United States: A Path Forward at 44–45 (The National Academies Press: 2009).

42. *See* Anita Hassan, *Harris County Plan Could Help Relieve HPD Crime Lab,* Hous. Chron. (Jun. 20, 2011), http://www.chron.com/news/houston-texas/article/Harris-County-

plan-could-help-relieve-HPD-crime-2078953.php.

43. *See* Ted Oberg, *Harris County Breaks Ground on New Crime Lab Center*, ABC13 EYE-WITNESS NEWS (Apr. 11, 2012), http://abc13.com/archive/8615789/.

44. *Id.*

45. *See* Timothy Oettmeier, Exec. Asst. Chief of Police, Houston Police Department, Email correspondence with author (Jun. 9, 2014) (on file with author).

46. *Id.*

47. *See* Federal Bureau of Investigation, *Testimony*, at http://www.fbi.gov/news/testimony/formation-of-an-mpd-laboratory (Sept. 22, 2006) (testimony of Dr. Joseph A. DiZinno, Ass't Dir. Laboratory Div., Federal Bureau of Investigation, before the House Committee on Governmental Reform).

48. *See* Maggie Clark, *D.C. Crime Lab: An Experiment in Forensic Science (Second of Two Parts)*, The Pew Charitable Trusts, State and Consumer Initiatives (Nov. 27, 2012), http://www.pewstates.org/projects/stateline/headlines/dc-crime-lab-an-experiment-in-forensic-science-second-of-two-parts-85899432291. For Dr. Houck's biography, see http://dfs.dc.gov/biography/max-m-houck-phd.

49. *See* Jeffrey Anderson, *D.C.'s New Forensics Lab Not Living Up to Expectations*, WASH. TIMES, Feb. 26, 2013, http://www.washingtontimes.com/news/2013/feb/26/dcs-new-forensics-lab-not-living-up-to-expectation/?page=all; Peter Hermann & Keith L. Alexander, *D.C. Police Crime Lab Technicians Ordered Transferred, to Be Replaced by Civilians*, WASH. POST, Sept. 21, 2012, http://www.washingtonpost.com/local/crime/dc-police-crime-lab-technicians-ordered-transferred-to-be-replaced-by-civilians/2012/09/21/af5eaeba-0419-11e2-9b24-ff730c7f6312_story.html.

50. *See* Hermann & Alexander, *supra* note 49.

51. Alan Blinder, *D.C. Opens $210m Crime Lab after Years of Delays*, WASH. EXAMINER, Oct. 1, 2012, http://washingtonexaminer.com/d.c.-opens-210m-crime-lab-after-years-of-delays/article/2509527.

52. *See* Jeffrey Anderson, *Conditions at New D.C. Forensic Lab Found to Be below Par*, WASH. TIMES, Mar. 21, 2013, http://www.washingtontimes.com/news/2013/mar/21/conditions-at-new-city-forensic-lab-found-to-be-be/?page=all.

53. *Id.*

54. *See* Richard Connelly, *Pat Lykos's Loss Brings Joy to Lots of Ex-Prosecutors,* HOUSTON PRESS BLOGS, May 30, 2012, http://blogs.houstonpress.com/hairballs/2012/05/pat_lykos_loses_da_race.php; Chris Moran.

55. *See* City of Houston, Texas, Res. No. 2012-17 (Jun. 6, 2012), http://www.houstonforensicscience.org/Formation%20Documents/COH%20Res.%20No.%202012-17%20%28Approving%20LGC%29.pdf. The entity actually went by the name "Houston Forensic Science LGC, Inc." from 2012 to 2014 when it was changed.

56. Tom Allen, FAQ, Houston Forensic Science LGC, Inc. (Mar. 14, 2012) (on file with author).

57. *See* Houston Forensic Science LGC, Inc., Meeting Minutes (June 20, 2012), http://www.houstonforensicscience.org/Board%20Meeting%20Files/Minutes/minutes_120620.pdf.

58. *See* Chris Moran, *City Council Agrees to Hand Crime Lab to Independent Board*, HOUS. CHRON., June 6, 2012, http://www.chron.com/news/houston-texas/article/Council-hands-crime-lab-to-independent-board-3615078.php.

59. *See* Houston Forensic Science LGC, Inc., Certificate of Formation (Jun. 22, 2012), http://www.houstonforensicscience.org/significant/120626%5EHFSLGC%20Certificate%20

of%20Formation%20%28file-stamped%29.pdf.

60. *See* International Organization of Standardization (ISO), *About ISO*, http://www.iso.org/iso/home/about.htm.

61. *See* Bureau of Justice Statistics, Census of Publicly Funded Forensic Crime Laboratories, NCJ 238252 at 7 (2009).

62. *See* Mayor's Office, Press Release: *President/CEO Named for Houston Independent Crime Lab* (Aug. 14, 2013), http://www.houstontx.gov/mayor/press/20130814.html.

63. *Id.*

64. *See* First Interlocal Agreement between the City of Houston and the Houston Forensic Science LGC, Inc. (Mar. 4, 2014), http://www.houstonforensicscience.org/Formation%20Documents/Interlocal%20Agreement.PDF.

65. This information is based on the author's notes from board meetings (on file with author).

66. *See* Houston Forensic Science LGC, Meeting of the Board of Directors Minutes (Jan. 10, 2014), http://www.houstonforensicscience.org/Board%20Meeting%20Files/Minutes/minutes_140110.pdf.

67. *See* Timothy Oettmeier, Exec. Asst. Chief of Police, Houston Police Department, Email correspondence with author (Jun. 9, 2014) (on file with author).

68. This information is based on private discussions between the author and other board members.

69. Matthew Slinkard, Houston Police Department, Assistant Chief, Personal notes from the inaugural celebration of the Houston Forensic Science Center, April 3, 2014 (on file with author).

70. *See* The Bromwich Group, *supra* note 31 at 44.

71. The information in this section is based on the author's personal notes of the event.

72. This information is based on the author's notes of the event.

73. *See* Houston Forensic Science LGC, Meeting of the Board of Directors Agenda (Oct. 12, 2012), http://www.houstonforensicscience.org/V_meetings/2012/oct__2012/1agenda_121010.pdf.

74. *See* Houston Forensic Science LGC, Meeting of the Board of Directors Agenda (May 9, 2014), http://www.houstonforensicscience.org/about-us/meeting-archive.

75. The information in this paragraph is based on the author's personal experience.

76. This information is based on a private conversation with Irma Rios, Dir. of the Forensic Analysis Div., May 2014.

77. Jennifer L. Mnookin, Simon A. Cole, Itiel E. Dror, Barry A.J. Fisher, Max M. Houck, Keith Inman, David H. Kaye, Jonathan J. Koehler, Glenn Langenburg, D. Michael Risinger, Norah Rudin, Jay Siegel, & David A. Stoney, *The Need for a Research Culture in the Forensic Sciences*, 58 UCLA L. Rev. 725, 731 (2011).

Chapter Eight

Conclusion: Reimagining the Practice of Forensic Science

The NAS Report (2009) calls for fundamental changes in how forensic science is researched and practiced, and it does so with full awareness of how high the stakes are.[1] Improvements in the forensic practice will not simply curb wrongful convictions in drug cases, rape cases, or even capital murder cases. The stakes also include dealing effectively with international terrorist attacks, like the Madrid train bombing case discussed in Chapter 4.

Congressional legislation has brought forth a national effort to address the lack of a research foundation for many disciplines and to make other changes in the interaction between forensic science and the judicial system.[2] The formerly fragmented governance of the forensic disciplines will now be coordinated within the National Institute of Standards and Technology, in a fashion similar to the NAS Report recommendation.[3] The Department of Justice has also undertaken a historic cooperative arrangement with the National Association of Criminal Defense Lawyers in conducting a massive review of cases involving "junk science" in the form of hair and fiber evidence.[4]

Some improvements have also been made at the state and local levels. Two states have formed Forensic Science Commissions that perform a variety of functions to regulate forensic science practice in those states, and other states have enacted legislation relating to the regulation of forensic laboratories. Texas has passed legislation allowing prisoners to file petitions challenging any forensic evidence, the validity of which has been newly shown to be unreliable but which played an important role in their convictions. Other states should consider doing the same. Additionally, the percentage of public forensic laboratories that have achieved accreditation has jumped from 71% in 2002 to 83% in 2009.[5] This means that more laboratories have implemented quality assurance programs and have otherwise met the accreditation standards, all of which bodes well for the quality of work done in these laboratories.

The judicial system is also showing signs of a growing awareness of forensic science's limits. Today judges are holding an increasing number of hearings at which defense attorneys are challenging the validity of certain forensic conclusions. Clearly, defense attorneys have begun to better recognize and appreciate the strength of such issues, and judges are beginning to listen. The NAS Report reserves some of its harshest criticism for the poor job that criminal courts had done in handling issues of forensic evidence in the past.[6] While this criticism was well deserved, the new attention to improving forensic science at the national level gives cause for optimism that criminal courts will also take notice and more seriously consider the evidentiary issues at stake.

The NAS Report's important recommendation, which it sees as key to solving many of the other problems it documented, is to make crime laboratories independent of their parent law enforcement agencies — at the federal, state, and local levels. Disturbingly, this recommendation has largely been ignored by most jurisdictions. The arguments against independence boil down to a defense of the ethical integrity and competence of forensic analysts as a group, but this argument misses the point. Even assuming that every forensic analyst is ethical, possessing high ethical standards would not solve the problems of underfunding, undertraining, backlogged workloads, and inadequate supervision. The practice of forensic science can still be improved by making the laboratories independent. Independence would not, in and of itself, solve the problems of budgets and training; but they would help solve those problems by taking laboratories out of direct competition with law enforcement for funding. More importantly, the close association with law enforcement currently makes crime laboratory managers and analysts vulnerable to conscious and unconscious cognitive biases, a problem that independence would greatly reduce. Moreover, history has shown that police chiefs are unlikely to have the credentials needed to properly supervise forensic laboratories. And finally, independence will foster the development of a genuine scientific research culture, encourage fundamental structural changes, and reorient these laboratories toward a clear and unencumbered scientific focus.

At the end of the day, law and science are imperfect. They constantly need improvement and reform. These improvements encouraged here will not stop all wrongful convictions, but each step in the right direction helps to keep the George Rodriguezes of the world safe from the horror of wrongful conviction. It is for this reason that we must not settle for a status quo that leaves much to be desired and should continue to strive for something better.

Notes for Chapter Eight

1. NATIONAL RESEARCH COUNCIL, STRENGTHENING FORENSIC SCIENCE IN THE UNITED STATES: A PATH FORWARD (National Academies Press, 2009) (hereinafter "NAS Report").

2. *See* U.S. Department of Justice. *Notice of Establishment of the National Commission on Forensic Science and Solicitation of Applications for Commission Membership.* Feb. 22, 2013, Federal Register, https://www.federalregister.gov/articles/2013/02/22/2013-04140/notice-of-establishment-of-the-national-commission-on-forensic-science-and-solicitation-of.

3. *Id.*

4. *See* Innocence Project, *News and Information: Innocence Project and NACDL Announce Historic Partnership with FBI and Department of Justice on Microscopic Hair Analysis Cases,* http://www.innocenceproject.org/Content/Innocence_Project_and_NACDL_Announce_Historic_Partnership_with_the_FBI_and_Department_of_Justice_on_Microscopic_Hair_Analysis_Cases.php#.

5. *See* BUREAU OF JUSTICE STATISTICS, CENSUS OF PUBLICLY FUNDED FORENSIC CRIME LABORATORIES at 1, NCJ 238252 (2009).

6. *See* NAS Report, *supra* note 1 at 95–98.

Epilogue

George Rodriguez's compelling story and the turmoil it caused for the City of Houston ultimately brought forth fundamental change in how forensic science is practiced in Houston. I spoke to George in September of 2014 and asked him to reflect on how he had passed the ten years since he was released from prison in October of 2004. How was life treating him today? He answered simply, "I'm doing okay." Before his arrest, George had worked in carpentry, but today a back injury he sustained after his release prevents him from working. I asked if the money from the lawsuit had made a difference in his life. The money had helped him get back on his feet, he said. He got about a million of the three-million-dollar settlement; "most of it went to the lawyers," he said matter-of-factly and without bitterness. Some of the money he gave to his daughters, who today were doing "okay."

His son, George Jr., remains incarcerated, serving his sentence for murder. He resides in a prison known as the Darrington Unit in Rosharon, Texas, about forty-five minutes south of Houston. As it happens, this is the same place I have toured many times with my students over the last twenty-four years. It is an old, dreary building with terrible ventilation and acoustics. It is deafeningly loud and musty, one of the worst prison environments I have encountered. George now goes back to prison regularly as a visitor to see his son. "I don't like going back," he says of the experience, "but I have to go to see him."

All in all, he seemed relatively happy with his life. George's father passed away while he was gone, but he has spent time with his mother since getting out of prison. He also lost his common law wife who left him after his conviction, but a new love awaited him upon release. He married a childhood friend, a woman he has known since the age of eleven. The two lived near each other as children but had gone their separate ways as adults. As George sweetly recounts it, when he was finally released in 2004, she was "waiting for me with a ring."

George's wife counseled him not to talk to me. He had tried so hard to put his ordeal out of his mind, and she dreaded his having to re-live it again. He said he felt ambivalent about giving the interview (which might explain why it took me a week to get through to him). Ultimately, he decided he liked the idea of my telling his story in this book. He had considered writing a book himself but had not followed through with it. It gave me an unexpected joy to have been able to tell his story for him. I am familiar with the common yearning of victims of all types to ensure that their suffering is not in vain. I did not set out to satisfy that yearning in George. I hoped only to explore issues in forensic science, and his story served as a literary vehicle to put the issues in human terms. Having talked to him, I now hope this book can bring George a more fulfilling sense of closure. I told him I appreciated how hard it must have been to talk to me and thanked him before saying goodbye.

Glossary*

Accreditation: The demonstration by forensic science testing laboratories that all forensic services are provided in accordance with accepted standards; applies to any laboratory performing forensic testing activities in the disciplines of Drug Chemistry, Toxicology, Trace Evidence, Biology, Firearms/Toolmarks, Questioned Documents, Latent Prints, Crime Scene and Digital & Multimedia Evidence. (American Society of Crime Laboratory Directors/Laboratory Accreditation Board, http://www.ascld-lab.org/international-testing-program/)

Certification: The testing process offered by professional organizations within most forensic disciplines by which individual practitioners may be "certified," a status that signifies an analyst's competence in the performance of the discipline.

Criminalist: The titles "criminalist" and "technician" are used interchangeably with "analyst" in police crime laboratories and indicate that these jobs require a background in science, typically including an undergraduate science degree. *See, e.g.,* California Association of Criminalists, *Criminalistics Information,* available at http://www.cacnews.org/membership/criminalistics.shtml.

Dry-labbing: When a researcher claims to have done research but in fact guessed the conclusion or copied the results from another's research and claimed them as their own. (Wiki answers, http://wiki.answers.com/Q/What_does_dry_labbing_mean?#slide=4) It is a form of cheating within a forensic laboratory by faking results rather than actually testing the evidence.

Forensic odontology: The application of the science of dentistry to the field of law; includes several distinct areas of focus: the identification of unknown remains, bite mark comparison, the interpretation of oral injury and dental malpractice. Bite mark comparison has often been used in criminal prosecutions and is the most controversial of the four areas just

---

* *Note*: All web citations are current as of June 2014.

237

mentioned. (National Academy of Sciences, Strengthening Forensic Science in the United States: A Path Forward at 173 (2009)).

Mitochondrial DNA: Mitochondrial DNA (mtDNA) testing is used to examine biological items of evidence from crime scenes to determine the mtDNA sequence from samples such as hair, bones, and teeth. Typically, these items contain low concentrations of degraded DNA, making them unsuitable for nuclear DNA examinations. Mitochondrial DNA is maternally inherited and multiple individuals can have the same mtDNA type. Thus, unique identifications are not possible using mtDNA analyses. However, mtDNA is an excellent technique to use for obtaining information in cases where nuclear DNA analysis is not feasible. (*Mitochondrial DNA testing*, FBI Laboratory Services at http://www.fbi.gov/about-us/lab/biometric-analysis/mtdna)

Nuclear DNA: Nuclear DNA testing is used to examine biological evidence from bodily fluids like blood and semen. The testing process generates DNA profiles sufficiently rare to be associated to a single individual to a reasonable degree of scientific certainty. (*DNA—Nuclear*, FBI Laboratory Services at http://www.fbi.gov/about-us/lab/biometric-analysis/dna-nuclear)

Proficiency testing: A solid proficiency testing program allows a forensic laboratory to satisfy accreditation requirements and confirm competent performance; compare performance with other forensic laboratories; identify improvement areas; and have increased confidence in the laboratory's work product. (American Society of Crime Laboratory Directors/Laboratory Accreditation Board, http://www.ascld-lab.org/overview-proficiency-review-program/)

Serology: Determination of the type and characteristics of blood based on analyzes of blood, blood testing, and blood stain examination. Forensic serologists may also examine semen, saliva, other body fluids left at a crime scene which may or may not also be involved with DNA typing. (Forensic medicine info, at http://www.forensic-medecine.info/forensic-serology.html)

Technician: The titles "technician" and "criminalist" are used interchangeably with "analyst" in police crime laboratories and indicate that these jobs requires a background in science, typically including an undergraduate science degree. *See, e.g.,* California Association of Criminalists, *Criminalistics Information*, available at http://www.cacnews.org/membership/criminalistics.shtml.

Toolmark examination: Toolmarks are generated when a hard object (tool) comes into contact with a relatively softer object. Such toolmarks may occur in the commission of a crime when an instrument such as a screwdriver, crowbar, or wire cutter is used or when the internal parts of a firearm make contact with the brass and lead present in the ammunition. Firearms and toolmark examiners believe that toolmarks may be traced to the distinct physical characteristics of an individual tool—that is the "individual characteristics" of toolmarks may be uniquely associated with a specific tool or firearm and are reproduced by the use of that tool and only that tool. (National Academy of Sciences, Strengthening Forensic Science in the United States: A Path Forward at 150 (2009)) Other examples of the types of examinations done by toolmark examiners includes: comparing stamps with stamped impressions for identification; fracture matching; and lock and key examinations. (*Firearms/Toolmarks*, FBI Laboratory Services at http://www.fbi.gov/about-us/lab/scientific-analysis/fire_tool)

Touch DNA testing: Developed in 2003, touch DNA testing involves the analysis of skin cells left behind when assailants touch victims, weapons or something else at a crime scene. (*What is Touch DNA?*, Scientific American at http://www.scientificamerican.com/article/experts-touch-dna-jonbenet-ramsey/)

Toxicology: Toxicology, as it relates to forensics, is the analysis of biological samples for the presence of toxins, including drugs. A toxicology report can provide key information as to the type of substances present in an individual's body and if the amount of those substances is consistent with a therapeutic dosage or is above a harmful level. (http://www.nij.gov/topics/forensics/evidence/toxicology/Pages/welcome.aspx)

Trace evidence: "Trace evidence" is generally thought of as any type of evidence occurring in sizes so small that it can be transferred or exchanged between two surfaces without being noticed. (http://dofs.gbi.georgia.gov/trace-evidence-0). Fibers, hair, soil, wood, gunshot residue and pollen are only a few examples of trace evidence that may be transferred between people, objects or the environment during a crime. (National Institute of Justice, http://www.nij.gov/topics/forensics/evidence/trace/Pages/welcome.aspx)

Validation studies: The empirical process of demonstrating that a laboratory procedure is robust, reliable, and reproducible. Validation studies also demonstrate the reliability of new instruments. There are generally considered to be two stages to validation: developmental validation and internal validation. *Developmental validation* involves the testing of new scientific procedures or instruments. *Internal validation*, on the other hand, involves verifying that established procedures examined previously under the scrutiny of developmental validation (often by another laboratory) will work effectively in one's own laboratory. (http://www.cstl.nist.gov/strbase/validation.htm)

Bibliography

ABA Criminal Justice Section, Ad Hoc Innocence Committee to Ensure the Integrity of the Criminal Process. *Achieving Justice: Freeing the Innocent, Convicting the Guilty.* Eds. Paul C. Giannelli and Myrna Raeder. (Washington, D.C.: American Bar Association), 2006.

AFTE Committee for the Advancement of the Science of Firearm and Tool Mark Identification. "The Response of the Association of Firearm and Toolmark Examiners to the February 2009 National Academy of Science Report *Strengthening Forensic Science in the United States: A Path Forward.*" *AFTE Journal* 41 (2009): 204.

Ake v. Oklahoma, 470 U.S. 68 (1985).

Alabama Department of Forensic Sciences. History of the Alabama Department of Forensic Sciences, http://www.adfs.alabama.gov/About.aspx (accessed Sept. 11, 2013).

Allen, Tom. "FAQ: Houston Forensic Science LGC, Inc." (Mar. 14, 2012). On file with author.

American Academy of Forensic Sciences. *The American Academy of Forensic Sciences Approves Position Statement in Response to the National Academy of Sciences: Forensic Needs Report.* Sept. 4, 2009, http://aafs.org/sites/default/files/pdf/AAFS_Position_Statement_for_Press_Distribution_090409.pdf (accessed Sept. 19, 2013).

American Society of Crime Lab Directors/Laboratory Accreditation Board. *Accredited Laboratory Index.* http://www.ascld-lab.org/accredited-laboratory-index/ (accessed March 27, 2014).

_____. *ASCLD/LAB-International. Program Overview* (2010 ed.). http://www.ascld-lab.org/wp-content/uploads/201 3/09/AL-PD-3041_Intl_2010_Program_Overview_v2.2_unmked.pdf (accessed Sept. 10, 2013).

_____. *ASCLD/LAB-International, ASCLD/LAB Guidance on the Estimation of Measurement Uncertainty–ANNEX C Firearms/Toolmarks Discipline Firearms Category of Testing, Example-Overall Length of a Firearm* (approved

May 22, 2013), http://www.ascld-lab.org/wp-content/uploads/2013/06/
AL-PD-3064-Guidance-Measurement_Uncertainty-Firearms_v1.0.pdf.

————. *History*. http://www.ascld-lab.org/history/ (accessed March 27, 2014).

————. *Legacy Program*. http://www.ascld-lab.org/legacy-program/ (accessed
March 27, 2014).

————. *Proficiency Testing and Review Program*, Oct. 31, 2011. http://www.ascld-
lab.org/wp-content/uploads/2013/04/AL-PD-1020_Proficiency_Testing_
Review_Program_v1.0.pdf (accessed Sept. 17, 2013).

American Statistical Association, *Position Statement on the NAS Report*, May
3, 2010. On file with author.

Anderson, Craig. "21 Defendants Get Notices of Tainted Evidence."
Delaware.newszap.com, Feb. 27, 2014. http://delaware.newszap.com/
centraldelaware/130023-70/21-defendants-get-notices-of-tainted-evidence
(accessed Sept. 8, 2013).

Anderson, Jeffrey. "Conditions at New D.C. Forensic Lab Found to be Below
Par." *Washington Times*, March 21, 2013, http://www.washingtontimes.com/
news/2013/mar/21/conditions-at-new-city-forensic-lab-found-to-be-be/
?page=all (accessed Aug. 14, 2014).

————. "D.C.'s New Forensics Lab Not Living Up to Expectations." *Washington
Times*, Feb. 26, 2013, http://www.washingtontimes.com/news/2013/feb/
26/dcs-new-forensics-lab-not-living-up-to-expectation/?page=all (accessed
Aug. 25, 2014).

Anderson v. State, 2014 WY 13, 317 P.3d 1108 (Wyo. 2014).

Associated Press. "Agency: Houston Crime Lab Worker Had History of Poor
Work." *ABC 13 Eyewitness News*, April 5, 2013. http://abclocal.go.com/
ktrk/story?section=news/local&id=9054336 (accessed Sept. 2, 2013).

————. "Defense Lawyer Group Calls for Investigation of State Crime Lab."
KOMO News, Oct. 16, 2007. http://www.komonews.com/news/local/
10590127.html (accessed Sept. 2, 2014).

————. "HPD to Take Second Look at Rodriguez Case." *Houston Chronicle*, Aug.
6, 2004, http://www.chron.com/news/article/HPD-to-take-second-look-
at-Rodriguez-case-1551669.php (accessed Sept. 2, 2014).

————. "No Criminal Charge for Manager of State Toxicology Lab." *Seattle Times*,
Nov. 9, 2007. http://seattletimes.com/html/localnews/2004005066_web-
gordon10m.html (accessed Sept. 6, 2013).

————. "Police: Eastern Washington Crime Lab Manager Falsified Work." *CBS
Seattle*, April 16, 2013. http://www.oregonlive.com/pacific-northwest-

news/index.ssf/2013/04/washington_state_patrol_says_c.html (accessed Sept. 2, 2014).

———. "7 W.Va. Ethics Commission Members Reappointed." July 1, 2014, http://www.herald-dispatch.com/news/briefs/x1116648612/7-W-Va-Ethics-Commission-members-reappointed (accessed May 4, 2014).

———. "WSP Crime Labs Slip Up." July 23, 2004. http://m.spokesman.com/stories/2004/jul/23/wsp-crime-labs-slip-up/ (accessed Sept. 22, 2013).

Associated Press Archives. "Ex-W. Va. Police Chemist Fred Zain Dies." Dec. 3, 2002. http://www.apnewsarchive.com/2002/Ex-W-Va-Police-Chemist-Fred-Zain-Dies/id-c3611a6bee2117e73b21992e16175e9a (accessed Sept. 23, 2013).

Association of Firearm and Toolmark Examiners, *AFTE Code of Ethics*, http://www.afte.org/AssociationInfo/a_codeofethics.htm (accessed Aug. 13, 2014).

———. *AFTE Contacts*. http://www.afte.org/AssociationInfo/a_contacts.htm. (accessed Aug. 11, 2014).

———. *AFTE Journal*, http://www.afte.org/Journal/AFTEJournal.htm. (accessed Aug. 12, 2014).

Association of Forensic DNA Analysts and Administrators, http://afdaa.org/2013/officers/. (accessed May 4, 2014).

Association of Forensic Quality Assurance Managers. http://afqam.org/wp12/. (accessed Sept. 25, 2013).

Bay City News, "Former SF Police Crime Lab Tech Pleads Guilty to Cocaine Possession." *San Francisco Examiner*, March 15, 2013. http://www.sfexaminer.com/sanfrancisco/former-sf-police-crime-lab-tech-pleads-guilty-to-cocaine-possession/Content?oid=2320882. (accessed Sept. 2, 2014).

Benos, Dale J., Edlira Bashari, Jose M. Chaves, Amit Gaggar, Niren Kapoor, Martin LaFrance, Robert Mans, David Mayhew, Sara McGowan, Abigail Polter, Yawar Qadri, Shanta Sarfare, Kevin Schultz, Ryan Splittgerber, Jason Stephenson, Cristy Tower, R. Grace Walton and Alexander Zotov, "The Ups and Downs of Peer Review." *Advances in Physiology Education*. 31 (2007): 145–152.

Berry v. City of Detroit, 25 F.3d 1342 (6th Cir. 1994).

Biographical Sketches of Key Players in the O.J. Simpson Trial: Barry Scheck. http://law2.umkc.edu/faculty/projects/ftrials/simpson/Scheck.htm (accessed Sept. 28, 2013).

Birke, Richard. "Reconciling Loss Aversion and Guilty Pleas." 1999 *Utah Law Review* (1999): 205.

Blackburn, Jeff, Gary Udashen, and Cory Session. "It is Time to Ban Junk Science from Texas Courtrooms." *Houston Chronicle*, Oct. 3, 2010. http://www.chron.com/opinion/outlook/article/It-s-time-to-ban-junk-science-from-Texas-1695901.php (accessed Sept. 30, 2013).

Blinder, Alan. "D.C. Opens $210m Crime Lab after Years of Delays." *Washington Examiner*, Oct. 1, 2012, http://washingtonexaminer.com/d.c.-opens-210m-crime-lab-after-years-of-delays/article/2509527. (accessed Aug. 25, 2014).

Brady v. Maryland, 373 U.S. 83 (1963).

Bromwich, Michael R. "Crime Lab Proposal Is a Major Step toward Independence." *Houston Chronicle*, March 23, 2012, http://www.chron.com/opinion/outlook/article/Crime-Lab-proposal-is-a-major-step-toward-3430904.php (accessed Oct. 9, 2013).

_____. "Final Report of the Independent Investigator for the Houston Police Department Crime Laboratory and Property Room (June 13, 2007)." http://www.hpdlabinvestigation.org/reports/070613report.pdf (accessed Oct. 22, 2013).

Bronner, Ethan. "Executed Texan's Family Seeks Pardon." *New York Times*, Oct. 25, 2012. http://www.nytimes.com/2012/10/25/us/willingham-family-seeks-posthumous-pardon-in-texas.html?_r=0 (accessed Oct. 23, 2013).

Brown, Darryl K. "Rationing Criminal Defense Entitlements: An Argument from Institutional Design." *Columbia Law Review* 104 (2004): 801.

Brown v. State, 01-12-01040-CR, 2014 WL 60965 (Texas App. Jan. 7, 2014).

Bullcoming v. New Mexico, 131 S.Ct. 2705 (2011).

Bureau of Justice Statistics. *Census of Publicly Funded Forensic Crime Laboratories.* (2009) at http://www.bjs.gov/content/pub/pdf/cpffcl09.pdf. (accessed Aug. 11, 2014).

Bush, Mary A., Peter J. Bush, and H. David Sheets. "Statistical Evidence for the Similarity of Human Dentition." *Journal of Forensic Science* 56 (2011): 118–123.

Bush, Mary A., Howard I. Cooper, and Robert B. J. Dorion. "Inquiry into the Scientific Basis for Bitemark Profiling and Arbitrary Distortion Compensation." Journal of Forensic Science 55 (2010): 1–8.

Cather, Karin H. "The CSI Effect: Fake TV and its Impact on Jurors in Criminal Cases." *The Prosecutor* (March/April 2004).

Center on Wrongful Convictions. *First DNA Exoneration: Gary Dotson.* http://www.law.northwestern.edu/legalclinic/wrongfulconvictions/exonerations/il/gary-dotson.html (accessed Jan. 4, 2014).

Chambers v. State, 424 S.W.3d 296 (Ark. 2012).

Chan, Sau, for Associated Press. "Scores of Convictions Reviewed as Chemist Faces Perjury Accusations: Forensics: Fred Zain's Expert Testimony and Lab Tests Helped Put Scores of Rapists and Murderers behind Bars. But College Transcript Shows He Flunked Some Chemistry Classes and Barely Passed Others. He Is Also Accused of Evidence-Tampering." *Los Angeles Times*, Aug. 21, 1994. http://articles.latimes.com/1994-08-21/news/mn-29449_1_lab-tests-fred-zain-double-murder (accessed Nov. 12, 2013).

Chu, Sarah. Email correspondence with Innocence Project Forensic Policy Advocate, May 16, 2014. On file with author.

City of Houston, Texas, Res. No. 2012-17 (June 6, 2012), http://www.houston-forensicscience.org/Formation%20Documents/COH%20Res.%20No.%202012-17%20%28Approving%20LGC%29.pdf (accessed March 11, 2013).

Clark, Maggie. "D.C. Crime Lab: An Experiment in Forensic Science (Second of Two Parts)." *The Pew Charitable Trusts, State and Consumer Initiatives*, Nov. 27, 2012. http://www.pewstates.org/projects/stateline/headlines/dc-crime-lab-an-experiment-in-forensic-science-second-of-two-parts-85899432291 (accessed May 10, 2013).

Clines, Francis X. "Work by Expert Witness Is Now on Trial." *New York Times*, Sept. 5, 2001. http://www.nytimes.com/2001/09/05/us/work-by-expert-witness-is-now-on-trial.html (accessed April 1, 2013).

Colaross, Anthony. "Defense Calls for New Trial in Rape Case." *Orlando Sentinel*, Nov. 26, 2002, B2.

Cole, Simon A. "Individualization Is Dead, Long Live Individualization! Reforms of Reporting Practices for Fingerprint Analysis in the United States." *Law Probability and Risk* 13 (2014): 117.

———. "More than Zero: Accounting for Error in Latent Fingerprint Identification." *Journal of Criminal Law and Criminology* 95 (2005): 985–1027.

Cole, Simon A., and Rachel Dioso-Villa. "CSI and Its Effects: Media, Juries, and the Burden of Proof." *New England Law Review* 41 (2007): 435–444.

Collaborative Testing Services, Inc. *CTS Statement on the Use of Proficiency Testing Data for Error Rate Determinations*, March 30, 2010. http://www.cts-forensics.com/assets/news/CTSErrorRateStatement.pdf (accessed March 10, 2013).

Collins, John M. "A Reality Check on Crime Lab Backlogs." *Michigan Bar Journal*, (Oct. 2012): 36.

Colloff, Pamela. "The Guilty Man: Michael Morton Spent Almost 25 Years Wrongfully Imprisoned for the Murder of His Wife, Until DNA Recovered from a Blue Bandana Found Near the Crime Scene Helped Set Him Free. A Year and a Half Later, That Same Piece of Evidence Finally Brought Him Face-to-Face with the Real Killer." *Texas Monthly*, June 2013, http://www.texasmonthly.com/story/guilty-man/page/0/2 (accessed Feb. 9, 2013).

_____. "Innocence Found: Why Did Anthony Graves Spend Eighteen Years behind Bars—Twelve of Them on Death Row—for a Crime He Did Not Commit?" *Texas Monthly*, Jan. 2011. http://www.texasmonthly.com/story/innocence-found. (accessed Sept. 2, 2014).

_____. "Innocence Lost." *Texas Monthly*, Oct. 2010. http://www.texasmonthly.com/story/innocence-lost. (accessed Sept. 2, 2014).

Comment: "Evidence. Confrontation Clause. Fourth Circuit Holds That 'Machine-Generated' Analysis Is Not Testimonial Evidence. United States v. Washington, 498 F.3d 225 (4th Cir. 2007)." *Harvard Law Review* 121 (2008): 1937.

Commonwealth v. Dyarman, 73 A.3d 565 (Pa. 2013), cert. denied, 134 S. Ct. 948, 187 Law Ed. 2d 785 (U.S. 2014).

Commonwealth v. Gatlos, 76 A.3d 44 (Pa. Super. Ct. 2013).

Commonwealth v. Lezynski, 466 Mass. 113 (Mass. S. Ct. 2013).

Commonwealth v. Vasquez, 462 Mass. 827 (Mass. 2012).

Connelly, Richard. "Pat Lykos's Loss Brings Joy to Lots of Ex-Prosecutors." *Houston Press Blogs,* May 30, 2012. http://blogs.houstonpress.com/hairballs/2012/05/pat_lykos_loses_da_race.php (accessed Feb. 13, 2013).

Cooper v. State, 434 Md. 209 (Md. Ct. App. 2013).

Corris, Steve. "Court Asks Officials to Consider Taking Crime Lab from State Police." *West Virginia Record*, June 28, 2006, http://wvrecord.com/news/180999-court-asks-officials-to-consider-taking-crime-lab-from-state-police (accessed March 30, 2013).

Crabb, John, Jr., Department of Justice Special Counsel, Re: Florida v. Gerald Murray, August 20, 2013. On file with author.

Crime Scene. *Forensic Detective Jacket.* http://www.crimescene.com/store/index.php?main_page=advanced_search_result&search_in_description=1&keyword=windbreaker&x=0&y=0 (accessed March 30, 2013).

Criminal Justice and Forensic Science Reform Act of 2014, S. 2177 at https://beta.congress.gov/113/bills/s2177/BILLS-113s2177is.pdf. (accessed Aug. 11, 2014).

Daubert v. Merrell Dow Pharmaceuticals, Inc., 509 U.S. 579 (1993).

"Defense Lawyers Call for Crime-Lab Investigation." *Seattle Post-Intelligencer*, Oct. 16, 2007. http://www.seattlepi.com/local/article/Defense-lawyers-call-for-crime-lab-investigation-1252662.php (accessed Feb. 14, 2014).

Department of Justice. Letter to District Attorney Allgood, May 6, 2013. Re: Manning v. Mississippi, 2013-DR-00491-SCT. On file with author.

——. "U.S. Departments of Justice and Commerce Name Experts to First-Ever National Commission on Forensic Science." January 10, 2014. http://www.justice.gov/opa/pr/2014/January/14-at-029.html (accessed Aug. 11, 2014).

DePrang, Emily. "Fake Lab Results Endanger Thousands of Drug Convictions." *Texas Observer*, July 8, 2013. http://www.texasobserver.org/fake-lab-results-endanger-thousands-of-drug-convictions/ (accessed May 10, 2013).

District of Columbia, Department of General Services, Consolidated Forensic Laboratory. http://dgs.dc.gov/page/consolidated-forensic-laboratory (accessed March 10, 2014).

"DNA Testing Mistakes at the State Police Crime Labs." *Seattle Post-Intelligencer*, July 21, 2004. http://www.seattlepi.com/local/article/DNA-testing-mistakes-at-the-State-Patrol-crime-1149846.php. (accessed Sept. 2, 2014).

Domash, Shelly Feuer, and Christopher Twarowski. "Nassau County Taxpayers Secretly Charged Millions for Police Crime Lab Scandal." *Long Island Press.com*, Dec. 31, 2012. http://www.longislandpress.com/2013/12/31/exclusive-nassau-county-taxpayers-secretly charged-millions-for-police-crime-lab-scandal/ (accessed Sept. 8, 2013).

Dror, Itiel E., David Charlton, and Ailsa E. Peron. "Contextual Information Renders Experts Vulnerable to Making Erroneous Identifications." *Forensic Science International* 156 (2006): 74.

Editorial. "Crime Lab: How Many Cases of Incompetent Analysis Must Come to Light?" *Houston Chronicle*, Aug. 9, 2004. http://www.chron.com/opinion/editorials/article/Crime-lab-How-many-cases-of-incompetent-analysis-1505063.php (accessed March 9, 2014).

Elias, Paul, and Terry Collins. "San Francisco Crime Lab Scandal Growing, Thousands of Criminal Cases May Be Dismissed." *Huffington Post*, April 8, 2010. http://www.huffingtonpost.com/2010/04/18/san-francisco-crime-lab-s_n_542102.html. (accessed Sept. 2, 2014).

"Ex-HPD Crime Lab Tech Convicted of Evidence Tampering, Felony Theft." *KHOU.com*, July 7, 2010. http://www.khou.com/news/Ex-HPD-crime-lab-tech-convicted-of-evidence-tampering-felony-theft-97976189.html (accessed March 14, 2013).

Ex Parte Donna G. Klohn, No. WR-81,294-01 (Ct. Crim. App.—Texas May 21, 2014) (per curiam).

Ex Parte George Rodriguez, 2005 Texas Crim. App. Unpub. LEXIS 399, Aug. 31, 2005.

Faigman, David L., Jeremy A. Blumenthal, Edward K. Cheng, Jennifer L. Mnookin, Erin E. Murphy, and Joseph Sanders. *Modern Scientific Evidence: The Law and Science of Expert Testimony*, Vol. 4: Forensics. (Eagan, Minnesota: Thomson Reuters 2013–14 edition).

Falkenberg, Lisa. "Innocent Man Waits for Compensation." *Houston Chronicle*, July 12, 2011. http://www.chron.com/news/falkenberg/article/Innocent-man-waits-for-compensation-1463532.php (accessed April 11, 2014).

———. "$3.1 Million Settlement Reached for Man Falsely Imprisoned." *Houston Chronicle*, Nov. 2, 2012. http://www.chron.com/news/houston-texas/houston/article/3-1-million-settlement-reached-for-man-falsely 4003901.php (accessed May 3, 2014).

Federal Bureau of Investigation. "Press Release: FBI Laboratory Announces Discontinuation of Bullet Lead Examinations," Sept. 1, 2005, http://www.fbi.gov/news/pressrel/press-releases/fbi-laboratory-announces-discontinuation-of-bullet-lead-examinations (accessed Feb. 10, 2014).

———. *Testimony*, at http://www.fbi.gov/news/testimony/formation-of-an-mpd-laboratory (Sept. 22, 2006) (testimony of Dr. Joseph A. DiZinno, Ass't Dir. Laboratory Div., Federal Bureau of Investigation, before the House Committee on Governmental Reform) (accessed Aug. 30, 2014).

Federal Rules of Evidence for United States Courts, P.L. 93-595; 88 Stat. 1926 (approved Jan. 2, 1975), Rules 607-14.

Fenton, Justin. "City Police Crime Lab Is Swamped." *Baltimore Sun*, March 14, 2010. http://weblogs.baltimoresun.com/news/crime/blog/2010/03/city_police_crime_lab_is_swamp.html (accessed Oct. 23, 2013).

Fergus, Mary Ann, "Josiah Sutton: One Year Later." *Houston Chronicle,* March 7, 2004. http://www.chron.com/life/article/Josiah-Sutton-One-Year-Later-1976295.php (accessed Aug. 19, 2014).

Findley, Keith A., & Michael A. Scott. "The Multiple Dimensions of Tunnel Vision in Criminal Cases." *Wisconsin Law Review* 2006 (2006): 291.

First Interlocal Agreement between the City of Houston and the Houston Forensic Science LGC, Inc., March 4, 2014. http://www.houstonforensicscience.org/

Formation%20Documents/Interlocal%20Agreement.PDF (accessed March 5, 2014).

Flood, Mary. "Jury Struggles in Case of Wrongful Conviction." *Houston Chronicle*, June 24, 2009, http://www.chron.com/news/houston-texas/article/ Jury-struggles-in-case-of-wrongful-conviction-1741108.php (accessed Sept. 2, 2014).

Forensic Quality Services (FQS). ANSI-ASQ National Accreditation Board, http://fqsforensics.org/ (accessed Oct. 24, 2013).

———. "Re: 'Strengthening Forensic Science in the United States: A Path Forward.'" On file with author.

Forensic Science and Standards Act of 2014, S. 2022, (113th Congress, 2013–2015) https://www.govtrack.us/congress/bills/113/s2022/text. (accessed Aug. 11, 2014)

"Former SFPD Lab Tech Sentenced for Drug Possession." abc7, July 19, 2013, www.abc7news.com/archive/9178786/ (accessed May 4, 2014).

Fradella, Henry F., Adam Fogarty, and Lauren O'Neill. "The Impact of Daubert on the Admissibility of Behavioral Science Testimony." *Pepperdine Law Review* 403 (2003): 30.

Francini, Simone Ling. "Note: Expert Handwriting Testimony: Is the Writing Really on the Wall?" *Suffolk Journal Trial and Appellate Advocacy* 11 (2006): 99–111.

Frankel, Jeffrey, and Peter R. Orszag. *Retrospective on American Economic Policy in the 1990s,* Nov. 2, 2001. http://www.brookings.edu/research/papers/ 2001/11/02useconomics-orszag (accessed Sept. 11, 2013).

Frye v. United States, 293 F. 1013 (D.C. Cir. 1923).

Furillo, Andy. "Crime Lab Overseers Split." *Sacramento Bee*, June 18, 2010. http://www.mcclatchydc.com/2010/06/18/96147/california-crime-lab-overseers.html (accessed Nov. 15, 2013).

Galloway v. State, 122 So. 3d 614 (Miss. 2013); United States v. Turner, 709 F.3d 1187 (7th Cir. 2013).

Garrett, Brandon L. *Convicting the Innocent: Where Criminal Prosecutions Go Wrong.* Cambridge, MA: Harvard University Press, 2011.

Garrett, Brandon L., and Peter J. Neufeld. "Invalid Forensic Science Testimony and Wrongful Convictions." *Virginia Law Review* 95 (2009): 1–15.

Garrett, Robert J. President, International Association for Identification (IAI). Correspondence to Senator Leahy, Chairman of the Senate Committee on the Judiciary, March 18, 2009. On file with author.

Gazal-Ayal, Oren, and Avishalom Tor. "The Innocence Effect." *Duke Law Journal* 62 (2012): 339.

Gee v. United States, 2012 D.C. App LEXIS 503 (2012).

General Electric Co. v. Joiner, 522 U.S. 136 (1997).

George Rodriguez v. City of Houston, 428 Fed. Appx. 367 (2011).

Gialamas, Dean (president), and Beth Greene (president-elect), American Society of Crime Lab Directors/Laboratory Accreditation Board (ASCLAD/LAB). Letter. http://www.gpo.gov/fdsys/pkg/CHRG-111shrg54304/pdf/CHRG-111shrg54304.pdf (accessed Dec. 17, 2013).

Giannelli, Paul C. "The Abuse of Scientific Evidence in Criminal Cases: The Need for Independent Crime Laboratories." *Virginia Journal of Social Policy and Law* 4 (1997): 439–475.

———. "Ake v. Oklahoma: The Right to Expert Assistance in a Post-Daubert, Post-DNA World." 89 *Cornell Law Review* 89 (2004): 1305–1312.

———. "Daubert and Forensic Science: The Pitfalls of Law Enforcement Control of Scientific Research." *University of Illinois Law Review* 53 (2011): 70.

———. "Independent Crime Laboratories: The Problem of Motivational and Cognitive Bias." *Utah Law Review* 2010 (2010): 247–260.

———. "'Junk Science': The Criminal Cases." *Journal of Criminal Law and Criminology* 84 (1993): 111.

———. "Regulating Crime Laboratories: The Impact of DNA Evidence." *Journal of Law Policy* 15 (2007): 59–68.

———. "Wrongful Convictions and Forensic Science: The Need to Regulate Crime Labs." *North Carolina Law Review* 86 (2007): 163–187.

Goodwyn, Wade. "Family of Man Cleared by DNA Still Seeks Justice." *NPR.org*, Feb. 5, 2009. http://www.npr.org/templates/story/story.php?storyId=100249923 (accessed Dec. 23, 2013).

Grissom, Brandi. "After 23 Years, A Suspect Emerges and a Family's Wounds Are Reopened." *New York Times*, Oct. 21, 2011. http://www.nytimes.com/2011/10/21/us/after-23-years-suspect-emerges-in-austin-murder-of-debra-masters-baker.html?pagewanted=alland_r=0 (accessed Dec. 14, 2013).

Grits for Breakfast, "Crime Lab Workers Suffer from 'Team Spirit' Mentality." July 10, 2008. http://gritsforbreakfast.blogspot.com/2008/07/crime-lab-workers-suffer-from-team.html (accessed Aug. 19, 2014).

———. "DPS analyst who faked results worked on 4,944 drug cases," July 28. 2012, http://gritsforbreakfast.blogspot.com/2012/07/dps-analyst-who-faked-results-worked-on.html (accessed May 4, 2014).

———. "Houston Crime Lab Found Hundreds of CODIS 'Hits' in Rape-Kit Backlog." April 6, 2014. http://gritsforbreakfast.blogspot.com/2014/04/houston-crime-lab-found-hundreds-of.html?utm_source=feedblitz&utm_medium=Feed BlitzEmail&utm_content=79553&utm_campaign=0 (accessed Mar. 9, 2014).

———. "Houston Crime Lab Reports Only Prosecution Friendly Evidence." April 30, 2009. http://gritsforbreakfast.blogspot.com/2009/04/houston-crime-lab-only-reported.html (accessed Apr. 1, 2014).

———. "Texas Should Conduct Review of Hair and Fiber Forensics Comparable to Feds." July 18, 2012. http://gritsforbreakfast.blogspot.com/2012/07/texas-should-conduct-review-of-hair-and.html (accessed March 14, 2014).

———. "The Weakest Link: TDCAA Agrees Nearly 5,000 Cases May All Be Jeopardized' by DPS Lab Worker Misconduct." March 15, 2013. http://gritsforbreakfast.blogspot.com/2013/03/the-weakest-link-tdcaa-agrees-nearly.html?utm_source=feedblitz&utm_medium=FeedBlitzEmail&utm_content=79553&utm_campaign=0 (accessed May 7, 2014).

Hammond, Larry A. "The Failure of Forensic Science Reform in Arizona." *Judicature* 93 (2010): 227.

Hansen, Mark. "Crime Labs under the Microscope after a String of Shoddy, Suspect, and Fraudulent Results." *ABA Journal*, Sept. 1, 2013. http://www.abajournal.com/magazine/article/crime_labs_under_the_microscope_after_a_string_of_shoddy_suspect_and_fraudu/ (accessed Jan. 19, 2014).

Harris, David A. *Failed Evidence: Why Law Enforcement Resists Science at 71–72.* New York: New York University Press 2012.

———. "The Constitution and Truth Seeking: A New Theory on Expert Services for Indigent Defendants." *Journal of Criminal Law and Criminology* 83 (1992): 469.

Hassan, Anita. "Harris County Plan Could Help Relieve HPD Crime Lab." *Houston Chronicle*, June 20, 2011. http://www.chron.com/news/houston-texas/article/Harris-County-plan-could-help-relieve-HPD-crime-2078953.php (accessed Feb. 8, 2014).

Hawkins, Bill. Fax to Mark Wawro, Oct. 3, 2005. On file with author.

Heinszerling, Lisa. "Doubting Daubert." *Journal of Law and Policy* 14 (2006): 65.

Hermann, Peter, and Keith L. Alexander. "D.C. Police Crime Lab Technicians Ordered Transferred, to Be Replaced by Civilians." *Washington Post*, Sept. 21, 2012, http://www.washingtonpost.com/local/crime/dc-police-crime-lab-technicians-ordered-transferred-to-be-replaced-by-civilians/2012/09/21/af5eaeba-0419-11e2-9b24-ff730c7f6312_story.html (accessed Aug. 14, 2014).

Houck, Max M., and Jay A. Siegal. *Fundamentals of Forensic Science.* (San Diego: Elsevier Science and Technology Books), 2006.

Houston Forensic Science LGC, Inc., *Certificate of Formation*, June 22, 2012. http://www.houstonforensicscience.org/Formation%20Documents/120626%5EHFSLGC%20Certificate%20of%20Formation%20%28file-stamped%29.pdf (accessed Jan. 28, 2013).

_____. Meeting of the Board of Directors Agenda, Oct. 12, 2012, http://www.houstonforensicscience.org/V_meetings/2012/oct__2012/1agenda_121010.pdf (accessed Aug. 25, 2014).

_____. Meeting of the Board of Directors Minutes, Jan. 10, 2014, http://www.houstonforensicscience.org/Board%20Meeting%20Files/Minutes/minutes_140110.pdf (accessed May 1, 2014).

_____. Minutes of the Board of Directors, June 20, 2012, http://www.houstonforensicscience.org/Board%20Meeting%20Files/Minutes/minutes_120620.pdf (accessed May 1, 2014).

_____. Minutes of the Board of Directors, May 24, 2013, http://houstonforensiccenter.com/files/minutes_130524.pdf (accessed Nov. 23, 2013).

Houston Police Department. "News Release: HPD Crime Lab Receives National Accreditation." (May 11, 2005) http://www.houstontx.gov/police/nr/2005/may/nr051105-4.htm (accessed Jan. 9, 2014).

Hsu, Spencer S. "Convicted Defendants Left Uninformed of Forensic Flaws found by Department of Justice." *Washington Post*, Apr. 16, 2012. http://www.washingtonpost.com/local/crime/convicted-defendants-left-uninformed-of-forensic-flaws-found-by-justice-dept/2012/04/16/gIQAWTcgMT_story.html (accessed Aug. 11, 2014).

In re Davis, 130 S. Ct. 1, 3 (2009) (mem.) (Scalia, J., dissenting).

In re Richards, Letter Brief of Amici Curiae in Support of Petition for Rehearing, 2012 WL 71060188, p. *3 (Cal. 2012).

Innocence Project. *Cases Where DNA Revealed that Bite Mark Analysis Led to Wrongful Arrests and Convictions.* http://www.innocenceproject.org/Content/Cases_Where_DNA_Revealed_that_Bite_Mark_Analysis_Led_to_Wrongful_Arrests_and_Convictions.php (accessed Feb. 8, 2014).

——. *DNA Exoneree Case Profiles.* http://www.innocenceproject.org/know/ (accessed Nov. 9, 2013).

——. *Fix the System: Access to DNA Testing.* http://www.innocenceproject.org/fix/DNA-Testing-Access.php (accessed Feb. 23, 2014).

——. *Fix the System: Compensation for the Wrongly Convicted.* http://www.innocenceproject.org/fix/Compensation.php (accessed March 15, 2014).

——. *Fix the System: Preservation of Evidence.* http://www.innocenceproject.org/Content/Preservation_Of_Evidence.php (accessed March 16, 2014).

——. *Fix the System, State Compensation Laws: Texas.* http://www.innocenceproject.org/fix/state1.php?state=TX (accessed March 16, 2014).

——. *Know the Cases: Browse the Profiles: George Rodriguez.* http://www.innocenceproject.org/Content/George_Rodriguez.php (accessed May 24, 2014).

——. *Know the Cases: Browse the Profiles: Ronald Gene Taylor.* http://www.innocenceproject.org/Content/Ronald_Gene_Taylor.php (accessed August 19, 2014).

——. *Know the Cases: Browse the Profiles: Timothy Cole.* http://www.innocenceproject.org/Content/Timothy_Cole.php (accessed March 16, 2014).

——. *Know the Cases: DNA Exoneree Profiles.* http://www.innocenceproject.org/know/ (accessed May 22, 2014).

——. *News and Information: Innocence Project and NACDL Announce Historic Partnership with FBI and Department of Justice on Microscopic Hair Analysis Cases.* http://www.innocenceproject.org/Content/Innocence_Project_and_NACDL_Announce_Historic_Partnership_with_the_FBI_and_Department_of_Justice_on_Microscopic_Hair_Analysis_Cases.php# (accessed Jan. 10, 2014).

——. *News and Information: Louisiana Man on Death Row for 15 Years Becomes 300th Person Exonerated by DNA Evidence.* Sept. 12, 2012. http://www.innocenceproject.org/Content/Louisiana_Man_on_Death_Row_for_15_Years_Becomes__300th_Person_Exonerated_by_DNA_Evidence.php (accessed Sept. 2, 2013).

——. *News and Information: Reforms by State.* http://www.innocenceproject.org/news/LawView5.php (accessed April 11, 2014).

——. *News and Information: Sequential Lineups Are More Accurate, According to Ground-breaking Report on Eyewitness Identification Procedures.* http://www.innocenceproject.org/Content/SAVE_Sequential_Lineups_Are_More_

Accurate_According_to_Groundbreaking_Report_on_Eyewitness_ Identification_Procedures.php (accessed March 23, 2014).

_____. *Press Release: DNA Test Proves Critical Hair Evidence in a Capital Murder Case Didn't Match Man Executed; General Counsel Memo to President Elect George Bush Hid the Fact That the Accused Sought DNA Tests That Could Have Spared Him from Execution*, Nov. 12, 2010. http://www.innocence project.org/Content/DNA_Test_Proves_Critical_Hair_Evidence_in_a_ Capital_Murder_Case_Didnt_Match_Man_Executed.php (accessed Dec. 2, 2013).

_____. *Understand the Causes: Unvalidated or Improper Forensic Testimony.* http:// www.innocenceproject.org/understand/Unreliable-Limited-Science.php (accessed Dec. 27, 2013).

Innocence Project of Texas. *State Arson Review.* http://www.ipoftexas.org/ statewide-arson-review (accessed Nov. 13, 2013).

"Inside Dateline, Wrongfully Convicted Man Awarded $9 Million after Spend-ing Almost 20 Years Behind Bars." *NBC News,* Feb. 4, 2014, http://inside-dateline.nbcnews.com/_news/2014/02/04/22574079-wrongfully-convicted-man-awarded-9-million-after-spending-almost-20-years-behind-bars (accessed May 12, 2014).

International Association for Identification. *History,* at http://www.theiai.org/ history/ (accessed May 30, 2014).

International Association of Chiefs of Police (IACP). *Forensics Policy, Approved by the IACP Governing Body on April 18, 2009.* On file with author.

International Organization of Standardization (ISO). *About ISO.* http:// www.iso.org/iso/home/about.htm (accessed April 14, 2014).

_____. *ISO/IEC 17025:2005* (2010), http://www.iso.org/iso/catalogue_detail.htm? csnumber=39883 (accessed April 14, 2014).

Jacobs, Sally. "Annie Dookhan Pursued Renown along a Path of Lies; Finally Found Fame, as Scandal Engulfed the State Drug Lab." *Boston Globe*, Feb. 3, 2013. http://www.bostonglobe.com/metro/2013/02/03/chasing-renown-path-paved-with-lies/Axw3AxwmD33lRwXatSvMCL/story.html (accessed Nov. 14, 2013).

Jenkins v. United States, 75 A.3d 174 (D.C. 2013).

Johnson, Alex. "Already under Fire, Crime Labs Cut to the Bone." msnbc.com. http://www.nbcnews.com/id/35319938/ns/us_news-crime_and_courts/t/ already-under-fire-crime-labs-cut-bone/ (accessed April 10, 2013).

Jones v. State, 982 N.E.2d 417 (Ind. Ct. App. 2013).

Jones v. State, 2013 Ark. App. 466 (Ark. Ct. App. 2013).

Jones v. United States, 27 A.3d 1130 (2011).

Justice Department. "FBI to Review Flawed Criminal Forensic Evidence." *PBS NEWSHOUR*, July 20, 2012. http://www.pbs.org/newshour/bb/law-july-dec12-fbi_07-11/ (accessed Jan. 4, 2014).

_____. "Notice of Establishment of the National Commission on Forensic Science and Solicitation of Applications for Commission Membership." February 22, 2013, FED. REG. http://www.federalregister.gov/articles/2013/02/22/2013-04140/notice-of-establishement-of-the-national-commission-on-forensic-science-and-solicitation-of (accessed Jan. 4, 2014).

Justice Project. *Improving the Practice and Use of Forensic Science: A Policy Review*. http://ag.ca.gov/meetings/tf/pdf/Justice_Project_Report.pdf (accessed May 16, 2014).

Kansal, Tushar. *Racial Disparities in Sentencing: A Review of the Literature*. Marc Mauer (Ed.). (Washington D.C.: The Sentencing Project) 2005. http://www.sentencingproject.org/doc/publications/rd_sentencing_review.pdf. (accessed Sept. 2, 2014).

Kaplan, Tracey. "Santa Clara County DA Criticized for Crime Lab Failures." *Mercury News*, March 15, 2009. http://truthinjustice.org/SantaClaralab.htm (accessed March 9, 2014).

_____. "Wrongfully Convicted San Jose Man to Receive $1 Million Settlement from Santa Clara County."*San Jose Mercury News*, August 15, 2009, http://www.mercurynews.com/ci_13118342?source=most_viewed (accessed May 4, 2014).

Kassin, Saul M., Itiel Dror, and Jeff Kukucka. "The Forensic Confirmation Bias: Problems, Perspectives, and Proposed Solutions." *Journal Applied Research in Memory and Cognition* 2 (2013): 42–52.

Kennedy, Donald. "Editorial: Forensic Science: Oxymoron?" *Science* 302 (2003): 1625.

Kershaw, Sarah. "Spain and U.S. at Odds on Mistaken Terror Arrest." *New York Times*, June 5, 2004, A1.

Khanna, Roma. "DA Unswayed by New Evidence in '87 Rape Case." *Houston Chronicle*, Aug. 24, 2004, http://www.chron.com/news/houston-texas/article/DA-unswayed-by-new-evidence-in-87-rape-case-1633824.php (accessed Aug. 14, 2014).

_____. "$5 Million Award Bittersweet for Wrongly Convicted: Jury Awards Rodriguez." *Houston Chronicle*, June 25, 2009, http://www.chron.com/news/

houston-texas/article/5-million-award-bittersweet-for-wrongly-convicted-1720657.php (accessed Aug. 14, 2014).

———. "Governor Pardons Josiah Sutton." *Houston Chronicle*, May 14, 2004, http://www.chron.com/news/houston-texas/article/Governor-pardons-Josiah-Sutton-1633572.php (accessed Aug. 14, 2014).

———. "Houston Man Walks Free after 22 Years in Prison." *Houston Chronicle*, August 29, 2009. http://www.chron.com/news/houston-texas/article/Houston-man-walks-free-after-22-years-in-prison-1736190.php (accessed Aug. 19, 2014).

———. "Judge Again Urges Moratorium." *Houston Chronicle*, Oct. 26, 2004. http://www.chron.com/news/houston-texas/article/Judge-again-urges-moratorium-1982619.php (accessed Nov. 14, 2013).

———. "Problems Persisted at Reformed HPD Crime Lab." *Houston Chronicle*, Feb. 22, 2008. http://www.chron.com/news/houston-texas/article/Problems-persisted-at-reformed-HPD-crime-lab-1610556.php (accessed Feb. 17, 2014).

———. "State Hires DNA Chief Despite Houston Crime Lab Probe." *Houston Chronicle*, Jan. 30, 2008. http://www.chron.com/news/houston-texas/article/State-hires-DNA-chief-despite-Houston-crime-lab-1785193.php. (accessed Sept. 2, 2014).

———. "2 Cases, 2 Opinions Equal Trouble for Crime Lab." *Houston Chronicle*, Aug. 29, 2004. http://www.chron.com/news/article/2-cases-2-opinions-equal-trouble-for-crime-lab-1974804.php (accessed March 30, 2014).

Khanna, Roma, and Steve McVicker. "Early Critic Named Director of Houston's New Crime Lab." *Houston Chronicle*, Oct. 9, 2003, http://archives.lists.indymedia.org/imc-houston/2003-October/007757.html (accessed Aug. 14, 2014).

———. "Fired DNA Analyst to Return to Work at Crime Lab." *Houston Chronicle*, Jan. 28, 2004. http://www.chron.com/news/houston-texas/article/Fired-DNA-analyst-to-return-to-work-at-crime-lab-1609733.php (accessed May 1, 2014).

———. "Panel will Review 180 HPD Crime Lab Cases." *Houston Chronicle.*, Oct. 12, 2007, http://www.chron.com/news/houston-texas/article/Panel-will-review-180-HPD-crime-lab-cases-1796314.php (accessed May 1, 2014).

Kingsnorth, Rodney, John Lopez, Jennifer Wentworth, and Debra Cummings. "Adult Sexual Assault: The Role of Racial/Ethnic Composition in Prosecution and Sentencing." *Journal Criminal Justice* 26 (1998): 359.

Kirk, P. L. "The Ontogeny of Criminalistics." *Journal of Criminal Law, Criminology and Political Science* 54 (1963): 235–238.

Koehler, Jonathan J., and John Meixner, eds. *Workshop on Cognitive Bias and Forensic Science.* (Chicago, Illinois: Northwestern University School of Law) June 22, 2011. http://www.law.northwestern.edu/faculty/conferences/workshops/cognitivebias/ (accessed Nov. 12, 2013).

Koppl, Roger. *CSI for Real: How to Improve Forensic Science.* Reason Foundation, Policy Study No. 364 (2007). http://reason.org/files/d834fab5860d5cf4b3949fecf86d3328.pdf (accessed Aug . 6, 2014).

——. "How to Improve Forensic Science." *European Journal of Law and Economics* 20 (2005): 255.

Krane, Dan E., et al. "Letter to the Editor: Sequential Unmasking: A Means of Minimizing Observer Effects in Forensic DNA Interpretation." *Journal of Forensic Science* 53 (2008): 1006.

Kumho Tire Co. Ltd. v. Carmichael, 526 U.S. 137 (1999).

Lazar, Ken. "How Chemist in Drug Lab Circumvented Safeguards." *Boston.com*, Sept. 29, 2012, http://www.boston.com/news/local/massachusetts/2012/09/30/how-chemist-drug-lab-scandal-circumvented-safeguards/A29LZnAw1eW4hvjn4xx7rL/story.html (accessed Jan. 8, 2014).

Lentini, John J. *The Mythology of Fire Investigation.* http://www.firescientist.com/Documents/The%20Mythology%20of%20Arson%20Investigation.pdf (accessed Sept. 11, 2013).

——. *Scientific Protocols for Fire Investigation.* (Boca Raton, Florida: CRC Press), 2006.

Leung, Rebecca, "DNA Testing: Foolproof?." *60 Minutes.* May 27, 2003, http://www.cbsnews.com/news/dna-testing-foolproof/ (accessed Aug. 19, 2014).

Liptak, Adam, and Ralph Blumenthal. "New Doubt Cast on Testing in Houston Police Crime Lab." *New York Times*, Aug. 5, 2004. http://www.nytimes.com/2004/08/05/us/new-doubt-cast-on-testing-in-houston-police-crime-lab.html (accessed Sept. 12, 2013).

Liptak, Adam. "Worst Crime Lab in the Country—Or Is Houston Typical?" *New York Times*, March 11, 2003. http://truthinjustice.org/suttonDNA.htm (accessed Aug. 14, 2014).

Littleton v. State, 372 S.W.3d 926 (Mo. Ct. App. 2012).

Locke, Mandy, and Joseph Neff. "SBI Fights District Attorneys' Attempts to Learn about Failed Tests: Agency Won't Release Data on 25 Analysts." *News and Observer*, June 14, 2012. http://www.newsobserver.com/2012/06/14/2137375/sbi-fights-district-attorneys.html (accessed Sept. 13, 2013).

Lott, Joshua M. "The End of Innocence? Federal Habeas Corpus Law After In re Davis." *Georgia State University Law Review* 27 (2011): 443–488.

Madigan, Nick. "Houston's Troubled DNA Crime Lab Faces Growing Scrutiny." *Houston Chronicle*, Feb. 9, 2003. http://www.nytimes.com/2003/02/09/us/houston-s-troubled-dna-crime-lab-faces-growing-scrutiny.html (accessed Sept. 13, 2013).

Mann, David. "DNA Tests Undermine Evidence in Texas Execution." *Texas Observer*, Nov. 11, 2011. http://www.texasobserver.org/texas-observer-exclusive-dna-tests-undermine-evidence-in-texas-execution/ (accessed Sept. 14, 2013).

Maricopa County District Attorney's Office. *CSI: Maricopa County, The CSI Effect and Its Real-Life Impact on Justice, A Study by the Maricopa County Attorney's Office*, June 30, 2005. http://www.ce9.uscourts.gov/jc2008/references/csi/CSI_Effect_report.pdf (accessed Sept. 2, 2014).

Martin v. State, 60 A.3d 1100 (Del. 2013).

Maxwell, Christopher D., Amanda L. Robinson, and Lori A. Post. "The Impact of Race on the Adjudication of Sexual Assault and Other Violent Crimes." *Journal of Criminal Justice* 31 (2003): 523.

Mayor's Office. *Press Release: President/CEO Named for Houston Independent Crime Lab*, Aug. 14, 2013. http://www.houstontx.gov/mayor/press/20130814.html (accessed May 12, 2014).

McCarthy v. State, 285 P.3d 285 (Ala. Ct. App. 2012).

McCarty v. State, 765 P.2d 1215 (Okla. Crim. App. 1988).

McKinley, Jesse. "Hundreds of Drug Cases Are at Risk in San Francisco." *New York Times*, April 3, 2010. http://www.nytimes.com/2010/04/04/us/04evidence.html?_r=0 (accessed April 27, 2014).

McMenamin, Jennifer. "Police Expert Lied about Credentials." *Baltimore Sun*, March 9, 2007. http://www.baltimoresun.com/news/maryland/balte.md.forensics09mar09,0,3664583.story?page=1 (accessed May 30, 2014).

McVicker, Steve. "Crime Lab Evidence Again Questioned." *Houston Chronicle*, Aug. 4, 2004. http://www.chron.com/news/houston-texas/article/Crime-lab-evidence-again-questioned-1482418.php (accessed April 27, 2014).

———. "Crime Lab Evidence Questioned Again: Experts Dispute Testimony in 1987 Sex Assault Case." *Houston Chronicle*, Aug. 5, 2004. http://www.chron.com/news/houston-texas/article/Crime-lab-evidence-again-questioned-1482418.php (accessed Nov. 14, 2013).

————. "DNA Test Review Casts Shadow of Doubt on 1987 Rape Conviction." *Houston Chronicle*, Aug. 22, 2004, http://www.chron.com/news/article/DNA-test-review-casts-shadow-of-doubt-on-1987-1983999.php (accessed Dec. 11, 2013).

————. "HPD's Crime Lab Faces Proficiency-Test Inquiry." *Houston Chronicle*, Oct. 5, 2007. http://www.chron.com/news/houston-texas/article/HPD-s-crime-lab-faces-proficiency-test-inquiry-1604493.php. (accessed Sept. 2, 2014).

————. "Officials Urge Special Probe of HPD Crime Lab." *Houston Chronicle*, Aug. 7, 2004. http://www.chron.com/news/houston-texas/article/Officials-urge-special-probe-of-HPD-crime-lab-1625012.php (accessed Dec. 20, 2013).

McVicker, Steve, and Andrew Tilghman, "More Crime Lab Troubles Possible, Chief Says." *Houston Chronicle*, Aug. 6, 2004. http://www.chron.com/news/article/More-crime-lab-troubles-possible-chief-says-1972139.php. (accessed Sept. 2, 2014).

McVicker, Steve, and Roma Khanna. "Early Critic Named Director of Houston's New Crime Lab." *Houston Chronicle*, Oct. 9, 2003. http://archives.lists.indymedia.org/imc-houston/2003-October/007757.html (accessed Aug. 14, 2014).

Melendez-Diaz v. Massachusetts, 129 S.Ct. 2527 (2009).

Memorandum of Understanding between the Department of Justice and the National Institute of Standards and Technology in Support of the National Commission on Forensic Science, signed March 25, 2013. On file with author.

Mendoza, Moises and Bradley Olson, "Major, Costly Overhaul Likely in HPD Fingerprint Unit." *Houston Chronicle*, Dec. 1, 2009, http://www.chron.com/news/houston-texas/article/Major-costly-overhaul-likely-in-HPD-fingerprint-1739953.php (accessed May 1, 2014).

Metzger, Pamela R. "Cheating the Constitution." *Vanderbilt Law Review* 59 (2006): 475.

Miller v. State, 2013 OK CR 11, 313 P.3d 934 (2013).

Mills, Steve, and Maurice Possley. "Report Alleges Crime Lab Fraud: Scientist Is Accused of Providing False Testimony." *Chicago Tribune*, Jan. 14, 2001, C1.

Mills, Steve, Flynn McRoberts, and Maurice Possley. "When Labs Falter, Defendants Pay: Bias toward Prosecution Cited in Illinois Cases." *Chicago Tribune*, Oct. 20, 2004, C1.

Minor, Joe. "Touch DNA: From the Crime Scene to the Crime Laboratory." *Forensic Magazine*, April 12, 2013. http://www.forensicmag.com/articles/2013/04/touch-dna-crime-scene-crime-laboratory (accessed Dec. 31, 2013).

Mitchell, Jerry. "Dentist Now Doubts Science of Bite Analysis." *Clarion-Ledger*, http://bitemarks.org/2012/08/06/dentist-now-doubts-science-of-bite-analysis/ (accessed Aug. 14, 2014).

Mnookin, Jennifer L. "The Validity of Latent Fingerprint Identification: Confessions of a Fingerprinting Moderate." *Law, Probability and Risk* 7 (2008): 127.

Mnookin, Jennifer, and David Kaye. "Confronting Science: Expert Evidence and the Confrontation Clause." *Supreme Court Review 2012* (2013): 99.

Mnookin, Jennifer L., Simon A. Cole, Itiel E. Dror, Barry A. J. Fisher, Max M. Houck, Keith Inman, David H. Kaye, Jonathan J. Koehler, Glenn Langenburg, D. Michael Risinger, Norah Rudin, Jay Siegel, and David A. Stoney. "The Need for a Research Culture in the Forensic Sciences." *UCLA Law Review* 58 (2011): 725.

Mondo, Michelle. "Freedom Comes to Three of the 'San Antonio 4.'" *San Antonio Express-News*, Nov. 18, 2013; updated November 20, 2013. http://www.mysanantonio.com/news/local/article/DA-drops-S-A-Four-cases-4985664.php (accessed Dec. 31, 2013).

Montanaro, Julie. "81 Drug Cases Possibly Affected by Former FDLE Chemist." *WCTV.com*, March 5, 2014. http://www.wctv.tv/home/headlines/FDLE-To-Hold-News-Conference-Regarding-Evidence-Tampering-243009311.html (accessed Nov. 22, 2013).

Montgomery County, Maryland. "Press Release: Duncan Welcomes Expansion of Germantown's Cellmark Diagnostics." http://www6.montgomerycountymd.gov/apps/News/press/PR_details.asp?PrID=11714 (accessed Jan. 14, 2014).

Moore v. State, 294 Ga. 682, 755 S.E.2d 703 (Ga. 2014).

Moran, Chris. "City Council Agrees to Hand Crime Lab to Independent Board." *Houston Chronicle*, June 6, 2012. http://www.chron.com/news/houston--texas/article/Council-hands-crime-lab-to-independent-board-3615078.php (accessed Jan. 15, 2014).

Moran, Greg. "Criminalist Who Testified on DUIs Falsified Résumé." *San Diego Union Tribune*, March 22, 2006. http://www.utsandiego.com/uniontrib/20060322/news_7m22duiguy.html(accessed Feb. 20, 2014).

Mueller & Kirkpatrick, *Evidence* (3rd ed. 2003).

National Academy of Sciences. *Mission Statement*. http://www.nasonline.org/about-nas/mission/ (accessed Feb. 13, 2014).

National District Attorneys Association (NDAA). *NDAA Comments Provided to the Consortium of Forensic Sciences Regarding the National Academy of Sciences Report* (Apr. 2009). On file with author.

National Fire Protection Association. *NFPA 921: Guide for Fire and Explosion Investigations*. http://www.nfpa.org/codes-and-standards/document-information-pages?mode=code&code=921 (accessed Nov. 23, 2013).

National Institute of Justice. *Status and Needs of Forensic Science Service Providers: A Report to Congress* (2004). https://www.ncjrs.gov/pdffiles1/nij/213420.pdf (accessed Feb. 23, 2014).

National Institute of Standards and Technology (NIST). *Organization of Scientific Area Committees, Role and Responsibilities* (April 11, 2014), http://www.nist.gov/forensics/osacroles.cfm. (accessed August 13, 2014).

_____. *Proposed Organization of Scientific Area Committees (OSAC) Presented to National Commission on Forensic Science* (Feb. 4, 2014). http://www.nist.gov/forensics/upload/NIST-OSAC-Plan-NCFS-Feb-4-2014-2-3-14-FINAL.pdf (accessed March 15, 2014).

National Research Council, *Strengthening Forensic Science in the United States: A Path Forward* (Washington, D.C.: The National Academies Press), 2009.

Neil, Martha. "Federal Jury Awards $5M to Texas Man Convicted on Bad Crime Lab Evidence." *ABA Journal*, June 25, 2009. http://www.abajournal.com/news/article/fedl_jury_awards_5m_to_texas_man_convicted_based_on_bad_crime_lab_evidence (accessed Nov. 13, 2013).

Neufeld, Peter J. "The (Near) Irrelevance of Daubert to Criminal Justice and Some Suggestions for Reform." *Public Health Matters* 95 (2005): S107.

New York State Justice Task Force, "Recommendations Regarding Discovery of Case File Materials." October 21, 2012 (on file with author).

New York Times Archives, "Court Invalidates a Decade of Blood Test Results in Criminal Cases." *New York Times*, Nov. 12, 1993. http://www.nytimes.com/1993/11/12/us/court-invalidates-a-decade-of-blood-test-results-in-criminal-cases.html (accessed March 29, 2014).

"Norwood Pleads Not Guilty in Debra Baker Death." KVUE.com, Jan. 9, 2014. http://www.kvue.com/news/Norwood-pleads-not-guilty-in-Debra-Baker-death-239457951.html (accessed Dec. 16, 2013).

Oberg, Ted. "Latest Large-Scale Reversal by DA Pat Lykos." *ABC13 Eyewitness News*, Feb.14, 2012. http://abc13.com/archive/8542367/ (accessed Dec. 17, 2013).

_____. "Harris County Breaks Ground on New Crime Lab Center." *ABC13 Eyewitness News*, April 11, 2012. http://abc13.com/archive/8615789/ (accessed May 12, 2014).

Oehling v. State, 109 So. 3d 1199 (Fla. Dist. Ct. App. 2013) review denied, 123 So. 3d 559 (Fla. 2013).

Oettmeier, Timothy. Correspondence with Executive Assistant Chief of Police Timothy Oettmeier. June 9, 2014. On file with author.

Office of the Independent Investigator for the Houston Police Department Crime Laboratory and Property Room, *Background of the Investigation*, http://hpdlabinvestigation.org/about.htm#From%20Home.http://www.hpdlabinvestigation.org/ (accessed May 12, 2014).

_____. *Scientific Advisory Board*, http://www.hpdlabinvestigation.org/sci_adv_board.htm (accessed May 1, 2014).

Office of the Inspector General, Oversight and Review Division. *A Review of the FBI's Handling of the Brandon Mayfield Case: Unclassified Executive Summary*, Jan. 2006.

Olson, Bradley. "Backlog Woes Continue at HPD Lab." *Houston Chronicle*, Jan. 26, 2010. http://www.chron.com/news/houston-texas/article/Backlog-woes-continue-at-HPD-lab-1709693.php (accessed Aug. 14, 2014).

Page, Mark, Jane Taylor, and Matt Blenkin. "Context Effects and Observer Bias—Implications for Forensic Odontology." *Journal Forensic Science* 57 (2012): 108–112.

People v. Bullock, 154 Ill. App. 3d 266 (App. Ct.—Ill. 1987).

People. v. Eleby, 2012 Cal. App. Unpub. LEXIS 3375 (2012).

People v. Farley, 2013 WL 6084198 (Mich. Ct. App. 2013) (unpublished).

People v. Givens, 2010 WL 5022731 (N.Y.S.Ct. 2010).

People v. Greenwood, L.A. Super. Ct. (2010).

People v. Leach, 980 N.E.2d 570 (Ill. 2012).

People v. Lopez, 55 Cal. 4th 569 (Cal. 2012).

People v. Pealer, 20 N.Y.3d 447, 985 N.E.2d 903 (2013) cert. denied, 134 S. Ct. 105, 187 L. Ed. 2d 77 (2013).

People v. Williams, Docket No. 107550 (Jul. 15, 2010), http://www.state.il.us/court/Opinions/SupremeCourt/2010/July/107550.pdf.

Peters, Jeremy W. "Report Condemns Police Lab Oversight." *New York Times*, Dec. 18, 2009, http://www.nytimes.com/2009/12/18/nyregion/18statepolice.html?_r=2& (accessed Aug. 14, 2014).

Pignolet, Jennifer. "Crime Lab Work Went Undone; Worker Accused of Lying about Completing Tests on Evidence." *The Spokesman-Review*, April 17, 2013. http://www.spokesman.com/stories/2013/apr/17/crime-lab-work-went-undone/ (accessed May 4, 2014).

Pinkerton, James, and Brian Rogers. "Crime Lab Analyst Kept on Job Despite Shoddy Work." *Houston Chronicle*, April 4, 2013, http://www.houstonchronicle.com/news/houston-texas/houston/article/Crime-lab-analyst-kept-on-job-despite-shoddy-work-4413046.php (accessed April 16, 2014).

Potterf, Tina. "Crime Lab Junkie? Alleged Theft and Tampering by State Patrol Chemist May Have Jeopardized Thousands of Drug Cases." *Seattle Weekly News*, Oct. 9, 2006. http://www.seattleweekly.com/2001-01-24/news/crime-lab-junkie/ (accessed Nov. 11, 2013).

Pratt, Travis C., Michael J. Gaffney, Nicholas P. Lovrich, and Charles L. Johnson. "This Isn't CSI: Estimating the National Backlog of Forensic DNA Cases and the Barriers Associated with Case Processing." *Criminal Journal of Policy Review* 17 (2006): 32–37.

Prosecutors Want Houston Man's Rape Conviction Dismissed." KHOU.com, Mar. 3, 2011, http://www.khou.com/news/local/Prosecutors-want-Houston-mans-rape-conviction-dismissed-after-17-years-behind-bars-117313038.html (accessed Sept. 11, 2013).

Quinn, Kathy. "New Police Crime Lab Could Suffer Due to Budget Woes." *Fox4kc.com.* http://fox4kc.com/2013/06/27/new-police-crime-lab-could-suffer-due-to-budget-woes/ (accessed Sept. 16, 2013).

Quinn, Kevin. "Effort to Ease Houston's Rape Kit Backlog Pays Off with Arrest of Suspect from 2004 Attack." *ABC 13*, Oct. 10, 2013. http://abclocal.go.com/ktrk/story?section=news/local&id=9282620 (accessed Feb. 15, 2014).

Reddy, L. Vamsi Krishna. "Lip Prints: An Overview in Forensic Dentistry." 2 *Journal of Advanced Dental Research* (2011): 17.

"Report: Crime Lab Delays Lead to False Drug Convictions." *Star-Telegram*, Apr. 20, 2014. http://www.star-telegram.com/2014/04/20/5751844/report-lab-delays-lead-to-false.html. (accessed Aug. 21, 2014).

Rice, Stephanie. "County Borrowing $10 Million to Pay Pair Wrongfully Convicted of Rape: Two Men Spent 17 Years in Prison for Crime They Didn't Commit." *The Columbian* (Vancouver, Canada), Oct. 22, 2013. http://

www.columbian.com/news/2013/oct/22/clark-county-wrongful-conviction-rape-northrop-dav/ (accessed March 12, 2014).

Rios, Irma, Assistant Director of the Crime Lab, City of Houston. Inter office Correspondence, Sept. 12, 2012, on file with author.

Risinger, D. Michael. "Navigating Expert Reliability: Are Criminal Standards of Certainty Being Left on the Dock?" *Albany Law Review* 64 (2000): 99.

Risinger, D. Michael, and Michael J. Saks. "A House with No Foundation." Issues in Science and Technology (Fall 2003): 35.

Robles, Frances. "Man Framed by Detective Will Get $6.4 Million from New York City after Serving 23 Years for Murder." *New York Times*, Feb. 20, 2014. http://www.nytimes.com/2014/02/21/nyregion/man-framed-by-new-york-detective-to-get-6-4-million-without-filing-suit.html (accessed May 11, 2014).

Rodriguez v. City of Houston, Daily Transcripts, June 15, 2008. https://docs.google.com/viewer?pid=explorerandsrcid=0B3ulC5gsGYV8ekxK-LVcxaG9BTHManddocid=c4d8cadd695f92dc3936643ab40ffaa0%7C620ff377d7eb1075808ae77ce557c238&chan=EQAAAMEZFKbzzVpATXwLTPW/m7S%2BAjk80sMd6EOGPiej2meZ&a=v&rel=zip;z2;June+16+2009+Volume+1+(2).pdf (accessed Feb. 11, 2014).

Rodriguez v. State, 766 S.W.2d 360 (Ct. App.—Tex. 1989).

Rogers, Brian. "Assistant DA Refuses to Testify about BAT Van Evidence." *Houston Chronicle*, Dec. 15, 2011. http://www.chron.com/news/houston-texas/article/Assistant-DA-refuses-to-testify-in-grand-jury-2405482.php (accessed August 20, 2014).

———. "Criticism Continues to Dog HPD Crime Lab." *Houston Chronicle*, July 29, 2011. http://www.chron.com/news/houston-texas/article/Criticism-continues-to-dog-HPD-crime-lab-2077794.php (accessed April 8, 2014).

———. "Harris County DA Testifies in Grand Jury Probe." *Houston Chronicle*, Jan. 17, 2012. http://www.chron.com/news/houston-texas/article/Harris-County-DA-testifies-in-grand-jury-probe-2584972.php (accessed Feb. 15, 2014).

———. "HPD Crime Lab Workers Quit over Faulty Testing Vans." *Houston Chronicle*, July 28, 2011. http://www.chron.com/news/houston-texas/article/HPD-crime-lab-workers-quit-over-faulty-testing-2081382.php (accessed March 30, 2014).

———. "Hundreds of Cases to Be Reviewed Because of Errors by Crime Lab Worker." *Houston Chronicle*, May 1, 2012. http://www.chron.com/news/

houston-texas/article/Hundreds-of-cases-to-be-reviewed-because-of-3525028.php (accessed May 13, 2014).

Rubin, Joel. "LAPD's Crime Lab Hampered by DNA Backlog, Money Woes." *Los Angeles Times*, Jan. 20, 2010. http://latimesblogs.latimes.com/lanow/2010/01/lapd-crime-lab-hampered-by-backlog-money-woes.html (accessed May 18, 2014).

Ruiz, Rosanna. "Rodriguez Out of Prison But Says, 'I'm Still Not Free.'" *Houston Chronicle*, Mar. 15, 2005, http://www.chron.com/news/houston-texas/article/Rodriguez-out-of-prison-but-says-I-m-still-not-1924980.php (accessed Sept. 2, 2014).

Ruiz, Rosanna, and Robert Crowe. "HPD Closes Lab's DNA Unit in Wake of Cheating Probe." *Houston Chronicle*, Jan. 26, 2008. http://www.chron.com/news/houston-texas/article/HPD-closes-crime-lab-s-DNA-unit-in-wake-of-1536283.php.

Sacramento District Attorney's Office, Crime Lab (Laboratory of Forensic Sciences), http://www.sacda.org/divisions/crime%20lab/crime%20lab.php (accessed Nov. 30, 2013).

Schechter, Marvin. Memorandum to the New York State Commission of Forensic Science, *ASCLAD/LAB and Forensic Laboratory Accreditation: An Analysis*, March 25, 2011. http://www.newenglandinnocence.org/wp-content/uploads/2011/07/ASCLD-Lab-and-Forensic-Laboratory-Accreditation.pdf (accessed Feb. 19, 2014).

Scheck, Barry C., and David R. Dow. "Falsification of Evidence Can Only Be Called Corruption: The Scope of the Scandal." Editorial. *Houston Chronicle*, July 10, 2005. http://www.chron.com/opinion/outlook/article/Falsification-of-evidence-can-only-be-called-1925384.php (accessed Sept. 11, 2013).

Schwartz, John. "Picked from a Lineup, on a Whiff of Evidence." *New York Times*, Nov. 3, 2009, http://www.nytimes.com/2009/11/04/us/04scent.html (accessed Dec. 12, 2013).

Schwartz, Victor E., and Cary Silverman. "The Draining of Daubert and the Recidivism of Junk Science in Federal and State Courts." *Hofstra Law Review* 35 (2006): 217.

Scientific Working Group for Firearms and Toolmarks (SWGGUN). *Criteria for Identification* (Adopted Guideline 2.2.2) (adopted June 4, 2012). http://www.swggun.org/swg/index.php?option=com_content&view=article&id=28:criteria-for-identification&catid=10:guidelines-adopted&Itemid=6 (accessed Dec. 30, 2013).

——. *SWGGUN Responds to SOFS* (May 20, 2011), http://www.swggun.org/swg/index.php?option=com_content&view=article&id=51:swggun-responds-to-sofs-request&catid=13:other&Itemid=43 and http://www.swggun.org/swg/attachments/article/51/SWGGUN_RDTE_Final.pdf. (accessed Aug. 11, 2014).

——. *The Foundations of Firearm and Toolmark Identification,* http://www.swggun.org/swg/index.php?option=com_content&view=article&id=66:the-foundations-of-firearm-and-toolmark-identification&catid=13:other&Itemid=43 (accessed May 4, 2014).

Scientific Working Group on Friction Ridge Analysis, *About Scientific Working Groups,* http://www.swgfast.org/AboutSWGs.htm (accessed May 4, 2014).

Scientific Working Group on Friction Ridge Analysis, Study, and Technology. *Document #4: Guideline for the Articulation of the Decision-Making Process for the Individualization in Friction Ridge Examination (Latent/Tenprint).* Posted April 27, 2013. http://www.swgfast.org/documents/articulation/130427_Articulation_1.0.pdf (accessed March 13, 2014).

Secret Service Forensic Services, *Forensic Services.* http://www.secretservice.gov/forensics.shtml (accessed Dec. 20, 2013).

Shauk, Zain. "More Rape Kits Than Thought Remain Untested." *Houston Chronicle,* Dec. 17, 2011. http://www.chron.com/news/houston-texas/article/HPD-rape-kit-backlog-more-than-6-000-2403903.php (accessed Sept. 15, 2013).

Shedlock, Jerzy. "Former Alaska Crime Lab Analyst Charged in Alleged Drug Thefts." *Alaska Dispatch,* March 6, 2014. http://www.alaskadispatch.com/article/20140306/former-alaska-crime-lab-analyst-charged-alleged-drug-thefts (accessed Oct. 11, 2013).

Senate Judiciary Committee. "'The Need to Strengthen Forensic Science in the United States: The National Academy of Sciences' Report on a Path Forward,'" Hearing before the Committee on the Judiciary, United States Senate (2009) http://www.gpo.gov/fdsys/kpg/CHRG-111shrg54304/pdf/CHRG-111shrg54304.pdf (accessed May 30, 2014).

Sichta, Rick. Email correspondence with author. May 30, 2014.

Sinha, Sudhir. "Re: 'Strengthening Forensic Science in the United States: A Path Forward.'" (2009) (on file with author).

Sixty Minutes. *Eyewitness Testimony, Part II.* Oct. 30, 2012. YouTube: http://www.youtube.com/watch?v=GtelV9lmzQc (accessed May 17, 2014).

Slinkard, Matthew, Houston Police Department, Assistant Chief. Personal notes from the inaugural celebration of the Houston Forensic Science Center, April 3, 2014. On file with author.

Smith, Tovia. "Crime Lab Scandal Rocks Massachusetts." *National Public Radio,* Sept. 20, 2012. http://www.npr.org/2012/09/20/161502085/state-crime-lab-scandal-rocks-massachusetts (accessed April 17, 2014).

St. Clair, Jami, Chair, ASCLAD/LAB Board. Letter read into the record of the United States Senate, Committee on the Judiciary. *The Need to Strengthen Forensic Science in the United States: The National Academy of Sciences' Report on a Path Forward.* (March 16, 2009).

Stacey, Robert B. "Report on the Erroneous Fingerprint Individualization in the Madrid Train Bombing Case." *Forensic Science Communications* (Jan. 2005): 7. http://www.fbi.gov/about-us/lab/forensic-science-communications/fsc/jan2005/special_report/2005_special_report.htm. (accessed Aug. 9, 2014).

State v. Alt, 504 N.W.2d 38 (Minn. Ct. App. 1993).

State v. Dennis, 303 P.3d 726 (Kan. Ct. App. 2013) (unpublished).

State v. Dixon, 2012 Minn. App. LEXIS 123.

State v. Dotson, 2013 WL 4728679 (Tenn. Crim. App. 2013).

State v. Harper, 2012 Wisc. App. LEXIS 629 (2012).

State v. Hayes, 108 So. 3d 360 (La.App. 4 Cir. 2013).

State v. Huettl, 2013-NMCA-038, 305 P.3d 956, cert. granted, 300 P.3d 1182 (N.M. 2013).

State v. Kinslow, 257 Or. App. 295 (Or. Ct. App. 2013).

State v. Lui, 179 Wn. 2d 457 (Wash. 2014).

State v. McGuire, 2011 WL 890748 (N.J. S.Ct. 2011).

State v. McLeod, 165 N.H. 42, 66 A.3d 1221 (N.H. 2013).

State v. Mercier, 87 A.3d 700 (2014).

State v. Ortiz-Zape, Case No. 329PA11 (NC S.Ct., June 27, 2013).

State v. Ramirez, 810 So.2d 836 (Fla. 2001).

State v. Rosario, 2012 WL 6027715 (N.J. Super. Ct. App. Div. 2012).

State v. Sheehan, 2012 WL 653653 (Utah App 2012).

State v. Solomon, 49 S.W.3d 356 (Tex. Ct. Crim. App. 2001).

State v. Whittington, 753 S.E.2d 320 (N.C. 2014).

Statement from the Office of State Senator Rodney Ellis. "DNA Testing Proves George Rodriguez Innocent: Forensic Scientists Call for an Audit of HPD's Serology Cases." Aug. 5, 2004. http://www.senate.state.tx.us/75r/Senate/Members/Dist13/pr04/s080504a.htm (accessed Dec. 6, 2013).

Stelloh, Tim. "Old Arson Cases Reviewed in Texas: Is Douglas Boyington an Innocent Man?" *NBCNews.com*, Nov. 20, 2013. http://usnews.nbcnews.com/_news/2013/11/20/21370404-old-arson-cases-reviewed-in-texas-is-douglas-boyington-an-innocent-man?lite (accessed April 18, 2014).

Striupaitis, Peter. Chair, International Association for Identification, Firearm/Toolmark Committee and Member, Scientific Working Group for Firearms and Toolmarks (SWGGUN). *The Foundations of Firearm and Toolmark Identification, prepared in response to 2005 request by the National Academy of Sciences.* http://www.swggun.org/swg/index.php?option=com_content&view=article&id=66:the-foundations-of-firearm-and-toolmark-identification&catid=13:other&Itemid=43 (accessed March 15, 2014).

Strom, Kevin J., and Matthew J. Hickman. "Unanalyzed Evidence in Law-Enforcement Agencies: A National Examination of Forensic Processing in Police Departments." *Criminology and Public Policy* 9 (2010): 381.

Stuzman, Rene. "Crime-Lab Worker Puts Cases in Doubt." *Orlando Sentinel*, July 19, 2002. http://articles.orlandosentinel.com/2002-07-19/news/0207190359_1_fitzpatrick-dna-sanford (accessed May 4, 2014).

Swierzbin, James. "RI Crime Lab Director Worried about Increased Caseload." *ABC6.com*, Oct. 15, 2012. http://www.abc6.com/story/19826411/ri-crime-lab-director-worried-about-increased-caseload (accessed July 22, 2014).

Teichroeb, Ruth. "Oversight of Crime-Lab Staff Has Often Been Lax." *Seattle Post-Intelligencer*, July 22, 2004. http://www.seattlepi.com/local/article/Oversight-of-crime-lab-staff-has-often-been-lax-1149961.php#page-3 (accessed Oct. 11, 2013).

_____. "They Sit in Prison—but Crime Lab tests Are Flawed." *Seattle Post-Intelligencer*, March 12, 2004. http://www.seattlepi.com/local/article/They-sit-in-prison-but-crime-lab-tests-are-1139478.php#page-2 (accessed Dec. 29, 2013).

Texas Forensic Science Commission and Texas Criminal Justice Integrity Unit. *Certification of Forensic Examiners in Texas: Our Path Forward.* Nov. 27, 2013. http://www.fsc.texas.gov/sites/default/files/documents/files/whitepapercertification.pdf. (accessed Sept. 2, 2014).

_____. *Defendant Notification after Major Forensic Nonconformance* (Nov. 27, 2013). http://www.fsc.texas.gov/sites/default/files/documents/files/whitepaper-notification.pdf. (accessed Sept. 3, 2014).

Texas Forensic Science Commission Stakeholder Roundtable Meeting Report, June 6, 2012. http://www.fsc.texas.gov/sites/default/files/documents/files/StakeholderRoundtableReport-June62012.pdf (accessed Feb. 16, 2014).

Tex. Gov't Code Ann. §§ 420.041-043 (West 2012).

Tex. Gov't Code Ann. § 411.0205 (West 2012).

Tex. Penal Code Ann. § 7.02 (West 2011).

Texas S.B. 344, http://www.capitol.state.tx.us/BillLookup/History.aspx?Leg Sess=83R&Bill=SB344, effective Sept. 1, 2013 (accessed May 15, 2014).

The Bromwich Group, "Looking Back to Move Forward: The Houston Police Department Crime Laboratory's Implementation of the Independent Investigator's 2007 Recommendations." June 29, 2014. On file with author.

The Lowell Sun. "State Crime Lab Chemist Pleads Guilty to Theft of Drugs." *Lowell Sun,* Jan. 6, 2014. http://www.lowellsun.com/breakingnews/ci_24856098/state-crime-lab-chemist-pleads-guilty-theft-drugs (accessed Nov. 18, 2013).

Thompson, Sandra Guerra. "Beyond a Reasonable Doubt? Reconsidering Uncorroborated Eyewitness Identification Testimony." *University of California, Davis, Law Review* 41 (2008): 1487–1491.

_____. "*Daubert* Gatekeeping for Eyewitness Identifications." *Southern Methodist University Law Review* 65 (2012): 593–637.

_____. "Eyewitness Identifications and State Courts as Guardians against Wrongful Convictions." *Ohio State Journal of Criminal Law* 7 (2010): 603–616.

_____. Judicial Blindness to Eyewitness Misidentification." *Marquette Review of Criminal Law* 93 (2010): 639–660.

_____. "Opinion: Brand New Era of Criminal Justice in Harris County?" *Houston Chronicle,* Aug. 5, 2010. http://www.chron.com/opinion/outlook/article/Brand-new-era-of-criminal-justice-in-Harris-1698085.php (accessed Feb. 6, 2014).

_____. "What Price Justice? The Importance of Costs to Eyewitness Identification Reform." *Texas Tech Law Review* 41 (2008): 33–53.

_____. "The White Collar Police Force: 'Duty to Report' Statutes in Criminal Law Theory." *William and Mary Bill of Rights Journal* 11 (2002): 3.

Thompson, William C. "The Potential for Error in Forensic DNA Testing (and How That Complicates the Use of DNA Databases for Criminal Identification)." Produced for the Council of Responsible Genetics' national conference (2008), http://www.councilforresponsiblegenetics.org/pagedocuments/h4t5eoyuzi.pdf (accessed May 4, 2014).

Thompson-Cannino, Jennifer, and Ronald Cotton, with Eric Torneo. *Picking Cotton: Our Memoir of Injustice and Redemption.* New York: St. Martin's Press 2009.

Tilghman, Andrew. "Rape Case Raises More Questions over Crime Unit." *Houston Chronicle*, Aug. 10, 2004. http://www.chron.com/news/houston-texas/article/Rape-case-raises-more-questions-over-crime-unit-1497561.php. (accessed July 24, 2014).

"Timothy Cole Dies in Prison While Serving Time for Rape He Didn't Commit." *Examiner.com*, Oct. 12, 2008. http://www.examiner.com/article/timothy-cole-dies-prison-while-serving-time-for-rape-he-didn-t-commit (accessed Sept. 16, 2013).

"Tops of 2013. TV and Social Media: Top Ten Primetime TV Programs of 2013—Regularly Scheduled." Nielsen, Dec. 17, 2013. http://www.nielsen.com/us/en/newswire/2013/tops-of-2013-tv-and-social-media.html (accessed Jan. 4, 2014).

"Tulia, Texas." *Wikipedia.* http://en.wikipedia.org/wiki/Tulia,_Texas (accessed Jan. 14, 2014).

Tyler, Tom R. "Viewing CSI and the Threshold of Guilt: Managing Truth and Justice in Reality and Fiction." *Yale Law Journal* 115 (2006): 1050–1083.

U.S. Army Criminal Investigation Command, *U.S. Army Criminal Investigation Laboratory.* http://www.cid.army.mil/usacil.html (accessed May 27, 2014).

U.S. Constitution, amendment 6.

U.S. Department of Justice. *Notice of Establishment of the National Commission on Forensic Science and Solicitation of Applications for Commission Membership.* Feb. 22, 2013, Federal Register, https://www.federalregister.gov/articles/2013/02/22/2013-04140/notice-of-establishment-of-the-national-commission-on-forensic-science-and-solicitation-of (accessed Dec. 18, 2013).

U.S. Department of Justice, Office of Violence against Women. *Eliminating the Rape Kit Backlog: A Roundtable to Explore a Victim-Centered Approach. Summary of the Proceeding.* (Washington, D.C.: U.S. Department of Justice), 2010. http://www.victimsofcrime.org/docs/dna-resource-center-documents/eliminating-the-rape-kit-backlog—-a-roundtable-to-explore-a-victim-centered-approach-%282010%29.pdf?sfvrsn=6. (accessed Sept. 3, 2014).

U.S. Departments of Justice and Commerce. *U.S. Departments of Justice and Commerce Name Experts to First-Ever National Commission on Forensic Science*, Jan. 10, 2014, http://www.justice.gov/opa/pr/2014/January/14-at-029.html (accessed Sept. 19, 2013).

U.S. Department of Labor, Bureau of Labor Statistics. *Occupational Employment and Wages*. http://www.bls.gov/oes/current/oes194092.htm (accessed Nov. 17, 2013).

U.S. Senate, Committee on the Judiciary. *The Need to Strengthen Forensic Science in the United States: The National Academy of Sciences' Report on a Path Forward*. (March 18, 2009), Sen. Hrg. 111-224 (Washington, D.C.: Government Printing Office), 2010.

United States v. Casey, 2013 U.S. Dist. LEXIS 34905 (2013).

United States v. Council, 2011 WL 1305247 (E.D. Va. 2011).

United States v. Dore and Barrett, No. 12 Cr. 45 (RJS).

United States v. Titus Faison, No. 2008 CF2 16636 (D.C. Super. Ct. May 28, 2010)

United States v. Jackson, 1:11-cr-411-WSD (N.D. Ga. July 25, 2012).

United States v. James, 712 F.3d 79 (2d Cir. 2013).

United States v. Llera Plaza, 179 F. Supp. 2d 492 (E.D. Pa., Jan. 7, 2002).

United States v. Llera Plaza, 188 F. Supp. 2d 549 (E.D. Pa., March 13, 2002).

United States v. Moon, 512 F.3d 359 (7th Cir. 2008).

United States v. Otero, 849 F.Supp.2d 425 (D.N.J. 2012).

United States v. Shanton, 513 Fed.Appx. 265 (4th Cir. 2013) (per curiam).

United States v. St. Gerard, United States Army Trial Judiciary, Fifth Judicial Circuit, Germany (2010).

United States v. Starzecpyzel, 880 F. Supp. 1027, 1038 (S.D.N.Y. 1995).

United States v. Stone, 2012 U.S. Dist. LEXIS 8973 (2012).

United States v. Turner, 709 F.3d 1187 (7th Cir. 2013).

United States v. Washington, 498 F.3d 225 (4th Cir. 2007).

United States v. Zajac, Slip Copy, 2010 WL 3489597 (D. Utah 2010).

University of Rhode Island, Rhode Island State Crime Lab, History, http://web.uri.edu/riscl/about/history/ (accessed Dec. 9, 2013).

"Unmoved by Injustice DA Should Give Same Weight to Forensic Analysis When It Exonerates or Convicts." Editorial. *Houston Chronicle*, Aug. 26, 2004, http://www.chron.com/opinion/editorials/article/Unmoved-by-injustice-DA-should-give-same-weight-1973533.php. (accessed July 24, 2014).

Valencia, Milton J., and John R. Ellement. "Annie Dookhan Pleads Guilty in Drug Lab Scandal." *Boston Globe*, Nov. 22, 2013. http://www.boston globe.com/metro/2013/11/22/annie-dookhan-former-state-chemist-who-mishandled-drug-evidence-agrees-plead-guilty/7UU3hfZUof4DFJGoNU fXGO/story.html (accessed Jan. 14, 2014).

Van Derbeken, Jaxon. "Problems of S.F. toxicologist not disclosed." *S.F. Gate*, May 26, 2010. http://www.sfgate.com/bayarea/article/Problems-of-S-F-toxicologist-not-disclosed-3263652.php#page-2 (accessed May 4, 2014).

———. "Toxicologist's Wash. History may taint Calif. cases." *Seattle Times*, May 26, 2010, http://seattletimes.com/html/nationworld/2011952994_coroner26.html (accessed May 4, 2014).

Vidmar, Neil, and Shari Seidman Diamond. "Juries and Expert Evidence." *Brooklyn Law Review* 66 (2001): 1121–1180.

Waggoner, Martha, Associated Press. "Review Finds Flawed NC Cases, Including Executions," Aug. 18, 2010, http://www.rawstory.com/rs/2010/08/18/review-finds-flawed-north-carolina-cases-including-executions/. (accessed Sept. 3, 2014).

Ward, Jennifer Inez. "Federal Funds Offer Limited Help for OPD Crime Lab." *Oakland Local*, Sept. 11, 2012. http://archive.oaklandlocal.com/article/federal-funds-offer-limited-help-opd-crime-lab (accessed Sept. 12, 2013).

Watson v. State, 828 N.W.2d 326 (Iowa Ct. App. 2013).

Webster v. State, 2011 OK CR 14 (Ok. Crim. App. 2011).

Wells, Gary L. "What Do We Know about Eyewitness Identification?" *American Psychologist*. 48 (1993): 553–571.

Whitehurst v. Commonwealth, 63 Va. App. 132 (Va. Ct. App. 2014).

Wicoff, Robert, Assistant Public Defender, Harris County Public Defender's Office, Email correspondence with author, September 28, 2014. On file with author.

Williams v. Illinois, 132 S.Ct. 2221 (2012).

Wilson, Paul. "Lessons from the Antipodes: Successes and Failures of Forensic Science." *Forensic Science International* 67 (1994): 79.

Wright, Ronald F. "Parity of Resources for Defense Counsel and the Reach of Public Choice Theory." *Iowa Law Review* 90 (2004): 219.

About the Author

Sandra Guerra Thompson is the Alumnae College Professor of Law and Director of the Criminal Justice Institute at the University of Houston Law Center. A graduate of Yale College and Yale Law School, she started her career as a prosecutor in the New York County District Attorney's Office where she practiced both trial and appellate criminal law until moving into law teaching in Houston. In 2012, she was appointed by Houston Mayor Annise Parker as a member of the Board of Directors of the Houston Forensic Science Local Government Corporation, a group charged with creating and overseeing an independent forensic lab and transferring such duties from the Houston Police Department's crime lab. She had previously been appointed to the Timothy Cole Advisory Panel on Wrongful Convictions in Texas, a panel created by the state legislature to propose statutory reforms to curb wrongful convictions.

Thompson teaches and writes in the areas of criminal law, criminal procedure, wrongful convictions and evidence. She has authored articles on causes of wrongful convictions such as eyewitness identification error, false testimony by police informants, and false confessions. She co-edited a book entitled *American Justice in the Age of Innocence,* an anthology about wrongful convictions that includes articles written by her seminar students.

A native of Laredo, Texas, Thompson today lives in Houston with her husband, Jim Thompson, a consumer marketing research analyst, and their dog, Simba. Her son, Andy Garcia, is a senior at Oberlin College in Ohio.

Index

toxicology, 86, 116n14, 207–08, 239
trace evidence, 86, 208, 239
training. *See* analysts.
Tulleners, Fred, 43–44
tunnel vision, 9–11

U
U.S. Bureau of Alcohol, Tobacco,
    and Firearms, 165, 218
U.S. Department of Commerce, 190
U.S. Drug Enforcement
    Administration, 190
U.S. Senate, Commerce, Science
    and Transportation Committee,
    202n53
U.S. Senate Judiciary Committee,
    184
U.S. Supreme Court, 150–61,
    158–61. *See* also Sixth
    Amendment.
UCLA Law School, xvi
unconscious bias. *See* bias.
underfunding. *See* funding.
understaffing. *See* staff.
United States v. Otero, 103–06
University of Arkansas Law School,
    xvi
University of Houston Law Center/
    Foundation, xv
University of Texas at Austin School
    of Law, xvi

V
validation studies, 96, 103, 239
Vasquez, David, 74
Veeder, Gary, 50–51, 57, 75n3
Velasquez, Eduardo, 74
victims
    bias for/against, 18, 47

guilt feelings for wrongful
    convictions, 20–21
manipulated by police/
    prosecutors, 20
Virginia, and independent crime
    lab, 182
voice comparison, 119n64

W
Walker, Sandra, 165–66
Waller, James, 74
Wardell, Billy, 74
Washington, Calvin, 74
Washington, D.C., independent
    forensic laboratory, 213
Washington, Earl, 74
Washington Post, on wrongful
    convictions, 112
Washington State, scandals in,
    41–42, 44, 60–61
Washington Supreme Court
    (*Williams* case), 164
Washington Times, and crime
    laboratory, 213
Watkins, Jerry, 74
Wawro, Mark, 8, 26
Webb, Thomas, 74
Webb, Troy, 74
Webster, Bernard, 74
Wells, Gary, 5
Werner, Anna, 205
West Virginia State Police
    Laboratory, 39, 61
whistleblowers, 51
White, Bill, 207
White, John Jerome, 74
White, Pamela, 49
Whitley, Drew, 75
Wiederhorn, Sheldon M., 190